THE SLAVE NEXT DOOR

THE PUBLISHER GRATEFULLY ACKNOWLEDGES
THE GENEROUS SUPPORT OF THE GENERAL ENDOWMENT FUND
OF THE UNIVERSITY OF CALIFORNIA PRESS FOUNDATION.

THE SLAVE
NEXT DOOR

HUMAN TRAFFICKING AND
SLAVERY IN AMERICA TODAY

Kevin Bales and Ron Soodalter

UNIVERSITY OF CALIFORNIA PRESS

BERKELEY   LOS ANGELES   LONDON

University of California Press, one of the most
distinguished university presses in the United States,
enriches lives around the world by advancing
scholarship in the humanities, social sciences, and
natural sciences. Its activities are supported by the UC
Press Foundation and by philanthropic contributions
from individuals and institutions. For more
information, visit www.ucpress.edu.

University of California Press
Berkeley and Los Angeles, California

University of California Press, Ltd.
London, England

Library of Congress Cataloging-in-Publication Data

Bales, Kevin.
    The slave next door: human trafficking and slavery
in America today / Kevin Bales and Ron Soodalter.
        p.   cm.
    Includes bibliographical references and index.
    ISBN 978-0-520-26866-1 (pbk. : alk. paper)
    1. Human trafficking—United States.   2. Slavery—
United States.   I. Soodalter, Ron.

HQ314B35 2009
364.15—dc22   2008044713O

Manufactured in the United States of America

19 18 17 16 15 14 13
10 9 8 7 6

This book is printed on Cascades Enviro 100, a 100%
post consumer waste, recycled, de-inked fiber. FSC
recycled certified and processed chlorine free. It is acid
free, Ecologo certified, and manufactured by BioGas
energy.

CONTENTS

Since we sat down to write *The Slave Next Door,* there have been some significant developments; and while many areas are still in serious need of improvement, a number of things have changed for the better. First, let's look at the good news.

POSITIVE DEVELOPMENTS

New Administration, Fresh Outlook

From all outward signs, the election of Barack Obama to the presidency has brought a fresh outlook to the issue of human trafficking and slavery in our country. This "debasement of our common humanity," he stated, "has to be a top priority." And Secretary of State Hillary Clinton echoed these sentiments. In a June 17, 2009, op-ed in the *Washington Post,* timed to accompany the release of the annual Trafficking in Persons Report, she wrote, "The Obama administration views the fight against human trafficking, at home and abroad, as an important priority on our foreign policy agenda." It's still too early to tell, but thus far, the new administration is saying and doing all the right things. In a move that demonstrated an understanding of the problem and how best to address it, President Obama nominated Luis CdeBaca as the State Department's ambassador-at-large to monitor and combat trafficking in persons. CdeBaca, arguably one of the most qualified people in America for the post, brings a career-long history of fighting human trafficking cases as

> Counsel to the U.S. House Committee on the Judiciary, on detail from the Civil Rights Division of the U.S. Department of Justice. On the Committee, his portfolio for Chairman John Conyers, Jr. includes national security, intelligence, immigration, civil rights, and modern slavery issues. At the Justice Department, CdeBaca served as Chief Counsel of the Civil Rights Division's Human Trafficking Prosecution Unit. During the Clinton Admin-

istration, he was the Department's Involuntary Servitude and Slavery Coordinator and was instrumental in developing the United States' victim-centered approach to combating modern slavery. He has investigated and prosecuted human trafficking cases in which victims were held for prostitution and other forms of sexual exploitation, farm labor, domestic service, and factory work. CdeBaca received the leading honor given by the national trafficking victim service provider community, the Freedom Network's Paul & Sheila Wellstone Award.[1]

For years CdeBaca has dealt with the broad spectrum of human trafficking, from the premise that all forms are equally egregious. As is evident from the various comments he has made throughout this book, he "walks it like he talks it."

Trafficking Victims Protection Reauthorization Act: The Latest Reauthorization

The most recent reauthorization of the Trafficking Victims Protection Act (TVPA)—officially dubbed the William Wilberforce Trafficking Victims Protection Reauthorization Act of 2008 (TVPRA)—took longer than expected to pass, but it was well worth the wait. The "Title 2" section of the law, which pertains specifically to human trafficking and slavery in America, offers a broad spectrum of improvements, many of which are structured to help both foreign-born and domestic victims and to enhance prosecutions. Shortly after the passage of the "Reauth," an extensive memo was circulated by Robert Moossy, director, and Hillary Axam, special litigation counsel, of the Department of Justice's Human Trafficking Prosecution Unit, summarizing the key points of the new law as it pertains to the United States. The memo is quoted below in its entirety:

> As many of you know, on December 23, 2008, the President signed into law H.R. 7311, the William Wilberforce Trafficking Victims Protection Reauthorization Act of 2008, which was passed by Congress on December 10, 2008.
>
> While this far-reaching Act addresses many aspects of human trafficking, including international aid programs, victim benefits, and immigration issues, we wanted to highlight some of the provisions that affect criminal prosecution of trafficking offenses here in the United States.
>
> Section 222 of the Act, available at http://www.govtrack.us/congress/bill.xpd?bill=h110-7311, includes several important enhancements to the anti-trafficking criminal statutes, which DOJ has supported since their introduction by the Senate in an earlier version of the legislation. As we noted in DOJ's July 2008 views letter, these enhancements are "help-

ful additions . . . that will enable more effective prosecutions and protections for victims." We are pleased to see these additions signed into law. Some of you have asked about the status of earlier legislative proposals that would have federalized commercial sex acts in or affecting interstate commerce with no requirement of force, fraud, or coercion. These proposals were not enacted in the final legislation.

We will be introducing more detailed and technical training materials in the coming weeks. For the moment, however, we wanted to provide a brief overview of some of the enhancements that will most directly affect criminal prosecutions.

NEW CONSPIRACY STATUTE

A new trafficking-specific conspiracy statute prohibits conspiring to commit the Peonage (§ 1581), Enticement into Slavery (§ 1583), Forced Labor (§ 1589), Trafficking (§ 1590), Sex Trafficking (§ 1591), and Document Servitude (§ 1592). In contrast to the general conspiracy statute whose maximum penalty is five years, the penalty for violating this provision is equal to the penalty for the underlying substantive offense, except that there is no minimum mandatory penalty for conspiring to commit Sex Trafficking (§ 1591). This statute therefore enhances the penalty for conspiring to commit trafficking crimes.

EXPANDED CRIMINALIZATION OF BENEFITTING FINANCIALLY FROM TRAFFICKING

The Act contains new provisions penalizing those who knowingly benefit financially from participating in a venture that engaged in trafficking crimes. Previously, only the sex trafficking statute, 18 U.S.C. § 1591, contained such a provision. The new legislation expands the prohibition against profiting from trafficking ventures to criminalize benefitting financially from a venture engaged in Peonage (§ 1581), Forced Labor (§ 1589), or Document Servitude (§ 1592), knowing or in reckless disregard of the fact that the venture engaged in such a violation.

CLARIFICATION OF FORCED LABOR STATUTE

The Act clarifies the application of the Forced Labor provision, 18 U.S.C. § 1589, by: 1) adding "force" as a fourth prohibited means of violating the statute in addition to serious harm, scheme/plan, and abuse of the law; 2) clarifying that the four prohibited means are alternate means of violating the same statute and that the statute may be violated by any one or any combination of these means; and 3) adding definitions of the terms "serious harm" and "abuse of the law" as discussed below.

EXPANDED CRIME OF SEX TRAFFICKING BY FORCE, FRAUD, OR COERCION

New language inserted into Section 1591 broadens the crime of sex trafficking by force, fraud, or coercion by expanding the *mens rea* requirement to include reckless disregard as well as knowledge. Previously, the government was required to prove that the defendant actually knew that force, fraud, or coercion would be used to cause a person to engage in a commercial sex act; the expanded statute can be satisfied by proof that the defendant acted in reckless disregard of the fact that such means would be used.

EXPANDED CRIME OF SEX TRAFFICKING OF MINORS

The Act broadens the reach of the crime of sex trafficking of minors by eliminating the knowledge-of-age requirement in certain instances. Previously, the government was required to prove that the defendant knew the person engaged in commercial sex was a minor. By contrast, the new legislation provides that where the defendant had a reasonable opportunity to observe the minor, knowledge of minor age need not be proven.

DEFINITION OF KEY ASPECTS OF COERCION

The Act clarifies the definitions of "serious harm" and "abuse or threatened abuse of the legal process," which are among the prohibited means of coercion in the Forced Labor (§ 1589) and Sex Trafficking (§ 1591) statutes. While the TVPA of 2000 did not explicitly define these terms, its legislative history called for a broad interpretation of the forms of coercion it proscribed, and the statutory language now codifies the broad definitions of these forms of coercion that had begun to evolve under the TVPA of 2000. Under the newly codified definitions, "serious harm" means any harm, including psychological, financial, or reputational harm, that would compel a reasonable person with the victim's background and in the victim's circumstances to perform labor, services, or commercial sex acts to avoid that harm. "Abuse or threatened abuse of the legal process" is defined as the use or threatened use the law or legal process in a manner for which it was not designed to cause a person to take or refrain from taking some action.

EXPANDED AUTHORITY FOR DETENTION

The Act expands the Government's authority to detain pending trial defendants charged with trafficking offenses. Under the new law, the charging of a Chapter 77 offense with a maximum term of imprisonment of 20 years or more raises a rebuttable presumption of pre-trial detention under 18 U.S.C. § 3142(e). These offenses include Peonage (§ 1581), Enticement into Slavery (§ 1583), Involuntary Servitude (§ 1584), Forced Labor (§ 1589), Trafficking (§ 1590), and Sex Trafficking (§ 1591).

NEW CRIMES OF OBSTRUCTING
HUMAN TRAFFICKING ENFORCEMENT

New provisions criminalize and severely penalize the obstruction or attempted obstruction of enforcement of any of the major Chapter 77 statutes, including Enticement into Slavery (§ 1583), Involuntary Servitude (§ 1584), Forced Labor (§ 1589), Trafficking (§ 1590), Sex Trafficking (§ 1591), and Document Servitude (§ 1592). The new obstruction violations are punishable to the same extent as the underlying crime. Previously, a similar obstruction provision applied only to enforcement of the Peonage statute, 18 U.S.C. § 1581.

EXTRA-TERRITORIAL JURISDICTION

The Act expands the reach of criminal anti-trafficking statutes by extending extra-territorial jurisdiction to trafficking crimes committed outside the United States, where the alleged offender is a national or lawful permanent resident of the United States or is present in the United States. The new law provides this extra-territorial jurisdiction for charges of Peonage (§ 1581), Enticement into Slavery (§ 1583), Involuntary Servitude (§ 1584), Forced Labor (§ 1589), Trafficking (§ 1590), and Sex Trafficking (§ 1591).

NEW FRAUD IN LABOR CONTRACTING CRIME

A new crime, codified at 18 U.S.C. Section 1351, prohibits fraud in foreign labor contracting. This provision imposes criminal liability on those who, knowingly and with intent to defraud, recruit workers from outside the United States for employment within the United States by means of materially false or fraudulent representations. The statute provides for a maximum term of 5 years' imprisonment.

We look forward to working with you to implement these new provisions, which we believe will enhance our ability to charge, convict, and punish human traffickers and vindicate the rights and dignity of trafficking victims. The Human Trafficking Prosecution Unit will be issuing more detailed guidance shortly, and please do not hesitate to contact us if we can provide further assistance in your efforts to serve trafficking victims and bring traffickers to justice.[2]

The advances in the law are indeed significant and will hopefully result in a major jump in the number of traffickers convicted and the number of victims of all forms of slavery rescued.

2009 Trafficking in Persons Report

The 2009 TIP Report was released with considerable fanfare from both Secretary of State Clinton and Ambassador CdeBaca. Although the United States still remains the only country not included in the State Department's global evaluation, the good news is that in 2010 it will be—although the level of objectivity the U.S. government can bring to its own evaluation remains to be seen. Also of interest will be the rest of the world's response to America's perceptions of its own anti–human trafficking efforts.

Domestics and Diplomats

It could be a coincidence, but one key recommendation of *The Slave Next Door* became government policy in October 2009. In chapter 2, we looked closely at the plight of domestic workers abused and often enslaved by foreign diplomats. These diplomats tend to escape scrutiny and, if they are found out, claim diplomatic immunity and quickly leave the country. We called for more protections for workers hired by diplomats, and now our government has provided just that. In a Diplomatic Note to all foreign embassies, Secretary of State Hillary Clinton issued two new requirements governing the employment of domestic workers. First, all embassies have to notify the State Department *before* they hire a domestic and apply for her visa. This allows the government the opportunity to examine the potential employee and ensure that the diplomat is ready to meet the second requirement—that of providing a safe and legal job. An important point of the new policy is the State Department's assumption that diplomats *will not* be able to provide the legally required wages and working conditions unless and until they provide evidence to the contrary. To meet the requirements, the diplomat must guarantee that there will be a contract stating hours and wages; a separate and independent bank account controlled by the worker where the wages will be deposited; overtime payments; travel provided to and from the United States; and the assurance that all relevant federal, state, and local laws will be obeyed. If diplomats violate these guarantees, their embassy will be denied visas for workers. And if there is serious abuse of workers, diplomats will be placed on notice that their immunity can be removed, making them liable to prosecution. We salute the State Department for establishing these rules, which we hope will become models for other countries as well.

Effective Advocacy for the
Anti-Slavery Movement on Capitol Hill

In 2007, a small, diverse coalition of antislavery and antitrafficking groups was formed with the intention of speaking with one voice to policy makers. The group, now called the Alliance to End Slavery and Trafficking (ATEST), was given crucial guidance and support by Humanity United, a foundation that supports work to eradicate slavery. Many of the significant changes featured in the above-summarized Reauthorization came about because of the unified efforts of this coalition.[3]

Counting Victims: Addressing the Issue of Quantification

Since its beginning, the movement against human trafficking in America has lacked an accurate and reliable system of quantification. For years, numbers of victims—both foreign born and domestic—have been put forth by both government and NGOs, only to be withdrawn, recalculated, and resubmitted. One major reason for this less-than-scientific approach is the hidden nature of the crime itself. By its very definition, modern-day slavery lives in the shadows, often making it impossible to locate, let alone count, the victims and their traffickers. Further, there is a temporal restriction built into the crime of modern-day slavery. Whereas other crimes, such as theft, assault, rape and murder, can be viewed as events—incidents that occur within a brief, fixed time frame— slavery, by its very definition, can extend over a period of years, and in some cases decades.

In 2010, a research team led by Northeastern University's Institute on Race and Justice—the same people who performed the extraordinary study on law enforcement responses to human trafficking (see chapter 7)—published an attempt to quantify human trafficking in the United States through a "meta-analysis." A meta-analysis is a study of existing studies, pulling together all previous estimates and seeking to build them into an overarching database; it is a technique commonly used in medical research. To attain accuracy, it must by its very nature rely on the completeness and reliability of these earlier studies. The soup, as it were, is only as good as the ingredients put into the pot. The Northeastern researchers found that many of the ingredients were lacking. The deficiencies in the previous research, they stated, were considerable, "making it problematic to derive a single estimate of the number of trafficking victims in the U.S."[4] Given these problems, the researchers were able to estimate an annualized minimum of somewhere between the 5,166 victims reported by national data collection programs and survey studies and the 60,467 victims reported by economic modeling studies. This analysis represents the most scientific attempt to determine the scope of the trafficking problem to date. The Northeastern study is significant, inasmuch as it lays the groundwork for more precise and accurate studies to follow.

Coalition of Immokalee Workers: On the Victory Trail

In chapter 3, we gave extensive coverage to the heroic actions of the Coalition of Immokalee Workers (CIW). Since that time the CIW has scored a number of major victories. They recently brought the East Coast Growers and Packers—a member of the Florida Tomato Growers Exchange (FTGE) and one of Florida's largest tomato growers—to the table, as well as the two organic growers Alderman and Ladymoon Farms, and all of them have agreed to pay the additional penny per pound of tomatoes, monitor against worker abuse, and refuse to purchase produce picked by slave labor. Meanwhile, the monolithic FTGE—about whom we also wrote, in less than flattering terms—is still holding out and refusing to recognize human rights violations in the fields. It is not alone; thus far, the list of holdouts includes Publix, Kroger, Sodexo, Aramark, Wendy's, Quizno's, Costco, and Wal-Mart.[5]

Then, on September 25, 2009, came the news that all but dwarfed everything that went before. An agreement was announced, and recognized by Secretary of Labor Hilda L. Solis, between the CIW and Compass Group, the world's largest food service and support services company. With 2008 revenues of nine billion dollars, Charlotte-based Compass manages over ten thousand accounts, including schools, corporations, hospitals, and cultural centers. The Code of Conduct stipulates, among other concessions, the penny-per-pound raise, payment for each hour worked, a reliable system of monitoring work hours, a forum for voicing worker concerns and reporting violations, third-party auditing, and a program of worker education, carried out onsite by the CIW. Compass Group's signature is binding to all its operating companies. Said their vice president of corporate communications Cheryl Queen, "We expect this code of conduct will improve the working conditions and create change within the industry." The CIW's Lucas Benitez took it a step further: "The future of Florida agriculture is contained within this agreement."[6] The road is long, but we believe that the CIW will ultimately bring every grower and purchaser in America to the realization that slavery and worker abuse will not be tolerated—not here, not now, not ever.

The American Civil Liberties Union Sues the U.S. Conference of Catholic Bishops: That Pesky Line between Church and State

In chapter 9, we presented our concerns regarding the blurring of the line between church and state, as exemplified by the policies of the U.S. Conference of Catholic Bishops (USCCB)—the organization given the government contract for allocating funds to survivors of human trafficking. It was—and is—of serious concern that such vital issues as sex education, contraception (many trafficking victims contract STDs as a result of the sexual assaults they suffer while enslaved), and funding for victims who have become pregnant through rape are not being addressed, and that the appropriate services are being withheld, on strictly religious grounds. Apparently, the American Civil Liberties Union agrees. In January 2009, it filed suit against the Department of Health and Human Services, the agency responsible for awarding USCCB's contract. The government, the suit alleges, "has allowed USCCB to impose its religious beliefs on trafficking victims by prohibiting sub grantees from ensuring access to services like emergency contraception, condoms, and abortion care." The case, *ACLU of Massachusetts v. Leavitt* (Civ. No. 09–10038), asks the court to "stop this misuse of taxpayer dollars and to protect the health and safety of trafficking victims. Trafficking victims need comprehensive and compassionate care to gain their freedom and lead safe and healthy lives."[7]

Case Updates

Within the past year, there have been some significant developments regarding some of the cases cited in *The Slave Next Door.*

TRAFFICKING SURVIVOR GIVEN KACHEPA: SOON TO BE A DENTIST NEAR YOU

You will remember the eleven-year-old Given Kachepa, who was brought to the United States in the late 1990s as part of a boys' choir and was enslaved by a Texas minister in a trafficking and charity scam. In May 2009, Given graduated from a university and is now training to become a dentist. He still takes time to speak out against human trafficking.[8]

NEW LEGAL STRATEGIES IN WISCONSIN

In chapter 2, we expressed outrage that Jefferson and Elnora Calimlim and their son, after being convicted of holding a woman in slavery for nineteen years in Wisconsin, had received sentences of only four years' imprisonment. In late 2009 lawyers Martina Vandenberg and Jerold Solovy, convinced that the district court had "undersentenced" the Calimlims, filed a civil suit against the couple and their son. The lawyers achieved a legal breakthrough when they demonstrated that the case met all the requirements to be treated as a violation of the Racketeer Influenced and Corrupt Organizations Act (RICO). Upheld by the federal court, this is a powerful new weapon to use against human traffickers.[9]

RETURN TO ASHLEY'S SALON

At the beginning of chapter 5, we got to know the young Togolese women who had been enslaved at Ashley's Hair Braiding Salon in East Orange, New Jersey. When the book went to press, the case had not yet been resolved, and one defendant was arguing that he couldn't understand the problem, since working at the salon was "better than in Africa." Testimony in court in August 2009 belied his assertion, demonstrating enslavement and sexual abuse. The case was so strong that all defendants ultimately pled guilty and are currently facing sentences of up to twelve years.[10]

LATEST ON THE CHINESE ACROBATS

The case involving a troupe of Chinese acrobats who had allegedly been trafficked into slavery in Las Vegas (see chapter 5) has been dismissed. According to the New York Times, "Steven W. Myhre, the acting United States attorney for Nevada, said a magistrate judge had initially approved the complaint. 'Upon further investigation, however, the United States has determined that it has been unable to develop evidence sufficient to prove those charges beyond a reasonable doubt,' Mr. Myhre told the Las Vegas Review-Journal." Our apologies to Mr. You Zhi Li if, in fact, he is blameless; thankfully, this is why we have updates like this Prologue.[11]

And now for the not-so-good news . . .

AREAS OF CONTINUING CONCERN

First You're Enslaved, Then You're Taxed on Your Slavery

In a number of recent cases, compensation for freed slaves has been ordered by the courts. This is right: their lives and labor were stolen, and the criminal slaveholders should pay them back. Yet incredibly, these slavery survivors then become liable for large tax bills on the compensation, no matter that they are destitute and struggling to rebuild their lives. We don't believe any lawmaker meant for this to happen, and the good news is that it can be fixed easily. All that is needed is an amendment to the TVPA that reads: "Crime victim restitution for human trafficking victims should be excluded from gross income under IRC §104(a)(2)." Okay, Congress, do the right thing.

One More Case Update: The Daewoosa Victims

In chapter 5, we also explored the largest case of human trafficking in America—the enslavement of hundreds of Chinese and Vietnamese workers on the island of American Samoa. By placing factories there, manufacturers were permitted to put "Made in America" labels in clothing supplied to major U.S. companies but were not required to obey the laws that protect other workers in America. One defendant, Kil Soo Lee, enslaved more than 250 workers, mostly young women. Ultimately he and others were convicted of federal charges and sent to prison. Some two hundred of the workers who survived enslavement were granted T visas and settled in twenty different states around the United States. Sadly, as reported by Monica Rohr in the *Houston Chronicle*, "Daewoosa survivors have put down roots in Vietnamese enclaves like Houston, Seattle and Orange County. . . . But they're stuck in a legal limbo, still waiting for their long-promised green cards and often mistakenly denied public assistance, college financial aid and other benefits." In this regard the Daewoosa workers are suffering the same unexplained delays that many trafficking victims face in receiving the green cards and survivor benefits to which they are entitled by law.[12]

State Laws

One by one, the states have been introducing and passing laws against human trafficking, presumably in response to the increasing presence the issue has had in the media over the past year. To date, nearly every state has its own version of antislavery laws; however, they all have similar problems. The laws are overwhelmingly—and in some instances, exclusively—concerned with the issue of sexual coercion, with either token attention or none at all paid to labor trafficking. Further, many of the laws focus on the punishment of the traffickers, while ignoring the challenge of providing a raft of vital services to the survivors: legal resident status, counseling, financial aid, health care both physical and mental, even concerns as basic as translation. The point we made when *The Slave Next Door* was first published still applies: it's not enough just to pass an antitrafficking law; unless it is centered on supporting victims and survivors, and unless it encompasses the broad spectrum of slavery in this country, it will accomplish little.

Nor is this deficit exclusive to the states. The area reflecting the most gaping lack at all levels of government is that of survivor services. There is simply not enough—of everything. In this regard, sadly, little has changed.

Child Sex Tourism

When we wrote about the case of convicted sex tourist Kent Frank, we were aware that sex tourism—the practice of Americans traveling to foreign, often developing, countries and buying or coercing sex with children—exists, and that it is egregious in the extreme. This we knew. However, we have come to a new understanding of the scope of the problem: it has become epidemic globally, and Americans are among the biggest offenders.

The nature of the crime defies credulity. In mid-September 2009, the U.S. Department of Justice announced the indictment of a thirty-nine-year-old former Connecticut man on charges of sexually abusing children in Haiti. According to the indictment, Douglas Perlitz allegedly obtained funding from a "religious organization"—the Order of Malta, under Jesuit leadership—to found an intake program for Haiti's street children, some as young as six. As head of the program, over a ten-year period Perlitz allegedly coerced the children to have sex with him. "In order to entice and persuade the children to comply with the sex acts," the indictment alleges, "Perlitz provided the promise of food and shelter and also provided monetary and other benefits, including cash, cell phones, electronics, shoes, clothes, and other items. If minors refused to engage in sex acts, it is alleged that Perlitz would . . . withhold benefits or threaten to expel them from the program."

It gets worse. For years, he maintained such strict control over the management of the program and its staff that no one dared blow the whistle; finally, however, word got out in 2007, at which point "Perlitz used his relationship with a religious leader and influential Board Members to continue to attempt to conceal his illegal sexual conduct." That he victimized children, unquestionably scarring them for the rest of their lives, is bad enough; the fact that high-ranking members of the church knew about it and collaborated in keeping it hidden makes it doubly horrific. The case is being prosecuted in Connecticut by Assistant U.S. Attorney Krishna Patel.[13]

Another case involving prosecutor Patel is that of Edgardo Sensi, a burly American in his fifties. Sensi, a maker of pornographic films—"kiddie-porn"—both here and abroad, was indicted in Connecticut in 2009. Among other charges, he allegedly filmed himself having sado-masochistic sex with a six-year-old girl. The indictment alleges that he then traveled to Nicaragua, where he used gifts of money, perfume, and a cell phone to persuade a twenty-three-year-old working mother to allow him sexual access to her four-year-old daughter. There are ten pages to the Sensi indictment, each page documenting in gut-wrenching detail the horrific acts this man forced children to perform.[14]

Acts such as these are as stunningly depraved as any crime can possibly be, yet these two men are not exceptions in the realm of child sex tourism, they are the rule. Ironically, the very nature of the crime makes them hard to catch. Often, the countries these men choose to visit lack sufficient police training or staff to pursue them; or worse, the authorities are corrupt. It is vital that our government begin to work with the governments of these countries in order to establish a level of cooperation that will lead to justice and care for the victims and, ultimately, to prevention. The very scope of the problem demands a massive commitment to action if this horror is to be addressed and eliminated.

NOTES

1. White House, Office of the Press Secretary, "President Obama Announces Another Key State Department Post," March 24, 2009.

2. Robert Moossy, director, and Hilary Axam, special litigation counsel, Human Trafficking Prosecution Unit, Civil Rights Division, Criminal Section, U.S. Department of Justice, internal memo, posted as "Congress Amends Federal Trafficking Laws; DOJ Summary of Changes," January 12, 2009, http://catfht .org/news/DOJLetter_2008Reauthorization.pdf.

3. In the interests of full disclosure, the organization Free the Slaves, of which coauthor Kevin Bales is president, helped to start the coalition and receives funding from Humanity United.

4. Northeastern University Institute on Race and Justice, with the Urban Institute, Justice Policy Center, and Michael Shively, Ryan Kling, and Kristin Wheeler, *Review of Existing Estimates of Victims of Human Trafficking in the United States and Recommendations for Improving Research and Measurement of Human Trafficking,* report to Humanity United, March 2010.

5. Amanda Kloer, "Victory: Chipotle, Tomato Growers Commit to End Slavery," September 11, 2009, www.humantrafficking.change.org.

6. Corporate Social Responsibility Newswire, "Compass Group and the Coalition of Immokalee Workers (CIW) Announce Sweeping Changes to Benefit Tomato Harvesters," press release, September 26, 2009, www.csrwire.com/ press/press_release/27757-Compass-Group-and-the-Coalition-of-Immokalee -Workers-CIW-Announce-Sweeping-Changes-to-Benefit-Tomato-Harvesters.

7. American Civil Liberties Union, "ACLU Asks Court to Stop Misuse of Taxpayer Dollars In Trafficking Victims' Program," press release, January 12, 2009, www .aclu.org/reproductive-freedom/aclu-asks-court-stop-misuse-taxpayer-dollars -trafficking-victims-program. See also Jessica Stites, "Strings Attached," *Ms. Magazine,* spring 2009, www.msmagazine.com/spring2009/StringsAttached.

8. Conversation with Given Kachepa and Sandy Shepherd, August 2009.

9. Andrew Longstreth, "Wisconsin Judge Okays RICO Suit in Human Trafficking Case" *AM Law Litigation Daily,* August 31, 2009, www.law.com/jsp/tal/digestTAL.jsp?id=1202433472112&Wisconsin_Judge_Okays_RICO_Suit_in_Human_Trafficking_Case, August 31, 2009.

10. Joe Ryan, "East Orange Man Admits Helping Run Human Trafficking Ring for Hair Salon," *New Jersey Star Ledger,* August 26, 2009.

11. Associated Press, "Slavery Charges Are Dismissed," *New York Times,* December 25, 2009.

12. Monica Rohr, "Trafficking Victims Try to Remake Lives," *Houston Chronicle,* April 12, 2009.

13. Reuters, "Former Connecticut Resident Charged with Sexually Abusing Children in Haiti," September 17, 2009, www.reuters.com/article/idUS169636+17-Sep-2009+PRN20090917.

14. *United States of America v. Edgardo Sensi, District of Connecticut,* Criminal No. 3:08cr253(WWE).

ACKNOWLEDGMENTS

Ron would like to thank his wife, Jane, for her invaluable insights that added so much to the clarity of this book. Kevin would especially like to thank Robert and Jane Hadfield for their wonderful friendship and for providing a special retreat where part of this book was written. A special appreciation goes to Humanity United, an independent grant-making organization committed to building a world where slavery is no longer possible, for their efforts empowering affected communities and addressing the root causes of conflict and modern-day slavery to build lasting peace.

Many people added to this book through sharing their experiences, ideas, and histories with us. Some of our informants wished to remain anonymous, and we thank them. Others allowed us to quote and recognize them and their work. We want to express our appreciation to Annie Sovcik, Lutheran Immigration and Refugee Service (LIRS); Joy Zarembka and Melanie Orhant, Break the Chain Campaign; Laura Germino, Greg Asbed, Lucas Benitez, Melody Gonzalez, Antonio Martinez, Romeo Ramirez, and others from the Coalition of Immokalee Workers; Mike Baron, Border Patrol, San Antonio, Texas; Allen Davies, law enforcement, Orlando, Florida; Doug Molloy, U.S. Attorney's Office, Florida; John Norris, U.S. Department of Labor, Ft. Myers, Florida; Armando Brana, formerly of the U.S. Department of Labor; Maggie Fleming, Office of Sen. Brownback; Jolene Smith, Peggy Callahan, Ginny Baumann, Meg Roggensack, Kate Horner, Malauna Steele, Austin Choi-Fitzpatrick, Kumiko Maemura, Raquel Stratton, Judy Hyde, Vithika Yadav, Helen Armstrong, Aashika Damodar, and Jessica Leslie of Free the Slaves; Andrew Kline, Department of Justice, Civil Rights Division; Lisa Butler, Florida Rural Legal Services; Dan Werner, Workers' Rights Law Center; Kevin O'Connor, U.S. Attorney's Office, Connecticut, and U.S. Department of Justice; Michael Wishnie, Yale University; Kathleen Kim, Loyola University of Chicago; Mary Bauer, Southern Poverty Law Center, Immigrant Justice Project; Kate

Woomer-Deters, Legal Aid of North Carolina; Patricia Medige, Migrant Farm Worker Division of Colorado Legal Services; James B. Leonard, volunteer attorney, Farmworker Justice Fund, Inc.; Krishna R. Patel and Tom Carson of the U.S. Attorney's Office, Connecticut; Florrie Burke, human trafficking consultant; Lou de Baca, counsel, U.S. House of Representatives Committee on the Judiciary; Jennifer Dreher and Gabriella Villareal of Safe Horizon; Sandy Shepherd and Given Kachepa; Jason Van Brunt of the Hillsborough, Florida, Sheriff's Office; Amy Farrell, PhD, Institute on Race and Justice, Northeastern University; Dr. Lois Lee, Children of the Night; Dorchen Leidholdt and Norma Ramos of the Coalition Against Trafficking Women; Bradley Miles, Polaris Project; Andrew Oosterbaan and Wendy Waldron of the Department of Justice's Child Exploitation and Obscenity Section (CEOS); Anna Rodriguez, Florida Coalition Against Human Trafficking; Rachel Lloyd, Girls Education and Mentoring Services, Inc. (GEMS); Christa Stewart, The Door; Carole Smolenski, ECPAT (End Child Prostitution and Child Pornography and Trafficking of Children for Sexual Purposes); Alison Boak, International Organization for Adolescents (IOFA); Ann Jordan; Mark Lagon of the State Department's Office to Monitor and Combat Trafficking in Persons (TIP); Andrea Powell, Fair Fund; Heather Moore, Coalition to Abolish Slavery and Trafficking (CAST); Jim Cross, U.S. Attorney's Office, Kansas; Leslie Wolfe, Center for Women Policy Studies; Anne Milgram, Attorney General, New Jersey; Cathy Albisa, National Economic and Social Rights Initiative (NESRI); Steve Wagner, Renewal Forum; Vanessa Garza, U.S. Department of Health and Human Services; Sister Mary Ellen Dougherty, Anastasia Brown, and Nyssa Mestes of the United States Council of Catholic Bishops; Kathryn Turman of the FBI's Office of Victim Assistance; Carlton Peeples of the FBI's Civil Rights Unit; Albert Moskowitz, formerly of the Criminal Section of the Civil Rights Division of the U.S. Department of Justice; Maria Jose Fletcher, Florida Immigration Advocacy Center (FIAC); Jane Rodas, International Institute of Connecticut; Juhu Thukral, Urban Justice Center; Omar Vargas, Pepsico; Ben Skinner; John Bowe; Alison Friedman and Julia Ormond of the Alliance to Stop Slavery and End Trafficking (ASSET); and Claude D'Estree, University of Denver. We also want to thank our excellent editor Reed Malcolm and our copy editor Elisabeth Magnus at the University of California Press, and Jill Marsal, our agent at the Sandra Dijkstra Literary Agency.

All errors and omissions are, of course, our own.

PART I

SLAVES IN THE LAND OF THE FREE

THE OLD SLAVERY AND THE NEW

The great thought of captains, owners, consignees,
and others, was to make the most money they could
in the shortest possible time. Human nature is the
same now as then.

Frederick Douglass, *The New National Era*, August 17, 1871,
recalling the Atlantic slave trade

Certain things we know to be true. We know that slavery is a bad thing, perpetrated by bad people. We also know that slavery not only exists throughout the world today but flourishes. With approximately twenty-seven million people in bondage, it is thought to be the third most profitable criminal enterprise of our time, following only drugs and guns. In fact, more than twice as many people are in bondage in the world today than were taken from Africa during the entire 350 years of the Atlantic slave trade. And we know that slavery is alive and more than well in the United States, thriving in the dark, and practiced in many forms in places where you'd least expect it.

Meet Sandra Bearden. Sandra was a twenty-seven-year-old homemaker in a comfortable suburb of Laredo, Texas—a neighborhood of solid brick homes and manicured lawns. Married, the mother of a four-year-old son, she lived a perfectly normal middle-class existence. By all accounts, Sandra was a pleasant woman, the sort you'd chat with at the mall or the supermarket . . . the sort who might live next door. Yet she is currently serving a life sentence, convicted of multiple offenses, including human trafficking and slavery.

It started innocently enough. At first, all Sandra wanted was a maid—someone to do the housework and help with her small son—but she didn't want to pay a lot. So she drove across the border to a small, dirt-poor village near Vera Cruz, Mexico, where she was introduced to Maria and her parents. Maria was only twelve when she met Sandra Bearden. She had very little schooling and dreamed of getting an education—a dream that her parents encouraged but could do nothing to achieve. Over coffee in their small kitchen, Bearden offered Maria a job, as well as the chance to attend school, learn English, and taste the rich life of "el Norte." The work, as Bearden described it, was much like what

Maria was already doing at home, and, with the promise of education and opportunity, Sandra's offer made a very enticing package. The fact that Sandra herself was Mexican born helped Maria's parents feel they could trust her, and they gave their permission. Sandra smuggled Maria across the border in her expensive car and drove her to her home in Laredo.

On arrival, Maria was dragged into hell. Sandra Bearden used violence and terror to squeeze work and obedience from the child. From early morning till midafternoon, Maria cooked, cleaned, scrubbed, and polished. If Maria dozed off from exhaustion, or when Sandra decided she wasn't working fast enough, Sandra would blast pepper spray into Maria's eyes. A broom was broken over the girl's back and a few days later, a bottle against her head. At one point, Bearden tortured the twelve-year-old by jamming a garden tool up her vagina. That was Maria's workday; her "time off" was worse.

When Maria wasn't working, Sandra would chain her to a pole in the backyard without food or water. An eight-foot concrete fence kept her hidden from neighbors. After chaining her, Sandra would sometimes force Maria to eat dog feces. Then Maria would be left alone, her arms chained behind her with a padlock, her legs chained and locked together till the next morning, when the work and torture would begin again. Through the long afternoon and night Maria would fade in and out of consciousness from dehydration, and in her hunger she would sometimes scoop dirt into her mouth. Like most slaves in America, Maria was in shock, disoriented, isolated, and dependent. To maintain control, Bearden kept Maria hungry and in pain.

About one-third of the handful of slaves freed in the United States each year come to liberty because an average person sees something he or she just can't ignore. Luckily, one of the Beardens' neighbors had to do some work on his roof, and that probably saved Maria's life. Looking down over the high concrete wall into the Bearden's backyard, the neighbor saw a small girl chained up and whimpering; he called 911.

The police found Maria chained hand and foot, covered in cuts and bruises, and suffering from dehydration and exposure. She was too weak to walk and had to be carried to freedom on a stretcher. Her skin was badly burned from days in the sun. (In Laredo, Texas, the *average* summer temperature is ninety-eight degrees.) Photos taken at the time show one of her eyes bloodied and infected and thick welts and scars on her skin where the chains had cut into her. She had not eaten in four days. The district attorney said, "This is the worst case I've ever seen, worse than any murder. It's tragic all the way around." Later, at Bearden's trial, the policeman who found Maria wept. "She was shaking and crying and had a scared look in her eyes. She was in severe pain," Officer Jay Reece testified. He explained that he had tried to remove the chains from Maria's arms with bolt cutters but couldn't. As he tried to move her arm to cut the chains, she twisted and whimpered because she was in so much pain. "I've never seen anything like it before," Reese said, and sitting in the witness box, this policeman began to cry.

It is hard to imagine, but Maria was one of the lucky slaves. In America, most slaves spend four to five years in bondage; Maria's enslavement lasted only seven months. Sandra Bearden was arrested, and the Mexican government brought Maria's parents up from Vera Cruz. Her father blamed himself for what had happened. "We made a decision that we thought would be good for our child, and look what happened. I made a mistake, truly, and this is all my fault," he said.[1] Unlike most slaveholders in America, Bearden was caught and convicted. Like most slaves, Maria got nothing, except the fare for the twelve-hour bus ride home. She had just turned thirteen.[2]

We all ask, "How could someone so abuse a child—to stake her in the sun, feed her excrement, beat her bloody. . . . Surely, only a monster could do this." Yet Sandra Bearden's treatment of Maria is not unusual. How a seemingly normal person can descend into a spiral of violent control and abuse of another is one of the mysteries of slaveholding—a mystery we have set out to solve in this book.

The simple truth is, humans keep slaves; we always have. To understand this, we must come to know what it is in the human heart that makes slavery possible. For this book we set out to uncover slavery in modern America. Our search for answers took us to slaves and slave masters, to experts, counselors, and doctors, as well as to leaders of government, law enforcement, and groups whose sole mission is to rescue and support victims. Some of these stories broke our hearts, sometimes the excuses and rationalizations made us boil with anger, and sometimes we met real unsung heroes who gave us hope that America can put an end to slavery once and for all.

EQUAL OPPORTUNITY SLAVERY

Most Americans' idea of slavery comes right out of *Roots*—the chains, the whip in the overseer's hand, the crack of the auctioneer's gavel. That was one form of bondage. The slavery plaguing America today takes a different form, but make no mistake, it is real slavery. Where the law sanctioned slavery in the 1800s, today it's illegal. Where antebellum masters took pride in the ownership of slaves as a sign of status, today's human traffickers and slaveholders keep slaves hidden, making it all the more difficult to locate victims and punish offenders. Where the slaves in America were once primarily African and African American, today we have "equal opportunity" slavery; modern-day slaves come in all races, all types, and all ethnicities. We are, if anything, totally democratic when it comes to owning and abusing our fellow human beings. All that's required is the chance of a profit and a person weak enough and vulnerable enough to enslave.

This is capitalism at its worst, and it is supported by a dramatic alteration in the basic economic equation of slavery. Where an average slave in 1850 would have cost the equivalent of $40,000 in modern money, today's slave can be bought for a few hundred dollars. This cheapness makes the modern slave easily affordable, but it also makes him or her a disposable commodity. For the slaveholder it's often cheaper to let a slave die than it is to buy medicine to keep the slave alive. There is no form of slavery, past or present, that isn't horrific; however, today's slavery is one of the most diabolical strains to emerge in the thousands of years in which humans have been enslaving their fellows.

SO HOW MANY SLAVES ARE WE TALKING ABOUT?

According to a U.S. State Department study, some 14,500 to 17,500 people are trafficked into the United States from overseas and enslaved *each year*.[3] They come from Africa, Asia, India, China, Latin America, and the former Soviet states. Nor are native-born Americans immune from slavers; many are stolen from the streets of their own cities and towns. Some sources, including the federal government, have put out extremely high estimates of the number of U.S. citizens—primarily children—caught in slavery. The fact is, the precise number of slaves in the United States, whether trafficked in from other countries or enslaved from our own population, is simply not known. Given the hidden nature of the crime, the best numbers on offer are rough estimates. We do know that slaves in America are found—or rather, *not* found—in nearly all fifty states, working as commercial sex slaves, fruit pickers, construction workers, gardeners, and domestics. They work in restaurants, factories, laundries, and sweatshops. Each year human trafficking and slavery in America generate millions upon millions of dollars for criminals who prey on the most vulnerable: the desperate, the uneducated, and the impoverished immigrant seeking a better life. Brutalized and held in slavery for years, those who survive face indifference, official confusion, stigma, and shame as they struggle to regain control over their stolen and deeply damaged lives.

While no one knows for sure how many people are enslaved in America, a conservative estimate would be around fifty thousand and growing. Even for those who have worked in this area for years, these numbers are staggering. More astounding is the fact that this is a crime that, as a rule, goes unpunished. This lack of punishment is reflected in a remarkable parallel in American crime rates. If we accept the government's estimates, about seventeen thousand people are trafficked into slavery in the United States in any given year; coincidentally about seventeen thousand people are murdered in the United States each year. Obviously, murder is the ultimate crime, but slavery comes a close second, especially considering the other crimes associated with it, such as rape and torture. Note that the national success rate in solving murder cases is about 70 percent; around eleven thousand murders are "cleared" each year. But according to the U.S. government's own numbers, the annual percentage of trafficking and slavery cases solved is less than 1 percent. If 14,500 to 17,500 people were newly enslaved in America in 2006, the fact is that in the same year the Department of Justice brought charges against only 111 people for human trafficking and slavery; 98 of them were convicted.[4] And those figures apply only to people trafficked from other countries; no measures exist for domestic slavery victims.

In July 2004 then-President Bush talked about the rate of arrests and convictions for human trafficking in the United States: "Since 2001, we've charged 110 traffickers. That's triple the number charged in the previous three years. We're beginning to make good, substantial progress. The message is getting out: We're serious. And when we catch you, you'll find out we're serious. We're staying on the hunt." Strong words, but the unvarnished truth is, with less than 1 percent of the offenders apprehended and less than 1 percent of the victims freed, the flow of human "product" into America continues practically unchecked.

AN UNBROKEN LEGACY OF BONDAGE

This book is about slavery in America today. Yet there has always been bondage in this country. That fact bears repetition—there has never been a single day in our America, from its discovery and birth right up to the moment you are reading this sentence, without slavery.

It began when the Spaniards landed. In 1493, on his second voyage across the Atlantic, and before even establishing a colony, Christopher Columbus enslaved hundreds of Taino Indians and shipped them home to Spain. The wave of armed and armored conquistadores following Columbus brought a plague of butchery and enslavement upon the Indians, destroying entire cultures. With the age-old rationale that any foreign society is inferior, the Spaniards used the "God-told-me-to-do-it" argument to justify a policy of rape, slaughter, and enslavement in their quest for riches.

When the Spaniards found that the Indians, not surprisingly, were dying in droves from brutality and European diseases, they began to sail to Africa for slaves—*bozales,* as they were called. In 1518, King Charles of Spain gave royal consent to begin what would become the 350-year trans-Atlantic slave trade. Ultimately, every European power claiming land in the New World followed Spain's example. French, Spanish, Dutch, Portuguese, and English settlers from the Canadian North to the bottom tip of South America owned slaves. There was a heavy concentration not only in the southern colonies of Virginia and Georgia but also on the farms and docks of the northern settlements of Massachusetts and New York. Slave labor in America became an accepted social and economic reality. Once again, the "heathen" state of the victims, along with the difference in their skin color, made for an easy—if false—moral distinction in the minds of the slavers.

Most of us are not aware that following the American Revolution Congress passed a series of increasingly stringent laws banning the international slave trade (while leaving the *institution* of slavery untouched), culminating in a law that made trafficking in slaves a hanging offense.[5] Congress, however, did little to enforce these laws, and both slavery and the slave trade flourished until the Civil War and the passage of the Thirteenth Amendment. It's a safe bet that a vast majority of Americans believes that slavery ended in 1865; nothing could be further from the truth. It continued more quietly and on a smaller scale, but without pause.

While legal emancipation might have come with the Thirteenth Amendment, that didn't stop the southern planters from re-enslaving countless thousands of African Americans. Crops in the South still needed planting, cultivating, and harvesting, and there was a vast population of unemployed former slaves. Planters instituted a system that was as close to the old slavery as possible, but with some new wrinkles. With the blessing of President Andrew Johnson, each southern state passed what were referred to as Black Codes. These laws were nothing more than legalized racial repression, dictating every aspect of the lives of the former slaves. The laws of each state varied, but in general, segregation was made mandatory, and African Americans were forbidden to vote, sit on juries, carry weapons in public, testify against whites, or hold certain jobs. Violations were punishable by fines and imprisonment.

This time, instead of the old-fashioned antebellum slavery, the rule was "peonage," a simple form of debt bondage slavery that took two forms. In the most blatant form of peonage slavery, local authorities were allowed to "bind out" to local farmers any violators convicted of a crime, often a misdemeanor, and unable to pay their fines. With the law on the side of the white farmers, court-imposed fixed terms of labor became the norm. The number of "violations" increased dramatically as the work called for it. At harvest time, sheriff's deputies were sent into African American neighborhoods and drinking spots to arrest a fixed number of the strongest men. Charged with being "drunk and disorderly," they would be ordered to "work off" a large fine for several months with local white farmers. Cotton production consumed a large part of the people enslaved through peonage, but local governments also worked this scam to serve other interests. This type of forced labor was used to build railroads, roads, and bridges, to clear forests, and to manufacture turpentine. It wasn't the long-term ownership of the antebellum South, but these slaves weren't expensive, and it still meant complete and violent control, no pay, and economic exploitation, the defining hallmarks of slavery. From the 1870s, white-controlled local governments all across the Deep South were essentially slave brokers, enslaving and then selling the labor of African Americans.

In the second form of peonage, African Americans were duped or coerced into signing contracts as field workers or sharecroppers. Farm owners would hold their pay, and the sharecroppers were obligated to make all their purchases from the "company store," using tickets or orders rather than money. When their annual contracts expired, they found that the crops they raised never paid the debts they owed. Although it was often apparent that these "debts" were fraudulent or impossibly inflated, the penalty for nonpayment was jail. The only alternative was to stay on the land and try to work off the debt, which never seemed to lessen or disappear. Worse, the debt passed from parent to child, binding families to the land with no hope of advancement or escape. Each year became a frustrating, spirit-crushing effort to break even. Historian Jacqueline Jones has said that "perhaps as many as one-third of all sharecropping farmers in Alabama, Mississippi, and Georgia were being held against their will in 1900."[6] Peonage was practiced across the South and upheld for decades by local and federal government. A full federal ban on peonage-based slavery was not passed until 1948, and it persisted across much of the South well into the 1960s.

THE MORE THINGS CHANGE,
THE MORE THEY STAY THE SAME

While both the federal government and the American people generally ignored peonage, another form of slavery was very much on the minds of Americans in the first decades of the twentieth century. Large numbers of foreign-born women immigrants were being exploited in many areas of the workforce, and some of them were being forced into prostitution. On the West Coast, young, Asian, immigrant females (some younger than the age of ten) were smuggled into the United States, thereby circumventing immigration laws that excluded them. Asian women were bought and sold as property in a system that became known as the "yellow slave trade." Bogus "contracts" were created to enforce this system of slavery in which Asian women became domestics or prostitutes. The contracts offered these women a chance to work to buy their freedom, but in ways that were impossible to achieve. In San Francisco alone the number of Asian immigrant women who died in enslaved conditions was in the thousands.

At this same time prostitution was rapidly expanding along with the cities and was controlled by the same criminal gangs who often ran corrupt local governments. Operating from the premise that white women— both immigrant and native born—were being either lured or abducted, sold, and forced into prostitution, reformers and religious groups mounted a nationwide campaign. Using the term *white slavery* to describe the systematic sexual coercion of unwilling young women, religious leaders and journalists waged war against pimps and procurers. The campaign captured the imagination of middle-class white America. The first attacks and exposés were highly anti-Semitic, portraying Russian Jews as the gravest offenders. The Jews, claimed the authors, were selling their own sisters and daughters to educate and advance their sons. The charges were preposterous and vicious, and they set an anti-immigrant tone that permeated the movement for years. But the biggest target of the reformers was the "urban machine," for it was in the cities that the evils of rape, seduction, and forced prostitution were most rampant.

Within a short time, the white slavery issue became a plank in Progressive election platforms, and candidates trumpeted their concern for the innocent young victims of the "vice combines." The whole question of "white slavery," however, became entangled (as it has today) with questions of race, ethnicity, and immigration. Inevitably, legislation for the safeguarding of endangered womanhood was introduced. The first of two laws, the 1907 Immigration Act, allowed the government to deport any immigrant engaging in any form of prostitution within three years of his or her admission to the country (thus deporting the victims of "white slavery"). The second law was the brainchild of Chicago congressman James R. Mann. In 1910, he introduced the White Slave Traffic Act, more commonly known as the Mann Act. Its provisions were simple: the federal government could prosecute anyone who transported young women and forced them into prostitution (or "any other immoral purpose"). The bill was signed into law with little resistance.

Sadly, these laws were also used as an excuse for racist oppression and the wholesale deportation of recent immigrants. Police systematically searched ghettos and other ethnic neighborhoods and raided brothels in several major cities across the United States, arresting recent immigrant clients and prostitutes for "moral turpitude" and deporting them. At the same time, many male immigrants were being caught up in forced labor in agriculture, mining, and construction, and American-born and immigrant women were still being enslaved in prostitution, but their existence or fate was rarely noted.

To this day, the debate continues as to how much "white slavery" actually existed. At the time, most Americans believed it was rampant, but there was no effective way to count victims. Ironically, the very situation that sparked fear and action one hundred years ago may have become a reality today. Thousands of foreign and native-born women and children are being enslaved in the United States by foreign and native-born human traffickers. Forced prostitution is, according to the federal government, the largest market for slave labor in America. This time there is no moral panic; most Americans are simply clueless.

Slavery in America probably hit its lowest ebb in the 1940s and 1950s. True, some states were still enslaving African Americans through trumped-up legal charges, and in remote areas Mexican and Chinese workers were locked away, abused and unpaid. Still, by the sixties, especially with the civil rights movement and farm mechanization undermining Southern sharecropping systems, slavery seemed all but dead. But beginning in the 1980s, and then exploding in the 1990s, slavery came back with a vengeance. With the end of the Cold War and the tripling of the global population, borders collapsed around the world and the traffic in people expanded exponentially. America, once again, became a prime destination for slave traders.

SLAVERY COMES IN MANY GUISES

The government, when it addresses the subject of human trafficking at all, focuses primarily on the area of forced prostitution, possibly because it makes the biggest splash. More visible than most other forms of slavery, it is thought to account for about half the trafficking victims in the country. These women and children are subjected to serial rape, physical injury, psychological damage, and constant exposure to sexually transmitted diseases, including HIV.

But what about all the other forms of slavery thriving right under our noses? If you don't see them, you're in good company; neither do many of our public officials. The plight of enslaved domestics, such as Maria, accounts for about one-fourth of all slaves in America. Agriculture is another major area of human trafficking. An unknown number of victims of forced labor are tending and picking our fruit and vegetables. They come here looking for a decent wage. Instead, they are enslaved by crime syndicates and families—and sometimes through our government's own unwieldy "guest worker" program—in such states as Florida, North and South Carolina, and Georgia.

What happened to seventeen-year-old Alejandro, an orphaned street kid from Guatemala, is typical. A trafficker, in the guise of a sympathetic neighbor, "loaned" Alejandro the money to come to America, promising good pay and the chance to get an education. When he arrived in the Southwest, he was immediately thrown into a barracks with twenty other trafficked workers, kept under guard by thugs with automatic weapons. Here he was told he had to work to pay off his "debt," which had suddenly doubled, with an interest rate of 75 percent. Of course the debt was never meant to be paid off; the money he earned went straight to his traffickers. Beaten, bound, and blindfolded, trucked from field to field, and threatened with torture and death should he run away, the disoriented and desperate boy finally managed to elude his keepers and found his way to a homeless shelter. Here the scars on his body were noticed, and he told his story. A "Good Samaritan" contacted a local refugee resettlement agency, and various nongovernmental organizations (NGOs) became involved. Finally, Alejandro was placed in a licensed foster home and worked with the Department of Justice to prosecute his traffickers. As with Maria, his story is unusual only in that he escaped his slavery; most do not.[7]

It turns out that slaves are all around us, hidden in plain sight—the dishwasher in the kitchen of the restaurant where you and your family dined last night; the kids on the corner of Forty-first Street, selling cheap trinkets for a dollar; the man in gray overalls, sweeping the floor of the big-name department store where you buy your Christmas presents. What they share in common is that their lives are not their own, and they deserve better. But without our help, their world will change only by getting worse.

Almost impossible to detect, slavery exists in our fields, in our towns, and, sometimes, in the house next door. And even if we did suspect a person of being a slaveholder, many of us would say it is none of our business. Be honest, nobody's listening; if you suspected that *your* next-door neighbor, your golfing buddy, or one of the women in your book club seemed to be keeping a "domestic" against her will, what, if anything, would you do? It's a tough question, not least because most Americans are not even sure what defines a slave.

BECOMING SLAVES

Slavery has been defined in various ways, but there are three essential criteria for knowing if someone is a slave. The first is the complete control of one person by another, through the use of violence—both physical and psychological. The second—hard labor for little or no pay—clearly applies as well. Slaves receive nothing beyond subsistence. The third criterion is economic exploitation—making a profit for the slaveholder. No one enslaves another simply out of meanness, at least not at first; slavery is about money. All three of these conditions are vital to the definition, but the most crucial is violent control and the resultant loss of free will. When we aren't sure if someone is, in fact, a slave, we can ask one basic question: "Can this person walk away?" In America, more and more frequently the answer is "no."[8]

That's why, ironically, most slaves in America are volunteers at first. Today the slave takers rarely have to coerce or kidnap their victims. All the criminals have to do is open a door to "opportunity" and the slaves walk in. Slave recruiters all over the world appear friendly and full of news about good jobs with good pay. There may even be a little money for the rest of the family as an "advance" on the big wages to be earned.

This helps ease the victims out of their homes and into the pipeline that will deliver them into slavery.

Once they are in the pipeline, their documents are taken away "for safekeeping." The transit house where they stay at night is locked up "to keep everyone safe." They are fed little, and the "boss" purposely keeps them awake most of the night. Within a few days, sleep deprivation, hunger, and isolation take their toll, and confusion and dependence set in. Disoriented, they are constantly reminded that soon they'll be working regular jobs in America.

They have no idea that they are, in fact, slaves, as they walk, ride, fly, or float further into bondage. Once inside the United States, far from family, without any proof of identity, unable to speak the language, hungry, confused, and now threatened, they become aware of their situation. If they resist or try to leave, they are punished. It is a story that is played out all over the world. There are variations on the theme; sometimes the recruiter is a friend of the family, sometimes the violence begins before the border is crossed. Some victims are brought into the country via major airports and harbors holding real or spurious documents, while others huddle in the backs of vans or wade across the Rio Grande. But ultimately, the result is the same.

A MELTING POT OF SLAVES

In 2004 the antislavery organization Free the Slaves teamed up with the Human Rights Center at the University of California, Berkeley to carry out the first large-scale study of slavery in America. They found people trafficked from at least thirty-five countries working against their will in the United States. Currently, the largest group of victims seems to be Chinese, followed by Mexicans and Vietnamese; but this can change, depending on shifts in global economics and politics.[9] Between 1999 and 2004, documented slavery cases were reported in at least ninety U.S. cities. These tended to be larger cities in states with sizable immigrant communities, such as California, Florida, New York, and Texas— all of which are on the transit routes for international travelers.

Most slaves in America, like Maria and Alejandro, come here hoping to start new and better lives. This is the terrible irony about American slavery. People are turned into slaves for doing what any one of us would do—in fact, what many of our own parents, or their parents, did. When many families today face the same circumstances they also pick up and move, inspired by desperation, courage, and determination. Some will succeed. But for many others, the land of opportunity includes a one-way ticket into bondage.

HOMEGROWN SLAVES

Not all slavery in America involves undocumented immigrants. Some victims are born and raised in the United States and find themselves pressed into slavery by deception or sheer violence. In January 2003, a terrified seventeen-year-old girl ran into a store in a suburban mall in Detroit and grabbed a security guard. She pleaded with him for help, as a group of men and women burst into the store pursuing her. Seeing that the girl was shaking and bruised, the guard stood up to the thugs and threw them out of the store. Once he had her safe, he called the police, and the girl told her story.

The teenager explained to authorities that a man and a woman had abducted her months before while she was waiting at a bus stop in downtown Cleveland, Ohio. Her captors drove her to Detroit, where she was held in a house with other female captives and forced to have sex with male visitors. The captives were never left alone, but were escorted around the house, even to the bathroom. An older woman kept the younger ones in line by threatening and sometimes beating them. Each day the girls were given a new assignment. Some would go to malls in the metro Detroit area to sell jewelry and trinkets; others would be forced to dance and strip for private parties and to perform sex acts.

The girls' captors "did that punishment-reward thing," a police investigator said. "They would get their nails and hair done. If they stepped out of line, they got beat down. Some of the senior women acted as enforcers."

One day, on a trip to the mall with several others, the girl managed to escape. After the security guard called the police, the young girl directed them to the house where she had been enslaved. The resulting bust led to the exposure of a multistate ring of forced prostitution involving midwestern women and girls, some as young as thirteen. Police discovered that the traffickers had been operating a forced prostitution ring since as early as 1995 by kidnapping teenage girls and transporting them to cities throughout the Midwest.

Not surprisingly, the victims are still experiencing severe emotional problems. "The devastation [this] has brought on these young women is just immeasurable," the prosecutor said.[10]

The young girl enslaved from the bus stop was a native-born American, with native-born parents and a life little different from that of most American children. When she left home that day, the last thing she expected was to be abducted and forced into prostitution. The parasitic traffickers are students of opportunity, seducing or stealing their victims where they can, all over America. One government official has asserted that about half the trafficking victims in this country are children.[11] And while studies point to runaway or throwaway children as the likeliest victims, no one is exempt.

Over and over, the story of enslavement plays itself out across our country. Every day our newspapers carry stories of human trafficking, yet we remain oblivious. Through our ignorance and worse yet, our lack of interest, we enable slavery. Unless we heed the wake-up call, slavery will continue to spread. Our children are also endangered by a different, subtler threat—apathy. Kids learn from their parents, and if noninvolvement is what we teach, by word or example, then that is exactly what they will learn and how they will live.

FREEDOM AND THE FUTURE

Federal law classifies tens of thousands of people in the United States as slaves, yet most Americans can't see them. If we are going to free slaves, ensure that they get to build new lives, and help our government enforce its own antislavery laws, we must understand what slavery is today and where it is going. We cannot solve a problem we don't understand. In writing this book, we have had to face up to some basic questions: How can any American, who began nearly every day of his or her young life with the phrase, "with liberty and justice for all," possibly enslave another? What is wrong with our country that it allows slave masters to live—and flourish—untroubled among us? What more can we as citizens do to fix this problem? And what will it take for our government, which serves at the will and for the good of its people, to dedicate the needed resources, both money and personnel, to destroying this evil?

On our journey we looked hard into the many faces of slavery. Now we can introduce you to the traffickers—from the single *coyote* to the crime syndicate. Victims of slavery will speak in this book, as well those who are struggling against terrific odds to find and free the slaves. We also want to share what we have learned about recognizing slavery in your own town or neighborhood. The more we learned, the more we've had to admit our own complicity. We discovered that the simplest daily purchases Americans make can contribute to keeping people in bondage. It turns out that all of us are responsible for perpetuating slavery by buying, wearing, eating, and using the products of slave labor, from cell phones and laptops, to the fruit and vegetables on our tables, to the clothes we wear.

Slavery is in our homes, neighborhoods, and cities, and little is being done about it. Together, we can change that. In these pages, you'll meet police officers on the street, high-ranking government officials, and Good Samaritans—everyday people, fighting to make an impact. Tough questions will be asked of government agencies whose roles include—or should include—the discovery, liberation, and support of slaves and the arrest and prosecution of their traffickers. While the problem is huge, our journey has taught us that it is within our power to end slavery in America; and we will offer ideas on how to achieve a final emancipation.

America was born with the congenital disease of slavery, and, legal or illegal, it has never left us. Today, we are still conflicted about our slaveholding past and its ugly aftermath. We study it, lament it, and argue it as a haunting presence from our darker history. Yet while we were looking the other way, slavery in America evolved into a whole new beast that lives in darkness among us and feeds on ignorance and misery. Only through our awareness, our concern, and our commitment can it be driven out. The aim of *The Slave Next Door* is to provide the awareness and hopefully inspire the concern and the commitment. It's both challenging and exhilarating to know that we really can be the generation to end this nation-long affliction.

2

HOUSE SLAVES

SLAVERY BEGINS AT HOME

Domestic slavery is unique among the many types of bondage in that it is less about *making* money than it is about *saving* money. The slaveholder, like Sandra Bearden, is stealing services for his or her own benefit rather than for profit. This form of slavery is also cheaper to operate than the others: bring in the victim, and she's yours for years.[1] Her keep requires minimal food and clothing, little or no medicine, and a mattress on the floor of the utility room. There are no start-up costs, as in a factory or on a farm; a domestic slave can be held very cheaply. What's more, U.S. government immigration policies have made the importation of a domestic slave remarkably easy for foreign diplomats and others.

It seems that the second-highest number of human trafficking victims in the United States are enslaved domestics.[2] But there are no large-scale domestic slavery rings; it is not the type of offense that lends itself to crime syndicates. Victims are sold one or two at a time, through "mom and pop" operations, requiring only an outside consumer who is complicit in the crime. Frequently, a woman becomes a domestic slave through legal channels, coming here on her own with a legitimate work visa. Only once she is under the slaveholder's roof does her life in bondage begin.

The underlying characteristic of domestic slavery is total control of mind and body. This normally involves threats and violence. That first beating goes a long way toward keeping an enslaved domestic in line. With the proper indoctrination, the slave soon becomes completely dependent and unable to leave. She is at the mercy of her keepers, and the degree of humiliation and abuse she suffers rests entirely with them.

SLAVES DON'T WEAR SIGNS

Most trafficked domestics remain under the control of their keepers for years, so well hidden behind the curtains of suburban homes that we never notice them. Joy Zarembka, who now directs the Break the Chain

Campaign, a Washington, D.C.–based NGO devoted exclusively to the rescue and support of abused domestic workers, discovered in the 1990s that she had, unknowingly, been living next door to a slave. "It is the reason I do the work I do now," she told us.

There's a very good chance that many of us have stood in grocery lines with an enslaved domestic and have simply taken her for a quiet, somewhat self-absorbed and timid foreigner if we noticed her at all. Perhaps we saw her sitting in the park, overseeing children obviously not her own, and thought she was simply a nanny. Often there is no more indication of involuntary servitude than a weeping woman sitting on a front step.

This is not like the old days of legal slavery in America. Then, a house slave was an expensive acquisition and, as such, a symbol of status and wealth. She—or he—would appear in the census, on property tax reports and inventories, and in wills. Far from being a secret, a house slave was an accepted—and sometimes envied—aspect of daily life. Nowadays, an enslaved domestic is cheaply acquired, cheaply maintained, and kept hidden. When she is allowed out of the house, it is rarely alone, and with her owners' certainty that she has nowhere else to go. The chains of bondage are formed by the victim's own inability to see beyond her prison. And often she won't even know she's the victim of a crime.

MORE THAN JUST A HOUSEKEEPER . . . AND LESS

For Ruth, the day starts like all the rest; the fact that it is Sunday makes no difference.[3] She wakes long before dawn and begins to clean the large house, careful not to disturb the family sleeping upstairs. If she wakes the man or his wife, they will beat her; they have done it before. Later, she gives the five children their breakfast and prepares lunch and dinner for the whole family. Between meals she works, and she continues to work well into the evening. At night she has to sleep with the one-year-old twins, caring for them whenever they wake. Between the twins and all the other jobs, her workday, except for catnaps, is essentially twenty-four hours long. If the family ever goes out, she is still not left in peace but is made to wait in the hallway of the apartment building until they return.

Ruth was a totally different person when she arrived in the suburbs of Washington, D.C., from West Africa, at the age of fifty-two. She had been promised a car and a house in return for serving as a housekeeper and nanny for the family of a man who worked for the World Bank. She was thrilled with a chance to help her impoverished family. That's what she was promised. Instead, both husband and wife beat her regularly, paid her nothing, and ignored her pleas to return to West Africa.

When neighbors heard Ruth screaming, they called the police. On the scene, the police turned to her "employers" to translate Ruth's broken French. When Ruth tried to act out the beatings she was suffering, the husband told the police, "See, she's showing you how she beats herself. She's crazy." And Ruth was taken to a local mental institution, where she was forcibly sedated, her arms and legs tied to the bedposts. By the time an interpreter arrived, the drugs had left Ruth unable to explain her situation, and the hospital staff called her employers and asked them to come get her.

When she was returned to her employers, they threatened her, telling her that if she tried anything again the police would come and take her to the hospital permanently. They told her that the security guard that patrolled the area was, in fact, there to watch her and make sure she didn't harm the children. Isolated, terrified, intimidated, Ruth believed them and spent many more months in slavery. Finally neighbors, who could still hear her cries when she was being beaten, helped her to escape. She was too traumatized to take part in the prosecution of her abusers, and she returned, penniless, to West Africa.

Ruth received no pay and never really knew anything of America except the site of her abuse. For Ruth, shock and despair replaced any sense of hope or self-esteem. The front door no longer represented the possibility of flight; it merely let her know when the man and his wife came and went. Ruth lacked the language skills to communicate outside the house; furthermore, she was terrorized with stories, fed her by the couple, of police and government brutality. If you go to the authorities, she was told, they will beat you, imprison you, and deport you. So Ruth remained a prisoner in the home. But unlike a convict, she had no fixed release date; she would remain until she was discarded, was rescued, or died. She was one of the thousands of enslaved "domestics" in today's America.

By now, it should be clear that domestic servitude is not simply about "housekeeping." Behind closed doors, it entails unrestrained physical, psychological, and sexual abuse. Victims are at the constant whim and call of their owners. Obviously, they didn't enter service to be enslaved, and it might not be why their owners first brought them here.

"Employers" often assert best of intentions, but the reality is a spiraling down to an enslaved girl and an abusive controller.

Most household slaves in America are teenage girls, but some are grown women whose hope is to earn money to send home to their families. Lakshmi was no longer a naive young girl; at thirty-four, she was the mother of five and wife to an ailing husband. She was her family's only breadwinner, but she couldn't find a job in her native city of Bangalore, India. So she traveled to Kuwait, where she found work as a domestic. After a few months, she was offered an opportunity to come to New York City and care for the new baby of a Kuwaiti diplomat. She was promised $2,000 a month; what she got was slavery.

When Lakshmi arrived in New York, the diplomat took her passport. She was worked fifteen hours a day, with no allowance for fatigue or illness, and was forced to oversee the man's two children. The diplomat's wife beat her daily, and she was serially raped. She was fed poorly and paid nothing. Locked in the apartment, denied any social contact, and afraid to leave, Lakshmi was a slave for four long years.

One day, after being so severely beaten that she feared for her life, Lakshmi decided to run. She was terrified, but she managed to find her passport and escape the apartment. Alone and overwhelmed on the streets of Manhattan, Lakshmi ran, frightened that at any moment she'd be caught by the man or his wife. Through luck, she found a sympathetic cab driver who spoke Hindi, and he drove her to a Hindu temple in Queens. From there, Lakshmi was introduced to Andolan, a charitable organization for the protection of South Asian women. They helped her and reported her case to the authorities. Lakshmi had just joined an exclusive club—the fewer than 1 percent of all trafficking victims who manage to escape or be rescued.

In time, the federal government offered Lakshmi a visa if she would testify against her keepers; despite her terror, Lakshmi agreed. In this, she was also an exception to the rule: many victims choose not to testify. Their traffickers make it perfectly clear what will happen to them—and their families in their home country—should they speak out. These victims need help: medical, psychological, legal. Yet fearing for their own safety, as well as that of their loved ones, victims will frequently choose to disappear before the trial, forfeiting the offer of sanctuary made by a government that often seems more concerned with convicting the trafficker than protecting the victim.

Despite Lakshmi's willingness to see her trafficker punished, the government declined to prosecute, citing the man's diplomatic status. This is an ongoing problem, since many trafficking cases involve foreign diplomats who, when caught, plead immunity or are simply whisked away by their governments. In cases such as this, the victim is often the one penalized.

Every year, foreign diplomats, as well as U.S. citizens and employees of such international agencies as the World Bank and the United Nations, legally import thousands of domestics, who are assigned work visas. Most are brought here from various parts of Africa and India; many are enslaved. The National Labor Relations Act (NLRA) doesn't include household workers in its definition of "employees." This, in combination with an immigration policy that ties the domestic to her employer via her visa, works in the slaveholder's favor and places in jeopardy any domestic who tries to escape. If he abuses her and she attempts to flee, she leaves herself open to deportation— unless she can prove abuse—since she has broken her contract, which can void the provisions of her visa. Should the case become public, as with Lakshmi, a foreign diplomat can simply claim immunity. In Lakshmi's case, the diplomat was transferred out of the country, and the Kuwaiti government stated that there would be no investigation. "I guess she just wanted to stay here in the States," said a Kuwaiti official. "You only see such cases in countries where they see a good opportunity."[4]

BUT WHY NOT JUST RUN AWAY?

Lakshmi escaped; the vast majority of slaves do not. How can a person's spirit be so broken that she accepts slavery over the risk of a bid for freedom? Why wouldn't she simply run away? As we read this, most of us harbor the conceit that we would rather risk all to escape than submit to such slavery. Certainly *we* would never put up with such treatment. But the reality is more complicated. A number of reasons—some more subtle than others—keep a slave from attempting escape, even in the "land of the free."

One of the main deterrents is fear, in its many forms. At the most basic level, the victim is afraid of being beaten or killed by the keeper should she attempt to flee. Most probably he has abused her in the past, so physical punishment is more than just a threat. The slaveholder is also effective at instilling in the victim a fear of the world outside his door. Often, he does this by showing her videos and television programs that feature an abundance of brutality and violence. By watching any one of hundreds of cop films and being told over and over that it represents a true picture of life on American streets, the victim develops a terror of leaving the house, let alone running away.

The victim is also taught to fear the police and the courts. The police are corrupt, she is told, just as they were back home. They will arrest you and beat you, and the immigration authorities will deport you. Finally, the slaveholder instills the fear of retribution against the victim's family in the country of origin: "If you run, I'll have your daughter killed."

Intimidation is powerful, but still other reasons keep a house slave under control. A surprising number of victims stay because they feel they are responsible for the repayment of their "debt." In all instances, this debt is inflated, sometimes purely fictitious, and it grows to amounts that are limited only by the traffickers' greed and imagination. Still, irrational though it might seem, some victims see it as an obligation they are bound to fulfill.

At times the victim stays because she develops a loyalty to her master. One of the more insidious effects of this loyalty is that the victim comes to feel that her enslavement is her own fault. This might grow out of her misplaced guilt, which engenders the belief that she deserves to be punished. An offshoot of this is the shame many slaves feel. By assuming responsibility for her state, the slave feels a deep sense of personal remorse, especially if she has been sexually abused. This shame keeps her from situations where she would have to share her condition with others; she wouldn't even tell her own parents. In this we see a parallel to the experiences of other women who are sexually assaulted or are victims of domestic violence. Rape victims often feel intense shame, though they know rationally that they have done nothing wrong. Slaves will also feel shame, even self-loathing, in a way that paralyzes them and prevents escape.

Language and geographic isolation are factors as well. The victim generally doesn't speak English, nor does she have any sense of location. One woman who was enslaved in Long Island, New York, later stated, "For three years, I lived around the corner from a Catholic Charities office and never even knew they were there." Outside the house is a frightening world full of hostility, babbling voices, and confusion to a woman who is, in every sense, isolated. And to ensure that she stays a stranger and a prisoner, her slaveholder takes her passport and any other form of identification.

Beyond the shame, the sense of obligation, the fear of arrest and deportation, the threat of physical injury to herself and her loved ones, the inability to communicate in a foreign language, and the confusion over not knowing where she is or where to go for help, other factors are at work. Two of them are things we all take for granted: food and rest. The slaveholder faces a difficult challenge: he must provide just enough of each to allow the victim to work the long, hard hours, yet remain totally subservient. Fed on scraps and leavings, most domestic slaves live in a constant state of malnutrition, a significant contributor to breaking their spirit. Sleep deprivation is another tool of the "employer": he must keep the victim tired enough to be confused and debilitated but not so tired that she can't perform her work. It is a delicate balance, and one at which the slaveholder becomes adept. On three hours of sleep per night a domestic slave can be kept confused and submissive for years, while still putting in fifteen to twenty hours of work a day.

There is another, more poignant reason why a domestic slave often chooses to remain in bondage. Over the course of time, she may form a bond with the children of her enslavers, and the thought of leaving them unprotected becomes unacceptable to her. Whether or not the parents are, in fact, abusive to the children isn't always a factor; frequently, the slave will project her own status as victim onto the children and assume the role of their protector. Time and again, this comes out in the victim's testimony in court: "How could I leave the children with those monsters?"

If we roll all of these factors together, it becomes easier to see how they forge a chain around the brain of the enslaved domestic. Fear, shame, confusion, depression, injury, hunger, and exhaustion all compound and reinforce a hopelessness and lethargy. Living in a nightmare, the minds of many household slaves take refuge by shutting down. Freed slaves talk of "going blank" or "not feeling anything," hallmarks of trauma, shock, and depression. These are coping mechanisms that help them get through their ordeal. The paralysis they feel is easier to understand when we glimpse the unrelenting abuse they suffer. What is much more difficult to understand is the behavior of the slaveholders.

MONSTERS AMONG US

It is tough to imagine how a person could be a slaveholder. For most of us the idea of maintaining, day after day and year after year, the systematic control and degradation of another human being is so unthinkable, so twisted, that it turns our stomachs. Our reaction in the face of enslaved domestic workers is disgust but also puzzlement. This is slavery in our homes, our most intimate space. These are slaves taking care of our *children*. How could we face our children, what would they be learning, if their care was entrusted to a slave? It is a fact so ugly that we want to reject it out of hand, to say, "These are monsters, not humans like us." But is it likely that Sandra Bearden was born and raised with the potential to enslave and torture Maria? Surely she possessed a vestige of humanity; no doubt she loved her husband and child, cried at sad movies, gave to charities. How could she have sunk so far as to chain Maria to a post and force her to eat dog feces? How can the thousands of slaveholders that live in the United States justify their crime to themselves, their families, and their children?

It may be easier to dismiss slaveholders as monsters than to look into our own hearts and ask, "How can a person do this?" But there is a very important reason why we should ask that question. Slaveholding is an affront that must be wiped out, rooted out of our economy and our communities, and that means confronting the mental gymnastics that allow some Americans to enslave. We need to be able to explain how someone could be a slaveholder in America today, but many of the reasons are locked in mystery. This is not surprising because many of the key questions about becoming a slaveholder have not been answered; indeed, some haven't even been asked yet.

This lack of answers reflects a pattern that has been played out in America with other crimes of abuse. Back in the 1960s, for example, there were no domestic violence shelters, almost no psychologists doing research or trained to work with domestic violence victims, no academic journals devoted to the issue, and no institutes where research could be centralized. Probably the biggest problem was that there was no education for police to help them identify when a "family spat" was actually a crime. In the 1970s people began to wake up to domestic violence in their neighborhoods and cities, and while domestic violence is still a serious problem today, we know a great deal more than we did in the past, and many people are working against it. This cycle repeated itself in the 1980s when torture victims began to pour into the United States from Central America and the Middle East. At first, confusion reigned; clearly there were enormous needs, but there were no experts, journals, institutes, or training programs. In time, expertise grew and with it a dedicated body of psychologists, doctors, social workers, and others who built the comprehensive response that torture victims need. Now thirty-one clinics or institutes in America provide support and rehabilitation for survivors of torture.

We are repeating that pattern again, beginning with the "discovery" of human trafficking and slavery in the United States in the 1990s. Not surprisingly, most of the effort—especially on the part of nongovernmental agencies—has gone into understanding and supporting the immediate needs of trafficking victims, not the psychology of slaveholders and traffickers. Today, there is only a glimmer of an organized response to our need to study and understand the lives of slaves and slaveholders in America. We have no journal, no institute, no accepted body of knowledge, only the first few college courses and a loose handful of experts who are learning on the job and piecing things together as best they can. The analogy to domestic violence and torture teaches us that the sooner we build the institutions that will lead us to a deeper understanding of slavery in the United States, the sooner we will be able to crack this crime.

UNDERSTANDING EVIL

Until we really understand the lives and the psychology of slaveholders and traffickers, we have to be careful not to fall into the well-worn grooves of modern myth and simply condemn them all as "evil." Of course, enslaving anyone is a terrible thing to do, but simply saying someone is "evil" does not explain his or her actions. If we look past such easy answers, we find that there doesn't seem to be a common thread of personality or circumstance running through all slaveholders. They are both men and women, rich and poor, foreign and native born. Some are gangsters, and some seem nothing more or less than housewives. There is no standard or single type of slave master, any more than there is only one reason, or one type of personality, responsible for committing murder. Some slaveholding is clearly premeditated, with brutality and enslavement being planned from the beginning. But in some American homes domestic slavery begins with what is thought of as an act of charity.

The slaveholder's rationalization is simple: by bringing a person from a poor country to the United States, the slaveholder says he is opening the door to education and opportunity. Perhaps he actually believes this, or at least some of the family believe it. Then a vulnerable and confused young person is injected into the complex arrangement of emotion and power that makes up any home. Many families are healthy and mutually supporting, but others are sick and in conflict. When a family already marked by anger, recrimination, and violence takes in a vulnerable and powerless young woman, is it surprising that she might be victimized? Perhaps she isn't the willing and happy servant they had expected her to be. Perhaps she is frustratingly ignorant of manners and customs. Perhaps she is sexually attractive to the men of the family and powerless to fend off their advances. Perhaps her sexual victimization offends and threatens the women in the house. Perhaps a housewife finds that for the first time in her life she has total control over another person who is not her own child. All of these situations have been described by counselors who work with freed domestic slaves.

In trying to explain the mind of the slaveholder, the handful of experts working with survivors of domestic slavery tell us that power is a key variable in two ways. For some slaveholders, gaining and maintaining total control over someone is intoxicating and addictive. The historian John Acton said that power corrupts and that absolute power corrupts absolutely. He might have been referring to despotic rulers, but this maxim also applies to the minds of some slaveholders. For them, the chance to achieve and enjoy absolute power over another person is enough to wipe out any reluctance to be a slave master.

For other slaveholders, the power of control works in a different way. These are the masters whose abuse of a slave reflects their own sense of powerlessness. Those working with freed domestic slaves in the United States say that when the woman of the house feels powerless she is more likely to take it out on the slave. The slave, after all, sees and knows everything that goes on in the house. If the wife is a victim of domestic violence or is regularly humiliated by her husband, now someone else, a possible sexual rival, knows these ugly secrets as well. In such cases, fear, frustration, and anger can all be redirected into abuse and control.

Some light can be shed when we see that the process of becoming a slaveholder is similar to that of becoming a torturer. Research into how people become torturers gives us hints about how middle-class housewives can become brutal slave masters. Often the person selected to be a torturer is first tortured and brutalized. In the past, when young Brazilian police officers were selected for the interrogation squad they were put through an extreme, dehumanizing, and cruel "boot camp." The instructors drove and beat the recruits, had them crawl through excrement, and ordered them to assault each other. Once their will was broken, they were told that only they were truly strong and pure enough to be trusted to torture and interrogate the criminal enemies of decent people. Then they were guided in torturing "enemies" by their superiors, officers who had built into the new torturers a dependence and instant obedience, as well as a redefinition of the "enemy" as subhuman. They were told that by carrying out the orders of their superiors they were defending everything they held dear. This transformation of the torturer into a just and moral authority opens the door to rationalized abuse. Slaveholders also redefine the slave as subhuman and use their imagined superiority to "correct" and "guide" the slave through punishment.

Other situations can also foster the exploitation of control over other people. These can include taking small steps into cruelty that are slowly increased until the enslaved worker is being severely abused. There seems to be a sort of intoxication that comes with acts of greater and greater violence and control. The powerlessness of slaves means that they cannot fight against abuse, and each act of cruelty they suffer can be a step up to even greater abuse the next time. Slaveholders will also define innocent actions by slaves as rebellious or dangerous. Enslaved domestics often report being beaten for seemingly minor mistakes: spilling a drink, bumping into the slaveholder, or even falling asleep. Since the victim of domestic slavery is normally dehumanized, treated like an animal, for example, by being forced to eat from the floor, the slaveholder can redefine his own actions from "hurting" to "helping" through corrective discipline.

The brutalization of slaves also occurs because of the anonymity of the slaveholder. Behind locked doors, the slave is invisible to the rest of society. Anything done to the slave exists outside the moral sphere of the community. Anonymity is known to allow and increase aggression; torturers and executioners routinely wear hoods or masks. In 1974, the anthropologist John Watson studied twenty-three cultures to determine whether warriors who changed their appearance, using war paint or masks, for example, treated their victims differently from those who didn't. He found that masked warriors were more likely to be destructive, by killing, torturing, or mutilating their victims, than unpainted or unmasked warriors. Phillip G. Zimbardo, the psychologist who conducted the famous "Stanford Prison" experiment that showed university students engaging in torturous abuse when randomly assigned to be "prison guards," explains it this way: "It's not just seeing people hurt, it's . . . controlling behavior of other people in ways that you typically don't."[5]

There is recrimination in the very existence of a slave. Every slaveholder, even if he does not feel he is doing something wrong, knows that he is committing a crime. If a slaveholder has any sense of guilt, then the slave is both the constant reminder of his culpability and the evidence on which punishment could be based. That brutal people will blame their victims and punish them is no surprise. For slaveholders, their silent and cowed accuser is always present and available for abuse.

We also know that when a slaveholding couple is having marital problems, there is a greater likelihood of physical and sexual abuse of the victim. High levels of stress feed into abusive slaveholding. But it would be wrong to assume any one of these patterns fully explains the mindset of a slaveholder. Whether a person is drunk with power or acting out powerlessness or stress, we have to consider the preexisting mental states that he or she brings to the situation. A sense of inferiority and the need to dominate can shape interaction with a domestic servant. By expressing that domination, masters routinely dehumanize slaves. One middle-class family forced a domestic slave to wear a dog collar and crawl around the house. Fed only leftovers, she was forced to sleep on the floor and was regularly called "creature" or "dog." Racial and ethnic differences will also feed into this process. If a victim behaves in a subservient way, either because that is what is expected of young people in many parts of the developing world, or simply out of fear, this confirms the slaveholder's sense of superiority.

Many slaveholders throughout history have worked hard to reclassify their slaves as less than human; that pattern continues today, sometimes in surprising ways. In one family in California, one job required of a domestic slave was to carefully slice meat and fruit to feed to her mistress's dogs, though she wasn't allowed to eat any herself. Her mistress had her dogs "write" greeting cards to her domestic slave and forced her slave to write back to the dogs. At one point the dogs and the maid were carefully arranged for a portrait photo. The mistress was building a fantasy of happy pets, both canine and human, a rationalization that allowed her to think all was well with her subhuman charges.

Sadly, such photos can work against the slave if her master or mistress is brought to trial. The slaveholder's lawyers will introduce photos taken at family celebrations. In them, usually in the corner of the picture, will be the slave, smiling. The lawyer says, "See, how can this woman be a slave? She was invited to the party and is obviously happy!" Of course, the slave is there to care for the children or serve at the table, nothing more. Nor do slaves smile from contentment; they smile because they are ordered to and because they are afraid not to. Yet such photos can help to shore up the slaveholder's self-deception that the slave is happy and appreciative. Strangely, a party can also be part of the mind control exercised over the slave. Abused one day and included in a celebration the next, the enslaved domestic is kept off balance and confused about her true role within the family.

"I AM AS EVIL AS I AM GOOD"

We still have a lot to learn about the psychology of slaveholders, but one thing about the enslavement of domestic workers is clear. Like rape, this is a crime of power. The "profit" from enslaving a maid, the wages not paid, the overtime she can be forced to work do not add up to vast sums. It is nothing like the kind of money that can be made from forcing trafficked women into prostitution. The families that hold and abuse domestic slaves can afford to pay for the same services in the normal way. For this kind of slavery, at least, the allure is power itself.

Americans are uncomfortable when it comes to household workers; there is something about that relationship of power over a servant that just seems out of place in the land of the free. Treating servants as if they are invisible is a way to avoid this discomfort, and—on a more sinister level—one of the reasons household slaves can be hidden in plain sight. In many upper- and middle-class homes, pretending that servants aren't in the room is standard behavior. The "help" are expected to perform their work invisibly, even if they live on the premises. And with the expectation of invisibility, slaveholders can more easily prevent visitors from having meaningful interaction with, or becoming aware of, their house slaves.

We might say this is a class issue, but that does not fully explain it. Many people who employ domestics do not act in this way—so maybe it's really about people who want to feel superior to and exercise control over "the help," as opposed to those who don't. While the psychological source of that need for superiority is complicated, the need exists, and when it involves a household slave it carries a particular danger. Because domestic workers (as well as janitors, hotel maids, and many other service workers) in the United States are often ignored, this can cause a slave to remain unseen. And we know that this is exactly the type of worker most likely to be caught in the web of trafficking and enslavement.

How that power is played out is another story. If we look back into our slaveholding past to the time when slavery was legal and accepted, we can see that slaveholders were as various and complex as the rest of the population. Even ex-slaves admitted that there were a few kind slave masters, though there was always a limit to their kindness. In the past, Americans agonized, in ways that we can barely understand today, over the fact that "good" people could take part in slavery. While we tend to think about slavery in terms of innocent slaves and cruel masters, before the Civil War it was not unusual to know someone who was a slaveholder, or even for your sweet old Aunt Sally to own a slave herself. After all, these good citizens, who believed in the rule of law, were living in a country where slavery was legally vouchsafed by the Constitution. Some slaveholders understood the moral sink they lived in. In Mozart's antislavery opera *Zaide,* the slave master Soliman sings: "I am as evil as I am good." That amazing book *Uncle Tom's Cabin* is deeply concerned with the impact of slavery on the slaveholders—the decent, devout, and highly conflicted Shelby family—and how it degrades and brutalizes them as well as their slaves. When slavery was both legal and, for some, morally and socially acceptable, slaveholders ran the gamut from kind to cruel, dehumanizing to uplifting, sexually exploitative to tenderly affectionate. Today we tend to lump all slaveholders together under the label of "evil" and criminal. That they are criminal there is no doubt; that they are committing evil acts is equally certain. That said, it is worth looking to the past, to the time when there were millions of slaveholders in America, to learn what we can about the motivations and mind-set of slaveholders today. We need to look deeply into those minds if we want to understand slavery in a way that helps us to truly eradicate it.

FIT THE CRIME?

On those rare occasions when a victim escapes or is rescued, it falls to the government to prosecute the slaveholders. As in Lakshmi's case, this is not always as immediate—or as successful—as it would seem at first glance. Aside from the obvious impediments such as diplomatic immunity, flight from the country, and the victim's disappearance or refusal to testify, the government faces certain legal issues that make conviction—or even indictment on serious charges—far from certain. For one thing, psychological coercion is extremely hard to prove. Despite years of involuntary servitude involving humiliation, mental and physical torture, sexual abuse, and debasement, there is rarely enough hard physical evidence to support the charges that *should* be brought and that carry the heavy penalties: rape, assault, kidnapping, torture. Instead, to improve their chances of a conviction, the prosecutors frequently water down the charges.

The incongruity between the unthinkable offenses and the relatively minor charges comes out in case after case. In 2005, a Saudi couple in Aurora, Colorado, was arrested for "keeping a young Indonesian woman as their slave—forcing her to cook, clean, and care for [their] children. She was frequently threatened and repeatedly sexually assaulted."[6] The woman was locked in an unheated basement room when not working and slept on a thin mattress on the floor. The U.S. government charged the couple with domestic servitude, forced labor, and harboring an illegal immigrant. Separate charges of sexual assault were brought by the state of Colorado. This case had several twists: the government of Saudi Arabia provided $400,000 as bail for the husband, who argued that he was the victim of anti-Muslim prejudice. While the husband was given a lengthy prison sentence for the sexual assaults, the wife received probation. All federal charges were dropped after the couple was convicted on state charges.

In late May 2006, the Justice Department announced the conviction of a Wisconsin couple for human trafficking. According to the charges, they had "held the victim in a condition of servitude for 19 years, requiring her to work long hours, seven days a week. . . . [The couple] threatened her with deportation and imprisonment if she disobeyed them" and forced her to hide in the basement when people entered the house.[7] *Nineteen years!* The government convicted the couple on charges of forced labor and harboring an undocumented alien. In November 2006, the couple were sentenced to each serve four years in prison, and their thirty-one-year-old son received three years' probation.[8] Meanwhile, where does this woman go to reclaim all those lost years?

In the same month, in Fort Myers, Florida, a man, his wife, and his brother-in-law faced sentencing for "harboring a 13-year-old girl kept as a sex slave and house keeper." According to investigators, the man had bought her from her parents for $260, after which "she was enslaved, raped, beaten and impregnated." All three pleaded guilty to charges, not of rape or assault, but of harboring an illegal immigrant.[9] The wife admitted to forcing the girl to help her prepare meals. The man, who also pled guilty to a charge of sex trafficking, received only sixteen months, the wife was sentenced to twenty-two months, and her brother got ten months.

In 2004, Ellilian de Leon Ramos, a thirty-five-year-old resident of Edinburg, Texas, paid a smuggler to bring two Guatemalan women across the Rio Grande. Ramos and her husband offered them each $125 a week for domestic work. Once the couple had the women in their home, however, they refused to pay them, abused them, and threatened them with deportation or worse if they complained or tried to leave. Two years later, Ramos stood in court to face sentencing for human trafficking; the judge gave her a four-year suspended sentence. Her husband, who had been charged with "acting with the intent to promote or assist in a crime," was found not guilty.[10] These four cases are not unusual, and they all raise the question of why slaveholders are consistently given prison sentences far shorter than the time they held their victims in slavery.

THE NANNY NEXT DOOR

If it were just a matter of running down the criminals and locking them up, solving the problem of domestic slavery would be somewhat less of a challenge. Sadly, the roots of domestic slavery grow right out of our law books, allowing "employers" to easily bring slaves into the United States for exploitation. And while a person's economic vulnerability often contributes to her chances of becoming a slave, ironically, the type of visa she is given by the U.S. government helps set the stage for enslavement.

Three types of visas for workers from overseas lead to many cases of domestic slavery. The A-3 visa is for household employees of diplomats. The G-5 visa is given for domestic workers attached to the households of employees of international agencies such as the United Nations, the World Bank, and the International Monetary Fund (IMF). The B-1 visa serves a larger group, since it covers the domestic workers who "belong" to businesspeople, foreign nationals, and American citizens with permanent residency abroad. All of these visas cover such household workers as housekeepers, nannies, cooks, drivers, and gardeners. These servants are linked to named individuals and are clearly in a situation of control and dependence, yet once they have passed through border control they are lost to view. No records are kept of the whereabouts of B-1 workers, and while an address is listed on the A-3 and G-5 application forms, there is normally no follow-up. Nearly four thousand of these visas are handed out each year; the largest proportion—about a thousand—are G-5s, for the servants of UN, World Bank, and IMF employees. To add further spice to this recipe for enslavement, a worker with an A-3 visa lives in legal limbo. Since her employer has diplomatic immunity, he can't be charged with criminal or civil violations. The State Department can investigate and request that immunity be waived, but in every case where this has happened the diplomat has been whisked out of the country and the domestic worker has been dumped or deported.

A case that unfolded on Long Island, New York, points to the risks faced by domestic workers brought in on B-1 visas. Early on the morning of May 13, 2007, a woman was found wandering outside a doughnut shop on Long Island wearing only pants and a towel. This woman, an Indonesian, was agitated and muttering, saying that she had been injured and wanted to return to her own country. Apparently, while taking out the trash, the woman had escaped the night before from the home—usually described as a "mansion"—of Mahender and Varsha Sabhnani, American citizens originally from India. After questioning the woman, police went to the Sabhnani home, where they discovered another Indonesian woman in distressed circumstances. Shortly after, the Sabhnanis were arrested.

In this case, the police played a vital role in the rescue of both women. Police have to deal with disturbed people regularly, and there's a good chance that the woman at the doughnut shop might have been institutionalized, jailed, or taken straight back to the couple that had enslaved her. Instead, she was freed—because of a police officer's homemade video. The story bears telling.

A few years ago, John Birbiglia, a local police detective, was called in by his boss and told, "You're in charge of human trafficking," even though his boss didn't know of any cases and the detective had no awareness of the problem. Consequently, Birbiglia attended a series of training programs given by Long Island's newly created Anti–Human Trafficking Task Force, and—electrified by what he had learned—decided to share it with his fellow officers. Frustrated while waiting for government training videos, he made his own—a rough, short tape that described what a trafficking case might look like—and showed it at roll call to the officers with whom he worked. Eventually his superior noticed the time and resources he was putting into the training and thought Birbiglia might be wasting time on it, since there weren't any trafficking cases in their bailiwick anyway.

But just a few days later, one of the policemen who had seen Birbiglia's video received a call from the doughnut shop, reporting that a distraught, scantily clad Indonesian woman was attracting attention. Had he not been given a modicum of training in human trafficking, the officer might well have responded by arresting the woman or returning her to her abusers. Instead, recognizing a possible trafficking case, he called Birbiglia, who had made and shown him the tape, and the woman was rescued. As the result of a little training, two women were freed. Ideally, this is the way it is supposed to happen.[11]

After investigation, it was determined that the two women, identified as Samirah and Enung, had been legally brought into the United States by the Sabhnanis in 2002 on B-1 visas. Once Samirah and Enung were inside their home, the Sabhnanis confiscated their passports and locked them in. Both were made to sleep on mats in the kitchen and given so little to eat that they were forced to steal food and hide it from the Sabhnanis. The Indonesian women described punishments ranging from being forced to eat large numbers of chili peppers, to being sliced behind the ears with a knife, to having scalding water thrown over them. They were in slavery for five years. At the Sabhnanis' trial in December 2007, Assistant U.S. attorney Mark Lesko said that Samirah and Enung were subjected to "punishment that escalated into a cruel form of torture." Enung testified that Samirah's nude body once was covered in plastic wrapping tape on orders from Varsha Sabhnani, who then instructed Enung to rip it off. "When I pulled it off, she was screaming," the housekeeper said through an interpreter before breaking down in tears on the witness stand.[12] Just before Christmas 2007, the Sabhnanis were convicted on all charges in a twelve-count federal indictment that included forced labor, conspiracy, involuntary servitude, and harboring aliens—convicted of enslaving two women brought into the country legally on B-1 visas. In June 2008, Varsha was sentenced to eleven years in prison, fined $25,000, and ordered to forfeit the family home, worth around $2 million.[13] Her husband, Mahender—who didn't actually participate in the brutality but who, according to the prosecutors, "allowed the conduct to take place and benefited from the work of the women"—was given a sentence of three and a half years and fined $12,500.[14]

This is worth a recap: about four thousand foreign workers are brought in each year with no contract requirements. To get the visa, the employer just has to state that he will provide "reasonable living and working conditions." Whatever paperwork is filed to get the visa can be disregarded as soon as the worker walks out of the airport; no one is checking. If a domestic worker ends up abused and enslaved, there are several possible outcomes, most of them bad. If she has an A-3 visa, her diplomat "employer" can't be arrested or prosecuted. If she has a B-1 visa, no one knows where she is anyway, so her best chance is to try to escape; but if she does, she is officially defined as "out of status" and will be deported if found. With a G-5 visa, escape can also mean deportation, and while her employer doesn't have immunity, he can simply leave the country if it looks as if he might be caught. Our visa system, far from being used to the advantage of the household workers, stacks the deck against them from the beginning. The ugliness of this situation is exacerbated by the fact that the U.S. government already *has* a system in place that can fix most of these problems.

A TALE OF TWO NANNIES

If you are a poor Filipina, Indonesian, or West African woman who desperately needs a job to support your family back home, then you are likely to end up in the unmonitored and dangerous world of the domestic worker in America. On the other hand, if you are a middle-class French, English, or Belgian girl interested in "educational and cultural exchange," you can come to the United States as an "au pair" and do the same type of nanny job some enslaved domestics were promised, but with a system of protections in place.

Unlike the ignored servants receiving B-1 visas, these young women, educated, middle class, and European, will be granted a J-1 visa, which is a ticket to safe and protected household work. With a J-1 visa each au pair or nanny is flown to New York for an orientation session and is introduced to a group of other nannies who will be located in the same geographical area. In this way, the women can form a network of friendships and have contacts from their own country whom they can call if they want to. After joining their host family, the nanny attends another orientation program to learn about educational opportunities, community resources, and contacts for a local support network. The nanny and her employers are required to discuss their situation with a counselor every month to report any problems and resolve disputes. The law stipulates that the host family has to pay the au pair a weekly stipend of at least the minimum wage, topped up with another $500 for academic expenses. Rules state that the au pair is not allowed to work more than forty-five hours a week and must have a private bedroom. Another rule requires a $500 fee to be paid by employers to cover inspection and enforcement costs. There is also a review of the suitability of the employers and their families and a requirement that "all adults living in the host family must pass a background investigation, including employment and personal character references." No limit is imposed on the number of J-1 visas that can be granted each year. For the U.S. government to operate these two systems in parallel is at best puzzling and at worst callous and exploitative.

Several nonprofit groups are currently seeking the same benefits for other household workers that the government offers European au pairs. They fight uphill battles against bureaucracy, and, if they are lucky, they will be allocated federal funds—which are always too meager to meet the medical, psychological, housing, food and clothing, and legal needs of ex-slaves. One of the most highly respected of these NGOs is the Break the Chain Campaign in Washington, D.C., the salvation of many enslaved A-3 and G-5 visa holders. The campaign was set up in late 1997, when Sarah Anderson and Martha Honey of the Institute of Policy Studies organized a meeting to consider the plight of domestic workers living in the Washington, D.C., area. Honey had carried out an investigation resulting in a feature article in a Washington newspaper. In it she listed and exposed abuses of domestic workers dating back to the 1970s. She discovered that many domestic workers, nannies, and maids, mostly from overseas, were being mistreated, sometimes enslaved. At the meeting, a number of organizations that had been informally helping these domestic workers came together for the first time. These churches, social service agencies, and law offices, as well as concerned citizens, had operated a pathway to rescue and help reminiscent of the Underground Railroad. The groups decided to form a coalition that would campaign for the rights of abused domestic workers.

Today, the Break the Chain Campaign locates, rescues, and supports abused and enslaved household workers. Often the only way to get any compensation for these workers is to bring suit against their "employers," since the campaign has found that law enforcement often takes no action. Lawyers acting on behalf of the Break the Chain Campaign carry out these lawsuits pro bono, but compensation is generally not available for freed domestics.

The current system is strikingly iniquitous. If the same laws that benefit the advantaged children of middle-class foreign families were applied equally to those who need them most—the disadvantaged poor, seeking their chance for improvement—the number of household slavery cases would drop significantly. As it is, our government has no idea of the number of victims enslaved as domestics in America, and—with no oversight program in place—they seem to have no pressing desire to find out. With a system of assigning visas that works against the recipients, no programs to monitor them once they are here, and a catch-22 of negative options should they attempt to escape, the plight of the household slave cannot improve. The situation cannot change without a serious redirection of the government's priorities away from the "employer" and toward the oversight and protection of the domestic worker. The fact that the State Department keeps no record of B-1 domestic workers would be simply bizarre if it were not so dangerous. Today it is not even possible to know how many of these workers are in the country. Is it surprising that this backdoor into the America workforce is regularly exploited by criminals?

The importation of domestic workers on special visas by foreign diplomats and employees of the World Bank, United Nations, and IMF also needs radical changes. It is estimated that some thirty thousand workers have come to the United States on these visas over the past ten years, but no one knows how much abuse occurs at the hands of diplomats, since no government agency tracks cases. In 2007 the State Department issued one thousand visas for personal servants of diplomats.[15] Some diplomats brought in two or even three servants. While the diplomat has to show a contract for the worker in order to get the special visa, no one ever checks to see if the terms of these contracts are kept. Carol Pier of Human Rights Watch explained, "The special visa program allowing international agencies and embassies to sponsor the workers is at the heart of the problem. It leaves migrants very vulnerable to serious abuse.... Most workers do not speak English and do not know where to go or how to complain. But if they do complain, and they're still with their employers, they risk being fired, losing their legal status and being deported, which scares them more."[16] When a foreign diplomat is discovered to be enslaving his servant, he's protected by diplomatic immunity. Normally, in the event of a scandal, diplomats will simply be called home or reassigned outside the United States, with the care and support of the domestic slaves they have victimized falling on charities and the taxpayer. Occasionally, a freed slave is able to win a judgment for back wages in a U.S. court, but collecting that award usually proves impossible.

Why should foreign diplomats have the right to import their own servants without legal accountability? If other foreigners working in America want to hire a maid or gardener, they have to go to an employment service like everyone else. Is the suburban home of a World Bank or IMF employee so secretive, sensitive, or precious that an American worker (or labor inspector) cannot be trusted to enter it? A special and unmonitored class of visas for "personal servants" for diplomats who cannot be prosecuted or punished is a system doomed to abuse and injustice. The fox has not just been put in charge of the henhouse; it has been given immunity from punishment. There is an easy way out of this: end the system of special visas. There are a number of sound legal arguments for ending immunity in slavery cases.[17] If foreign diplomats want servants, let them hire servants from employment agencies like everyone else. Abolishing the special servant visas would go a long way to ending the dilemma faced by prosecutors over diplomatic immunity and would reduce the number of people caught in domestic slavery.

THE COST OF DOMESTIC SLAVERY

Three poor women from India alleged that they had been held in the rich Washington, D.C., suburb of McLean, Virginia, by a Kuwaiti diplomat. They reported working sixteen-hour days and receiving rough treatment. One of them, Kumari Sabbithi, told of being beaten with a wooden box and a package of frozen chicken. "They would beat me with their hands. They would push me against the wall. They would hold my head and drag me," she recalled.[18] When, after yet another physical assault, the abuse became too much, Sabbithi ran into the night. Clad only in a summer maid's dress against the winter cold, she knocked on the door of a nearby house. The neighbor, Hector Rodriguez, took her in. After the police were called, Sabbithi's Kuwaiti "employers" denied everything and stood on their diplomatic immunity. Rodriguez asked the question that the government needs to answer: "How is it possible—in the country where freedom is relished—that these atrocities are allowed to happen under the umbrella of diplomatic immunity?"[19]

Because of people like Rodriguez more enslaved domestics are emerging, but the toll on their lives is high. Xiomara Salgado, a psychotherapist, counsels abused domestics in the Washington, D.C., region. Testifying before Congress, she explained, "Most people living in slave-like conditions develop what is known as PTSD [posttraumatic stress disorder], a pattern of responses involving among other symptoms: recurrent and intrusive thoughts and images of the traumatic experience, nightmares, flashback episodes, intense psychological distress, insomnia, and hypervigilance. It is common for these domestic workers to experience self-blaming and guilt."[20] Salgado also talked about how, for the ex-slaves she treated, the impact of domestic slavery continues long after they are freed:

> After feeling betrayed by their employers—and some of them by their own parents who gave them to these "patrones"—it is hard for them to trust strangers. The social isolation they have been subjected to has made them

even more distrustful and vulnerable. Their self-esteem suffers considerable damage after prolonged periods of maltreatment, exploitation, and humiliation. They feel inadequate, powerless, and worthless. The sustained abuse and exploitation also generate anger. Anger they do not dare to direct to their abusers out of fear of retaliation; anger that builds inside aggravating their anxiety and depression and worsening their psychological and physical conditions.[21]

And here we come to the ugly end of an ugly story of household slaves in America. While enslaving people is made easier through government regulations and immunities that shield slaveholders, provisions for the care of their victims are scant and arbitrary. Remember that enslaved domestics are not just robbed of years of labor; they are often tortured, assaulted, starved, and raped. Once freed, they often have to rely on strangers and the help of a few charities dedicated to their aid. If they are lucky enough to be recognized as victims of human trafficking, they become eligible for certain supports like health care, psychiatric help, housing, and food. But the agencies that are tasked with delivering this help say that the low level of funds awarded means that they, and the victim of slavery, are forced to make the devil's own choices: psychiatric help *or* housing; legal support *or* medical care. So while their employers have cheated them of their wages, our government tries to run their rehabilitation on the cheap.[22]

WHAT ARE WE GOING TO DO ABOUT THIS?

Scattered across our country, hidden in lovely suburban homes, are house slaves. These enslaved domestic workers share a number of characteristics. They are almost universally female; they have virtually all come to America on the promise of fair and legal work; they have taken a chance on working away from home to better themselves and better support their families, but instead are isolated and alone, no longer control their own lives, and suffer degradation, assault, and slavery. They are believed to make up more than a quarter of all the slaves in America.[23]

Remarkably, these slaves are in many ways easier to find and free than many of the other types of slaves in the country. Traffickers who enslave women in prostitution will regularly move them from place to place to keep them confused and law enforcement off track, but domestic slaves are sedentary for long periods, even decades. While they are regularly hidden away, their duties often have them hanging out washing, walking children to school, taking out garbage, or doing other household tasks that place them, however fleetingly, in public view. A number of domestic slaves come to freedom each year through the actions of "Good Samaritans"—neighbors or community members who reach out to a woman who seems troubled, frightened, or in danger. Often they are motivated by a vague but strong feeling—sometimes lasting months, or even years—that "something isn't right," only to be shocked when they discover just how wrong the situation really is.

What is discouraging is that for every person who takes the risk of reaching out to someone who might be enslaved, there are countless others who choose not to get involved—"countless" because we have no idea how many people are seeing situations that don't look right, seeing slaves without knowing it, but then looking the other way. A neighbor might fail to act because he or she doesn't know the warning signs of slavery. In fact, they are pretty simple:

- Is this person unable to move freely, or is she being watched or followed?
- Does she seem frightened to talk in the presence of others?
- Does this person look to be of school age, but is she regularly seen working during school hours?
- Are there signs of assault—bruises, cuts, bandages, limping?
- Does she seem disoriented, confused, malnourished, or frightened?

If it is possible to approach a likely slavery victim, then it is worth asking if she feels free to leave the house of her "employer" or if she has had her passport taken away or if she has ever been paid. Louis Etongwe was shocked to find an enslaved domestic worker in his own extended family after he had noticed her during a Thanksgiving dinner at a relative's house. In time he helped this girl to freedom and she led him to two other enslaved domestics. His advice for all Americans is simple: "Know your neighbors, ask them questions!"

If you think you might know of an enslaved person, you can call the Human Trafficking Information and Referral Hotline: 1–888–373–7888 (it is a free call). You could also call your local, county, or state police. But do *something*—someone's life may be at stake. Calling in the professionals—trained victim service providers—is always the right thing to do; don't try to intervene if you think the situation would endanger you or the person you think might need help. Just having read this chapter gives you an awareness you probably didn't have before; and even a little bit of knowledge can go a long way to freeing a slave.

Local, state, and federal government have a number of things to fix, none of which is difficult or expensive. For starters, local and state police need training about slavery and human trafficking. The good news is that this training, in the form of educators, films, manuals, workbooks, handbooks, pamphlets, and posters, already exists; it just needs to be delivered to the right people. It is actually pretty easy to ask others in your community the following questions, perhaps in a letter to the local newspaper: How can we ensure that everyone who is most likely to come into contact with a person in slavery—police, firefighters, health inspectors, nurses, doctors—learns to spot the warning signs? How can we help neighborhood groups to learn these warning signs as well? At the end of this book is a resource list of groups, Web sites, and sources for information on slavery and human trafficking.

Christina was one of the enslaved domestics found and helped by the Good Samaritan Louis Etongwe. She was a slave for five long years. In her words we hear the truth of household slaves in America—both the tragedy and the hope for the future:

> I consider myself a slave because I worked for so many hours without getting paid, and without going to school. And I couldn't leave. I feel like they stole my life from me. We didn't know anything like this happened. It's like we were brainwashed so we didn't know the laws, we didn't know the rules. All we knew was what they were telling us. And we believed all that they were saying. We were blind then. Anybody in my situation shouldn't take that long to get help. There's help out there. They shouldn't believe it when their employers are telling them it's scary out there. There are good people out there. They should reach for help immediately if they're not getting what they were promised. And no matter what, you shouldn't send your child away, especially with strangers.
>
> The people were found guilty. They pleaded guilty and they did some community service. They were asked to pay me some money for the years that I worked for them. They are paying bit by bit, but not that much. Right now I'm just trying to keep away from them. I just want to live my life. I don't want to even see them. But if it happens, I would say, look at me now—here, look at me now.
>
> I'm proud of myself now because now I have a job, I have a roof over my head, I have a car, I can do whatever I want. I'm building a house for my parents and I paid my siblings' school tuition. My mom is always sick so I pay her medical fees—send her to a bigger hospital so she can get more tests. What I dream now is to be a registered nurse. I love helping people. With the help of God I'm going to do it and I'll be a registered nurse. Everything is possible. I'm trying to work hard, save some money, go to school. I'm going to do it. I have to do it.[24]

3

SLAVES IN THE PASTURES
OF PLENTY

California, Arizona, I harvest your crops,
Then it's north up to Oregon to gather your hops.
Dig the beets from your ground, cut the grapes
from your vine
To set on your table your light sparkling wine.
Woody Guthrie, "Pastures of Plenty"

A STUDY IN CONTRASTS

About thirty miles due south of the Southwest Florida International Airport is the town of Naples. It sits on its own bay off the Gulf of Mexico, not far from Sanibel, Vanderbilt Beach, and the Isles of Capri. Naples is a lovely town—a rich town—attracting wealthy retirees and men of industry. A palm-lined walk down Fifth Avenue will take you past art galleries offering everything from contemporary sculpture to portraits of your pets; chic restaurants featuring a variety of ethnic and exotic cuisines; high-end clothing and jewelry stores; and a fair smattering of Bentleys and Rolls Royces.

A small tour boat offers a sunset cruise of the bay. The area is rich in animal and bird life, brightly colored flowers, and lush plants, but the guide points out only the houses and properties, proudly ticking off for the tourists the astronomical values of each. No number is below seven figures, and several are higher. One empty lot, we are told, recently sold for $18,000,000. It sits, like a missing tooth, between two massive structures of questionable taste but stunning worth. Many of these houses serve as second, third, or fourth homes and are occupied for only a few weeks a year.

The boats that line the pier are studies in sleekness and speed. Long, shark-shaped Cigarettes and Scarabs, with their two and three outboards of 250 horsepower each, give the illusion of motion even at the dock. Looming over the pier walk are elegant new apartment buildings, painted various pastel shades, as are many of the homes and shops of Naples. There is nothing here to jar the senses. There is everywhere an air of money and complacency.

If, however, you left the airport and drove forty minutes to the south-*east,* along narrow state roads, you would enter the town of Immokalee. You could never confuse the two.

Driving into Immokalee, you become instantly aware that this is not a town concerned with its appearance. There is no movie theater, no outward indication of social activity, except for the Seminole Casino, where out-of-towners from Naples and Fort Myers come to gamble. Many of the buildings of Immokalee are low, basic, carelessly maintained. Most of the signs—many roughly hand-painted—are in Spanish, as well as a language that looks familiar, almost French, but spelled phonetically. This is Haitian Creole. In many of Immokalee's homes, English is neither spoken nor understood. The languages are Spanish, Creole, and more than a sprinkling of indigenous tongues—Quiche, Zapotec, Nahuatl, Ttzotzil, Mam, Mixtec, Kanjobal.[1]

There is a handful of restaurants—mostly Mexican—with names like la Michoacana, el Taquito, Mi Ranchita. The décor is minimalist, the food just acceptable; dining out is not a major activity in Immokalee. There are a couple of nail and hair salons, housed in tiny storefronts. One turquoise-and-yellow painted structure advertises "Mimi's Piñatas." Chickens run wild, their crowing a backdrop you stop hearing after a while, and the vultures crowd the roads outside of town in such profusion that they present a driving hazard. Many who live here walk from point to point or ride one-speed bicycles. They can't afford cars. There is not much vehicle traffic in Immokalee itself, with the exception of the trucks that haul the produce to the packinghouses and the long school-type buses that carry the workers to and from the fields.

THE PRICE OF TOMATOES

Immokalee is a migrant town—actually, "more a labor reserve than a town."[2] There are many such communities in Florida, but this is the epicenter. Immokalee—an unincorporated community—was built in the first decades of the twentieth century for the growing, picking, packing, and shipping of tomatoes and oranges. Old-timers can still remember the days when teamsters drove horse-drawn wagons from Fort Myers to haul the produce from the fields.[3] There are other crops—lemons, grapefruit, watermelon—but these are the big two, and the tomato crop is the biggest by far. The crews who work in the fields come from Mexico, from Guatemala, from Haiti. Most are young—in their early twenties—small in stature and dark skinned, both by birth and by long exposure to the sun. Many have the Mayan features of the "Indio puro." There is a shyness—a reserve—shown a stranger and, usually, a smile.

Immokalee's year-round population of twenty-five thousand swells to forty thousand during the nine-month harvest season. There are surprisingly few women among Immokalee's farmworkers; around 95 percent of the workforce is male. They have left their home countries and crossed our borders into Texas, Arizona, or New Mexico—most with the help of a *coyote,* or "guide"—in the hope of finding a way to support their families, since no such opportunities exist at home. Instead, they have found jobs that are unrelentingly hard, under the rigid control of crew leaders, for the lowest wages imaginable. Every day, often seven days a week, the workers walk through the 4:00 a.m. darkness to begin gathering at parking lots around town; here they wait for buses that will take them—at least some of them—to the fields. Some carry their lunch from home in white plastic bags, while others choose to buy their daily food in one of the several convenience stores, with names like La Fiesta #3 and La Mexicana #2, that open early to accommodate them. The prices are high, often twice what they are elsewhere; the workers have no choice.

Nor do they have much option as to where they live. The town is honeycombed with parks of broken-down trailers, enclaves of tiny huts, and depressing little apartments. The rents are staggering. A dilapidated single-wide trailer, with dented, dingy yellow corrugated siding that is separating from the frame, accommodates twelve men, who sleep on bare mattresses abutting each other on the floor. Each of them pays a rent of $50 a week. There are perhaps fifteen such trailers on a single lot. The few individuals who own most of these enclaves would qualify as slumlords in any community in America, but their tenants pay the rents and live in their hovels; again, they have no choice.

Picking tomatoes is brutal; it requires working bent over in the southern sun for hours on end, straightening only long enough to run 100 to 150 feet with a filled thirty-two-pound bucket and literally throw it up to the worker on the truck. Lunch is a hurried affair, and water breaks are few. But at least nowadays there's clean water; not so very long ago, it wasn't uncommon for pickers to be obliged to drink from the canals and ditches, taking in the bacteria and the runoff of insecticides and fertilizer along with the water. And until fairly recently, a picker ran the risk of being beaten if he stopped picking long enough to drink.[4]

The pickers are not free to decide when or how much to work; they must work however many hours and days a week the crew chief mandates or weather and conditions permit. For this, they are paid a piece rate—so much per full bucket. The going rate—which has barely changed in nearly thirty years, despite the steady rise in the cost of living—is $25 per ton of tomatoes picked. This means filling around 125 buckets of tomatoes a day just to gross $50. But to make the equivalent of minimum wage, the worker has to fill around *two hundred* buckets—or two and a half tons—of tomatoes; this often entails working twelve or thirteen hours a day, if and when the work is available.

Why aren't these workers paid the minimum wage? The term *minimum wage* is misleading; realistically, although the 2008 rate in Florida is $6.79 per hour, the worker stands no real guarantee of earning it. Conditions are against him. There are no fixed hours, and what records are kept are often doctored in favor of the crew leader and the grower. The worker is also at the mercy of the weather; the market; pestilence; the availability of harvesting equipment; the yield due to the relative richness of a field's soil; the number of times a field has been picked; the distance from the picker to the truck; personal stamina; and, most frustrating, time lost traveling to and from the field and waiting unpaid hours on the bus for the dew to dry or the weather to change.

Because harvesting is by nature unpredictable, the picker must be available every day at around five in the morning; if it turns out there is no work that day, he's just out of luck. This precludes his ability to take a second job. And on days when the work is slack and few pickers are required, he's likely to go home with nothing in his pocket. If he gets to the field and it rains, he earns nothing. The days spent on buses to other regions when the local crops have been picked is unpaid time; and if he and his fellow workers arrive at the new fields before they are ready for picking, they're paid nothing as they wait for the crops to ripen. They are paid only when they are picking, and they are paid little at that. It is no wonder that the Department of Labor (DOL) has described farmworkers as a labor force in "significant economic distress."[5]

The only true measure of the pickers' compensation is their annual earnings: workers average $7,000 to $10,000 per year. On a good day, the best they can accomplish is to reach the poverty level, but their yearly earnings are well below it. There are no benefits—no overtime, no health care, no insurance of any kind. "You can only get sick in Immokalee," says Coalition of Immokalee Workers (CIW) co-founder Lucas Benitez, "between 8:00 a.m. and 4:00 p.m., which are the hours of the clinic." If a picker does get sick, he works nonetheless. If he becomes seriously ill or breaks a limb, not only is he without income, but he must pay his medical bills himself—more often than not an impossibility, since nearly all his money goes to food and rent, with perhaps a few dollars put aside to send home. "You wait until you are half dead to go to a doctor."[6]

SCORE ONE FOR THE DIXIECRATS

There is no point in looking to the government for help: farm labor is practically the only type of work not covered by the National Labor Relations Act of 1935, the law that protects workers, gives them the right to organize without fear of retaliation, and fixes wage, health, and safety rules. Yes, farmworkers can organize a union or strike for better pay, but they can be fired for doing so. This exclusion of farmworkers from the rights given to almost all other American workers came from the power of Deep South congressmen in 1935, when the law was passed. These Dixiecrat politicians were adamant that black field hands should never be allowed to organize. Not surprisingly, household servants were also excluded from full rights. Some DOL wage and hour rules do apply to farmworkers, but with only two wage and hours inspectors for the entire Southwest Florida region—which includes tens of thousands of farmworkers, as well as other types of laborers—there is little hope of help there either.[7] For years, the local inspector for that section of Florida generally spoke only English—in the midst of workers who did not—and spent more time in the grower's office than in the fields, where he might witness firsthand the treatment of the pickers. With the law on their side, the crew leaders and the growers hold all the cards.

With conditions so dismal, and the pay so low, why would anyone come to Immokalee to work? Or to nearby towns like Lake Placid, Wimauma, or LaBelle? There is simply no real choice: wherever a worker goes to pick America's crops, he meets similar conditions. With the trend toward consolidation and expansion of agribusinesses, it has become increasingly difficult to find work on the old-style family-owned farms of twenty-five years ago. Instead, the small farms are being gobbled up by huge companies. Competing with each other and with foreign suppliers, these megagrowers are themselves being caught in a cost/price squeeze. On the one hand, they face constantly rising costs of gasoline, pesticides, fertilizer, and a couple dozen other items necessary for production. On the other hand, the buyers—fast-food giants such as MacDonald's, Subway, Taco Bell, and Burger King, and market corporations like Shop Rite, Wal-Mart, and Costco—are dictating the prices they are willing to pay for tomatoes and other crops. The buyers have turned their corporate backs on the small growers who supplied them faithfully for years. In the words of one worker advocate, the buyers "each have a purchasing company, looking to buy high volume at the lowest possible price. They are price *setters,* not price *takers.*"[8] Rather than purchase from several smaller growers, as in the past, these megabuyers have decided to work with the largest suppliers, who can provide ready, uniform, year-round supplies of product. Only the huge agribusinesses, such as Gargiulo, Pacific, Nobles Collier, and the Six L's, can meet the demanding production requirements while weathering the rising costs and the squeeze on their profit margin. Size counts: even with the cost/price pressure they manage to make a tremendous amount of money, and they are growing exponentially.

As large as these agribusinesses are, they pale in the shadow of the companies that supply their needs—giants such as Exxon, John Deere, and Monsanto. Against these multinational corporations the growers have no bargaining power. So, with nothing to say about their escalating costs or the buyers' shrinking prices, the only way they can hold on to profits is by cutting labor costs. Their aim is to keep at gutter level the amount they pay—and for decades have paid—their workers, and they do. As a 2004 Oxfam America report put it, "Squeezed by the buyers of their produce, growers pass on the costs and risks imposed on them to those on the lowest rung of the supply chain: the farmworkers they employ."[9] And because these privately held Florida-based grower corporations are constantly expanding, a worker can move to North Carolina, Delaware, California, or even Puerto Rico and still be working in the same grower's fields—for the same pay, and under the same conditions. There is no refuge. While the large grower corporations compete, they have also banded together to control the labor market by forming the Florida Tomato Committee. The committee and the Florida Fruit and Vegetable Association are powerful lobbies with the state government; this is not surprising, since some of the large growers are themselves members of the Florida legislature.

This situation is not new. In her excellent history of Atlantic Coast farmworkers, Cindy Hahamovitch writes of Florida in the 1930s: "While the rest of growers' expenses rose over the course of the decade—the cost of seed, fertilizer, and equipment all went up—farm wages remained stagnant or fell, depending on the crop. . . . As a veteran of harvests in thirty-three states put it, 'Florida is the sorriest wages in the United States.'"[10] In those days, the workers were mostly African American and Bahamian; today they are most likely to be Latino. Otherwise little has changed, with one ugly exception.

SLAVERY IN THE FIELDS

As bad as most pickers have it, there is a rung on the ladder that is lower still—the *enslaved* farmworker. Antonio Martinez came from a family of five younger siblings, in Hidalgo, Mexico. His parents were sickly, and Antonio was unable to make a sufficient living to support them all. He met with a contractor—a *coyote*—who promised that he would smuggle Antonio into the United States and find him construction work in California for a fee of 16,000 pesos—about $1,700 American. Antonio told the man that he didn't have that much money, but the *coyote* assured him that he could pay it off once he started to work. Two weeks later, he was on a bus along with forty others, heading north toward the border.

When the bus arrived at a sparse border camp in the Sonora desert, the workers were separated and given to other *coyotes*. The man in charge of Antonio's group was called Chino. He led them through the desert for three days, despite having water and supplies for only one day, crossing the border to a whistle-stop called Tres Puntas. From there they were driven to a house in Tucson, where Chino demanded additional money from them or their families, on pain of violence. Some of the others complied, but Antonio had no money to give. At this point, without money or papers, under violent threat, he realized he was trapped.

Antonio was told that instead of going to a construction site in California he would be put to work in the tomato fields of South Central Florida, at the pay rate of $150 per day. The promised amount went far toward allaying his misgivings. Chino then handed him over to a van driver, or *raitero*, called "el Chacal"—the jackal. Antonio was crowded into the back of the van along with seventeen other Mexican workers. On the long drive to Florida, the van stopped only for gasoline; the migrants in the back were told to urinate in a bottle when the need arose. Twice on their journey police stopped the van; on neither occasion did the officer question the presence of eighteen Mexicans packed like cargo in the back.

When el Chacal arrived in Florida, he drove to the camp of two labor contractors, Abel and Basilio Cuello. Here, Antonio overheard el Chacal negotiating with the Cuello brothers for the sale of the workers. El Chacal was demanding $500 apiece, whereas the Cuellos were willing to pay only $350. At this point, Antonio realized, "We were being sold like animals."[11]

Antonio's life was tightly controlled. The door of the shack in which he and the other workers slept was locked at night and was unlocked in the morning by Abel Cuello only when it was time to go to the fields.

Cuello never left them alone; he stayed with them as they picked and threatened violence and death should they attempt to escape. The promised pay was whittled away to practically nothing as Cuello deducted for rent, food, water, even the cost of transportation to and from the fields. With the tiny amount left to them, the workers bought food or toiletries when taken by the bosses on rare trips to a small local grocery store.

After four months in slavery, Antonio saw his chance. While he and a few others were shopping, Cuello, on guard outside the market, dozed off, and the workers ran to the highway and escaped. The subsequent case against the Cuello trafficking operation was one of Florida's first contemporary cases of forced labor. Cuello was convicted and sentenced to prison on slavery charges.

Antonio still works with the crops—but under his own volition, and not with tomatoes. He also travels throughout the country, speaking about the slavery in America's fields and in the food we eat. He has marched in several campaigns against corporate abuse and participated in the ten-day hunger strike against Taco Bell. At one point, he taught a training session to law enforcement officers and government officials in Chiapas, Mexico, through the U.S. Department of Justice (DOJ). This author spoke with Antonio while he was participating in a late-2007 workers' march against Burger King, and his motivation was clear. Taking action against the offending corporations, he said, "is extremely important; there is more and more consumer participation in the struggle, and it makes the campaign that much stronger. The big companies buy so much produce that they must take responsibility for the conditions under which the people who harvest it are suffering. It infuriates me that some of these corporations are still ignoring the plight of the farmworkers.

"I just want you to know," he states, "why I'm out here today. For four and a half months, I was held in forced labor in the fields against my will, and it seemed like an eternity for me. They were watching me all the time, controlling all I did. I thought I was going to die. Thanks to God, I was able to escape, and it allowed me to become more and more aware. I'm out here learning more every day."[12]

HIDDEN AMONG THE CROPS

In the words of one human rights activist, "It is, of course, almost too obvious to state that the deprivation of liberty typical of agricultural slavery operations is the most extreme violation of human rights in the fields today."[13] Obvious though it might be, agricultural slavery is virtually unknown to most Americans. In a country where the plight of millions of migrant workers—suffering the nation's lowest wages and worst conditions—fails to hold the public's attention, agricultural slavery finds no place at all. Yet slavery on America's farms is one of the three largest forms of human trafficking in America today. Activist Laura Germino states the case well: "American consumers don't want to have slavery woven into the fabric of their daily lives; but, unknown to most, it already is. They drink orange juice in the morning, they eat tomatoes with their burger for lunch."[14]

Slavery in the fields is especially common in the southeastern United States; one DOJ official referred to this part of Florida as "ground zero for modern slavery."[15] Enslavement usually takes the form of debt bondage. The trafficked worker is an easy target—socially disconnected, recently homeless, and without resources. He is literally sold by the *coyote* to the crew leader, or contractor, who then puts the purchase price—or whatever price the crew leader decides—back on the head of the worker. He is told that he must work to pay off his debt, which is often quoted in the thousands of dollars; but in most cases, no matter how hard he works, the debt just increases. Kept isolated with other trafficked workers—often under armed guard or open threats of violence—he is forced to work when, where, and for however long the crew leader decides. In some instances, whatever necessities he requires—food, clothing, medicines—are purchased from the crew leader's own store and deducted from his wages or added to his debt. As time passes, the debt grows, and the worker sees no hope of liberation. Lucas Benitez describes the process of enslavement: "Debt begins when the *coyote* turns you over to the crew leader. So many of our *companeros* have suffered in this way and say being sold . . . feels worse than being an animal. . . . You get sold for $500, but next day the debt is $1,000. Then they add on rent and food, and your debt increases. . . . If you have a slow day in the fields, the crew leader will say, 'You owe us more now; you didn't work well.' You never see the check stubs, so you have no idea where you stand with your debt." And workers can stay indebted, and enslaved, for years. A single trafficking operation can keep hundreds of people in bondage; as Benitez points out, "The more workers enslaved, the greater the profits."[16] By convincing the worker that he is responsible and might someday pay off this debt, the slaveholder diverts his attention from the real situation: he is a slave and if he tries to leave he will be hurt.

Agricultural slavery is a very hands-on form of bondage, often involving the use of weapons.[17] Workers are clearly warned that any attempt to run or to report their situation will result in injury or death, and the bosses can—and often do—make good on their threats. In addition to threatening or beating the worker, his captors tell him that any efforts to escape will result in violence for his family back home. This is a particularly terrifying threat, and it quells the desire to run. Even if the worker is outside the immediate physical control of the crew leader, he can never be free to leave, or to speak out, as long as his family is under threat. The workers know these are not idle threats; many slaveholders have family or associates in Mexico, or other Central American countries, positioned to carry them out.

The workers are also trapped by isolation; they usually have no idea where they are, have no knowledge of English, and wouldn't begin to know what to do, where to go, or whom to trust should they escape. While some of the houses and trailers in which they are kept are in the fields or swamps far from civilization, a surprising number of slave dwellings have been on major roads. One was alongside a golf course and another right in the middle of Immokalee. Yet the enslaved worker, a veritable stranger in a strange land, is as isolated as if he were on Mars.

There is one more subtle reason why enslaved workers don't attempt to escape. They feel honor-bound to pay their debt. Dishonesty feeds on honesty. The very rules of trust and integrity that most of these poor farmworkers use to guide their dealings with each other are a key tool used to enslave them. From small rural communities, where a man's reputation may be all he has, the workers carry a very strong sense that debts *must* be repaid, that a person who does not pay his debts is the lowest of the low. The slaveholder uses this sense of honor against the workers as an alternative to violence. He will string them along by appealing to their sense of "fair play." They are trapped in a situation where they believe that while trying to run away will accomplish nothing, trust *might* pay off. If this is how it is here, they reason, if working to pay off a debt is how things are done in America, what choice is there but to remain and toil? With no idea that conditions can be different, what is there to escape to?

The chain of slavery in the fields has several links. It begins with the *coyote*, who, rather than simply deliver the worker to the crew leader, sells him outright. The crew leader then becomes the slaveholder, keeping people against their will, refusing them payment, and using violence as his primary tool. He may act alone, or with his family, or as part of a syndicate. Handled efficiently, the possibilities for rich profits are endless. These are the primary criminals, with the greatest guilt, but the responsibility climbs right up the product chain.

Big growers tend to deny all knowledge of the labor conditions in their fields, leaving it to the subcontracted crew leaders. Yet a big grower is likely to know about the trafficking cases in his own backyard, and he deals directly with the crew leaders, some of whom make their way into the news and the courts. It seems that the grower disassociates himself from the men in the field only when it suits him to do so. In denying the workers' efforts to organize, the grower will claim that he maintains direct daily communication with his laborers and that this closeness precludes any need for a union. The degree to which a grower is willing to acknowledge the conditions in his fields seems to be a matter of personal convenience and economy.[18]

But the responsibility continues up the product chain, up to the megacorporations that buy the crops from the growers. In fact, an argument can be made that the buyers are accountable both by contributing to the harsh conditions that have given rise to trafficking and by refusing to take responsibility. By pushing down the prices at which they buy up the crops, the fast-food and supermarket chains have created an environment where the only predictable savings the grower—and by association, the *coyote* and the contractor—can realize are from squeezing workers or, in the worst cases, enslaving them.

According to Lucas Benitez, until recently the growers and buyers have been able to ignore the situation because the subcontracting crew leaders have done the actual enslaving.[19] Nonetheless, as one activist puts it, "What kind of work atmosphere is it when, after the first five [slavery] cases are uncovered, you can still claim you don't know what's going on? The silence from both the growers and the buyers was deafening. Nobody stood up and said, 'Oh, my God, this is just awful! We have to do something about this!' None of the buyers came forward and said, 'Why, we were buying from this very farm!' You have to ask why they didn't know, and once it was brought to their attention, why there was no outcry."[20]

As more cases of slavery in the production of the food we eat came to light, consumers remained in the dark. The consumers are the last link in the product chain, and what Americans eat sometimes comes from the hands of slaves. So where is the consumer demand for clean food? And what is being done to end slavery in our fields?

EARLY ANTISLAVERY EFFORTS

Throughout the country are NGOs that actively root out cases of agricultural trafficking. One that has taken aggressive and effective action against slavery in the southern fields is the Coalition of Immokalee Workers (CIW). Founded in the early 1990s, the CIW is a worker-based organization devoted to improving the lives of farm laborers. Many of its members brought from their native Mexico, Guatemala, and Haiti experience in labor organizing, which they put to use through programs—in their words—of popular education, leadership development, and powerful protest actions.[21] Confronted with the horrific conditions in Immokalee, they set about uniting the workers—most of whom had little in common except the inhumane conditions under which they lived and worked. The CIW set out to combat known labor violations: the subpoverty wages; impossibly long hours; denial of health benefits, pension, meal and break time, sick days, and holidays; injury from the hard labor; danger from exposure to pesticides; slum-level, high-priced housing; and blacklisting of any workers who dared to complain or attempt to organize. And in the course of their efforts, they discovered slavery in their midst.[22]

In hindsight, it was not a great leap; as CIW member Laura Germino says, "Slave operations don't occur in a vacuum. It's at the end of a spectrum of labor violations."[23] The same conditions that give rise to the abuse of migrant workers with at least the freedom to leave, taken a step further, make slavery possible. When the philosophy is "The less you pay, the more you make," the ultimate objective is to pay nothing. And what better way to achieve this goal than to enslave the workforce?

The coalition didn't set out to free enslaved workers; in fact, in the beginning, they weren't aware, any more than the rest of us, that there was such a thing as human trafficking in the fields. As foreign, vague, and misunderstood as trafficking is to Americans today, fifteen years ago it was virtually unknown. Poor labor conditions, yes; low wages, of course; but slavery in America? Never.

Then came the word that Miguel Flores had enslaved scores of workers in South Carolina. Working with his partner, Sebastian Gomez, Flores recruited his victims—mostly indigenous Mexicans and Guatemalans—both in Latin America and in the United States. They were forced by gun thugs to work ten to twelve hours daily, often for no pay except what went toward bare subsistence. The few who attempted to escape or defy their captors were beaten; at least one was shot.[24] By the time the CIW heard of Miguel Flores, his slavery ring had been operating for years.

"The Boss Shot a Worker"

Often the awareness that one is enslaved comes abruptly. One day, a newly arrived worker in Miguel Flores's South Carolina labor camp inadvertently "tested the boundaries" when he took a leisurely stroll along a cornfield that bordered the compound. Within minutes, a pickup truck roared up, and Sebastian Gomez ordered him inside at gunpoint and drove him back to the camp. The message was unmistakable: you cannot leave.

Sometimes the awareness of slavery comes gradually, as it did when the newly formed CIW first learned of Miguel Flores's activities. A few CIW members were on an outreach trip in South Carolina in July 1992 when six laborers approached them. One of the workers, a small Mayan woman named Julia Gabriel, told a CIW member that they hadn't been paid for their work at the last camp. Ah, thought the member, a non-payment of wages issue.

"Why didn't you get paid?" he asked.

"Because we had to leave the camp in the middle of the night."

"Why did you have to leave?"

"Because the boss shot a worker who owed him money and was trying to leave to find work elsewhere."

Gabriel revealed the name of the boss, Miguel Flores, and told the CIW members that the compound was called "Red Camp" and lay three hours to the north, in the little dirt-poor town of Manning. Red Camp consisted of three barracks and was situated among fields and woods at the end of an unlit dirt road; it was the largest of many Flores encampments in that part of the state.

"That's all we had to go on," says Germino. She and her two colleagues drove to Manning, and since it was Sunday, they assumed that the workers would be at the town's one laundromat. They were, under the watchful eyes of guards and informants. The CIW members asked for Miguel Flores and were greeted with an ominous "Who wants to know?" Flores's wife was there, and—at the request of the CIW people—agreed to give the six workers their back pay, so as to avoid a public scene. Then, curiously, she volunteered the information that Sebastian Gomez, who had recently been arrested for fatally shooting a worker, was out of jail, since the police had been unable to find the man's body. "Another piece of the puzzle came together; we learned that Miguel Flores's partner was Sebastian Gomez, and we had heard before we even left Florida . . . that Gomez and his people had shot a man up in the Carolinas who'd wanted to work elsewhere. . . . So you see, something vague that you can't really act on becomes clear once additional information comes in."[25] Adds Greg Asbed, a CIW member, "It's like when you have radio static, and suddenly you're tuned to the right station."[26]

The CIW members returned to Immokalee and spoke with DOJ agents to try to push the case. Over the next year, the CIW interviewed several witnesses to Flores's atrocities—including some of the original six escaped workers whom they'd met in South Carolina—and gave their names and statements to the DOJ. Nothing was done.

At one point, sheriff's deputies from Hendry County, Florida, contacted the CIW to discuss Flores's activities in and around LaBelle, a small agricultural town twenty-five miles from Immokalee, where the contractor had maintained a strong and growing presence for years. The bodies of Hispanic men had been turning up in the nearby Caloosahatchee River, and the deputies suspected that Miguel Flores was behind it, but no evidence was ever found to connect Flores to the killings. However, one deputy later commented that once Flores was in jail the killings miraculously stopped.[27]

It gradually became apparent that Flores had camps in a number of locations in Florida, Georgia, and South Carolina, holding a captive workforce that numbered between four hundred and five hundred. As months passed, the CIW continued to grow the number of leads, escapees, and witnesses, and still the DOJ dragged its heels. In late 1993, the case was reassigned to another DOJ prosecutor, but human trafficking was apparently on neither his nor the FBI's radar. It seems the feds just didn't know what to do with it, and consequently the case didn't progress for a year. Time and again the CIW would contact the federal authorities with a list of witnesses, and time and again they were met with resounding silence.[28]

Another year passed, and in August 1994 a third prosecutor was put on the case who finally, slowly, painfully, started the wheels in motion. He interviewed Julia Gabriel, the woman who had first told the CIW of the Flores ring. In Laura Germino's words, Julia, at 4′ 10″, was "a tiny woman with a big story to tell."[29] By early 1995, DOJ prosecutors had reinterviewed several of the witnesses with whom the FBI had spoken, in some instances, several times. Availability for interviews was a major issue: the DOJ and the FBI never quite seemed to understand that the workers traveled with the harvest, often ranging from Florida to Pennsylvania, and working very long days. Even when the workers were in the vicinity, it was absurd to schedule an interview at, say, ten o'clock in the morning and assume a worker would be there; yet that is precisely what the agents did, so that the interviews would conform to their own schedules. Still, the workers would manage to show up, over and over again, to give their testimony. Meanwhile, the number of men and women Flores had enslaved continued to grow, as did the stories of his violence against workers, translators, informants, and witnesses.

Despite all the efforts being put forth by the CIW and the dozens of witnesses and escapees who had come forward, life went on undisturbed in Flores's camps. Many mornings, Sebastian Gomez woke the workers by firing his nine-millimeter semiautomatic Smith and Wesson pistol in the air, and his partner, Miguel Flores, would punctuate his curses in the fields with shots from his own gun. When vendors or visitors approached his camps, he drove them off by brandishing his pistol or firing over their heads. On one occasion, he shot out a visitor's tires. Over the years, Flores was arrested periodically on firearms and abuse charges, and sometimes he was bailed out by the local growers for whom he supplied the workers. He was never prosecuted. Former DOL senior investigator Armando Brana states, "In my files, I have seven reports of workers who disappeared or died while working for Flores. Even for those who were shot, it was listed as 'death by natural causes.' Some, it seemed, fell off a bridge, or were hit by a tractor or a bus." Investigations were cursory. "In one case," recalls Brana, "the coroner on the case was the farmer Flores was working for!"[30]

In January 1996, the DOJ was still evaluating the situation and had not yet committed to fully pursuing it. It was, however, still reinterviewing witnesses. Meanwhile, it had become apparent that the case would be helped by introducing additional investigators beyond the FBI, and the DOJ asked the Border Patrol to step in. For the first time in more than three years, a dedicated, bilingual agent was on the case. Agent Mike Baron was given his own budget and free rein to conduct his own investigation. Baron had picked crops as a boy, and he knew the business from the inside. He reached out to the CIW and the workers and provided an interest and an understanding that had been lacking. One significant change he made was to interview workers only on the weekends, to avoid stirring suspicion by their absence and to allow them the weekdays to keep earning.

Finally, in October 1996, an indictment was brought in the U.S. District Court in South Carolina against Miguel Flores, Sebastian Gomez, and two of their recruiters on charges of conspiracy, involuntary servitude, extortion, illegal possession of a firearm, use of a firearm in the commission of a violent crime, transporting and harboring aliens, and unlawful entry into the United States after deportation. The judge considered the defendants a high flight risk and ordered them held without bail.[31]

In May 1997—nearly five years after the CIW started its campaign against the Flores slavery ring—the defendants entered a plea of guilty. This left only the sentencing hearing. Julia Gabriel, the tiny woman with the big story to tell, came forward to speak for a severe sentence. She told her story, and that of friends and co-workers who had been threatened and brutalized, and when she finished, she said,

> That's what I saw. And everything they did to others, they had no compassion for them. A lot of people were hurt. And there were a lot of victims, because they were very sure of themselves, and they could do anything. And they took advantage of the people, and that's why I'm here, so that they will receive a harsh sentence, because they hurt a lot of people . . . and these people did nothing to them. These people are victims. . . . And now is the moment of sentencing, and what I want is for them to see that . . . if they are prisoners . . . they will see what they did to other people. And if they are given a short sentence then they can, once they are out . . . go for revenge, and no, that shouldn't be. They are bad people. And that's the truth I'm telling you.[32]

The court believed her. Flores and Gomez were each sentenced to fifteen years in federal prison.

Although there had been other cases of slavery in the fields, some going back to the 1970s, the Miguel Flores case was the first contemporary agricultural trafficking case to gain national prominence. It had caught the government flatfooted. The government simply wasn't prepared for modern slavery, and the result was hesitation, confusion, lack of interest, and constant misunderstandings on the government's part in pursuing it, as well as the inordinately long time it took to bring the traffickers to justice.[33] At one point, the FBI actually conducted a brief investigation of Flores and found him to be "in full compliance with the law."[34] Former DOL senior investigator Armando Brana recalls that when he began working with Border Patrol agent-in-charge Mike Baron his bosses resented the time he spent on the Flores case. "Dealing with my supervisors was harder than conducting the actual investigation. They'd ask me sarcastically, 'So, have you joined the Border Patrol?'"[35]

The conviction of Flores was a landmark case and instrumental in bringing about the Victims of Trafficking and Violence Protection Act in 2000, with its sets of definitions, charges, and penalties for dealing specifically with cases of sex and labor slavery in the United States. And from a time when, in the words of Mike Baron, "you could fit the whole antislavery movement in the back of my patrol truck," it helped spark the anti–human trafficking effort in the country today.[36] Baron is lavish in his praise of the coalition's efforts: "If law enforcement had the same dedication and tenacity as the CIW, and weren't bound by our restrictions, there wouldn't be a place for the criminals to hide. They maintained contact with the workers and tracked the movements of the crew leaders. Without the CIW, we wouldn't have had any witnesses; we never would have found the victims."[37]

More Bad Apples to Pick

With the awareness that slavery existed in the fields, there was no going back. "It became clear," says Germino, "that this wasn't a one-time bad apple employer. This was something . . . the community decided we had to fight back against."[38] The CIW made the liberation of enslaved, as well as oppressed, workers a priority. Now, with its deep-rooted, community-based network of over three thousand members, the CIW sometimes receives word that a crew leader is operating a slave camp, and they begin to investigate. In their words, "Workers are well-placed to understand, analyze, investigate, and operate within the parallel and totally separate world that captive workers and their employers inhabit in rural agricultural communities."[39]

By 2009, the CIW had contributed to the uncovering, investigation, and prosecution of several trafficking operations in four states, resulting in the liberation of well over a thousand workers and long sentences for the offenders. Among those cases was that of the notorious Ramoses— two brothers and a cousin—who enslaved hundreds of workers. To gather information, a young CIW member, Romeo Ramirez, volunteered to infiltrate one of the Ramos camps, pretending to seek work. He lived in squalid conditions with several other workers, and when he left he took with him enough information to justify an investigation. When asked if he feared for his safety while among the Ramoses' crew, Ramirez replied, "When you're afraid, you can't get anything done." Eventually, the Ramoses were sentenced to lengthy prison terms, their land and property were confiscated, and they were fined $3,000,000—the amount the judge determined they had earned off the labor of their enslaved workers.[40]

In early 2007, the CIW was helpful in bringing about the arrest and conviction of a man who owned labor camps in Palatka, Florida, and Newton Grove, North Carolina. For over fifteen years, Ronald Evans recruited workers from homeless shelters and kept them in debt by providing them with overpriced crack cocaine and alcohol, coupled with exorbitant charges for rent and food. Aside from the horrific nature of the offense, what makes this servitude case unusual these days is the fact that Evans was not preying on foreign migrant workers; nearly all his victims were American born. Once again, the coalition was instrumental in investigating the case, traveling to Palatka and North Carolina several times to gather information. Along with advocates from advocate organization Touching Miami with Love, "The Coalition hit laundromats, gas stations, and convenience stores. They talked to workers, clinic officials, priests, waitresses and growers" in their search for witnesses and victims.[41] They then turned their findings over to the DOJ, which brought Evans to justice. In attempting to minimize the slavery aspects of the case, Evans's attorney callously argued, "This was the best situation most of these people ever had in their lives." The judge disagreed and sentenced Evans to thirty years in federal prison.[42]

MULTITASKING AGAINST SLAVERY

The CIW defines its antislavery campaign as a "worker-based approach to eliminating modern-day slavery in the agricultural industry."[43] Members work on multiple fronts. In their attempts to deal with existing slavery situations, they combine community outreach, investigation, and counseling. They hold member meetings on a regular basis. To help get the word out, the CIW has its own radio station in Immokalee—Radio Conciencia—which broadcasts locally in the various languages spoken by the workers. Its programs combine music with vital information on workers' rights.

Because the coalition is worker-based, members have access to situations and places that would be inaccessible to government and law enforcement agents. As a member states, "The CIW members know how slavery camps operate, and often become aware of such operations due to being tapped into networks in the world of migrant labor."[44] When they uncover slavery, the coalition works closely with the DOJ—which has made tremendous strides since the days of the Flores case—to bring the captives to freedom and the perpetrators to trial.

Because of the complex, violent nature of agricultural slavery, the investigative techniques used by the CIW are many and varied. As in the case of Romeo Ramirez, they will send a member into a slave camp to gather evidence. (Mike Baron credits them with perfecting their techniques for "covert operations.")[45] They frequently travel to various states, visiting remote camps, looking for evidence of forced labor, and speaking with the workers. In the course of their investigations, some of which have taken years, they have spoken with "workers, growers, store owners, flea market vendors, police, motel owners, priests, nurses, gunmen, and crew leaders."[46] They have combed the Internet, performing criminal background checks and license plate searches; they have studied police records and court documents. And when they've discovered workers in a slavery situation, they've helped them escape.

Once a worker is free, the CIW provides counseling, as well as education and peer support. The freed worker can train in slavery awareness, labor rights, and organizing techniques. He or she can, in turn, become a peer educator for others coming out of slavery, calming their fears of retaliation, and addressing the shame many feel for having been "bought, sold, and treated like an animal."

The CIW has provided training on agricultural slavery for many organizations, including the FBI in Quantico, Orlando, and Miami, for both supervisors and field agents; the North Carolina State Troopers Training Academy; the Florida Coalition against Domestic Violence; and the North and South Carolina U.S. Attorney's Offices, where the training included local, state, and federal officials and was attended by such agencies as Immigration and Customs Enforcement (ICE).

HOLDING THE BIG CORPORATIONS ACCOUNTABLE

But it is not enough just to uncover slavery and bring the bad guys to account: while prosecution is vital, it addresses an abuse only after it has occurred. The CIW takes the view that, while it is necessary to address trafficking cases as they arise, new ones will just keep coming up. As the CIW sees it, the true key to ending slavery is to prevent it from happening in the first place by targeting the big corporations that buy the produce because they have power over the growers and their subcontractors. "Our goal," says Germino, "is to get them to take responsibility and say, 'We are no longer going to tolerate sweatshop conditions and slavery.'" Many of the current labor violations—including a steep increase in the number of trafficking cases—are indirectly driven by the demand for lower and lower prices by the buyers from the big corporations. So now, says Germino, "Let them use their power in the market for good. . . . [If] they can say to a supplier, 'We want 'x' and 'y' health and safety standards, we want this size tomato, we want this color,' they can do the same for labor standards as they do for animal rights. They could say, 'We don't want these particular kinds of abuses in our supply chain.'"[47]

By going after the big buyers, the CIW is looking to reverse the process of falling wages and worsening conditions. They see criminal prosecution as a short-term means of dealing with existing slavery cases, while the concept of corporate accountability aims at removing the conditions that give rise to abuse in the first place. Many activist organizations choose to address labor abuses by concentrating on what goes on inside the farm gate; the coalition's approach takes the issue beyond the gate, to the offices of America's biggest market and fast-food corporations. The ultimate objective is to convince the buyers to eliminate sweatshop conditions and slavery from their supply chain.

Ringing Taco Bell's Bell

In 2001, the CIW began what would become a four-year boycott aimed specifically at Taco Bell and its parent company, Yum Brands. The "Boot the Bell" campaign included marches and media events, including a ten-day hunger strike on the lawn of Taco Bell's corporate headquarters. It also saw a groundswell among college students that resulted in the closing or blocking of a number of Taco Bell restaurants. The result, which gained national attention, was a concession from Taco Bell to pay a penny more per pound of tomatoes directly to the workers, to adopt a genuine policy of zero tolerance for slavery, and to establish an "enforceable code of conduct," drawn up with the participation of the workers.[48] In early 2007, Yum Brands added its other companies—including KFC, Long John Silver, Pizza Hut, and A&W—to the agreement.

On April 9, 2007, after a two-year campaign, McDonald's followed suit—along with their suppliers—and agreed to pay the additional penny per pound. They also consented to work with the coalition in a "collaborative effort to develop a third party mechanism for monitoring conditions in the fields and investigating workers' complaints of abuse."[49]

Initially, the response from Burger King was not as positive. In late 2007, Burger King—after nearly two years of discussions with the coalition—issued a public response that has baffled and frustrated CIW leadership. As one coalition leader has stated, "It's as if they're repeating every failed tactic Taco Bell had tried to use."[50] They refused to pay the additional penny per pound, claiming no connection with the workforce. And rather than focus on the issue of wages and working conditions—the true root issues—the Burger King spokespeople expressed dismay at the workers' *housing* situation: "The workers' living conditions are, in fact, substandard, and we are sympathetic and concerned about the housing." Burger King offered a counterproposal for improving the lives of the workers: "We have offered to send Burger King recruiters to the area to speak with the CIW and with workers themselves about permanent, full-time employment at Burger King restaurants."[51] Lucas Benitez of CIW responded: "Burger King was never acting in good faith. How else could one explain their absurd offer to solve the ongoing exploitation of farm workers by training all of Immokalee's tomato pickers to work in their restaurants? Who, exactly, would be left to pick their tomatoes? This kind of answer isn't even serious; it's a slap in the face."[52]

In lieu of paying a penny more per pound, monitoring field conditions, and refusing to buy slave-harvested produce, Burger King offered charity: "We have . . . spoken with the CIW about the strong interest from the charitable arm of Burger King Corporation, the Have It Your Way Foundation. . . . The Foundation is keenly interested in working with the CIW and others to identify charitable organizations that could improve the lives of the workers."[53] The CIW membership feels that Burger King has missed the point. The workers never requested, or wanted, charity; they are seeking a small but long overdue wage increase for the paid workers and freedom for those enslaved. CIW members saw the offer of charity as an insult.

Ironically, just a few weeks after issuing their position statement denying concessions to workers, Burger King was the subject of an article on the front page of the *New York Times* Business Section, under a banner reading, "Burger King Pledges Cage-Free Food." "Animal rights activists praised Burger King," the article states, "for its new commitment to begin buying eggs and pork from suppliers that do not keep their animals in cages or crates." Burger King, the article continues, "has told egg suppliers that it will look favorably on cage-free eggs when making purchasing decisions."[54] As Lucas Benitez said during the Taco Bell boycott, "Taco Bell has a policy that it will not buy food from contractors that mistreat animals. All we are asking is that they have the same policy for humans."[55]

Instead, Burger King resorted to dirty tricks. First, a spate of vicious comments and false allegations against the CIW began to appear on the Internet, signed only by the writer's online names. "The CIW is an attack organization," read one, submitted under the name surfxaholic, "lining the leaders' pockets. . . . They make up issues and collect money from dupes that believe their story." Other submissions referred to the CIW as "bloodsuckers" and "the lowest form of life." As it turned out, the smear campaign was ultimately connected to Stephen Grover, a Burger King vice president, who used his young daughter's computer and online name to wage his nasty little war. He was finally unmasked in April 2008 when his daughter spilled the beans. A CIW member commented, "When you realize the person posting those things is actually Burger King's vice president in charge of the ethical operation of the company's supply chain, it makes you wonder just how high up does this whole thing go."[56]

Around the same time, it was discovered that Cara Schaffer, the twenty-five-year-old owner of a private security firm hired by Burger King, had infiltrated the CIW and the Student/Farmworker Alliance, a nonprofit student activist organization, by pretending to be a student at Broward Community College. She attended two planning sessions by phone before her true identity became known. Schaffer, a loose cannon who had apparently been denied her Florida private investigator's license because of lack of training, had nonetheless been employed on other such projects by the fast-food giant. John Chidsey, the CEO of Burger King, was aware of the long-term use of Schaffer's company, but as one Burger King executive stated, "It is both the corporation's right and duty to protect its employees and assets from potential harm." Why the massive organization felt the need to protect itself from two pacifist nonprofits was not explained.[57]

Burger King's indiscretions made the national news, including the *New York Times*. In late May 2008, smarting under the exposure, the corporation issued a public apology to the CIW and signed an accord along the lines of those approved by Yum Brands and McDonalds. Since then, Subway and Whole Foods have followed suit. There are still a number of Goliaths, including Chipotle and Wal-Mart, that have yet to acknowledge their involvement in the exploitation of workers; the CIW's long-term game plan includes them as well.

The CIW's antislavery efforts have not gone unrecognized. In 2003, three CIW members received the Robert F. Kennedy Human Rights Award for their work in combating slavery. They are CIW co-founder Lucas Benitez, "undercover operative" Romeo Ramirez, and the courageous Julia Gabriel. It was the first time this prestigious international award was given to recipients within the United States. In 2007, the CIW was given the annual Anti-Slavery Award by London-based Anti-Slavery International, the world's oldest and original human rights group. In April 2008, Lucas Benitez joined farmworkers, growers, and law enforcement officials in testifying at a U.S. Senate Health, Education, Labor, and Pensions Committee hearing entitled "Ending Abuses and Improving Working Conditions for Tomato Workers." The hearing was held by U.S. Senators Ted Kennedy, Bernie Sanders, and Richard Durbin.

Hitting Them in the Pocketbook

In addition to campaigns and the criminal prosecution of traffickers, another avenue is open to antislavery workers: civil litigation. The goal is to obtain financial compensation and emotional and psychological satisfaction for former slaves by suing the traffickers and everyone associated with them. As the U.S. district judge in the Ramos case said at their sentencing, "There are others . . . at a higher level, that . . . are complicit in one way or another in how these activities occur. . . . They . . . create a legal fiction or corporation that insulates them . . . so they can be relieved from any liability. . . . I think there is a broader interest out there that the government should look at as well."[58] If the feds won't prosecute, the human rights groups bring civil lawsuits.

Occasionally, a lawsuit is brought alongside a criminal prosecution. In the case of Ronald Evans, who enslaved residents of homeless shelters with booze and crack cocaine, Lisa Butler of Florida Rural Legal Services sued the growers. By 2008, she had brought three separate suits against two growers for failing to provide either employment or the wages promised, for substandard housing, and for extortion and forced labor. Typically, for her case to succeed, she needs the victims' testimony. "All cases," she explained, "turn on what the workers want to do." In the Evans case, several of her clients have testified.[59] At this writing, two of the cases had settled to the workers' satisfaction.

Besides gaining recompense for the victims, attorneys see civil litigation as a way of fighting demand. Dan Werner, legal director of the Workers' Rights Law Center of New York, states, "We want to make it costlier to use slaves than to hire paid workers."[60] Civil courts, he adds, are the only system where the victim can actually confront his abuser directly, and as such, they become part of the healing and empowering process. Werner is himself pursuing civil lawsuits in a recent New York State agricultural slavery case involving the Garcia-Botello family.

The Garcias were big western New York State labor contractors who had been running a trafficking operation for years. They were part of a network that smuggled illegal immigrants—men and teenage boys—across the Mexican border into Arizona, trucking them to the farms of three New York counties and enslaving them there. They were forced to work in the row crops of onions, cabbage, and tomatoes. The situation was typical of those found in such cases: instead of receiving the promised favorable working conditions and decent wages, they were met with threats and acts of violence, squalid living conditions, and confiscation of their pay by the traffickers—in this case, various members of the Garcia family. Six of the workers finally escaped and blew the whistle; eventually the trafficking ring was busted, and five of the Garcias were arrested, prosecuted, and convicted. Werner then filed suit against not only the Garcias but twenty growers as well, on the premise that they were aware of the workers' servitude and had done nothing to stop it. The suit is ongoing.[61]

There doesn't have to be a criminal conviction before a lawsuit can start. This is good because criminal charges often languish. Time and again, in interview after interview for this book, legal aid attorneys and caseworkers commented on the government's unwillingness to take on trafficking cases—or at least the less "glitzy" ones. Many feel that limited resources of finances and personnel, and a lack of understanding of the subtle nature of most slavery cases, have led the DOJ to "cherry-pick" the cases they think they will win, as well as those with high visibility. This often means cases that involve sex and overt violence. Inevitably, according to the NGOs, the majority of trafficking cases go unprosecuted.

This view, say representatives of the DOJ, is unduly harsh and not very realistic. One U.S. attorney presents a practical explanation: "I think it has less to do with 'one version of trafficking is worse than another,' than with what could just be a lack of resources. We have to make tough calls about the types of cases we're going to follow through on. Because of the difficulty in proving many of these cases, my guess is, law enforcement may be going after the worst ones."[62] However, as experience has shown, in cases that the federal government chooses not to pursue, a civil suit can actually succeed. In a civil case, where the burden of proof is less rigid, the plaintiff can sue all the way up the ladder, to the CEO of the corporation that hires the contractor, as well as the contractor himself. A case currently in the Connecticut courts comes out of what had all the earmarks of a trafficking situation. A dozen Guatemalans were given legal work visas to plant trees in North Carolina; the contractors, however, allegedly packed them into a van, drove them to a nursery in Granby, Connecticut, confiscated their papers, and threatened them with arrest and deportation. According to the civil charges, they were forced to work eighty-hour weeks for practically no pay, denied emergency medical care, and clearly kept against their will.[63]

U.S. attorney Kevin O'Connor maintains that this situation does not represent a trafficking case, and the government has decided not to pursue it.[64] However, Yale University's clinical professor of law Michael Wishnie and four of his students brought civil suit on behalf of the workers, against not only the labor contractor (Pro Tree Forestry Services of North Carolina) but the grower (Imperial Nurseries) and the corporation that owns them (Griffin Land and Nurseries), personally naming the parent company's CEO, among others. Griffin trades on NASDAQ, and Imperial Nurseries is one of the twenty largest in the country. Wishnie contended that "Imperial was responsible for what happened on their fields, and they profited from the fact that these workers weren't paid."[65] Regarding Wishnie's civil suit, U.S. attorney O'Connor says, "We're perfectly fine with Mike going ahead with his suit; it's not an issue."[66]

In June 2007, Griffin Land and Nurseries and its subsidiary, Imperial Nurseries, settled the suit by agreeing "to provide the workers with financial compensation out of concern for the hardship they allege they experienced." According to a Griffin spokesperson, the corporation fired Pro Tree as their labor contractor immediately on learning of the worker abuses they allegedly inflicted.[67] Although the suit against Griffin and Imperial was resolved, the action, citing human trafficking and forced labor, would take another year and would result in a judgment in excess of $7 million against three defendants, including Pro Tree.[68]

Federal law didn't permit bringing a civil suit on the grounds of trafficking until 2005; before that time lawyers used federal and state wage and hour laws, the racketeering law (RICO), the Alien Tort Claim Act, the Migrant and Seasonal Agricultural Worker Protection Act (AWPA), and the Thirteenth Amendment. They sued on the basis of assault, false imprisonment, involuntary servitude, outrageous conduct, and emotional distress.

Many see civil action as a viable means of attacking the trafficking problem. In 2005, attorneys Kathleen Kim and Dan Werner wrote a manual for lawyers, *Civil Litigation on Behalf of Victims of Human Trafficking*.[69] They see lawsuits as a way to "make the victim 'whole' again." In these civil suits, the perpetrator is made directly accountable to the victim rather than to the criminal charges of the prosecution. In addition, third parties who allegedly profit from human trafficking, such as Imperial and Griffin, can be made liable, and damages are allowed to exceed restitution.

Currently agriculture-based civil suits are in progress in various states, including Colorado, Georgia, North Carolina, New York, and Connecticut. (One recent New Hampshire case, involving trafficked Jamaican workers, actually resulted in the successful *criminal* prosecution of the traffickers.)[70] But the road to civil litigation is by no means a sure one. It presupposes certain conditions and inherently incurs certain difficulties. Federal law states that the prosecutor in a *criminal* case can seek damages for the victim through a requisition order. If the court awards the plaintiff damages in amounts exceeding the defendant's ability to pay, it is pointless for a civil attorney to seek further payment: his clients will never see a nickel, especially once a defendant is in jail. Also, to bring suit against the bigger fish, the attorney has to be able to demonstrate the buyer's direct involvement in the labor process. Another drawback is time: like all civil actions, these suits can take years to resolve, and the workers, in all likelihood, will have long since moved on. In cases where the victims' testimony is crucial, this is an obvious drawback. Realistically, the chances of winning against a large corporation are daunting, considering that they will invest heavily in skilled lawyers. And should they lose, they can afford to go through an endless series of appeals and chalk it up to the cost of doing business. At the other end of the spectrum, some companies, like labor recruiters, are small and virtually without assets, making civil litigation difficult. Some of these companies are criminally "connected," and by naming them in a civil suit the victim puts himself—and his family—at risk. Further, in cases where workers have been through the emotional wringer of a criminal trial, they may not want to see the inside of a courtroom again. And because the trafficker remains at large, the victims may never feel safe. Still, given how few trafficking cases face criminal prosecution, a civil lawsuit may be the only legal satisfaction open to the victims.

"GUESTS" IN THE FIELDS

It's bad enough when slavery exists and the government is either unaware or unwilling to address it. But how about an ongoing federal program that makes it much too easy to bring people into the United States to be enslaved? Welcome to the "Guest Worker Program," also known as the

H-2 program, after the type of visas assigned. Temporary agricultural workers from Latin America, Asia, eastern Europe, and the Caribbean are lured here by the *official guarantee* of good working conditions: so many hours a week at a fixed and acceptable wage, government-inspected living conditions, and medical benefits, including "payment for lost time from work and for any permanent injury." Guest workers are also entitled to "federally funded legal services for matters relating to their employment." According to the rules, any employer who receives DOL approval to import guest workers must compensate them for their travel expenses—the plane or bus fare and food costs incurred on the way to the promised job. Finally, the worker is guaranteed three-fourths of the total hours promised in his contract for the period of employment specified.[71] The conditions of the program also stipulate that the worker is obligated to stay with the employer who sponsored him; he cannot leave to seek a job elsewhere. Some employers adhere to the conditions of the law. But in a large number of cases, not a single one of these promises is honored because of employer abuses and government neglect.

The Guest Worker Program is not a new concept: the United States has been taking in foreign workers almost since its inception. Our attitude toward them—at least over the last hundred years—has been ambivalent. America welcomed them when we needed them—during the two World Wars, for example, when most of the permanent work-force was in the service—and limited or simply ousted them when we didn't. In 1943, to provide workers for the southern sugar cane fields, the government established the H-2 program. From its beginning it was characterized by inequity and brutality. As recently as 1986, cane cutters who attempted a work stoppage over poor conditions were beset by armed police with dogs, acting at the employers' behest. The incident became known as the "Dog Wars." In that same year, the H-2 program was expanded to include nonagricultural workers, but the number of mainly Asian and Latin American guest workers arriving for farm work under the program is still significant. The number of foreign workers certified by DOL as agricultural—or H-2A—laborers went from forty-eight thousand in 2005 to nearly seventy-seven thousand in 2007.[72]

The viability of a guest worker program has been endlessly debated, but one thing is clear: its lack of oversight provides a splendid opportunity for mistreatment and enslavement. In the words of Mary Bauer of the Southern Poverty Law Center, "The very structure of the program . . . lends itself to abuse."[73] Increasingly, employers use labor contractors to recruit guest workers for them. In this way they avoid technical responsibility for the workers, legally distancing themselves from any abuses that follow. The brokers recruit the workers in their home countries. Unrestricted by law or ethics, they make promises of work and wages that far exceed the provisions of the program—so much so that the workers go into massive debt, often in excess of $10,000, to pay the recruiter's inflated fee.

Employers often bring in more workers than they need. They exaggerate the number required, as well as the period of employment, since they know the government isn't paying attention. Employers know they can get away with not paying the three-fourths of the wages or meeting the other conditions the contract stipulates. The worker, heavily in debt and doomed to few work hours and pay fraud, is indentured even before he leaves home. When he arrives in America, he finds himself at the mercy of his employer. The promised forty-hour week turns out to be only twenty-five hours, and his looming debt becomes instantly insurmountable. Sometimes the workweek is eighty hours long, but the promised pay is withheld or radically reduced. The "free housing in good condition" can turn out to be a lightless, heatless shack with no bed or blankets, and sometimes no windows to keep out the cold, shared with twenty or thirty other workers. In some cases, he is locked in or kept under armed guard.[74] If transportation to the job is required, a travel fee is deducted from his pay. Fees are illegally charged for food and sometimes rent, both of which are guaranteed him by law. The program also promises him worker's compensation for hospital or doctor's costs and lost wages, but the moment he gets sick or hurt on the job he finds this is a lie. Ignorant of the system and the language, he has no clue how to seek medical help, and his employer, far from being solicitous in the face of losing a laborer, pushes him to keep working.

To enforce control, the employer confiscates or destroys the guest worker's passport and visa, making him an illegal alien. In this way, he faces the threat of arrest and deportation should he attempt to leave or refuse to work. If he manages to escape and find his way to the local police, the likelihood of the authorities taking the word of an undocumented migrant worker, with little or no English, over that of an established local grower is slim to none. Without his papers, the worker is at considerably greater risk than his employer. And once he has made waves, he runs the risk of being blacklisted and destroys any chance of coming back in the future for a decent job.[75] The Carnegie Endowment for International Peace reported in 1999, "Blacklisting of H-2A workers appears to be widespread, is highly organized, and occurs at all stages of the recruitment and employment process."[76] The large North Carolina Growers Association has blatantly kept a blacklist, which in 1997 was titled "NCGA Ineligible for Rehire Report," listing over a thousand workers' names.[77]

All in all, there is little about this that doesn't fall under the definition of slavery. Workers are often kept against their will, held by the threat of violence, paid as little as their employers wish, and denied every basic right guaranteed by law. In fact, there is little to distinguish these thousands of guest workers from the crews held in slavery by Miguel Flores—except for the stunning fact that this particular form of bondage occurs within a government-sponsored program. Admittedly, this scenario doesn't play itself out in every instance: many employers honor the conditions of the H-2A laws, providing the work promised at the agreed-upon wage. Nonetheless, this doesn't change the fact that because of the program's lack of oversight the result can be coercion and peonage.

Flying in New Victims for Katrina

In 2005, a small, fly-by-night labor contracting company calling itself "Million Express Manpower, Inc." brought thirty Thais to the United States on agricultural guest worker visas. Two of the three owners of Million Express Manpower were Laotian; the third was an American who worked for the state job service and was "familiar with the process of licensing farm labor contractors."[78] The three planned to use the Thais—all from small villages, with no knowledge of English—as cheap labor with which to compete with the larger, established labor brokers, such as the North Carolina Growers Association.[79] The contractors' associates in Thailand promised the workers steady work for three years and charged them a fee of $11,000 each "to secure the promised employment."[80] By putting up their houses and bits of farmland as security, the Thais borrowed enough to pay the fee. But as case records show, the guest workers "were victims of trafficking. When they arrived in North Carolina, Defendant Million Express Manpower, Inc. confiscated their passports and visas. Defendants did not provide plaintiffs with the promised work, and kept plaintiffs in seriously substandard housing. Defendants warned plaintiffs they would be arrested if they left their employment, monitored their movements constantly, and showed plaintiffs they possessed guns. Plaintiffs were fearful of leaving . . . and also were bound to continue working to pay off the massive recruitment fees they had [incurred]."[81]

Although they were initially put to work in the potato and tobacco fields around Benson, North Carolina, the work quickly ran out. Shortly after Hurricane Katrina, the contractors drove them to a flooded New Orleans and lodged them—several to a room—in a condemned motel. There were no lights or heat, and the water was polluted. Far from the crops of North Carolina, they forced the Thais to "work in atrocious conditions, and failed to pay them for their work. Plaintiffs eventually sought help and escaped."[82]

This is the sanitized version of the horrors these guest workers suffered. A civil lawsuit states that Million Express Manpower was founded "to capitalize on (1) the need of impoverished people in northern Thailand to get employment abroad in order to support their families; and (2) the desire of some North Carolina farmers to obtain H2-A workers more cheaply, and with less accountability, than if they made application on their own behalf or used a more established H-2A labor provider."[83] Subsequently, Legal Aid of North Carolina sued for damages on behalf of twenty-two of the workers under the 2000 Trafficking Act, the Fair Labor Standards Act, RICO, and North Carolina common law. Asserting a strong connection between the contractors and the growers, Legal Aid is suing *both* groups.[84] Since there is a high likelihood that Million Express Manpower has no money, whatever compensation the workers receive will have to come from the growers, who are being sued for violations of the Fair Labor Standards Act and breach of contract.[85]

Meanwhile, what becomes of the workers once they're freed but before the government certifies them as trafficking victims? This is a big problem. In general, there is a lack of both funding and social services for rescued or escaped victims. In this instance, though they were victims of serious crimes, North Carolina had nothing to offer them. No shelters would accept them. In the end, they were sent to Washington, D.C., where they were cared for by a victim service organization called Boat People SOS.[86]

A T visa—and frequently funds and support—are available to certified trafficking victims, but the certification process can be a nightmare. According to Kate Woomer-Deters, an attorney with Legal Aid of North Carolina, although various government agencies can certify a person simply by filling out a form qualifying him as a victim of human trafficking, "This is where they drag their feet." Neither an investigation nor a

prosecution is required for certification, but many law enforcement officials will refuse to certify in the absence of one or the other, or both. Yet
as Woomer-Deters states, "Without a slam dunk case—with barbed wire
and beatings to place before a jury—there is less likelihood of prosecution."[87] As a result, victims hang in limbo—no social services, no housing or food allowance, no acknowledged place in the world of people.
Victims are ghosts, and ghostlike, they will often simply disappear.

So Who's Minding the Store?

We would assume that the DOL would be involved in the process of
approving and tracking agricultural guest workers, given the ease with
which they can become trafficking victims. But the DOL has expressed
its intention to become *less* involved in the program by removing itself
from the approval process of employers' applications. There are already
too few wage and hour inspectors, and in the words of Mary Bauer,
director of the Southern Poverty Law Center's Immigrant Justice Project
and the author of "Close to Slavery: Guestworker Programs in the
United States," "I have never seen a DOL inspector in the field."[88] The
"Close to Slavery" report further explains: "The number of wage and
hour investigators in the . . . DOL has declined by 14 percent between
1974 and 2004, and the number of completed compliance actions
declined by 36%."

In July 2008, the federal watchdog, the Government Accountability
Office (GAO), reported to the House Education and Labor Committee
in Congress that the Wage and Hour Division of the DOL—the agency
responsible for investigating complaints of wage, hour, and child labor
violations—was failing to fully investigate and properly address violations of the law. They concluded that the agency "does not sufficiently
leverage its existing tools to increase compliance."[89] The GAO calcu-
lated that actions initiated by the department on wage and hour violations had dropped from approximately forty-seven thousand in 1997 to
fewer than thirty thousand in 2007, a smaller number of complaints
than were investigated in 1941, the year of the department's founding.
And the use of fines that punish repeat or egregious offenders had
declined by nearly 50 percent from 2001 to 2007. Anne Marie
Lasowski, a GAO investigator, told lawmakers that there had been a
sharp decline in enforcement during the tenure of the Bush administration
and that the number of wage and hour inspectors had been slashed during
that period from 942 to 732. Lasowski explained, "It's not working for

low-wage workers; they are becoming victims because the law is not being enforced."[90]

When you combine this information with the fact that the number of workers has grown radically over the past several years, the conclusion is obvious: the government is abdicating its responsibility to protect these people from employers who ignore or abuse the laws as a matter of course and as a way of doing business.[91] Mary Bauer adds, "Government enforcement has been largely ineffective. . . . Though violations of federal regulations or individual contracts are common, DOL rarely instigates enforcement actions." Despite the alarming number of employers who have violated the legal rights of workers, there is hardly a single recorded instance of the DOL taking action to stop any of them from importing more workers.[92]

The DOL's position regarding enforcing the rules of the Guest Worker Program became clear after the Federal Appeals Court handed down its verdict in the Arriaga case. The issue, which came out of Florida, concerned the payment of workers' transportation costs, and the court ruled that the employer was, in fact, liable for the reimbursement of travel expenses. This was an important case because it took a step toward easing the workers' burden of debt. The DOL, however, responded by stating that it would continue to maintain a position of nonenforcement. After opening the door to the exploitation of guest workers, the government was saying, "I don't want to get involved."[93]

Of course, governmental noninvolvement is preferable to harassment and interference. In Northwest Colorado's Moffat County, the Vermillion Ranch Limited Partnership—a large multigeneration stock operation—for years brought guest workers from Chile on H-2A visas to work with cattle. Once on the ranch, however, the workers were made to surrender their documents. Instead of herding, they were put to maintenance chores, corral building, gardening—various types of non-H-2A work for which they should have received the minimum wage, instead of the much lower pay the government allows under the Range Production of Livestock law. In fact, they received *no* money; their employer told them it was being deposited in individual accounts set up for them at a local bank. Deductions were taken from these accounts for overpriced food, medicine, and other daily necessities, which they were forced to buy from their employer. The guest workers were allowed no visitors, and the rancher opened their mail. Having taken their documents, the rancher threatened them with deportation if they tried to run. The two workers who mustered the courage to ask to leave were sent to a remote part of the ranch, with no phone or means of transportation.[94]

In 2006, a group of workers escaped and sought help from Colorado Legal Services, who sued the ranch not only for breach of contract but also for false imprisonment and outrageous conduct. Members of the ranch family had served as county commissioners, and presumably they inspired the county sheriff to take the next step. Claiming that the workers had "absconded," the sheriff notified Colorado Legal Services that their attorney was under investigation in a missing persons case! The sheriff's office began a campaign of intimidation aimed directly at her, digging up all the personal information they could find. Rather than gearing their resources toward uncovering a trafficking operation, local law enforcement elected to support the home boys and harass the trafficked workers' legal team. This is the same law enforcement agency whose Web site promises, "The men and women of the Moffat County Sheriff's Office believe that our fundamental duty is to serve and protect the citizens of Moffat County. . . . We will uphold the law fairly and firmly. . . . We believe that life and individual freedoms, as guaranteed by the Constitution of the United States, are primary guidelines in performing our duties."[95]

Obstruction by local law enforcement is not all that uncommon. In referring to another rural agricultural trafficking case, one federal agent commented, "You had to be careful because sheriff's offices are sheriff's offices. . . . You know, in small communities—loyalties run deep in some of those places."[96]

The federal government declined to prosecute the Vermillion Ranch case. The problem, according to Colorado Legal Services attorney Patricia Medige, lies in the fact that "federal law enforcement in general—FBI, ICE . . . is still adjusting to the concept of 'psychological coercion.' Because there is a subjective element to it, I think it makes law enforcement uncomfortable. . . . To them, sex and violence are more tangible than 'abuse of the legal process' or threats."[97] As Mary Bauer understates it, "Most of the time we don't see the government as an ally."[98]

The Bush administration expressed its intention to expand the Guest Worker Program. However, the Southern Poverty Law Center's "Close to Slavery" report concludes that the "H-2 guestworker program is fundamentally flawed. Because guestworkers are tied to a single employer and have little or no ability to enforce their rights, they are routinely exploited."[99] CIW member Laura Germino puts it succinctly: "There are two ways to keep [the workers] down on the farm; one is by force, and the other is by a government-sanctioned program that locks the worker to the employer."[100] The report goes on to suggest that the Guest Worker Program as it now exists "should not be expanded or used for a model of immigration reform."

The program could be brought closer to the spirit and letter of the law with structural changes to the H-2A agricultural category and the H2-B visa program that covers other labor categories, such as seafood processing, landscaping, and construction.[101] Flexibility could be woven into the program to allow workers to choose to work for another employer. Above all, diligent monitoring by responsible government inspectors is vital to ensure that the workers whom we have welcomed into our country are housed, fed, paid, and cared for as the law stipulates. Otherwise, expanding the Guest Worker Program will simply perpetuate a situation that invites abuse and enslavement.

SLAVERY IN YOUR FACE

At the very beginning of the trans-Atlantic slave trade some Africans were tricked into slavery.[102] A slave ship might sail upriver and find an isolated village; if the people didn't run away, the slaver might trade with them and invite them on board the ship. He might tell them about the land on the other side of the water where food was abundant, land was there for the taking, and everyone lived like kings. Excited about the chance to see the enormous "canoe" up close, villagers would flock aboard, and while they were being shown the lower decks, they would be captured, beaten, and chained. The trap was set with lies and sprung with violence, and the new slaves would be on their way to the fields of North America. Once sold to farmers, the slaves who survived would usually be put to work growing and gathering crops: cotton, sugar, fruit, vegetables, timber, all to supply the growing nation's demand for food, clothing, and building materials. All over the United States, in slave states and free states, families would eat the food grown and picked by slaves in the South.

Today, the same things occur. Farmworkers are being ensnared by deception and enslaved through violence. And we Americans obliviously munch away on the slave-picked fruit and vegetables we bring home from the grocery store or order in fast-food restaurants. The slaves tend to come from Asia and Central and South America instead of Africa, but they are tricked with the same sorts of lies and promises. And while the U.S. government tended to just ignore the illegal antebellum slave trade, today it swings through the bipolar reaction of prosecuting some cases while propping open the door to human trafficking through the Guest Worker Program.

The idea of putting slave-grown food in the mouths of our children should make us sick. Putting a stop to this travesty should be an immediate concern. The good news is, we know how to bring this slavery to an end—through greater public awareness, an enhanced system of government inspection, a complete overhaul of the Guest Worker Program, a governmental willingness to root out and prosecute cases of trafficking in the fields, and—most vital—a solid respect for the rights and humanity of the people whom we put to growing and harvesting our crops. But none of this will happen until we all decide that slave-picked food is just too bitter to swallow.

4

SUPPLY AND DEMAND

OF DIFFERENCES AND SIMILARITIES

Thousands of women and children are trafficked into prostitution and other forms of sex slavery in the United States. Many are immigrants. They come from every corner of the world, by plane, car, truck, bus, van, boat, or on foot. They share few outward characteristics. Some are Russian high school graduates; others are Mexican indigenous women who have spent more time in farm fields than in school. Others are Cameroonians whose main interest is in attending college. Some have legitimate papers, others falsified documents, and still others no papers at all. Yet what they do share is the hope and the promise they felt at the beginning of their journey. In story after story, a trafficker, often a known member of the community, a friend of the family, or sometimes a relative, offers a better life in America. He or she promises steady work with enough pay to send some back to the family, a good home, maybe an American education: in short, all the things we as Americans assume as our birthright.

These women and children share a dream, and when it all goes wrong for them, it usually does so in heartbreakingly similar ways as well. Anyone who has ever felt the sudden cold stab of panic can imagine the first moment when a woman or child realizes the true nature and the hopelessness of his or her situation. It is often a moment of brutal shock involving beating and rape, often gang rape, intended to remove any resistance. As the body is subjugated, in shock the psyche follows, leaving the victim without the will to resist. Traffickers know this. They are expert at their work, and they use the victim's disorientation, inability to communicate in English, and fear of the outside world to drive the message home: I control your body now, and your life. If you try to reassume control, you will be punished.

FROM GUATEMALA TO HELL

The Lutheran Immigration and Refugee Service (LIRS), based in Washington, D.C., and Baltimore, works with survivors of sexual slavery. In their training sessions and public seminars, they present the story of a young girl whom they call "Maria."[1]

According to LIRS records, Maria grew up in a small country town in Guatemala. Her father, a farmer, struggled but failed to provide adequately for his family, and they often went hungry. For years, an uncle occasionally came by to bring some food—and to sexually abuse Maria. Her parents refused to believe the girl when she complained.

When Maria was sixteen, a man met with her parents and offered to send their children to America, where steady work awaited. They selected Maria because of her "maturity" and ability to work hard. At this juncture, the man treated her well. He flattered her, bought her gifts, made her "feel special." With her natural beauty and his contacts, he told her, he was certain he could make her a successful model. The prospect of removing her uncle from the picture by sending money home, and hopefully sparing her sisters the pain and shame of being molested as she had been, pleased the young girl.

The dream died abruptly. The night Maria was scheduled to make her journey north, the man picked her up in his truck, drove her to a border town, and rented a motel room. For the next four days, she was locked in the room and raped again and again. Then, she and four other girls were driven into the United States; their first stop was a ravine, where Maria was forced to have sex with nine men. Her "sponsor" told her that if she attempted to leave or speak to the authorities, she would be jailed as an illegal immigrant. In addition, he threatened the lives of her family. She was trapped, and it was about to get worse.

The trafficker sold the shell-shocked teenager to a Mexican organized crime group. They took her further north and installed her in an apartment with three other girls, to be sold for sex all day, every day. Sometimes she was forced to walk the streets under a trafficker's watchful eye. Not surprisingly, she contracted several sexually transmitted diseases (STDs) and was beaten regularly.

In time, the apartment was raided, and Maria was victimized yet again—this time by the authorities, in a "sting" operation. Maria should have been freed and helped toward the mental and physical healing she so desperately needed. Instead, she was arrested for illegal prostitution and eventually released back to her "uncle"—the trafficker who paid her bail. She was returned to her life as a sex slave.

There were several opportunities for Maria to be freed; all of them were missed. They came when she was taken to the health clinic for her STDs; when she was brought to the emergency room after a particularly vicious beating by a sadistic john; when a naive social worker failed to question how the trafficker's "wife" had fallen down a flight of stairs; and when she was picked up by the police. Training, sensitivity, and awareness would have made all the difference. A suspicion that all was not right, a few carefully phrased questions, and Maria's story would have ended differently. She could have received counseling, an education, and the chance to become a *free* resident of the United States. As it is, after her long-delayed rescue in another raid on the brothel, she was briefly placed in a foster care program, from which she ran away. This is not a story with a happy ending; the overwhelming majority of sex slavery stories aren't.

HOMEGROWN SLAVES

The government tends to quote only the estimated numbers of victims trafficked *into* the United States. For many people, it is somehow less jarring to think of all victims of forced prostitution as immigrants, but this is not the case. True, many of those sexually enslaved have come here from other countries. But some of the women and children trafficked into sexual slavery are Americans born and raised. Certainly there are similarities, but there are also major differences in the way domestic cases are approached and in the agencies empowered to address them. In the words of Kevin O'Connor, U.S. attorney for Connecticut, "These are cases of *domestic* trafficking victims; they're not about immigration, and ICE [Immigration and Customs Enforcement] is not involved. There are no issues involving the threat of deportation. Here, you're looking at straightforward coercion—either physical or psychological."[2]

Recently the federal court system in Connecticut dealt with two major cases, involving both the prostitution of minors and the forced prostitution of adults, in which all the victims were American by birth. In one case, involving a trafficking and prostitution ring, ten defendants were charged. Nine struck a plea bargain; the tenth, Dennis Paris, chose to try his luck in court. We decided this was a trial we should attend.

On a rainy late-spring morning, we entered the Federal Building in Hartford, Connecticut, to attend the first day of the trial of Dennis Paris.

Paris, whose street name is Rahmyti, had been indicted on sixty-four charges, including placing juveniles in prostitution and compelling adults into prostitution through force, fraud, or coercion: in other words, sex trafficking. In making its case, the government, represented by assistant U.S. attorney James Genco and the new federal Human Trafficking Prosecution Unit's special litigation counsel, Andrew J. Kline, described Paris's brutal treatment of his "girls": the handcuffs, humiliation, beatings, rapes, death threats, denial of money.

While driving to Connecticut that morning, and having already read the indictments against him, we had formed a mental picture of Dennis Paris as a monster. We arrived at the courtroom a little early, and most of the players had not yet taken their seats. At the table in front of us stood a thin, pale, white-haired man who looked to be in his sixties, dressed in a grey suit; next to him sat a very fat, friendly black man in his mid-thirties with close-cropped, thinning hair, dressed in a conservative blue shirt and striped tie. He asked if we were reporters for the *Hartford Courant*, at which point we gave our names, as did he—Dennis Paris. He was not what we'd expected.

Hearing a bit of our exchange, the older man—who turned out to be Paris's attorney, Jeremiah Donovan—asked what we were writing about.

"Trafficking," we responded.

With a knowing, somewhat condescending smile, he replied, "Well, this isn't about trafficking. This is about man's oldest profession. When I think of trafficking, I think of buying and selling babies in Bangkok!"

It was an interesting comment, especially considering that Donovan had, in fact, been a prosecutor before going over to the private sector and that he presumably knew the law.[3] We just hoped that the jury, by the time the trial was over, would have a clearer notion of sex trafficking as it applied to Mr. Paris.

Prosecutor Genco opened for the government, laying out for the jury the various ways in which Paris had violated federal law. He likened the trial to a jigsaw puzzle and promised the jurors that by trial's end all the pieces would fit. What stood out most was his brief account of how Brian Forbes, a fellow pimp, had sold Paris two women for $1,200 each, whereupon Paris had stripped, measured, and photographed them for marketing purposes. It was painfully reminiscent of antebellum slave auctions. Genco explained how Paris had maintained control over these women by keeping them addicted to heroin and denying them their "fix" when they balked. He forced them to have sex with him whenever he wanted and beat, bound, and threatened them regularly.

He achieved his objectives with the women through force, fraud, and coercion, the three key criteria of the trafficking law. In addition, Genco continued, Mr. Paris had prostituted two young girls—ages fourteen and sixteen—in direct violation of the law prohibiting sex trafficking of a minor.[4]

Mr. Donovan, when his turn came, painted quite a different picture: Dennis Paris was the women's savior. The pimp Forbes, he argued, was a brutal bully, and by buying the women from him Paris was "rescuing" them. No force, fraud, or coercion had been used; these women had come to Hartford, Connecticut, for the express purpose of making money, and he had provided them with the opportunity. Paris merely ran an escort service, and these women were, as Donovan described them, "stars! There was competition for their services!" They earned $180 in a half hour, he claimed, and although they had to split it with Paris and their driver they were still making quite a paycheck. In the defense attorney's argument, they had never had it so good. As for the charge of trafficking minors, Donovan claimed that his client had had no idea they were underage.

Then two of the girls—Maryanne C. and Ilene W.—took the stand, and they told a very different story.[5] They were both now twenty-one years old, and native New Englanders—one from Vermont, the other, New Hampshire. Both had run away from home at an early age, come to Hartford, and been introduced to Dennis Paris by a friend. Maryanne had been fourteen at the time, and Paris had promised to find her a housekeeping job in a hotel. The night she met Paris, he took her to a Days Inn motel, where they danced. Paris then stripped her, and they had sex. Within a short time, she was turning tricks for him.

Ilene was sixteen when she was introduced to Paris. She was a freshman in high school ("I should have been a junior, but I got kept back") and was recruited in much the same way. Both girls stated that in their recollection Dennis Paris knew their age at the time. One testified that he had told her to say she was nineteen.

Two other young women, Melissa P. and Jen D., testified that Paris had enslaved them to a life of prostitution by keeping them dependent on heroin. They had both been eighteen when they met Paris, and they were described by the Hartford *Journal Inquirer* as having been "pretty blond teenagers from neighboring towns in New Hampshire." They had two things in common: a friendship since childhood and heroin addiction. When Melissa was thrown out of the house because of her drug habit, her friend Jen introduced her to a Hartford pimp named

Brian Forbes, who in turn introduced her to "the life"—which Jen was already living. Soon both girls found that they were under Forbes's total control, which took the form of verbal and physical abuse and the withholding of drugs. The girls described how, in time, Forbes had sold them to his friend, Dennis Paris, who continued Forbes's methods of discipline and control. On one occasion, when Paris suspected Melissa of talking to the police, he handcuffed and raped her, wrapped her in a blanket, and put her face down on a bed, letting her know that he was about to smother her to death. She cried and begged for her life. "I just made myself deal with the fact that I was going to die," she told the jury. Paris suddenly left the room and soon returned with food from McDonald's. He laughed and joked and removed Melissa's handcuffs. Hysterical, the girl fled.[6]

On various occasions, the girls in Paris's charge were treated brutally by their johns. The common image of the pimp standing between his "ho" and a john's abuse is a myth. Instead of protecting them, Paris forced them to endure whatever physical pain and damage the men chose to inflict, some of which required medical attention. At his trial, Paris testified that as far as he was concerned he merely arranged "dates," not sex, and that anything that followed was simply a matter of agreed-upon relations "between two consenting adults."[7]

After a little over a week of testimony, closing statements were made—Andrew Kline delivering the summary for the prosecution—and the jury retired to consider its verdict. Within a day, they came in with their findings: "guilty of knowingly using minors . . . in his prostitution business and also of using force, fraud, and various coercive means to compel two adult victims to perform commercial sex acts for his financial benefit." Paris was also convicted of conspiracy and "13 counts related to the use of interstate facilities to promote and conduct a prostitution business [Paris regularly used cell phones to arrange "dates"], as well as three counts of money laundering."[8]

Since cases involving the sex trafficking of minors do not require the use of force, fraud, or coercion, even if the girls had willingly gone to work for Paris, they would be trafficking victims according to law, and he would be their trafficker. Conviction on charges of sex trafficking a minor carries a maximum sentence of forty years. If he had been convicted solely on the two charges involving force, fraud, and coercion, Dennis Paris would have faced a possible life sentence and a fine of $250,000 on each count. But given all the other charges upon which he was found guilty—such as money laundering and violations of the

Mann Act—there was the possibility that he would never see the outside of a prison. But he got off relatively lightly; on October 14, 2008, Dennis Paris was sentenced to 30 years in prison, plus five years of supervised release, and ordered to pay over $46,000 in restitution. In a DOJ press release dated October 20, 2008, Director Robert Moossy of the Human Trafficking Prosecution Unit stated, "The victims . . . continue to receive medical and psychological treatment. . . . [They've] been able to move on with their lives: All victims who were drug-dependent have been drug free for over a year; the victims have obtained high school diplomas; some victims are attending college; they have obtained driver's licenses; and, they are finding employment in jobs that they never dreamed they could obtain." Moossy might have added that they are no longer victims; they are survivors.

BARBIE AND THE GORILLA PIMP

Not all victims are minors, runaways, or drug addicts. The second of the two Connecticut cases involving the sexual enslavement of American-born women, *United States v. Corey Davis, a.k.a. "Magnificent," and Shamere McKenzie, a.k.a. "Barbie,"* makes this abundantly clear. Shamere McKenzie was an attractive, intelligent young woman, a model student, and, as far as her parents knew, a well-adjusted, happy teenager. She had attended a New York college on an athletic scholarship and had won numerous awards and medals. She was a "normal" girl from an average American home.[9]

Corey Davis—street name "Magnificent"—was a pimp who maintained his control through an inordinate reliance on violence; in street jargon, he was a "gorilla pimp." One day he pulled up alongside Shamere in his Mercedes and "sweet-talked her." Within a short time they were seeing each other regularly. This part of the pimp's process, according to Dr. Lois Lee, founder and president of the California NGO Children of the Night, is referred to as "copping." "The 'straight' woman who has been 'copped' by a pimp," states Lee, "perceives the relationship as a 'normal' man-woman relationship. [She] usually lacks knowledge of the pimp's involvement in prostitution at the beginning."[10]

Sensing that Shamere needed money, Davis convinced her that she could make upwards of $3,000 a weekend by stripping. Soon he was beating her and forcing her into prostitution. This step in the process is called "turning out."[11] The final step involves both the physical and psychological manipulation of the woman to better maintain the relationship and direct her "career."[12] Pimps are masters of the various techniques required to keep a woman in "the life." Under Davis's control, Shamere's life took an interesting but not uncommon turn; she formed a strong emotional bond with her pimp and went from being just another girl in Davis's "stable" to becoming his "bottom." According to street vernacular, a "bottom," or "bottom female," is a pimp's most trusted prostitute; she collects his money from the other girls, recruits new prostitutes, and deals with legalities such as posting bond when they are arrested.[13] The elevation of one girl is a divide-and-conquer strategy a pimp uses to increase his control, creating competition to become his "bottom." Shamere—or "Barbie," as she was now known—had become "Magnificent's" most trusted associate, and along with her other jobs she helped him traffic minors into prostitution. By the time Shamere saw the inside of a courtroom, she was a defendant, not a victim. In such cases, it's up to the prosecutor to determine the nature and number of charges. Corey "Magnificent" Davis was sentenced to over twenty-four years for trafficking minors and women into prostitution, but Shamere was allowed to plead guilty to just one count of the indictment.[14] Had the prosecution chosen to bring the hammer down, Shamere could have faced indictments for sex trafficking and forced labor.

Shamere's story is a tragedy turned back upon itself. She was, in the truest sense, a victim, for whom the system now offers little sanctuary. Women like Shamere, in one victim advocate's words, "are victims, survivors, and perpetrators."[15] Of course in this sad story a large cast of unknown characters were crucial to the plot—the men who paid Corey Davis to use women and children for sex.

THE JOHNS

It is obvious that without the demand for the sexual services of women and young girls there would be no need to write this chapter. Yet the demand exists, and it is vast. Rachel Lloyd, director of Girls Educational and Mentoring Service (GEMS), which offers shelter and direction to sexually exploited girls, says, "A girl or woman might belong to five, or maybe even ten pimps over the course of a few years; but how many men have had her in that time? For every twenty kids out there every night, there are maybe thousands of johns."

Who are the men who pay for sex, often with enslaved women and children? They go by several euphemistic names, but for the sake of this discussion we'll call them "johns." They are ubiquitous and have been for thousands of years. According to Rachel Lloyd, "There seems to be an unspoken understanding that men have the right to buy sex. The government wants to believe this, despite the fact that the law forbids it. Remember, men in public positions have private flaws."[16] Consider all the sex scandals surrounding our celebrities and officials, says Lois Lee. "When the mayor of Syracuse is caught trying to buy sex from a fifteen-year-old girl, or a famous movie star's name appears on the client list of a Hollywood brothel, the news is often met with a wink and a nod. It's just guys being guys."[17]

Whatever the cultural and political ambivalence, the "Pretty Woman" scenario happens only in the movies. There is no similarity between a smiling, carefree Julia Roberts and a serially raped thirteen-year-old girl, forced into service to a gorilla pimp, with no choices and no exits but one. And let's face it: most johns are not Richard Gere. Not only is the "It's-not-such-a-bad-life" message spread in the media fallacious; it stands directly in the path of the public understanding the realities of "the life."

Still, according to the sociologist Ronald Weitzer, not all johns are ruthless villains: "As in other moral crusades, the perpetrators are presented as 'folk devils.' Customers are labeled 'sexual predators' that brutalize women." Weitzer quotes Michael Horowitz, senior fellow at the Washington, D.C., headquarters of the conservative Hudson Institute and an acknowledged leader in the antiprostitution campaign: "We want to drive a stake through the heart of these venal criminals. This is pure evil."[18] However, Weitzer points out, "Research on customers cautions against sweeping characterizations and generalizations. Customers vary in their background characteristics, motivation, and behavior, and they buy sex for different reasons. There is no doubt that some . . . act violently, that some seek out underage prostitutes, and that some travel to other countries for this purpose." But we would be jumping to conclusions, states Weitzer, to presume that this is the norm. In fact, "some analysts make the counterargument that only a small minority of clients mistreats prostitutes."[19] An opposing view states that the very act of buying sex in and of itself debases the person in prostitution.

Whatever the john's motivation, it is clear that prostitution is potentially damaging for any woman involved. Given that prostitution is illegal in most areas of the United States, one approach to reducing the demand for commercial sex is the "john school," an intervention program pioneered in San Francisco. In the spring of 2008 the first in-depth assessment of john schools was published.[20] This approach is designed to reduce the demand for commercial sex and human trafficking by educating men arrested for soliciting prostitutes about the negative consequences of prostitution. Normally, the men are first-time offenders and are given the choice of paying a fee and attending a one-day class (the "john school") or being prosecuted. The curriculum in the school focuses on the legal consequences of subsequent offenses; on johns' vulnerability to being robbed or assaulted while involved in prostitution; on johns' elevated risk of HIV and STD infection; on the vulnerability of women serving as prostitutes to rape and assault, health problems, drug addiction, and various forms of exploitation; on pimps' and traffickers' recruitment, control, and exploitation of women and girls for profit; on the links between local street prostitution and larger systems of human trafficking; and on the drug use, violence, health hazards, and other adverse consequences that co-occur with street prostitution. The 2008 report was extensive, but two findings are worth noting here: first, that the schools have been effective in substantially reducing recidivism among men arrested for soliciting prostitutes; and second, that this approach is cost-effective, operating for over twelve years at no cost to taxpayers and generating nearly $1 million for recovery programs for providers of commercial sex.

Meanwhile, in most cities, the police generally don't pursue the john at all, and when they find him at the scene they'll usually let him go. It's different for the woman or child he's been abusing. Trafficking victim or not, child or adult, she's likely to be arrested, while the john goes home to his wife and kids—a little shaky but none the worse for wear. And the pimp who put that woman or child on the street has become one of the new heroes of American popular culture.

THE PIMPS

Pimps as Folk Icons

It is a cruel twist that victims are often punished by the system that should protect them while the pimps who victimize them enjoy widespread glamour. As the NGO Polaris Project regularly points out, from Hollywood, to the major record companies, to the front-stoop stories of wide-eyed school children, pimps have acquired a glitzy, dangerous, "outlaw" persona. The 2006 Academy Award for best song went to "It's Hard Out Here for a Pimp," from a Sundance Film Festival award-winning movie about a pimp with dreams of making it as a rapper. Its star was Oscar nominated for his sympathetic, if unlikely, portrayal of a pimp in turmoil. Some rap and hip-hop music has been criticized for denigration of women and glorification of the pimp lifestyle. In 1999, HBO produced *Pimps Up, Ho's Down*, an "up close and personal" study of pimps. Apparently, it was popular enough to justify a sequel.

Every year, pimps hold a "Players Ball" in various cities throughout the nation, sometimes with the public endorsement of local mayors. These events serve as showcases for outlandish and expensive clothes and cars, and, aside from the usual drinking and dancing, include awards for "No. 1 International Pimp of the Year" and "No. 1 Super Player." The Players Ball, first reputedly held in Chicago in 1979 to celebrate a famous pimp's birthday, represents a tradition that grows in popularity and mystique every year, with music and film celebrities attending and joining in the festivities.[21] Some of the balls have even been covered by national television. The myth of the pimp has so captured the popular imagination that middle-class teens, college clubs and fraternities, and adults hold themed "pimps and ho's" parties. The lore of pimps permeates our daily lives.

The Dark Side

The Players Ball is, in the words of one club owner, "strictly a dress-up costume party that is wild and crazy," having nothing to do with pimps, prostitutes, or trafficking.[22] Yet the pimps who attend are often facing indictments for sex trafficking, involuntary servitude, sexual abuse of a minor, kidnapping, assault with a deadly weapon, and racketeering.[23] They are men responsible for the kinds of damage listed on a Department of Health and Human Services (HHS) fact sheet: the physical damage of "drug and alcohol addiction; physical injuries (broken bones, burns, concussions, genital/anal tearing); traumatic brain injury resulting in memory loss, dizziness, headaches, numbness; sexually transmitted diseases (e.g., HIV/AIDS, gonorrhea, syphilis, urinary tract infections, pubic lice); sterility, miscarriages, menstrual problems; other diseases (e.g., TB, hepatitis, malaria, pneumonia); and forced or coerced abortions," and the psychological damage of "mind/body separation/ disassociated ego states, shame, grief, fear, distrust, hatred of men, self-hatred, suicide, and suicidal thoughts . . . Post-traumatic Stress Disorder (PTSD)—acute anxiety, depression, insomnia, physical hyper-alertness, self-loathing that is long-lasting and resistant to change . . . [and] suffer[ing] from traumatic bonding," in which victims fall in love with or grow dependent upon their traffickers.[24]

Pimps frequently take a lax approach to safe sex; more often than not, they don't provide condoms, yet at the same time they expose their victims to hundreds, perhaps thousands, of men. The law of averages works against the victim; inevitably, she will acquire, and transmit, STDs. A study released in late 2007 highlights "the link between HIV-AIDS and human trafficking" and goes on to say, "We have been encouraging U.S. health officials over the past several years to incorporate strong and clear policies that address this link, and to devote greater energies and resources to the health aspects of human trafficking, or modern-day slavery.... Health officials have just begun to recognize this link, and stronger emphasis is needed."[25]

The pimps don't care if their "girls" contract a life-threatening disease so long as they can continue to make them money. A recent case, successfully prosecuted by Innocence Lost, involved a Florida pimp named Justin Evans who was accused of "enticing a minor to engage in prostitution." His indictment states that he set up "dates" for the child at various hotels, checked up on her constantly, and kept every cent she made. Then, in February 2005, the girl—referred to in the indictment as "Jane Doe"—was hospitalized for nearly two weeks and diagnosed with AIDS. Shortly after she left the hospital, Evans put her back to work.

The government secretly recorded a telephone conversation between Justin Evans and an associate identified as CW, in which they discussed the girl's condition:

> CW: She in her last stages, dog. You fucked that girl up, man.... When I told you she was sick, dog, don't put her on the street ... you was like, fuck it. I need the money.... That whore was too sick, dog.
>
> . . . . . .
>
> EVANS: What? You don't think she can still make money?
>
> . . . . . .
>
> CW: That girl dying, dog. Right now, that girl dying.

Apparently, Evans had stripped and beaten the child, knowing she was seriously ill. CW took him to task, and Evans responded:

> EVANS: That's part of being a pimp[,] man. In the pimp rulebook it says when you beat 'em like that. You strip them down naked and beat them. They respect you more.... You're supposed to strip 'em butt naked ... and beat her ass.
>
> CW: You shouldn't did that girl like that, dog. I feel sorry for that girl, Justin.... Basically, it's not about her having AIDS.... It's basically about ... You know what I'm saying? ... when she was sick, dog. How she was treated, dog. She shouldn't been treated like that, dog.

EVANS: Listen. Even though you're sick, you can still get out there and pull tricks. If you're so sick where you can't walk that's one thing. But if you're still physically able to walk . . . she should be able to go get that money.[26]

The child worked for Evans until May 2005, when she was again hospitalized for AIDS treatment. Her body was covered with blisters and sores. "Jane Doe" was fourteen years old.[27]

There is nothing glamorous or romantic here. Behind the flashy clothes and expensive cars, these are bad guys. They degrade, exploit, and brutalize the girls and women they control. All three trafficking qualifiers—force, fraud, and coercion—are here. Pimps claim and display ownership of their victims, sometimes by tattooing their name on them, sometimes by branding.[28] They control them through beatings with bats, chains, belts, coat hangers, and ropes; they burn them with heated wire hangers; they have them gang raped, tortured, locked in car trunks. They feign affection, even love; they make promises that they have no intention of keeping; they withhold money. They pump girls and women with addictive drugs, then use that addiction to control them. They threaten serious physical injury or death to the girl or her family; they create an atmosphere of terror; and they exercise total control over the girl's life.[29] There is no glamour here, only misogynistic brutality, carried on for profit and power.

AMERICA'S DIRTY LITTLE SECRET

Pimps are equal opportunity exploiters: age, color, gender, and ethnicity are irrelevant. And the jagged iceberg just below the surface of the human trafficking issue in America is the sexual exploitation of children. According to federal law, children get special status. Just by prostituting an underage person, the pimp becomes a trafficker in the eyes of the law. Yet the pimps and traffickers are apparently unimpressed; the trend toward trafficking children is on the rise. In 2005, the FBI issued the text of a statement made in Congress on "the exploitation of children and others in the United States." In it assistant director Chris Swecker drew upon what has been the largest and most complete study of sexual exploitation so far of children in the United States, Canada, and Mexico. This study concluded that "between 244,000 and 325,000 American children and youth are 'at risk' each year of becoming victims of sexual exploitation, including as victims of commercial sexual exploitation (e.g., child pornography, juvenile prostitution, and trafficking in children for sexual purposes)."[30] The report explained that the most vulnerable children, those at special risk of sexual exploitation, are "runaways, thrownaways, victims of physical or sexual abuse, users of psychotropic drugs, members of sexual minority groups, [and] illegally trafficked children."[31] What is chilling is the fact that this estimate of children at risk of sexual exploitation is in addition to the more than 105,000 children that annually are substantiated or indicated to be victims of child sexual abuse.[32]

Rachel Lloyd states that to the government, "as a concept, domestic trafficking [of children] is a new development" and that the government is having a hard time with it. "The tremendous amount of money being spent by Washington, compared to the minimal impact it's having in the streets, is alarming."[33] Says former assistant attorney general for the Civil Rights Division Wan J. Kim, "All too often, these crimes occur right in our own backyards."[34]

"The average age range of a child first used in prostitution is 11 to 14," FBI assistant director Chris Swecker says, "with some as young as 9 years of age."[35] It's another unsupported statistic, but regardless, it is clear that children are being prostituted. "I got an eleven-year-old the other day," says Rachel Lloyd. "The police picked her up at Port Authority and brought her to me. It really shouldn't be more shocking than finding a thirteen-year-old, but it is. And I keep asking myself, who in the hell would want to buy this child, who hasn't even reached puberty? What kind of person are we talking about?"[36]

Child prostitution is, in the words of one victim advocate, "America's dirty little secret."[37] Here, and elsewhere in the world, the sellers of children are innovative and entrepreneurial. And given our increasingly umbilical connection to the Internet, they can frequently be found online, peppering the ether with every kind of child pornography. Once in a great while, they get caught. A Boise, Idaho, man was recently convicted of producing a video of a toddler suffering sexual abuse and of sharing it on the Internet. This unthinkably horrible crime is known as "baby rape," and for it, he received a sentence of life plus sixty years. The prosecutor, U.S. attorney Tom Moss, summed up the current state of affairs: "At any given time, 50,000 predators are prowling for children on the Internet. It is not an exaggeration to say that we are in the midst of an epidemic of sexual abuse and exploitation of our children."[38]

Carlos Curtis is typical of those who traffic children into prostitution. Curtis was a pimp who picked up a twelve-year-old runaway in New York City's Times Square and took her to a Brooklyn hotel, where he forced her to have sex with an older prostitute as he took pictures. He then drove her to Washington, D.C., where he put her on the streets as a prostitute. She was not the only minor to be prostituted by Curtis.[39]

Curtis was arrested in Washington and indicted on seven counts, including sex trafficking, transporting a minor in interstate commerce for prostitution, and producing child pornography. He was the first defendant in the District of Columbia to be tried for trafficking juveniles under the Trafficking Victims Protection Act of 2000 (TVPA). Assistant U.S. attorney Cynthia G. Wright wrote to the judge on the case, "The defendant is a dangerous person. All children, particularly vulnerable children, need to be protected from this predator." Curtis already had a conviction for pimping an underage girl in New Jersey. Although his lawyer argued that this crime was not a violent one, the judge disagreed—as vehemently as the law allowed. Viewing the crime from the trafficked girls' position, the judge stated, "Putting a girl out on the street for prostitution exposes her to beating, to assault, to murder. It . . . creates a serious potential risk." She prefaced her sentencing by saying, "They suffer psychologically and emotionally, and they suffer physically. And they often suffer for a lifetime—as Mr. Curtis is going to suffer for a lifetime." As the defendant looked on in stunned disbelief, Judge Kessler sentenced him to life in prison. Sadly, there was to be no happy ending for the twelve-year-old girl. She was locked in a detention center during the trial to prevent her running away, and when the trial ended, she went off the radar. According to an article in the *Washington Post*, "The authorities do not know where the troubled teenager is [she was thirteen by this time]. . . . Prosecutors have not been able to find her of late. They suspect that she is back on the street, making money the way Curtis taught her to." Although the law punished Carlos Curtis with the maximum sentence allowed and for all the right reasons, it failed utterly in the second vital part of its job: to protect and heal his underage victim.[40]

How He Spent His Summer Vacation

On the surface, one form of trafficking doesn't seem to meet the definition; but don't let appearances fool you. When Americans travel to foreign countries to buy sex with children, it is categorized as human trafficking in U.S. law. Norma Ramos of the Coalition Against Trafficking in Women (CATW) asserts that a number of sex tourists are American men. Asks Ramos, "What could possibly inform males' sexuality, that leads them to children?"[41] For years, outwardly respectable citizens—husbands, fathers, businessmen—have gone abroad in search of the cheapest kinds of thrills, knowing there was little or no chance the law could touch them. According to Andrew Oosterbaan, chief of the Department of Justice's Child Exploitation and Obscenity Section (CEOS), until recently, they were right: it was almost impossible to make a case against these predators. In the past, the biggest obstacle was the requirement to prove that a man *intended* to have sex with children when he formed his plans to go abroad. The PROTECT (Prosecutorial Remedies and Other Tools to end the Exploitation of Children Today) Act of April 2003 eliminated that particular impediment. Nonetheless, the path to arrest and conviction is still a rocky one, placing a strain on the government's most crucial resources: money, time, and staff.

Building a sex tourism case usually involves several agencies, such as ICE and the FBI. It can take years, and the pretrial work and the trial can be very expensive. And there's the risk that with time the evidence can become corrupted. To make a case, it can be important to have the child victim in court and willing to testify against the defendant. "Children," says Oosterbaan, "are the same [in court] as any other victim; they have to be able to stand up and tell what happened to them." Yet the difficulties in bringing a child victim to the United States, housing or detaining him or her until trial, and providing services for the child's mental and physical rehabilitation, are massive. Understandably, a child victim can be hostile and suspicious, and, as Oosterbaan states, "Unless you give them the help they need, you can't bring a victim from an uncooperative to a cooperative witness. There is no case without a victim."[42]

Still, some cases have to be made without the help of the victims. Such a case went to trial in Miami in 2007. Kent Frank, a heavyset, fiftyish, financially comfortable native Floridian with two teenage sons, traveled to Phnom Penh in late 2003 and early 2004 to buy sex with underage girls; but for a quirk of fate, he probably would have gotten away with it. The local captain of the Cambodian National Police, a diligent and dedicated officer named Keo Thea, was on the lookout for a different American sex tourist when a taxi driver told him about Kent Frank, whom he had seen taking four very young girls into a hotel. Thea got authorization to search the room, where he discovered photos taken by Frank of his underage companions, "posing naked and in sexually explicit positions." In one photo, Frank was having sex with one of the girls.[43]

The Cambodian police arrested Frank and notified ICE criminal investigator Gary Phillips, who happened to be in Phnom Penh on another case. "The Cambodian government," says CEOS trial attorney Wendy Waldron, "lacks the resources to effectively prosecute the many foreigners who are exploiting their children."[44] Still, the Cambodians brought Frank up on charges of debauchery, a crime in Cambodia if the girls are under fifteen years of age. For reasons that remain unclear, the charges were dismissed. Once released, rather than return to the United States, Frank traveled to Vietnam. Meanwhile, Phillips contacted and updated Wendy Waldron at CEOS, who went to the U.S. Attorney's Office and volunteered to help build a case against Frank. She was paired with an assistant U.S. attorney for Florida's Southern District. Phillips shipped the evidence to Miami, and together they began to work up their case.

Although Frank was indicted in the United States in 2004, it took years to bring him to trial. The prosecutors faced serious obstacles. The most frustrating was finding three of the girls Frank had initially purchased and photographed. Sadly, Frank's defense team found them first, and by the time the government was ready to go to trial, the girls were listed as witnesses for the defense. Their pimp and their mothers—who knew the girls' occupation and were anxious for them to return to work—pressured them into saying the police had beaten them and that they had been eighteen or older at the time of the offense. At one point the pimp even passed himself off as a girl's father. None of them seemed to be looking out for the girls' interests; it was all a matter of profit and loss. Two of the girls gave their testimony through depositions; a third was flown to the United States for the trial. Ironically, the prosecution had to make its case *around* the girls, treating them as hostile witnesses, while still seeing them as victims of sex trafficking—on whose behalf, in fact, the whole trial had been initiated.[45]

Frank was brought back from Vietnam to face ten charges. Medical experts testified as to the girls' probable age on the basis of their physical development, and a strong case was made. In April 2007, Frank was convicted of eight of the ten counts, including engaging in illicit sexual conduct with a minor (a new provision of law resulting from the PROTECT Act), and purchasing or otherwise obtaining custody or control of a minor with the intent to promote the production of child pornography. Four months later, he was sentenced to forty years in prison, as well as fifteen years of supervised probation, and was fined $25,000.[46] As for the underage girls, a Cambodian NGO sheltered and provided them with social services.[47] But perhaps because of pressure from their pimp or their mothers, or because they found "living the life" more lucrative, or simply because this was the way they had come to see themselves, the girls returned to the streets. In all, it took three and a half years and a considerable investment of money and personnel to catch, try, and sentence one American sex tourist.[48]

According to Anna Rodriguez, head of the Florida Coalition Against Human Trafficking, you can find *American* children for sale outside our borders as well. Rodriguez recalls a trip she took to Tijuana, Mexico, with other antitrafficking workers, as well as Mexican and American law enforcement officers: "As we walked," she says, "I saw American kids trafficked and sold for sex for $15. We identified a couple of kids who had been listed as missing." Rodriguez described corrupt members of the local police, "standing next to the traffickers, promoting specific brothels. We had two undercover Mexican *federales* walking with us, and still it felt dangerous. We reported it to the FBI and were told it wasn't in their jurisdiction. We made numerous phone calls—to ICE, the San Diego TIP [Trafficking in Persons] office, and the State Department—but no one helped. They told us it wasn't as easy as just going in and taking them out." Rodriguez states that efforts within Mexico itself can often end badly: "The head of the federal police in Tijuana, who had been actively investigating trafficking, was shot and killed."[49]

A Long, Hard Road

Andrew Oosterbaan is not ambivalent about stopping child sex crime; he believes strongly in the mission of his agency: "I'm not a politician, never will be. This is an easy job for me, because we're dedicated to the kids. We're prosecuting cases that no one else will take." But it is an uphill struggle, with the number of offenses against children multiplying yearly. Oosterbaan sees the government's problem as simply "not enough" of everything: money, time, and resources. CEOS, says Oosterbaan, has been seeking to link with service providers and other government agencies for the express purpose of providing support for the child victims of sex crimes. Oosterbaan is proud of the task force he helped set up in the District of Columbia in partnership with the U.S. Attorney's Office. It consists of several governmental organizations, including ICE, the FBI, and the DOJ, and a long and impressive list of NGOs. It covers several jurisdictions and opens lines of communication for sharing perspectives and information.

Innocence Lost, a joint initiative created by CEOS, the FBI, and Washington's National Center for Missing and Exploited Children, also prosecutes sex trafficking cases. It has set up task forces in twenty-four cities known to have extensive child trafficking problems, and the group stages awareness and sensitivity training for government and NGOs. Still, there are huge gaps in the response to child sex crime. For example, there might not be service providers, or informed law enforcement, in the places where these crimes take place. Word is slow to spread, training even slower.

Meanwhile, what is to be done for the victims? What is needed, says Oosterbaan, is to take the model of the D.C. task force on the road. It's an ambitious idea, he states, but one that could only improve things. "It's our short-term objective to put a broad-based, national working group together to assist in setting up and supporting all of the individual task forces. . . . It won't happen overnight, but with the help of this working group, eventually all of the task forces will be operating effectively. This is really world-changing stuff."[50] As Wendy Waldron emphasizes, fighting child sex crime "has to be done city by city, agency by agency, agent by agent. Rather than wait for someone to be busted, we have to gather intelligence and share databases on the bigger pimps. Although efforts are being made at all levels, there's tons of room for growth."[51]

WHO CARRIES THE CAN?
THE VIEW FROM THE NGOS

This all sounds like progress, but the government doesn't get high marks from most groups that serve the child or adult victims of sex trafficking. Rachel Lloyd places much of the blame with the police: "There's a handful of really great cops who approach it thinking, 'This could be my child.' But this doesn't represent the attitude of law enforcement as a whole. Most cops are ignorant and prejudiced on the issue. Although force, fraud, and coercion have no legal place in a situation involving child trafficking, the police will approach it with the attitude, 'Well, she's not chained to a bed.'"[52]

CATW co-executive director Dorchen Leidholdt agrees: "Pretty much, the police response that I've encountered has been extraordinarily obtuse. Whether it's international or domestic, they're not recognizing it as such. The victims are treated as criminals. If they're not seeing bruises, . . . overt fear, indicia of 'force, fraud and coercion plus,' then it's not human trafficking."[53]

The organization ECPAT, based in Bangkok, was the first to blow the lid off child sex tourism in Southeast Asia, and since the mid-1990s it has grown into an international agency of some seventy-three groups.[54] Carole Smolenski is the executive director of ECPAT USA, the Brooklyn-based office that addresses the trafficking of children both to and within the United States, as well as child sex tourism by Americans. For three years, beginning in 2002, her organization—in partnership with the International Organization for Adolescents (IOFA)—conducted a program called the Community Response to Trafficking Project, paid for by HHS. This project called on law enforcement, community members, and other NGOs to reach into various ethnic neighborhoods and offer printed material in seven languages. It was, in Smolenski's words, "incredibly successful"; then its funding was cut and the program ended. She points out that, despite the wide range of agencies dedicated to rescuing and helping child victims of slavery, "since the passage of the TVPA in 2000, very few immigrant children have been officially identified as trafficking victims and afforded the protection due them."[55] Even so, says Smolenski, foreign-born child prostitutes tend to be accepted as victims more often than prostituted American children. There seems to be the assumption that native-born child prostitutes are there by choice; they are seen as "bad," and "in need of punishment and reform," whereas immigrant child prostitutes are more likely to receive help as trafficking victims.[56] Rachel Lloyd agrees: "Despite the growing number of American children forced into prostitution, Americans tend to view sex trafficking as an international problem. And despite the progress that the Trafficking Victims Protection Act of 2000 represents, young people trafficked within the United States are still often treated as criminals rather than victims."[57] Smolenski feels that much of the responsibility for this misperception lies with the local police and the courts. Few child prostitution cases ever make it to the federal level; and further victimization of these children by the legal system is likely to continue until police and state and local courts get the training they need to recognize and help child trafficking victims.[58]

Christa Stewart worked at the victim assistance agency Safe Horizon and now serves as director of legal services for an organization called the Door. Based in New York, the Door provides health programs, education (such as English language classes), counseling, and legal services to at-risk young people between the ages of twelve and twenty-one. Around one-third of the nine thousand young people helped each year are foreign born. Child trafficking cases, generally involving debt bondage and sex slavery, pop up regularly. Stewart takes a hard view of the government's response. "Just to get the government to take on a case relating to the prostitution of a minor can be a daunting, and often fruitless, effort," she says. "It's extremely frustrating to get the feds involved in a case. They have such a strict view of what constitutes prostitution that they wouldn't bother with a situation . . . if it's not a brothel, charging X number of dollars for specific services. They take kind of a limited view. I had one case that was going on over a year, and I made thirty-four calls [to ICE] to get a young victim certified. And *that* was a case that you would have thought they'd be interested in, because it did involve prostitution of a minor." Either no one responded to Stewart's calls, or she was told, "We're looking into it," or the ICE agent would make an interview appointment for Stewart and the girl: "We'd come in—again and again—and they wouldn't be there. There's supposed to be a victim witness coordinator, but they're just as hard to get in touch with. The whole thing was just a travesty!"[59]

Stewart was also trying to get the girl certified as a trafficking victim: "Although they said repeatedly they'd get it for me, and had already granted the girl continued presence with work authorization, they simply wouldn't do it. They told me the investigation was still 'young,' although it was over a year and a half old. Finally, I filed for an affirmative T visa on my own."[60]

The FBI, says Stewart, can be just as frustrating: "They're hard to convince. There's a general lack of belief in a victim's story, which is especially frustrating when the victims are so young—twelve or thirteen—that they just don't remember." As for HHS's community awareness-raising "Rescue and Restore" program, "I'm aware that there's supposedly this campaign, and I've been to a few of their press conferences. . . . I've asked that we be involved, and they said they'd keep me apprised, but they're 'reviewing what's going on.' I for one don't *know* what's going on with them, but as a concerned advocate, I'm disappointed that they've poured a lot of money into that campaign and there's no kind of tangible product from it."[61]

On federal government's efforts to date, Stewart says, "Some excellent efforts were initially made to effect training, but it's all become muddled." Asked what she would like to see changed, she replies, "Everything. More outreach to foster general awareness, let people know what trafficking encompasses. I'd like to see more dialogue around the contributing factors—the global issues—why this is happening. I'd pour funding into services, and I'd rewrite the law, to remove the distinction between sex and labor trafficking!"[62]

The "distinction" to which Stewart refers is in the legal definitions of the TVPA. Unlike other laws or international treaties, the key U.S. law distinguishes between two types of "severe forms of trafficking" and a third form called, simply, "sex trafficking." The two forms of severe trafficking separate sex and labor trafficking: the first is any commercial sex act induced by force, fraud, or coercion, or one involving a minor; the second includes obtaining labor or services, also by force, fraud, or coercion, with the purpose of "involuntary servitude, peonage, debt bondage, or slavery." "Sex trafficking" is defined as the "recruitment, harboring, provision, or obtaining of a person for the purpose of a commercial sex act" but does not include the proviso of "force, fraud, or coercion." If this seems confusing, imagine being a lawyer or prosecutor and trying to determine if a twenty-one-year-old who has been enslaved in a brothel is a victim of a "severe" form of trafficking or simply "sex trafficking." Of course, a good deal of the confusion arises because the crime being defined as "trafficking" is slavery pure and simple. The TVPA defines severe "trafficking" by its outcome—a state of enslavement—but then seems to rule that any recruitment or "obtaining" of a person for prostitution is also "trafficking." Not sure how to handle this subtle difference in the legal definition, local law enforcement tends to fall back on local statutes, or worse, as when enslaved trafficking victims are charged with "solicitation." The NGOs that try to make sense of this, and to support trafficking victims, build up experience and understanding over time but are often unable to benefit from this experience since the necessary funding is capricious.

Funding is, understandably, a big issue among NGOs. Lois Lee, of Children of the Night, observes, "There's so much competition . . . and, go figure—there's no money to compete for!"[63] Alison Boak, president of IOFA, also finds the federal government's criteria for the distribution of funding wrongheaded: "The dollars are given out not on the basis of who will have the greatest impact, or who's most appropriate, but as paybacks to the groups who support the [Bush administration's] political agenda."[64] A high-ranking administration official, who asked to remain anonymous, agrees: "The 'company view' is that a lot of money was going out, with no results. In reality, it's just a way for the federal government to take money away from the more worthwhile NGOs—the actual progressive service providers—and hand it over to the advocacy groups, typically not service providers, who are aligned with the neoconservative, values-driven antiprostitution clique."

"None of the money flow makes sense," says Florrie Burke, a well-regarded expert on the treatment of trafficking victims, "with arbitrary time lines, one source of funding for certified clients and one for uncertified clients."[65] An anonymous senior law enforcement source takes it a step further: "There needs to be a return to the old infrastructure, wherein grants went to service providers."

YOU CAN'T GO HOME AGAIN

When sex trafficking victims are found and liberated, they need a safe and secure place to stay. Security and comfort are crucial to their recovery. Yet a key issue raised by every NGO is the lack of adequate housing. Once an adult or underage sex trafficking survivor is in the system, it is imperative to provide a suitable living situation, but this hardly ever happens because of the lack of available or appropriate space. According to Lois Lee, it borders on the impossible: "There are only thirty-nine beds allocated for sexually exploited children—in the entire country! And we have twenty-four of them." She adds that six are in Atlanta, at a probation center called Angela's House, and the rest are at GEMS, in New York City.[66] Christa Stewart states the Door's policy: "If a victim is, say, under sixteen, we'll probably advise that they go into foster care, just for safety reasons."[67] Without a place for the sex trafficking victim to live, the greatest fear—and likelihood—is that she will return to the streets and become victimized once again.

Ann Jordan, formerly of Global Rights, points to the lack of adequate housing as the federal government's biggest failure in addressing the needs of trafficked children. "Unaccompanied children," she states, "are languishing in inappropriate housing. . . . They have no guardian or parent or any supervised living situation." To further complicate matters, "Unaccompanied minors are forced to meet the same requirements as adults to cooperate with law enforcement." This often means testifying against their traffickers. Incredibly, it is up to the child to decide. "Unaccompanied minors who are unwilling to speak with law enforcement are pushed into a legal limbo in which they can either try to fend for themselves or be held as a 'material witness' and be forced to testify. In some cases, it could result in the child being faced with possible deportation." Jordan tells of a trafficked child sent to detention and given the option of either speaking with law enforcement or losing the possibility of benefits. "She decided not to talk to law enforcement. As a result, she was sent back to her home country, where she had nobody to take care of her and had no social support."[68]

To CATW's Dorchen Leidholdt, domestic violence shelters offer the best option. "This is the best model for trafficking victims, whether they're domestically or internationally trafficked, sex or labor. If domestic violence service providers start opening their doors, it's a great resource for trafficking victims. . . . The shelters' provision of confidentiality is exactly what trafficking victims need . . . and shelters are usually not filled to capacity."[69]

CarlLa Horton, executive director of New York's Northern Westchester Shelter for over a decade, disagrees:

> Domestic violence shelters, sadly, may be the "best place" for these victims, but that says more about our government's pitiful response to the issue than it does about the appropriateness of domestic violence agencies. In my opinion, our shelters are not a good option for trafficking victims. . . . Many of us, our agency included, do not have extensive security systems . . . and other needed protections. Also, our agency, as with so many other domestic violence agencies, is already challenged in meeting our mission of sheltering domestic violence victims . . . and we cannot allow our very limited resources to be diverted. We already turn away far too many domestic violence victims due to lack of room. Our shelter averaged 100 percent capacity for the last seven years; and over the last five years alone, we had to deny shelter to 4,197 victims due to lack of room.[70]

Along with the lack of housing goes a severe shortage of psychological and social services. Those who have been sexually victimized desperately need help. However, to award benefits, social service providers must have authorization. Again, Ann Jordan: "Despite the fact that a large number of trafficking victims are children, only thirty-four letters granting eligibility for benefits to child trafficking victims were issued in 2005." Jordan sees the "mandatory requirement for minors to cooperate with law enforcement" as one of the underlying reasons for this paucity of acknowledged child victims. And when benefits *are* assigned, it is often after a wait of several weeks or months, during which time the child is "receiving no treatment for the serious trauma of trafficking and not receiving dental or medical care."[71] Being subjected to the brutality of prostitution can require a lifetime of physical, mental, and spiritual care to overcome. As Lois Lee describes the purpose of Children of the Night, "We get them fundamental social security, give them bed and board. We're in the business of raising these kids; this isn't a thirty-day fix."[72] Yet the official response to trafficking into prostitution is often arrest and detention. Florrie Burke puts it bluntly: "Lock-ups are not acceptable shelters!"[73] Says Lee, "Children are spending more time in jail than their pimps."[74]

The treatment of children who have been liberated from sexual abuse and exploitation should be guided by our sense of decency, not by concerns over government budgets or policy. To require a child who has been raped and assaulted to make mature decisions about participating in a prosecution before he or she gets desperately needed care is both cruel and misguided. To take a child out of violent slavery just to lock her up in a detention center calls into question our humanity. Children are not criminals. Our national response to the needs of enslaved children is disorganized, harmful, and an ineffective way to address this crime. It is time for the lawmakers to fix this mess, and as they do so to ask themselves, "What would I do if this were my child?"

FOREIGN-BORN VERSUS DOMESTIC VICTIMS: A QUESTION OF PARITY

One issue that seriously affects the quality of the government's response is whether the victims are foreign-born or domestic. Although this could be said about all forms of modern slavery in America, the discrepancy is felt most strongly in the area of sex-related trafficking. It influences prosecutions of traffickers and funding of survivor services, and, not surprisingly, opinions on it are widely divided.

When the TVPA was passed in 2000, it defined U.S. child victims as such for the first time; yet its provisions favored foreign-born as opposed to U.S. or domestic victims of trafficking. Imbalances in the allocation of funding and benefits still exist. One activist points out, "Clearly, if you look at the TVPA, the focus is on international trafficking victims. The services are provided to international victims. And although I don't see it as a competition, I would suspect that there's a higher incidence of domestic than international trafficking— I suspect largely because it's become so hard these days to cross the borders—and I think it's being largely ignored."[75]

Several antitrafficking groups are calling on the government to provide more money to domestic in addition to foreign-born victims. In the view of some NGOs, the disparity in the numbers is massive. These groups argue that hundreds of thousands of American women and children are at risk, compared to the federal government's estimate of up to 17,500 foreign victims of trafficking per year. These groups assert the existence of an inordinately large number of *American* sex trafficking victims—both minors and adults.

So what funds does the government provide for their unique service needs? According to Bradley Myles of Polaris Project, "Very little, when compared to the scope and size of the problem. All federal funds created under the TVPA for direct services to trafficking victims have been used to assist noncitizen victims. Trafficking services grantees have been required to serve only noncitizen victims with their grants, leaving no federal funds for specialized services for U.S. citizen victims. We need to reach a new paradigm where grants, policies, organizations, and task forces can address both U.S. citizen and noncitizen victims without divisiveness and with the freedom to serve and protect all victims."[76]

State allocation of funds and services can also be difficult because of the constant mobility of the victims, whose pimps move them from state to state, and the fact that their pimps will often confiscate or destroy their identity papers. "This problem," says Polaris's Myles, "is exacerbated when dealing with U.S. citizens, who also frequently present complicated custodial issues as minors." Myles points out that such problems as underdeveloped life skills, societal tendencies toward victim blaming, mental and drug-related problems, and criminal histories also hinder the assignment of money and services to survivors of sex trafficking. To further complicate matters, domestic victims are often shut out of government benefit programs, including welfare. As we've seen, there is no provision for housing; victims are placed in detention or drug rehabilitation centers, or in homeless shelters, where they not only suffer the stigma of having been prostituted but are often easily found by their pimps and traffickers. Additionally, most states' crime victim compensation programs do not address trafficking and reimburse only for medical bills directly resulting from a specific list of crimes. In many individual states, the victims are seen as criminals.[77]

In pointing to what he sees as a lack of parity in the provision of services for U.S. citizen victims, Myles states, "In Polaris's current caseload, we are servicing far more U.S. than foreign victims. And yet, when we try to enroll them in the federal government's per capita system for serving trafficking victims, we're told that the system is currently only available to foreign-born victims." In many ways, the process of sexual enslavement for a U.S. citizen parallels that of the foreign-born victim: often her documents are confiscated by her pimp or trafficker, she is taken from her home, initiated—or, "seasoned"—through gang rapes and beatings, assigned a quota to be filled nightly, and held through both threatened and real violence. And yet, forced into prostitution, she is blamed, and that blame contributes to both a lack of empathy from law enforcement and a lack of benefits and services available to her. "There's a gross misunderstanding among U.S. citizens," says Myles, "about the nature of sex slavery."[78]

An equally vocal and adamant group of service providers feel that this view of the reported volume of domestic victims of sexual trafficking is distorted and inaccurate. Much of the problem, they feel, can be attributed to the hidden nature of the crime itself. It is stunningly difficult to try to ascertain numbers—in *any* form of human trafficking— with any degree of accuracy when you don't know where to look or, for that matter, what you're looking *at*. As Mark Lagon, director of the State Department's Office to Monitor and Combat Trafficking in Persons (TIP Office), puts it, "It's a misconception that we're ever going to get a hard number of how many victims there are. By nature, the kind of exploitation below the surface that trafficking involves means they're always going to be estimates."[79] Simply put, if you can't find victims, you can't count them. According to one government official who asked to remain anonymous, "The claims are being made by advocates, not officials who might be in a better position to know. The truth is, nobody can prove at this point how many U.S. citizen victims are out there. It's the most underreported crime, and it carries with it its own reasons for not reporting it. The only number I trust is the number [of victims] that have been found."

Conversely, while funding exists for foreign-born victims, they generally don't receive it. Says Carole Smolenski of ECPAT, "The foreign-born kids are simply not being found. Nobody knows what to look for or what to do with them. Only one hundred foreign-born kids have been found and certified since the TVPA was passed in 2000." To those on the "domestic" side of the discussion, that might well be because they don't exist, at least in any significant number. According to their opponents, this is utter nonsense. They're out there; it's just a question of training people to know where to find them and how to help them once they're found.[80]

Unfortunately, we have no true idea of the number of foreign-born children and adults currently being sexually exploited in the United States today. IOFA's Alison Boak attributes this in part to the fact that foreign-born survivors, to obtain victim certification, are encouraged to cooperate with the police and aid in the prosecution of their traffickers— a step many of them are fearful and unwilling to take.[81] Sometimes a young girl or woman refuses to view *herself* as a trafficking victim, for various reasons. She falls in love with or grows dependent on her pimp and sees herself as the girlfriend in a loving relationship and not as a commodity. Or perhaps she sees herself as sinner rather than sinned against. She feels guilty, ashamed. Or perhaps her trafficker has so indoctrinated her to fear the authorities that she doesn't come forward. As a result of this fear, a significant number of foreign trafficking victims are not counted.

And although the "domestic" advocates feel this country's foreign-born victims are receiving the lion's share of the services, "there are huge barriers in the assignment of benefits," says Boak. "The whole process is massive, daunting. Only a small percentage of those who are identified as victims by either government or service providers actually apply for these benefits. We . . . found that only one out of approximately four victims served by nonprofit agencies ended up taking the step to go through the government's process."[82]

The service providers see their efforts blunted by sectionalism and infighting. It benefits no one to promote or deepen the rift between advocates of foreign-born versus domestic victims; they all require the same degree of commitment for help and services from our government. Lou de Baca, counsel to the House Judiciary Committee, says of this kind of factionalism, "At the end of the day, all it does is hurt our ability to help slavery victims."[83] Andrea Powell, the executive director and co-founder of FAIR Fund, an NGO devoted to reducing gender-based violence in the lives of young women, similarly points out that although the TVPA was designed more to serve foreign-born than domestic victims, "There's a general lack of coordinated services available to *both* groups, and neither is getting the help they need."[84]

ARE WE GETTING OUR MONEY'S WORTH?

Beyond the question of who gets the money to perform these services is the issue of accountability for the tax dollars spent. Many NGOs that have had their federal funding reduced or cut off altogether point to what they see as a stunning lack of performance by some of the agencies that *are* receiving government monies. According to a high-ranking official who asked to remain anonymous, a number of these organizations were selected by the Bush administration "regardless of whether they ever helped anyone and without either peer-reviewed grants or bid contracts; they've been accountable to virtually no one." Andrea Powell sees accountability as a big issue. Overall—for service providers and government agencies—she "would hope to see more organizations moving forward by evaluating their programs so we can gauge the impact and see what's not working. There are a lot of programs out there, and without monitoring their success we'll have no idea how successful we really are."[85]

Some government agencies are making genuine efforts to institute training programs for all levels of government and to uncover and prosecute sex trafficking crimes. One federal prosecutor at the DOJ points to "an ever-increasing percentage of federal prosecutions."[86] Yet while they've shown an accelerated rate of success, not even they would dispute that, while their record of cases is in the hundreds, at least thousands of undiscovered cases of sex slavery remain. And beyond the arrests and prosecutions, the big question arises: What is being done for the victims? Attempts to work with service providers through the formation of effective task forces is certainly a positive step, but it should be a giant step, taken quickly.

The consensus among service providers is that the current state of governmental awareness, empathy, and services provided to trafficking victims is poor. For all the dissension among the various NGOs and for all the ideological differences among victim advocates, service providers, and researchers, one general thread of agreement seems to be that the government simply hasn't allocated sufficient funds, or designated them appropriately, for the ongoing service and relief of sex trafficking victims. Says Polaris's Myles, "Our collective response as a nation is so inadequate, and the recognition of the problems has so many shortcomings, that we need a total mind change in how we think about it and how we respond to it."[87]

CAN IT GET ANY WORSE?

So we have an unknown number (thought to be in the thousands) of people trafficked into the country each year to be made into sex slaves. We also have thousands more U.S. citizens, including children, ensnared into forced prostitution each year. The number of new victims of sex slavery in the United States annually is likely to be greater than the number of murder victims, but only a tiny fraction are rescued. And the ones who *are* rescued must jump through hoops to get help, rarely have a safe place to go, and encounter confusion and buck-passing from the authorities. Can it get any worse?

You bet it can. Just add to the mix a civil war, fought on deep philosophical grounds, between the groups dedicated to rescuing and supporting the victims. It is not the position of federal or state law that all forms of prostitution constitute slavery or that all pimps are engaged in human trafficking. In the words of Edward P. Reilly of Suffolk County, New York, police detective lieutenant and member of a federal antitrafficking task force, "Not every prostitute is a trafficking victim, and not every pimp is a trafficker."[88] But a battle has been raging for at least ten years over the exact relationship between slavery and prostitution.

According to the federal government and several advocacy groups, of all the forms of slavery in America today, human trafficking for sex is the most prevalent. While other forms of trafficking include sexual abuse as a standard feature, American law defines this form of slavery by the fact that someone is making money from it. "Sex trafficking," as it is sometimes known, covers a multitude of sins, ranging from forced prostitution, to involuntary work in strip joints and massage parlors, to child pornography. Of these, prostitution gets the most media attention, making it the form of human trafficking best known to most Americans. This is not surprising. According to a recent study, "The United States . . . ranks as the world's largest destination/market country (after Germany) for women and children trafficked for purposes of sexual exploitation in the sex industry."[89]

No question, forced prostitution is heinous. It is nothing less than serial rape for the enrichment of the trafficker. But what makes forced prostitution problematic is the difficulty that often arises in distinguishing between human trafficking and more conventional, "voluntary" prostitution, or "sex work." Even stating the difficulty in this way generates controversy. Of all the types of contemporary slavery, only forced prostitution engenders such radically divisive opinions. Much of the controversy centers on this question: Should prostitution, in and of itself, be considered a form of slavery? That question has become a battleground, with lines firmly drawn separating factions that answer it in different ways. To one faction, all prostitution is slavery, the very heart of slavery, and only by punishing panderers and pimps can it be eradicated. To the other side, this is nothing more than the old moralistic antiprostitution crusade given a new venue—a red herring, deflecting much-needed aid and resources from the real and broader issues of human trafficking.

180 DEGREES OF SEPARATION

The United States has debated prostitution for a long time. In the late nineteenth and early twentieth centuries, a panic over the "White Slave Trade"—white women being forced or sold into prostitution—swept the country and led to anti-immigrant laws and miscarriages of justice. The Mann Act, which came out of this swirl of racial protectionism, outlawed, among other things, taking a woman or girl across state lines "for the purpose of prostitution, debauchery, or for any other immoral purpose." One of the first people to be tried under this new law was the African American world champion boxer Jack Johnson, who was jailed for driving a white prostitute to another state. (The fact that they eventually married, and that he was taking her *from* a brothel, had no effect on the court's findings.) Today there continues to be sharp debate over the best way to respond to prostitution, and because many human trafficking victims are forced into sexual exploitation they are in the spotlight.

On one side of this argument, representing the antiprostitution perspective, are individuals and groups who believe that, except for the "teeny percentage of women who may have entered into it voluntarily,"[90] all prostitution is a form of slavery. Prostitution for this side is often defined as "illegitimate violence against women and girls driven by male sexual demand."[91] As one of the leading antiprostitution groups, CATW, makes clear, "Exploitation of prostitution and trafficking cannot be separated."[92]

Proponents of this view are often referred to as "abolitionists" because their ultimate aim is the "complete eradication of all forms of sexual exploitation."[93] Anthony DeStefano, in his 2007 book, *The War on Human Trafficking: U.S. Policy Assessed*, asks, "Why single out prostitution instead of, say, domestic, farm, or factory work, all of them settings for labor trafficking? The answer: abolitionists and certain feminists viewed prostitution as a special evil, a violation of women's rights, and by its nature an exploitation. Because prostitution involved sexual commerce, it was laden with enormous moral and religious implications, particularly for evangelical Christians, who saw it as sin."[94] One researcher has described the "abolitionists" as "having picked up the banner once carried by social purists and religious spokespersons."[95] Another compares them to the "moral entrepreneurs" of the late nineteenth century, who "were convinced of the immorality of prostitution, firmly believed that no woman could ever freely and rationally choose such a career, and sought the worldwide elimination of this traffic."[96] Says political scientist Barbara Ann Stolz, "Similar to [the] earlier trafficking movement, the contemporary 'antiprostitution sphere' focuses primarily, if not exclusively, on trafficking for the purpose of prostitution." For antiprostitution groups, the "legalization or decriminalization [of prostitution] should only make the situation worse." This side tends to include "conservative, faith-based, and some feminist organizations."[97] Stolz numbers among their members such organizations as Protection Project, CATW, Equality Now, the National Organization for Women (NOW), and the Planned Parenthood Federation of America.[98] To this group is often added the Salvation Army.

One of the foremost spokespersons of this group is Dorchen Leidholdt. Leidholdt, who serves as director of the New York–based Center for Battered Women's Legal Services at the Sanctuary for Families in New York City, has a long history of working within the antipornography and anti–sex trafficking movements. An attorney who has taken her beliefs into the courtroom, she teaches a seminar at Columbia University Law School on domestic violence and the law. She is also a co-founder and co-executive director of CATW. Leidholdt is a well-spoken woman who is not shy about voicing her beliefs: "We think the legalization of prostitution really creates a huge market for sex trafficking. It just confers on pimps and brothel owners the status of respectable businesspeople. It's the way governments put out the welcome mat for human traffickers." To Leidholdt and her colleagues, the model recently adopted by Sweden would work best for America.[99] This would result in "decriminalizing all the people who are being prostituted, . . . stepping up services, including health care, . . . developing and implementing strong laws against traffickers, including brothel owners and pimps, and holding buyers accountable through low-level criminal sanctions—and for repeat offenders, jail."[100]

Norma Ramos, co-founder and co-executive director of CATW, takes exception to the claim that the antiprostitution group excludes other forms of trafficking from their agenda. She defines their mission as the effort "to raise international awareness around all forms of human trafficking and to create an international culture that is hostile to human trafficking. But," she acknowledges, "given the fact that 80 percent of those who are trafficked are women and girls, and 70 percent of these end up as victims of sexual exploitation, that's our major focus."[101]

On the other side of the battle line, a "cluster of diverse individuals and groups—human rights, public health, labor, and migration—are categorized as the 'human trafficking sphere.'"[102] This group believes in a broad definition that does not differentiate between types of servitude but includes all forms of sexual slavery within the overall category of human trafficking. Their stance is that all "human trafficking is a crime in and of itself." It includes "any unfree labor, including children working as camel jockeys or soldiers; or men, women, boys, and girls working in the sex industry, so long as there is evidence of force, coercion, or deception."[103] Despite the assertions of antiprostitution groups, not every member of this group believes in the legalization of prostitution, but that, they argue, is beside the point. "By viewing 'human trafficking' as a crime, an organization's position on the legal treatment of prostitution is irrelevant, because any forced labor, including prostitution, is trafficking."[104] Some advocates, but not all, on this side have maintained that many women have few or no options for earning a living and that if prostitution is the best of the choices available to them they should be protected and allowed to do this "sex work." At the same time a handful of organizations, notably Free the Slaves and the International Justice Mission, have taken great pains to stand outside these two camps. This small but distinct group has often sought to act as peacemakers in the conflict between abolitionists and the anti–human trafficking movement.

Ann Jordan is one of the more outspoken representatives of the anti–human trafficking movement. Jordan, formerly director of Global Rights' Initiative Against Trafficking in Persons, was one of the founders of the Freedom Network, a loosely affiliated group of thirty independent organizations of service providers and victim advocates. She was battling trafficking long before most people knew there was a war. She points out that, while "current federal law enables prosecutions of all enslavers and provides protection for all victims," the broad scope of the law "is being eroded by a U.S. campaign that equates prostitution with trafficking, and is redirecting resources to end prostitution rather than to end trafficking." Her concern, and that of her colleagues, is that this focus on prostitution as the main—and to many the only—form of human trafficking to warrant government attention "is affecting delivery of services to victims." She suggests that the investigative and prosecutorial branches of the federal government are being diverted from their primary goals of eradicating all types of trafficking and protecting and serving the victims in order to pursue a dubious and legally questionable war on prostitution. This approach, Jordan argues, not only denies the government's protection to many victims of trafficking but is in direct conflict with the provisions of the Thirteenth Amendment.[105] Author DeStefano agrees and likens this "simplistic approach" of the antiprostitution movement to "the way Prohibitionists advanced a ban on alcoholic beverages as a way to cure social ills. . . . The Bush administration believed that eradicating prostitution would stop the evil of sex trafficking—though it would have no effect on other forms of trafficking."[106]

Of the two factions, the antiprostitution faction is by far the more vocal, and its influence on the legislative process—through both its continued lobbying presence and the alignment of certain conservative congressmen and religious leaders with its issues—has been strongly felt. Clearly, the shift in grant funding shows that the federal government is collaborating with an antitrafficking program that heavily emphasizes the issue of sex trafficking, to the detriment of labor trafficking efforts. "Changes in the 2003 and 2005 TVPA," writes Barbara Stolz, "as well as the later trafficking hearings to focus on aspects of trafficking for sex, would seem to suggest that Congress has paid greater attention to the reassurance of and conferring of deference on the 'anti-prostitution sphere.'"[107] The 2003 reauthorization of the TVPA included a clause—Section 7—"which required organizations to state that they do not 'promote, support or advocate the legalization or practice of prostitution' in order to receive funding."[108] Many NGOs and human rights groups "were worried that they might have to answer a U.S. demand for a prostitution policy even if they did not work on the subject."[109] The political stance of the Bush administration fell into line with the antiprostitution group in stressing sex trafficking over other forms of modern-day slavery. As DeStefano writes, "The government's emphasis on sex cases obscures the fact that labor cases may be just as rampant, and its continued focus on sex trafficking and the abolition of prostitution has become divisive."[110]

Ann Jordan sees this "gag rule" imposed by the 2003 and 2005 reauthorizations as standing in direct conflict with the First Amendment's right to freedom of speech.[111] So frightened are many of the NGOs and universities, she states, that they have compromised their services, practices, and policy positions so as not to give HHS an excuse to reduce or remove their funding.[112] A number of organizations "have purged prohibited words such as 'sex work' . . . from their materials and websites because they know that U.S. officials are scanning websites in search of prohibited words, alleged by U.S. officials to be evidence of 'promoting' prostitution."[113] There is a pervasive sense among many service providers in the anti–human trafficking movement that "Big Brother is watching." As Florrie Burke, human trafficking consultant and former director of international programs at the NGO Safe Horizon, points out, "Just because we're looking at sex trafficking as a crime doesn't mean we're supporting prostitution."[114]

The controversy came to a head in 2008 over four little words. In the process of reauthorizing and amending the TVPA, the fight over prostitution and slavery focused on the words "force, fraud, and coercion," the criteria used to define "severe forms of trafficking in persons." A coalition of antiprostitution groups pressed hard to delete these words so that all that would be needed to bring a charge of human trafficking was that a person had performed a "commercial sex act." Groups as diverse as Equality Now and the Southern Baptist Convention's Ethics and Religious Liberty Commission were concerned that unless the law was amended it would remain necessary for federal prosecutors to prove that pimps used "force, fraud, or coercion" in order to establish that an adult prostitution case was also trafficking. The DOJ, a number of anti-trafficking groups, and the bill's key sponsors in the Senate, Senators Biden and Brownback, resisted this.

It was right that they did so. Human trafficking is the process of delivering a person into enslavement. It is a process defined by its end result. If a person is smuggled into the United States and then left free to find a job, the crime is smuggling. If a person is brought here and then held against his or her will and forced to work without pay, the crime is human trafficking, which is to say slavery. The original drafters of the bill made this clear; they defined the crime as including "force, fraud, or coercion for the purpose of subjection to involuntary servitude, peonage, debt bondage, or slavery." Without these criteria any act of prostitution becomes trafficking and thus slavery. Over the years many groups have tried to use the word *slavery* to accentuate or dramatize their issue. In the 1990s one group even urged the United Nations to name incest as a type of slavery. Low-wage workers and economic migrants are sometimes termed slaves, but the dilution of the word *slavery* serves no one. Slavery is based in violence. *Slavery,* throughout all of human history, has meant holding people against their will through the threat or reality of violence, forcing them to work, and paying them nothing beyond subsistence. To attempt to expand the definition of slavery to include anyone who can walk away, who can make a choice about his or her situation, is to rob the word of its meaning and to demean those who have suffered in slavery over the centuries. Congress may choose to pass a law that makes prostitution a federal crime. There are many forms this law might take, including the Swedish model that leaves the sale of sex as legal while making the purchase illegal. But gutting an existing antislavery law that applies to all forms of human trafficking is not the way to go.

SEX SELLS

It is not accidental that when most Americans think of human trafficking they think of sex slavery. It comes, in large measure, as a direct result of the efforts and the influence of the antiprostitution faction. The government has frequently made it clear that when it talks about human trafficking it really means sex trafficking. And although there have been cases involving servitude in homes, fields, and factories, when the government touts its victories, the majority are sex cases, and the subject of labor trafficking makes scarcely a ripple.[115] As stated in a 2006 article in the Tulane University law journal, "What's enthralled the media, the Christian right and the Bush administration is not the demanding, multi-layered narrative of migrants, but the damsels in distress, the innocents lured across borders for the purpose of prostitution. In other words, their concern over human trafficking has become, in practice, a concern over what they deem sex trafficking."[116] This attitude was given voice by John Miller, who, while serving as the Bush administration's director of the TIP Office, referred to trafficking in women as "the sex pillar of slavery."[117] In 2007, this trend manifested itself in the structuring of the New York State trafficking law, in which the difference between penalties for sex trafficking (a "B" felony) as opposed to those for labor trafficking (a "D" felony) is vast. Dorchen Leidholdt is adamant that this was not the intent of the antiprostitution group and that rather the pressure of the New York State Assembly was responsible for the disparity. "We advocated for comparable penalties for labor and sex trafficking. We wanted to see [the traffickers] punished at the same level."[118] Says Norma Ramos of CATW, "The truth is, we fought as hard for labor as for sex trafficking, but the legislators kept saying, 'You're never going to get that.'"[119] Still, the influence of the antiprostitution group was strongly felt throughout the campaign for the passage of this law. It's a chicken-egg question: Would the legislators—and the governor—have been so disposed toward a sex-weighted law had the pressure from this group not been so great?

Mark Lagon, Miller's replacement as ambassador at large and director of the TIP office, sees New York's law as superior to any other state antitrafficking statutes passed thus far. It is, he states,

> without a doubt, the model that I look to. It finds a way of dealing with all aspects of human trafficking, and in particular on the sex trafficking front, not being flummoxed by the limits of federalism for dealing with prostitution. We know—reasonable people know—left and right, pragmatists and

moralists know—that the sex industry and legal prostitution breed an enabling environment—a legitimate cover in which sex trafficking can occur. And [the New York State law] finds a way to . . . look at the ways that victims are enticed into sex trafficking. . . . It's a model law for other states and . . . for other countries.[120]

The emphasis on sex trafficking is interesting considering that New York State has seen not only clear examples of agricultural and domestic servitude but such highly visible cases as New York City's deaf Mexicans and the dozens of Peruvians trafficked into labor on Long Island. And now, according to one high-ranking government official who asked to remain anonymous, "The abolitionists are trying to make the New York State law the model for the rest of the country."

At the heart of the debate is whether a woman can freely and truly choose to become a prostitute and should be allowed to continue under meaningful protections, or whether all the pressures that drive her into prostitution should be considered coercion and call for serious corrective legal action. Both sides point to the overarching conditions of poverty, sexism, discrimination, violence against women, and lack of education as factors that push a woman toward prostitution. The fight over this issue is bitter and has been for over twenty years. The abolitionists have said that their opponents represent "pimps and procurers," whereas their opponents paint the abolitionists as dogmatic and ideologically rigid propagandists who are willing to ignore the immediate health and safety needs of "sex workers." The advocates who see the legalization or criminalization of prostitution as distracting from the larger issue of slavery in all its forms, including forced prostitution, are often caught in the middle. On all sides, the pain and degradation suffered by sexually exploited women drive the intensity of the debate. Both groups project anger and urgency, and the gulf between them is wide and perhaps unbridgeable. On at least one point, however, there is consensus. For those women—and children—who have been kidnapped, sold, and/or forced into the control of pimps or brothels, no one questions the absence of free choice. No one disputes the scope, or the barbaric nature, of true sex slavery.

MOVING FORWARD

As for the service providers, victim advocates, philosophers, religious leaders, and partisan intellectuals, they must all recognize that too often the very trafficking victims they purport to be "saving" are neglected when energy goes to dissension and political maneuvering. Any case or argument can be better made through objective analysis and viable research than through vilification and fear-mongering. Ultimately, there must be a common goal and a single, unified effort to reach it. Otherwise, we will continue to show a failure rate that is as tragic as it is embarrassing.

Yet the likelihood of détente seems remote at best. Feelings are strong and often bitter and the players intractable. When asked whether she envisioned a coming together of the factions or an increased polarization, CATW's Dorchen Leidholdt replied, "I don't think it could get any more polarized. . . . We can't gloss over differences that may result in the denial of services to victims or legislation that provides a loophole to traffickers. So, honestly—do I think that the people who think the sex industry is beneficial to women . . . and that prostitution is a job like any other are going to sit down with organizations like the Coalition Against Trafficking in Women and break bread and join in a common effort for legislation any time soon? No. I don't see it as happening. . . . These are very different, almost antithetical perspectives, and I don't think they could be—or should be—resolved any time soon."[121]

Ann Jordan has a different perspective:

I would like to believe that people of goodwill can unite around efforts to stop the use of unfree labor in prostitution, homes, construction, agriculture or any other site; to prevent the use of minors in the worst forms of child labor, particularly prostitution and pornography; to prosecute all acts of violence against sex workers; and to develop further research and funding to support evidence-based programs to help youth stay out of sex work and provide sex workers with training for other types of work. Collaboration breaks down, however, around the question of whether adults have the right to choose to engage in sex work (and to expect their rights to be protected at work) or whether sex workers are, by definition, victims who do not have the right or ability to choose, from among good or bad options, the type of work they will do. The "anti–right to choose" advocates believe that no woman freely consents to sell sex. They insist that criminalizing prostitution and clients is the means to stop women from selling sex and to stop trafficking into the sex sector. The pro-rights advocates note that all human beings have the same rights, including the right to make choices that others might not like. Even the International Labour Organization recognizes the reality that some "adult individuals" may "freely choose sex work" and calls for the application of human rights protections: "the policy concerns should focus on improving their working conditions and social protection and on ensuring that they are entitled to the same labour rights and benefits as other workers." It may be that the only way to move forward, despite our differences, is for policy makers and advocates to agree that policies and programs must be based upon objective, apolitical, peer-reviewed, evidence-based research and not on anyone's opinions or anecdotes.[122]

The Los Angeles–based NGO Coalition to Abolish Slavery and Trafficking (CAST) recently put out a position paper that takes a broad view: "We are at a pivotal point in this still early stage of America's modern abolitionist movement. What is needed now, more than ever, is a holistic, human rights-based framework, to guide our next steps to ensure that *all* victims—including those forced into commercial or non-commercial sex, sweatshops, agriculture, domestic servitude, hotels or restaurants, construction, even boys' choirs—have access to assistance that is equitable, non-paternalistic, survivor-centered, and client-driven."[123] Heather Moore, CAST's social services director, adds, "We need an approach that's reasonable, and responsible—an approach based on integrity."[124] Amen.

5

NEW BUSINESS MODELS

IT SOUNDS LIKE A JOKE

What do acrobats, naked gardeners, hair braiding, boy's choirs, deaf Mexicans, and the shirt on your back all have in common? In a word: slavery. While most slaves in America today fall into three categories— agricultural labor, forced prostitution, and domestic servitude—there is no lack of ingenuity on the part of traffickers in exploiting their victims. Slave traffickers are imaginative and innovative businessmen. Where an opportunity exists for exploitation, however strange or unlikely, there's a good chance there is a hidden slave.

Ashley's Salon

Ashley's Hair Braiding Salon looked like any one of hundreds of similar establishments across America. Located on Central Avenue in East Orange, New Jersey, it offered hair care at a reasonable price, primarily serving the needs of African American women. Service was good, and the braiders were authentic West Africans with the lovely French accents of their native Togo. The irony was that they had made their own middle passage into slavery.

In late 2007, federal agents arrested the two men and a woman who ran Ashley's Salon and another braiding shop in Newark. All were charged with harboring illegal aliens, and the woman was charged with smuggling illegal aliens for financial gain. Immigration and Customs Enforcement (ICE) agents stated that at least twenty young women had been smuggled into the country and put to work with no pay. The scheme rested on fraud linked to existing U.S. visa procedures. Some Togolese citizens had participated in the U.S. Diversity Immigrant Visa Program. This congressionally mandated program makes available fifty thousand permanent resident visas each year, drawn by a random selection from applications, submitted by people from countries with low rates of immigration to the United States who meet strict eligibility requirements. After arriving as part of this program and becoming a permanent resident or citizen of the United States, a person is allowed to apply for admission for his or her close relatives as well. So far, so good, but some of the Togolese lottery winners began to have surprisingly large families, made up primarily of young women.

After posing as relatives of visa recipients, the young women were excited about a chance to build a new life in America, but the reality was not what they had expected. On arrival their passports were taken, and they were put to work for up to fourteen hours a day, six or seven days a week. They were not paid. Once freed, the women told officers that if they complained or did not follow the rules they were beaten. The special agent in charge of the investigation, Tom Manifese, explained, "This is a case of modern-day slavery. These women were promised a better life in the U.S. but instead ended up becoming victims of human trafficking."[1] All twenty young women were taken into care and provided with emergency housing and counseling. Meanwhile, the son of the woman who had enslaved them offered the classic rationalization for human trafficking when interviewed by reporters. "They got everything they needed and it was better than Africa," he said. "Everybody was treated well. We helped them."[2] How strange that this young man, himself an African American, would so closely follow the logic of Thomas R. Dew, key southern apologist for American slavery before the Civil War: "The condition of the negro slave in the South is far better than that of the native African."[3]

Viva Las Vegas!

There's a moment in the lives of most Americans, possibly a moment of maturity, that comes when, while watching performing animals in a circus, one suddenly thinks, "They're fun to watch, but I wonder if *they* are having fun?" Interestingly, the same thought rarely occurs to us when it comes to the *human* circus performers; after all, they chose this glamorous if grueling profession, right? So it is not surprising that people in and around Las Vegas were shocked to discover that a locally based troupe of Chinese acrobats was, in fact, enslaved.

The break in this case came when one of the enslaved women, who also served as interpreter for the troupe, escaped and went to the police. She told them that she and others were being held against their will in a suburban home in Las Vegas. After a short investigation federal agents raided the house and arrested three men. The ringleader seemed to be You Zhi Li, aged thirty-eight. Immediately after the raid, agents interviewed fourteen people, five of them juveniles. Talented acrobats, they had taken a chance on a good-paying job in America and lost.

The acrobats told the agents that they were hungry. They'd been restricted to small servings of instant noodles, rice, and vegetables twice a day. They explained that they had to perform twice a day, were awakened early, and didn't get to go to sleep until very late. Li had confiscated their visas and passports and had warned the team members that he would eavesdrop on phone calls made to their families. One of the juveniles told authorities that he feared for his family's safety in China and that he had seen Li's assistant Jun Hu beat up another performer. In the suburban house Li had them sleeping four to six per bedroom. When they were not performing, Li rented the acrobats out to another man, who used them to clean and renovate houses and do yard work. The performers had been promised up to $1,600 per month; most received no pay at all, though some were given $50 or $100 per month as pocket money. Though most of the acrobats had very limited English, FBI spokesman David Staretz explained they were overjoyed at being liberated—"They literally hugged the investigators when they arrived."[4]

Though he told investigators he made only $30,000 per year, You Zhi Li seemed to be doing well with his acrobats. After a little digging, police found that he owned a $320,000 home, had paid off and owned another $170,000 home, had $110,000 in his business bank account and $30,000 in his personal bank account, and owned four vans worth about $25,000 apiece.

The reactions of Li's neighbors to the revelation that twenty people were being held in his house are typical of American suburbanites when they first meet the slave next door—puzzlement and confusion as they attempt to understand how slavery fits within the workings of a normal neighborhood. A man living next door said that he had noticed "excessive amounts of trash put out for collection" but added that his neighbors "weren't very noisy and were always friendly." Across the street a man stated that he had often seen the acrobats exercising in the garage but explained, "They were not boisterous. They were model citizens. I wouldn't have known anything was happening over there that wasn't on the up and up."[5]

If there was anything odd about the case of the trafficked acrobats—besides the fact that they were *acrobats*—it was the quick action on the part of the Chinese government to deny that any such crime had taken place. Normally when foreign nationals are trafficked into the United States their home government will either offer help or simply ignore them, leaving their care and rehabilitation to U.S. service agencies. But in this case, the Chinese government quickly went on record supporting the traffickers. Articles on the government Web site China.org, "China's Official Gateway to News and Information," rolled out a remarkable set of reasons why these acrobats were not trafficking victims. According to a report by Zou Di, the acrobats' passports weren't confiscated; they were just "kept away from the members in case they were lost." Di's report also argued that the "accusation of using child labor is groundless as well, since acrobatics is, to a large extent, an art of the young" and that it was "difficult to find evidence for human trafficking, because all performers have valid visas and passports."[6] American law, of course, doesn't exempt exploitative child labor for any reason, and many trafficking victims are brought into the country with valid visas and passports. Why the Chinese government wants to deny this case is unclear, but their report ends by asserting, "Some believe the complaints are false and were made by acrobats trying to find a way to stay in the US." The "some" who believe this are never identified.

The Best Offer They Never Heard

A beautiful young woman in expensive clothing and costly jewelry goes to the door of a dilapidated shack in a small Mexican village. The little hut, or *jacal*, has no amenities, and the toilet is a hole in the backyard. The woman enters and immediately begins to play what one activist refers to as her "psychological war game" with the family within.

"How can you live like this?" she demands, shaming them with the squalor.

Taking from her purse an album of photographs, she shows them pictures of the luxuries she enjoys in "el Norte": the big house in Queens, New York, the expensive car, the elegant clothes. She tells them that the simple job she holds in New York enables her to live at this level. "You, too, can have this, and money to send home besides, to help your family."

The young woman repeats this performance in many such homes, varying the story as the situation requires. She tells one family she works in a restaurant; another, that she works as a cleaning woman. The lie is apparent, unless you don't know to look for it. Perhaps they believe her because of the single characteristic she shares with them: the woman and all the people she is recruiting are deaf.

She convinces them by the busload to accompany her across the border, where their lives will improve a hundredfold. She dresses up some of them to look like average tourists and teaches them how to sign ignorance to the border guards, who more often than not wave them through. Others make the long trek on foot, but they come by the hundreds over a ten-year period, clinging to her false words of promise.[7]

The woman's name is Adriana Paoletti, and she was a major player in a particularly vicious family-run human trafficking ring. For ten years, the Paolettis, a deaf family from Mexico, made a business of illegally importing deaf and hearing-impaired men and women into California, transporting them to Chicago and New York City, and enslaving them there as street peddlers.

Sometimes the family would vary its methods by recruiting deaf teens out of school.[8] In Mexico, the future held little promise for deaf youths—special education was available only through junior high school—and they had virtually nowhere to go; frequently their own families would reject them. The promise of a better life in the United States made them easy victims, and, according to Jose Badillo Huerta, director of Mexico City's National School for Deaf Mutes, "There are dozens of families like the Paolettis in Mexico who exploit the deaf."[9]

In New York City, fifty-seven of the deaf Mexicans were crammed into small, rundown apartments in two Queens houses and forced to sleep on the floor or on bare mattresses. They were threatened, abused, and beaten as a matter of course. Some of the women were systematically raped. Every day, seven days a week, they were each given one hundred cheap trinkets—which the Paolettis had purchased for $3 per dozen from a novelty company—and sent out to sell them for a dollar apiece.[10] Some of the men were given two hundred trinkets a day. They were all told not to return until every trinket was sold. For twelve to eighteen hours, they would walk the city's streets or stand on corners staring at the sidewalk and holding out their trinkets; or they would ride the subways, eyes cast down, leaving with the riders a trinket—a pen or a key chain—and a small, worn card reading, "I am deaf," then returning to collect either the trinket or a dollar. If they came home at night with any trinkets left, they were beaten, shocked with stun guns, denied food and water, or locked out. One woman later told the judge, through a translator, that there were days "when she walked down subway cars with the bruises and bumps from the frequent beatings the ringleaders delivered."[11]

The Paoletti family members were masters of psychological manipulation. They featured an "incentive program," in which the peddlers who sold the most trinkets were given prizes, such as a trip to Disneyworld. One man was told he had won a van; he had no license, couldn't drive, and wouldn't have known where to go if he could, but from time to time his controllers let him sit behind the wheel of "his" van. Those who performed well tended to always perform well, and they continually won the prizes. The others received harsh treatment; they were constantly abused. Ironically, because of their limitations, those who suffered the most at the hands of the Paolettis eventually had the hardest time explaining the exploitation they had suffered to the police and prosecutors.[12]

The Paolettis were smart. They knew that the victims' families back in Mexico would worry if they received no word, so once in a while they took everyone to Disneyworld or to other tourist attractions. Here they would take dozens of photos showing their victims smiling and would mail them home, saying, "Your son is doing well, and working as a [fill in the blank]." The Paolettis also had a paid contact working in the Mexican consulate, who would call the families with imaginary "updates."[13]

The Paoletti family made a fortune. Do the math: with each of the fifty-seven victims bringing home at least $100 a day, the family was taking in a minimum of $5,700 daily in New York City alone. And there was also the Chicago ring. The two cities frequently exchanged victims who failed to meet quota, to give their associates the chance to "straighten them out." Following a familiar slaveholder's pattern, some victims were made enforcers or overseers and were coerced into informing against—and beating—their friends. This had a severe psychological effect all its own on both the enforcers and their victims.

The peddlers' knowledge of the city's streets and subway routes was staggering, yet their freedom to roam at will was an illusion. The victims couldn't communicate with the world outside their group. They didn't speak, write, or sign English—and in more than a few cases couldn't read or write at all. And they were living under constant threat. According to a *Time* magazine article, neighbors later told the authorities of "a nightly horror show of barefoot women, clad only in nightgowns, fleeing from the houses with men in pursuit; of babies crying, their squalls unattended; of walls vibrating from slamming doors and pounding fists."[14]

Various opportunities on the part of New York City agencies to help these victims came—and went. On at least one occasion, police and emergency workers arrived at one of the houses to give medical attention to a woman. The fire and building departments made inspection appearances as well. No one blew a whistle. When the trafficking ring was finally uncovered, it was not because the various public servants who had witnessed the conditions in which these people lived took action. It was because the victims finally decided they'd had enough. Choosing four men from among their number—a hard choice, since they all felt those chosen would come to harm—they sent them off to find the police. With no language skills, the four tried several times, unsuccessfully, to make themselves understood to the police in the local Queens precincts. Finally, an older deaf man—an American—working at Newark Airport befriended them. Although he spoke no Spanish, he helped them write a letter describing their enslavement. At four in the morning on July 19, 1997, they walked into a Queens police station and handed the letter to the desk sergeant.[15]

The police followed the four men back to the houses and staged a predawn raid; what they found was heartbreaking. As *Time* magazine reported, "Police discovered 57 Mexicans, most of them deaf-mute illegal immigrants, crammed into two top-floor apartments."[16] To build a case, communication with the victims was essential—and nearly impossible. At this juncture, Lou de Baca was called in. De Baca was the involuntary servitude and slavery coordinator at the Department of Justice and the department's most experienced trial attorney on slavery cases. "They called me on the Sunday following the Friday raids. I had just finished the Miguel Flores case [described in chapter 3], and I thought I'd take some time off. Instead, I was flown to New York as a trafficking expert."[17]

During the course of the investigation, which was conducted by both the FBI and Immigration and Naturalization Services, a wide array of agencies and service providers was introduced to the case. De Baca worked closely with Sandy Cohen, chief of civil rights for the U.S. Attorney's Office, and assistant U.S. attorney Leslie Cornfeld. Legal Aid of New York was brought in by the city to represent the victims. And counseling was provided by an experienced victim advocate, Florrie Burke, through the New York–based Lexington Center for the Deaf. At the time, Burke was executive director of the center's Lexington Center for Mental Health, and she immediately set about assembling an on-site team to work with law enforcement and city officials to develop a social service program for the victims.

Some of the Mexicans could read lips, and since de Baca spoke Spanish he was the natural choice to establish a line of communication. He learned some sign language and worked with the trial team to set up a system of bilingual "relay interpreters," frequently utilizing a deaf Latino sign interpreter. Over time, some of the Mexicans learned American Sign Language (ASL).[18] Through a combination of signing, writing, and drawing, the victims—"among them pregnant women and children and infants"—told how they'd been exploited by the Paolettis, lured with "promises of a sweeter life," only to have their papers and documents taken, making it virtually impossible for them to flee.[19]

By the time the "Deaf Mexicans" case made the news, various private organizations and political figures had become involved. Several civil lawyers volunteered to work on the case. Congressman and Senate candidate Chuck Schumer and Mexico City mayor and presidential hopeful Cuauhtémoc Cárdenas both made an appearance. New York mayor Rudy Giuliani ordered the city to help with resources and placed the Mexicans in city housing.[20] Meanwhile, several of the Paolettis, as well as their henchmen and relatives, were arrested; they pled guilty and were sentenced to long terms in federal prison. Adriana was given a sentence of fourteen years. As for the vast sums of money the Paolettis made from the work of these people, very little has been found. There is conjecture that it was smuggled to Mexico, although Lou de Baca feels that much of it simply went to support the family's rich lifestyle.

Two of the higher-ups in the family—Jose Paoletti Moreda and his son, Renato Paoletti Lemus—could not be found and initially were presumed to be on the run. As it turned out, they were serving time in a Mexican prison, but by late September 2006, when they were finally sentenced in U.S. District Court in Brooklyn, twenty survivors of the Paoletti slavery ring were there to witness it. Some submitted letters to the court expressing their outrage at their traffickers. And—through a translator—angrily, passionately, ten of them told their stories. "We were slaves," signed one, "and we have nothing to show for it. I am very angry. We did not want this to happen. I just wanted to let you know this."[21] In signing, the broader and more energetic the hand and arm movements, the more emotional is the message.[22] On sentencing day, the signing was marked by "waving, wild hand motions, convey[ing] anger and sadness."[23]

For the two years following the deaf Mexicans' liberation, Florrie Burke and her team provided counseling, eventually helping to create an education program and provide job training and placement. Of the nearly sixty survivors, around fifteen chose repatriation; the others decided to stay and make their lives in the New York area. Because their case predated the passage of the 2000 Trafficking Victims Protection Act (TVPA), they were given S visas. This was an unusual application of this type of visa, generally used in cases involving organized crime and terrorism, that is employed to protect the witness from possible retaliation in the home country. Some of the survivors took jobs in retail stores or as baggage handlers. The same pattern that existed under the Paolettis has reemerged in freedom: those who were continually high performers for the traffickers continue to be star employees in the world, while those who performed poorly still function at a lower level and, in the words of Lou de Baca, "will need a support network all their lives."[24]

The survivors are clear as to what happened to them: "They see themselves as having been enslaved, as victims of fraud, and now, as survivors. The most important concept to them is *estar*—the Spanish verb 'to be'—but in this case it translates to mean 'to matter, to signify.' They want people to understand who they are and that they exist."[25] Florrie Burke explains, "They are proud of the fact that they're now 'legitimate.' They have status here and the ability to learn new skills, they can send their children to school and no longer be ashamed of what they're doing. On the flip side, there's real loneliness. They're separated from their families and by their disability. Still and all, they're free."[26]

Sing a Song of Slavery

Trafficking, more often than not, entails a betrayal of trust. When the betrayer is a minister of the church and the victims are children, the crime is particularly egregious. In the 1990s, a Texas missionary group calling itself "Teaching Teachers to Teach" (TTT) set out to fund and build schools in Zambia, South Central Africa. At one point, TTT staff members traveled to the village of Kalingalinga, Zambia, where they heard a group of boys singing in an a capella choir. Impressed with their voices and their harmony, one of the TTT staff, a Baptist minister from Sherman, Texas, named Keith Grimes, decided to bring the boys home with him. In the United States he planned to set up benefit concerts, ostensibly raising money to build the schools and provide living essentials for the members of the boys' village. For their part, the boys would receive a good education and be well taken care of.[27]

Grimes immediately began scheduling venues for the group, which he named the ZABC—Zambian Acapella Boys Choir. This choir would be only the first of several boys' choirs he would bring over—and enslave. As predicted, the choirs did well, filling halls wherever they performed, and the money began to pour in. Little of it ever reached Zambia; no schools were built, and each of the boys' families received only $20 a month. Grimes, working with his daughter, kept nearly every dollar the choir earned. He also forced the boys to sing as many as seven concerts daily and locked them in a trailer when they weren't singing. He denied them medicine when sick and food if they dared to complain or refused to sing. He forced them to dig him a swimming pool by hand in the hot Texas sun. And he told them that if they tried to escape they would be severely punished. When any of the boys resisted his control, they were deported in shame to Zambia—along with Grimes's report to the parents that their sons had been "bad"—and replaced with "good" boys.[28]

At one point, the Department of Labor, alerted to labor abuses, ordered Grimes and his daughter to pay the boys; they did so, giving each of them $645—then taking back $600 of it, as payment for "home schooling" (nonexistent), medicine (denied), and food (cooked by the boys themselves in their trailer, when Grimes deigned to turn on the gas). Nothing had changed.[29]

By January 2000, Grimes had died of a brain tumor, and his daughter and her husband were running the operation. The most recent choir group consisted of eleven boys, who had believed that despite the harsh conditions at least their friends and families in Zambia were being well provided for as a result of their concerts. When they discovered the truth, they resisted. In the interest of damage control, Grimes's daughter acted to deport the four boys she saw as the prime "troublemakers." At this point, the whole choir demanded to be deported, in support of their friends. When officials of the U.S. Immigration and Naturalization Service—through close questioning of the boys—found out what had been occurring at the minister's house, they were incredulous. A church choir, enslaved by a man of God—such things simply didn't happen, and certainly not here! The facts were borne out, however, and the group was rescued. Of the eleven boys in the choir, ten elected to remain in the United States. Most of them have not done well. Alcoholism is a common thread, and they have little or no contact with their families in Zambia.

One of the boys, Given Kachepa, is a rare exception. Orphaned at nine, Given had lived with his cousin in the village of Kalingalinga. As was common in the village, the house in which he lived had no door and no running water. A fire built on the floor of the hut provided for both heat and food preparation. Given, along with most of the residents of Kalingalinga, lived on one meal a day. Only eleven and an orphan when trafficked by Grimes (who falsified the boy's age on his passport), Given lived in slavery for two years; after the Grimes ring was shut down, he was adopted by a family in Colleyville, Texas, and introduced to a new life as a middle-class American. Since then, he has graduated high school and will soon graduate college, where he is studying to be a dentist. Given also travels throughout the country with his legal guardian, Sandy Shepherd, sharing his experience and lecturing on the realities of slavery in America. He was instrumental in helping Texas draft an anti-trafficking law in 2003. Given is extremely bright, expresses love and gratitude to the Shepherds, and bears no outward signs of bitterness. When describing Rev. Grimes, he says, "He was a different man in Zambia—well-dressed, polite, and he made promises. . . . When he got here, he became pushy, intolerant. When a boy comes to a new country, he will make little mistakes because he doesn't understand its ways; but Mr. Grimes would get extremely angry over the smallest things."[30] When asked whether conditions in Kalingalinga have improved in the past twelve years, Given replied, "Nothing has changed."[31]

The choir was freed in January 2000; the TVPA didn't pass until October, so Grimes's daughter and her husband were not charged, since no one seemed to know what to charge them *with*. In those early days of trafficking awareness—and without the legal provision of psychological coercion to lean on—unless there were the physical marks and scars associated with slavery, officials were reluctant to pursue a case. Sandy Shepherd tells of the frustration when she and several involved neighbors repeatedly tried to contact members of law enforcement in hopes of helping the boys and punishing the couple. According to Shepherd, their efforts to connect with the FBI, then–attorney general Janet Reno, and various federal senators and congressmen, as well as such media figures as Oprah Winfrey, brought only frustration. The boys' alleged traffickers will never spend a day in prison.[32]

Enslaving the Mentally Ill

Arlan Kaufman and his wife, Linda, took slavery to a whole new dimension. Both in their sixties, the Kaufmans were, as far as their neighbors in Newton, Kansas, knew, an upstanding couple—doting parents and grandparents and solid members of their community. They regularly attended Sunday services at the Faith Mennonite Church and played an active part in church activities. In the eyes of those who thought they knew them, the Kaufmans also performed an admirable service for the community. Arlan held a doctorate in clinical social work, and Linda was a registered nurse. For twenty-four years, they operated Kaufman House, which encompassed three residential facilities for mentally ill patients. Arlan had refused to obtain a license for his homes, but this struck no one as anything beyond an eccentricity. Several such homes throughout the state operated without licenses.

But gradually, over the course of years, a grim pattern of enslavement and mental and physical abuse emerged. The Kaufmans had broken trust with their patients and sunk to an almost incomprehensible level of behavior. The first glimpse of scandal came in November 1999, when children on a school bus passing the Kaufman's farm saw people working in the fields—in the nude. The bus driver complained to the Butler County Sheriff's Office. When investigators questioned Arlan Kaufman, he explained that these people—residents of his facilities—were "naturalists" who practiced nudity as part of their philosophy. The truth was that the residents were deprived of their clothing as "punishment" for often-imaginary infractions and without their clothes were made to tear down a barn, repair barbed-wire fences, and unload cement blocks from a pickup truck. Besides talking to Kaufman, the sheriff's office did nothing in response to the complaint.

Two years later, acting on suspicion that the Kaufmans were systematically defrauding Medicare, the residents, and their families, agents of the U.S. Department of Health and Human Services (HHS) raided the Kaufmans' home, searching for records. They found more than they bargained for—more than thirty videotapes, explicitly showing the Kaufmans conducting "nude therapy sessions." At Arlan's direction, residents were "forced and coerced"—in the wording of the subsequent indictment—to engage in activities that "included, but were not limited to: massaging each other; exhibiting their genitalia; masturbating; shaving each other's genitalia; fondling each other's genitalia; and having defendant Arlan Dean Kaufman fondle the residents' genitalia."[33]

Amazingly, in spite of the videos, Kaufman House was allowed to stay open. The only fallout was the suspension of Arlan's license to practice social work in Kansas. Linda's nurse's license was suspended—three years later. (An attorney for the Kansas Regulatory Board of Nursing was at a loss to explain why the nursing board failed to act on Mrs. Kaufman's license until 2004.)[34] There was a twenty-four-year-long period of official nonaction, beginning in the 1980s, as local, state, and federal agencies examined the operations of Kaufman House but never closed its doors. In addition to the response—and subsequent inactivity—of the sheriff's office and HHS, local Newton police responded to disturbance calls "multiple times," and the Kansas Department of Social and Rehabilitation Services (SRS) "received at least a half-dozen complaints about exploitation of Kaufman clients but repeatedly tried to shift responsibility to others."[35]

Over the years, any attempt by police or social services to enter the facilities was rebuffed by the Kaufmans; no one defied them. Residents who were questioned by authorities were "manipulated . . . into making statements that were favorable to the [Kaufmans]."[36] Not until February 2004 did a persistent Newton police detective finally manage to gain entry into one of the residences when the Kaufmans were away and interview a patient in her fifties. She told the detective that Arlan Kaufman, "while serving as her legal guardian, landlord and therapist, had victimized her for decades." She painted a verbal picture of the Kaufmans' activities and ended by stating, "I want to go home."[37]

Rather than go to SRS, which had proved ineffectual in the past, the policeman turned the case over to the state attorney general, who then went to the Disability Rights Center of Kansas. Their subsequent report regarding this woman—whom they referred to as "Pam"—allowed the detective and the Disability Rights Center's attorneys to brace Arlan Kaufman at his door with a change-of-guardianship court order for Pam. Once free of the Kaufmans' domination, Pam provided sufficient information to light a fire under the federal government's stalled investigation into their illicit business dealings. As Rocky Nichols, director of the Disability Rights Center, stated, "We got the first person out, and the rest fell into place."[38]

Further investigation revealed the Kaufmans' depravity. One forty-two-year-old resident testified that Arlan had "used him as a guinea pig to demonstrate [a stun gun] to Linda and two female residents." The female residents shocked his testicles, and the Kaufmans "zapped" his penis. As a result, he said, his testicles bled. So complete was the Kaufmans' psychological control that the man actually told police that he had deserved it. The stun gun was subsequently found in Kaufman's desk.[39]

In October 2004—eight months after the detective first spoke with Pam, and twenty-four years after the Kaufmans opened their facility—two dozen FBI agents served warrants at the Kaufmans' group homes and their personal residence. The agents found residents housed in deplorable conditions. The homes were generally grimy, were infested with roaches and mice, had nonworking bathrooms and appliances, and had live electrical wires running through a basement area where people took showers. Arlan and Linda Kaufman were arrested and charged with involuntary servitude—slavery. The indictment was amended to include thirty-four criminal counts, including health care fraud, mail fraud, forced labor, and obstructing a federal audit. (It seems when the Kaufmans learned the feds were looking into their false Medicare claims they sold all their property to their three sons for one dollar apiece.)[40] The indictment charged, among other things, that the Kaufmans "purported to provide care and therapy to mentally ill adults . . . but in truth and in fact, subjected them to serious harm, including, but not limited to: sexual abuse; psychological abuse; physical abuse; coercion; isolation; denial of proper psychological treatment; deprivation of property; substandard living conditions; forced or prolonged nudity; and threats of institutionalization."[41]

The indictment states that the Kaufmans "obtained the labor and services of the Kaufman House residents by: the use and threatened use of physical restraint; the infliction of physical injury; the use and threatened use of serious harm; use of a scheme, plan, and pattern intended to cause the resident to believe that failure to perform such labor and services would result in serious harm or physical restraint; and the abuse and threatened abuse of the law and legal process."[42] So here was a case that involved all three of the legal criteria for human trafficking: force, fraud, *and* coercion. And not content with enslaving and brutalizing their helpless charges, the Kaufmans submitted nearly a million dollars in claims to Medicare for their bogus "therapy" sessions—more than any other such care provider in the state. Over a ten-year period, Medicare paid them well over $200,000.[43] The government, in effect, was financing both their perversions and their enslavement of patients. Tucked away on page six of the forty-two-page indictment is an admirably concise, one-sentence morality lesson: "A provider of medical and clinical services, including a licensed clinical social worker and a registered nurse, should 'first do no harm' and should provide honest services, as opposed to providing services driven by a desire to enhance the provider's income, to entertain the provider, or to satisfy the provider's prurient sexual interests."[44]

The Kaufmans, according to the indictment, "created and encouraged the creation of sexually explicit video tapes with the intent and purpose of profiting, selling, and otherwise sharing the tapes with others outside of the Kaufman House."[45] Federal prosecutors showed that Arlan Kaufman took such pride in his video "documentations" that he offered them to the American Nudist Research Library in Kissimmee, Florida. The library director declined.[46]

One of the Kaufmans' defense attorneys stated, "They are not dangerous to anyone. These are gentle people. They're churchgoing people."[47] The court disagreed, finding Arlan guilty of thirty-one counts of the indictment and sentencing him to thirty years in prison. Linda was found guilty on seven counts; she received a seven-year sentence. In June 2006, the Kaufmans were further ordered to pay $534,810 in compensation to former patients and to reimburse Medicare for fraudulent claims. In his ruling against the Kaufmans, the judge noted, "A sad irony is that defendants' conditions of confinement [in prison] will be better than the conditions endured by many of the Kaufman House residents."[48] At this writing, the case has been appealed by both the Kaufmans and the federal prosecutors, who are asking that Linda Kaufman's sentence be increased.[49]

"Made in America"—by Slaves

Clothing does not have to be fabricated in New York, or Los Angeles, or Gary, Indiana, to bear the tag "Made in America." Some of our most prominent clothing manufacturers and vendors contract to factories in American territories, where labor is cheap.[50] These factories pay a fraction of what they would in the States, since minimum wage law doesn't apply, but they can still put "Made in America" on the product. Yet despite how little the garment workers are paid, to some factory owners it's still too much.

Kil Soo Lee was the Korean owner of the Daewoosa garment factory in Tafuna, American Samoa. He secured contracts to provide garments for Wal-Mart, JCPenney, Target, and Sears, and he trolled for laborers by using familiar bait: the promise of steady work, good pay, and decent housing. In this way, he caught over 250 Chinese and Vietnamese workers, mostly young women. Beguiled by Lee's promises, they each paid him and his fellow traffickers between $5,000 and $8,000 for the opportunity of being enslaved. Since this was the equivalent of five to ten years' pay at home, many of the women and their families took on massive debt to make the payment.

In return for the "recruitment fee," Kil Soo Lee and his thugs beat the women, starved them, sexually assaulted them, locked them—thirty-six to a room—in a rat-infested barracks in a gated compound, and forced them to work long hours in heat that reached well over one hundred degrees every day. He paid them nothing for months at a time. In addition to the physical abuse, he threatened them with deportation. And on at least one occasion, this went beyond mere threats. When workers complained about the conditions, Lee withheld food for two days, then had four of them arrested and deported. While deportation might seem preferable to abuse, remember that their families in China and Vietnam were counting on these young women to make good the debts they had taken on and to use their earnings to support their brothers and sisters at home. To return a failure was to betray their families.

This treatment went on for nearly two years. When one woman was courageous—or desperate—enough to complain, one of Lee's overseers blinded her in one eye with a piece of broken pipe. On one occasion, as a show of control, Lee and his henchmen staged a mass beating of the women with chairs and pipes. Lee and two of his thugs were finally arrested and charged with various crimes, including extortion, money laundering, conspiracy to violate individual civil rights, and eleven counts of involuntary servitude. Lee was sentenced to forty years in prison.[51]

As for the workers, the FBI reported that around two hundred of them were given T visas and "settled in some 20 different states around the country." Others fled, and "some were deported to their native lands [by immigration services] before investigators arrived." Wherever they have gone, they all doubtless carry with them a mental tag that reads "Enslaved in America."[52]

CHILDREN OF MYSTERY

Connecticut residents are proud of their state's reputation as the wealthiest in the nation. And in 2002–3, even after the U.S. attorney and his assistants assembled a solid antitrafficking task force composed of representatives from Immigration, the FBI, the Coast Guard, the Department of Social Security, and the IRS, as well as members of local NGOs, it was still hard to believe that slavery could happen there. Then one day a Meriden policeman, summoned to a house on a complaint, accidentally knocked on the wrong door.

A woman answered, and the officer saw that a number of school-age children were inside, at midday on a school week. He also noted that both the woman and the children were speaking in a foreign language, which turned out to be Swahili. Sensing that something was amiss, the police officer reported his suspicions—and nothing further was done. Inside the house, however, panic ensued, as the woman and her male partner got rid of the children. How they did so and where the children went is still unknown. A third adult, who called himself the "Bongo Man," felt sorry for one young girl; he kept her and at one point tried to enroll her in a local school. Alarm bells went off when it became apparent to school officials that he knew nothing of the girl's history and that she spoke only French and Swahili. The girl was taken into custody by the Department of Child Services. "Bongo Man" was picked up and held by the authorities. Sensing a larger issue, the police contacted the U.S. State Department, who notified ICE in Washington, D.C., who called ICE Connecticut, who in turn got in touch with assistant U.S. attorney Krishna Patel. She sent ICE agents to the Meriden house to interview the couple who were passing themselves off as the girl's parents.

The immigration officials suspected they had uncovered a child smuggling ring. The couple, who were from the Congo, had been using the woman's own children's passports to smuggle in other children, bringing them first to Meriden and from there across the border into Canada. But suspicion was one thing, evidence and proof quite another. Records kept by the couple indicated that groups of children had arrived from Rwanda, but no record showed that they had left Connecticut. At the time ICE interviewed the couple, only two children were still in their control, ages seven and twelve, in addition to the girl whom "Bongo Man" had taken in.

The U.S. Attorney's Office ordered surveillance on the couple, and one day ICE agents followed the woman to Newark Airport. Here she was observed meeting a young boy, and she and the boy were taken into "secondary inspection." They both maintained—falsely, as it turned out—that he was her son; both were paroled into the country and ordered to appear within the week at the U.S. Customs and Border Protection Office in Hartford. Instead, the woman ran, taking the boy with her. Patel correctly assumed she would try to enter Canada with the child, and she issued a warrant. They were caught at the border and returned to Connecticut.[53]

Meanwhile, "Bongo Man" became an informant, giving up the operation as far as his knowledge of it allowed. He admitted that the woman and her partner had been operating a trafficking ring, importing children from Rwanda and selling them across the Canadian border. At first blush, it would appear that the government had a solid case of human trafficking. They had the couple, the testimony of an accomplice, and at least a few of the children. But certain essential ingredients were missing. Authorities hadn't a clue as to the identity or location of the trafficker who had been receiving the children in Canada; there was no record of a transaction and no clear purpose for which the children were allegedly sold. "Bongo Man" lacked information on this crucial aspect of the scheme, and with his impressive criminal record he made a less than credible witness.

Almost certainly, many children had been smuggled into the country and trafficked and sold into Canada. But the remaining few children—clearly terrified of being returned to Rwanda—would say nothing to implicate their "mother," and without victims, buyers, or even a hint as to what they were being trafficked *into,* the burden of proof was simply too weighty to make a case for human trafficking. The couple, Hussein Mutungirehe and Abiba Kanzayire, were charged with thirteen counts of smuggling children into the United States and harboring aliens.[54] By the time the verdict was delivered, they'd been in custody for a year; Hussein was sentenced to an additional six months, while Abiba was sentenced to time served. Both were deported to Rwanda.[55] Had the Department of Justice been able to charge and prove child trafficking, they would have faced the possibility of life in prison.[56]

As the trial was taking place, the U.S. Attorney's Office—suspecting that the children had been stolen from, or sold by, their families in Africa—had the FBI contact the U.S. embassies in Canada and Rwanda, as well as various nongovernmental organizations and clergymen, in an attempt to find relatives of the remaining children. Word was put out that if people would agree to give a DNA sample no charges would be filed against them; there was not a single response. The number of children trafficked by this Congolese couple, and their subsequent fate, will probably never be known.

The fact that these children are lost, casualties in the battle against slavery, points to a crucial dilemma. Human trafficking is a crime that regularly transcends borders but is normally combated with laws that stop at the border. There is little doubt that Canadian law enforcement would be willing to do its part to find these children and help build a case against their traffickers. Even the poor and shaky government of Rwanda would likely help out if given some support to do so. International cooperation is critical, and treaties and agreements have been forged that support that cooperation, but as with so much of the work against human trafficking and slavery, the dedicated resources are simply nowhere near what is needed to get the job done. Yet when we're talking about children being sold as commodities, resources should hardly be a question.

WHAT'S WRONG WITH THIS (MENTAL) PICTURE?

A lot of jobs simply don't exist anymore. Social change and especially technological revolution can cause traditional occupations to disappear from our lives and our memories. Take the "umbrella translator," for example, a job that has gone the way of the dodo. Translators provided a one-man umbrella recycling service working from stalls or barrows on city streets. If the wind turned your umbrella inside out and snapped its struts, you'd simply hand it, along with a little cash, to the next umbrella translator you met, and he'd hand you a new (well, rebuilt) umbrella. Yet one ancient occupation never seems to go away—that of slave. Maybe this is because, unlike the specialized umbrella translator, slaves can be put to any use imaginable.

One of the greatest challenges America faces in ridding itself of slavery is that nearly all Americans think they know exactly what slavery looks like: an African American, in chains, picking cotton under the hot southern sun. The problem is that this picture of American slavery is older than, and pretty much as dead as, the umbrella translator. Both are artifacts of the nineteenth century. But while one job has completely disappeared from our memories, the image of the other is as clear and bright in our minds as if we ourselves had seen slaves in the fields. It is right that we should never forget the horrors of antebellum plantation slavery. But if all we can see when we hear the word *slave* is a picture from *Gone with the Wind,* our eyes will be shut to the slaves of the present.

Of course, the slaves in this chapter also have their echoes in the past. Slaves were singers and acrobats in ancient Greece and Rome as well as America in the nineteenth century. Such afflictions as mental illness and hearing loss have never been a protection against exploitation; if anything, such disabilities simply open another avenue to control by the ruthless. Slaves have been assembled in sweatshops to make clothing for thousands of years. The importation and sale of little African children across borders is nothing new, and neither is the use of slaves as body servants or hairdressers. What's wrong with our mental picture is that *these* jobs are left out of our common image of how slaves are used.

This is America, land of the freethinker. We applaud the innovator and entrepreneur who comes up with new ideas, angles, and products. We're amazed and impressed when someone makes a fortune from doing something as simple as writing software that helps us auction off the junk in our garage over the Internet. And again, perhaps that's how we picture the innovator—as someone doing something clever, original, and useful. But we need to remember that criminals can be clever too. They're often pushed much harder toward innovation than the rest of us, since failure in their business can mean prison, while success can mean huge profits.

The fact is that slavery can be used in almost every job that we can dream up and then some. We have to be just as observant and imaginative as the criminals if we are going to recognize the slaves next door, singing to us in the choir, selling us a trinket for a dollar, or braiding our hair. One of the neighbors of You Zhi Li assumed his house was just a "flophouse for legal or illegal immigrants who were new to Las Vegas," so he looked no deeper, and since the residents "weren't boisterous" or "very noisy" they were just left alone. We tend to have our attention drawn to the noisy and the dramatic, but slaves are usually silent, timid, and retiring. They know that if they speak out or draw attention to themselves they will be punished. Slaveholders make this clear—that slaves should never answer questions, offer help, show themselves to strangers, or reach out in any way. And if the safety of your own family back home is on the line, or you already know the kind of beating you'll get, you keep quiet. To see the slave next door, we have to look past the silence and offer that hand or word that could be the key to someone's freedom.

But there is another way slaves reach into our homes. Yes, people come to America with hopes of a better life and find themselves enslaved, but all around the world are people in slavery who, though they will never come to the United States, produce raw materials and goods that *will*. As the next chapter shows, in our homes and our lives every day we touch, hold, use, value, share, and give to our children goods made by the hands of slaves.

6

EATING, WEARING, WALKING, AND TALKING SLAVERY

Slavery probably crept into your life several times today, some before you even got to work. Rolling off your bed, standing on that pretty handwoven rug, maybe you threw on a cotton T-shirt. In the kitchen did you make a cup of coffee, spoon in a little sugar, and then kick back with a chocolate croissant and your laptop to check the headlines? After a shower, maybe you drove to the station. Waiting for the train, perhaps you made a couple of calls on your cell phone.

All in all a normal day, but slavery was involved in almost every step. Hundreds of thousands of rugs are handwoven by slaves in the "carpet belt" of India, Pakistan, and Nepal. Cotton is grown with slave labor in India, West Africa, and Uzbekistan, the world's second largest producer. Coffee cultivation also encompasses slave labor, mainly in Africa. Enslaved Haitian workers harvest the sugar in the Dominican Republic, the largest exporter of sugar to the United States. The chocolate in that croissant can also be the product of slavery, from the cocoa farms of the Ivory Coast. Even the steel and iron in your car can be polluted by slavery. From a quarter to a half of all U.S. imports of raw iron in different forms come from Brazil.[1] In that country slaves burn the forests to make charcoal, which in turn is used to smelt ore into pig iron and iron into steel. In America, the single largest consumer of Brazilian iron and steel is the automotive industry, though the construction industry also uses a large amount. Pressed against your ear, that cell phone keeps you connected to friends and family but also to slavery. Cell phones (and laptops and other electronics) just don't work very well without a mineral called tantalum. In the Democratic Republic of Congo poor farmers are rounded up by armed gangs and enslaved to dig tantalum out of the ground. Every one of us, every day, touches, wears, and eats products tainted with slavery. Slave-made goods and commodities are everywhere in our lives but, paradoxically, in small proportions. The volume is unacceptable but rarely critical to our national economy or quality of life.

And slavery in our lives is not restricted to cotton, coffee, cocoa, steel, rugs, and cell phones. The list goes on and on, with new commodities and products turning up all the time. Some of them, such as shrimp, might surprise you.

HUCKLEBERRY FINN IT AIN'T

If there is an archetypal picture of rural youth, it is the barefoot lad with the fishing pole over his shoulder. The dusty riverbanks, the lazy heat, the straw dangling from his lip, it all says that halcyon days are possible in our youth. Today even this picture out of Mark Twain is spoiled by bondage. Across Africa and Asia children are enslaved to catch, clean, package, and dry fish. They feed a global demand for everything from shrimp cocktail to cat food. One of the world's largest consumers of seafood is Japan, but the United States isn't too far behind. Americans imported 2.5 million tons of seafood in 2006, worth over $13 billion.[2] And when it comes to shrimp, the United States imports significantly more than the seafood-loving Japanese. Americans love shrimp, and the little crustacean that was once an expensive specialty food is now as ubiquitous as chicken. More than three million tons of frozen shrimp were imported to the United States in 2006.[3] The huge demand for shrimp in the United States and other rich countries has generated a gold rush along the coastlines of the developing world. From India to Bangladesh, from Indonesia to Ecuador, Guatemala, and Brazil, coastal forests, mangrove swamps, and natural beaches are ripped up to build hundreds of thousands of acres of shrimp farms. In all of these places adults and children are enslaved to cultivate and harvest the shrimp.[4] In some cases whole families are caught in debt bondage slavery; in others children are kidnapped and hustled off to shrimp and fish farms on remote islands. Children are regularly enslaved in fishing and shrimping, since kids can do the work and are easier to enslave and control.

In Bangladesh, boys as young as eight are kidnapped and taken out to remote islands like Dublar Char off the southwest coast. Sold to the fishing crews for about $15, they are set to work processing fish on shore for eighteen hours a day, seven days a week. If the boats return with a large catch, they may work several days with no sleep at all. Like robots they clean, bone, and skin fish; shell mussels, shrimp, and crab; and wash squid to remove the ink. Other children sort, weigh, check, and load the haul, processing and preparing the fish for freezing and shipment. The slaveholders sexually abuse the boys and beat them regularly. They get little food and no medical care, and they sleep on the ground. If they sicken or are injured and die, they are thrown into the ocean.[5] Dublar Char was raided and the children were freed in 2004 when researchers linked to the U.S. antislavery group Free the Slaves discovered the situation. They worked with the State Department's antitrafficking office to bring diplomatic pressure on the Bangladeshi government, which led to a raid by military police. (The local police were on the take from the gangs running the island.)

No one knows how many other remote islands conceal such slave camps. Much of the fish and shrimp from these islands enters the global markets and then comes to the United States. Dublar Char is just one example of the slave operations that supply our hunger for seafood. Around the island of Sumatra in Indonesia the sea is dotted with what appear to be ramshackle rafts. They are actually fishing platforms, crudely lashed together and moored up to twenty miles off the coast. There are some 1,500 fishing platforms in this region, each holding three to ten children whose only avenue of escape is a twenty-mile swim. Promised a good job, they are left on the platform to cast nets, catch fish, and clean and dry the catch. In heavy weather the platforms can break up; then children can be swept overboard or may simply fall through the holes in the rough bamboo deck. On irregular visits, the boss collects the fish and administers beatings to increase productivity. As in Dublar Char and so many other places, the children are sexually abused, and if they become ill there is no relief. If they die of illness or injury, they are simply rolled into the water. The revenues from Indonesian fish exports reached $5 billion in 2006; America is one of the top destinations for frozen shrimp, canned tuna, tilapia, and sea crab from that country.[6]

HARD TO AVOID

The products of slavery don't stop with fish, cotton, coffee, and steel. Criminals around the world look for ways to cut costs and increase profits, and what better way to cut labor costs, especially in labor-intensive industries, than slavery? Mining in North America is generally done with enormous machines and skilled workers; mining in the developing world tends to use many of the same techniques known in the Bronze Age. In Ghana, boys and men dig shafts into the earth searching out flecks and nuggets of gold. Crawling through narrow makeshift tunnels, they work in cramped, poorly lit mines where the air is thick with dust and they are constantly at risk of deadly accidents due to falling rock, mine wall collapse, and explosions. Outside the mine, the gold is separated from rock using mercury, a deadly poison. Handling mercury and breathing its fumes damages organs and especially nervous systems. Recall that in the eighteenth century, before mercury's toxic effect was fully understood, hat makers used mercury salts to shape and treat felt for hats. The high incidence of nerve and brain damage and the resulting uncontrollable shaking and tremors are the source of that common expression "mad as a hatter." In the gold fields some miners receive a little money based on the gold they find, while others are locked into debt bondage slavery.

Gold mining in Ghana is just the tip of the iceberg. Primitive mining consumes people, and especially children, in many other countries as well. Enslaved men, women, and children mine gold in Brazil, the Philippines, and Peru. It is estimated that some twenty-five thousand people pan gold from the Amazon, producing seven metric tons a year.[7] Juan Climaco is a judge based in the Amazonian town of Huepetuhe in Peru. "We are talking about people forced to work in the worst conditions imaginable," he said, "without pay, and they really have no way out."[8] Amazonian gold flows into the global market and can end up in anything from electrical parts to gold bars to the ring on your finger.

That ring might also have a gemstone that comes from the hands of slaves. In Sierra Leone adults and children are enslaved in the diamond fields in the Kono district. Olara Otunnu, the special representative of the secretary general of the United Nations, stated, after visiting the mines, "I was horrified by what I saw."[9] These diamonds also flow into the global market. Better-quality stones go to traditional diamond-cutting centers like Antwerp, where they are graded and cut for jewelry. Lower-quality gems, more than half of global production, are sent to India, where, in Gujarat, hundreds, perhaps thousands, of children in debt bondage slavery cut and polish the stones. These gems move into the market for less expensive jewelry along with the cheaper zirconium gems the children also process. Set in jewelry or exported raw, these zirconium gems end up in the United States, pushed at us in television ads, at jewelry stands at the mall, and in advertisements in the back of budget magazines.

Not far from the Peruvian and Brazilian gold mines, slaves are cutting timber. A report by the International Labour Organization in 2005 estimated that thirty thousand people are enslaved in Amazonian logging camps; the Peruvian government endorsed the report.[10] Geyner Pizango and his brother were enslaved to illegally cut mahogany along the Brazil-Peru border in July 2004. His brother was seriously injured by a skidding log and lay untreated in the camp for more than a month. In October 2004 a Brazilian army patrol raided the camp. The patrol destroyed the camp and all of the mahogany logs and then jailed Pizango, his brother, and other workers for two months. Deported back to Peru, his brother died eight months later, aged twenty-two. "It's hard to think of worse exploitation than what we went through," Pizango said, "The Brazilians called us modern day slaves, and they were right. We were sent to the jungle, imprisoned for trying to make an honest wage and treated like animals." The head of Peru's antislavery commission said slavery in logging was "widespread and there's very little anyone can do about it."[11] The two largest timber import companies in the United States imported more than three million board feet of mahogany in 2006.[12] American manufacturers then purchase this wood to make high-quality furniture, cabinets, window frames, and musical instruments.

In addition to raw materials like timber, a constant trickle of manufactured goods, made with slave labor, enters the United States. For example, most of the fireworks used to celebrate the Fourth of July come from China and some from India, where child slavery in fireworks is well documented. Also from India come shoes, clothes, jewelry, household goods, sporting goods, craft items, and hand-rolled *beedi* cigarettes made with slave labor.

At the end of 2007 news reports pointed to child slaves in textile factories in New Delhi, making embroidered shirts for the Gap and other retailers. Hand-embroidered clothing came into fashion in America around 2004, and articles extolled the look in *Vogue,* the *Face,* and *I-D* magazines. But as Ginny Baumann, who manages antislavery projects in India and Nepal for Free the Slaves, explained, "In 2006 and 2007 there have been numerous raids on factories where hundreds of children were enslaved to embroider this fashion clothing."[13] In late October 2007, British reporters found children working in filthy conditions and describing long hours of unpaid work, threats, and beatings.[14] Beaded children's blouses found in the sweatshop were marked with serial numbers that the Gap admitted corresponded with its own inventory. To be fair, this was not a Gap factory but an Indian company that had been subcontracted to produce the blouses by one of the Gap's Indian suppliers and that did so in violation of the Gap's contracts and rules about child labor.

But when it comes to slave-made products in our shops, the largest amount by far comes from China. The Chinese government has found a remarkable way to boost its income. Over the past twenty years the national prison system has been converted into a system of prison *factories*. These factories produce goods for the lucrative export market, and most of these goods flow to the United States. Glancing at the stickers on products in any American "big box" retail store will identify thousands of Chinese-made goods. These products sell for prices that seem impossibly low. How, for example, can a desk lamp be made from wires, glass, metal, and electrical fixtures, assembled, packaged, shipped across the Pacific Ocean, and then shipped within the United States and stocked onto shelves and still generate a profit for the company when it sells for only $4? Could one part of the answer be that the person who assembled and packaged that lamp was enslaved?

It might seem reasonable that convicted criminals serving their sentences should work to pay their keep, but that is far from the situation in Chinese prison factories. In China, a person can be arrested and imprisoned *without trial* for "crimes" such as professing a forbidden religion or expressing opinions in disagreement with the government. Though sentenced for as long as fifteen years, these prisoners have never been tried, have never had the benefit of the due process of law, and once imprisoned have no rights or protections. Ramin Pejan, writing in a journal of American University's school of law, explains:

> The PRC [People's Republic of China] uses *Laojiao* [the prison factory system] to detain individuals it feels are a threat to national security or it considers unproductive. . . . Because those in *Laojiao* have not committed crimes under PRC law, they are referred to as "personnel" rather than prisoners and they are not entitled to judicial procedure. Instead, individuals are sent to the *Laojiao* following administrative sentences dispensed by local public security forces. This vague detainment policy allows the PRC to avoid allegations that the individual's arrest was politically motivated and to assert that they were arrested for reasons such as "not engaging in honest pursuits" or "being able-bodied but refusing to work."[15]

Clearly the prison factory system is a cruel injustice and is often used to crush any opposition group, such as Tibetans who object to the Chinese occupation of their country, members of the Falun Gong religion, or Christian churches that have stood against government controls. And while it is illegal under U.S. law to import goods made by slaves or convicts, the Chinese government has a way around that as well. Ramin Pejan again:

> Each *Laogai* camp has both a camp name and a public name. For example, the Shanghai Municipal Prison is also called the Shanghai Printing & Stationery Factory. Financial information on 99 forced labor camp enterprises collected by Dunn and Bradstreet was released on June 30, 1999. According to this data, the 99 camps had total annual sales of U.S. $842.7 million. These camps represent only 9 percent of the roughly 1,100 known *Laogai* camps. The extremely cheap cost of labor in the *Laogai* system creates a very low-priced, competitive product to export, providing the PRC additional incentive to continue its use of the *Laogai* system.[16]

That "very low-priced competitive" product range includes the $4 lamp and thousands of other consumer goods. Once we know the origin of these goods, most of us would rather not buy them, but it is difficult to trace which of the cheap goods from China come from the hands of workers enslaved by their own government, since the Chinese government works hard to conceal which exports are prison made and which come from other factories. Slave labor has been known to produce toys, lamps and other electrical items, tote bags, clothing, and kitchen goods, but whenever a case is exposed by the press, human rights groups, or U.S. Customs, the Chinese government closes the prison factory and then either moves it or reopens it under a new name. Many of the Chinese exporters, American importers, and "big box" companies know which goods are made by slaves, but they're not telling.

The United States is the richest country in the world, and goods flow from everywhere trying to tap into its lucrative market. Is it any surprise that criminals are making huge profits by using slave labor for the insatiable American consumer? The goods literally surround us, and we give them to our children to wear, eat, and play with. It is hard to imagine that things could be worse, but they are—the slaves that feed our consumption are also being forced to destroy the environment.

DESTROYING LIVES, DESTROYING THE EARTH

Slaves grow, mine, and produce what we eat, use, and wear, but the story doesn't stop there. In many cases, a major by-product of the slave labor feeding into the American economy is environmental destruction. Not surprisingly, criminals who destroy the lives of slaves don't mind wreaking havoc on nature. Forests are illegally cut, strip mines are carved into protected areas, reefs and coastal environments are destroyed, and it is slaves who do the work. In the Amazon rain forests, slaves—not bulldozers—cut the lungs from the planet. The mangrove swamps destroyed to build shrimp farms are ecological "sponges" protecting the coastline from being overwhelmed by the rushing wall of water that is a tsunami. In the devastating tsunami of December 2004, the areas of Sri Lanka that suffered the greatest loss of life were where natural coastal ecosystems had been ripped up to install fish and shrimp farms. This was especially the case when outlying coral reefs were broken up, thus removing a natural buffer.

The two thousand gold mines of Amazonian Peru and Brazil have turned 125 miles of rain forest into ravaged mounds of raw earth and ponds choked with mercury-tainted water and silt. To get at the gold flecks, tons of topsoil and riverbanks are dug up and hauled into troughs, where jets of water wash through it. The thick brown and yellow runoff clogs streams and pollutes whatever lies downriver. With the topsoil and vegetation removed, nothing grows on the barren moonscape that remains. In the camps, mercury is applied to a slurry of minerals, dirt, sand, and flecks of gold. Mixed together, gold and mercury form a bond, called an amalgamation, and the sand or other minerals float to the surface of the liquid mercury, where they can be skimmed off. The mercury-gold amalgamation, a waxlike mass, is then heated, and the mercury evaporates, leaving the gold dust behind. While efficiently separating the gold from all the other sand and dirt, this process also means that unprotected miners handle mercury and breathe it in when it is evaporated. All the used mercury is ultimately left in the air, soil, or water to poison the earth. Another method used to refine gold is even more dangerous to the workers. This involves leaching gold-bearing ore with a cyanide solution that is extremely poisonous and polluting.[17] The next time you consider buying that stylish South American gold "Inca" figurine or piece of jewelry, think of the real cost—to the environment and to the slaves who mined and processed the ore.

ALIEN ATTACK!

Outside of Amazonia, a bizarre double-whammy has been inflicted on Brazilian forests to provide the steel needed for our cars, furniture, toys, and thousands of other products. It's like a story out of science fiction. For thousands of years, a particular corner of planet Earth was dense forest. The people who lived in it were just one of the many species that existed in balance with the thick tangle of trees. A mature ecology of plants and animals, it was about as stable and long-lasting as any natural place can be. One day, machines of enormous power appeared. In hours, they scraped away the ancient forest as if it were no more than foam on the earth's surface. Within days the sterilized land was replanted with a single, alien species. This planting was invincible and voracious. None of the native insects and animals that survived the attack could eat or live on the new species. Those that tried learned the hard way: a noxious poison oozed from its leaves and branches when cut or broken. Meanwhile, any surviving plants starved as the alien sucked all the nutrients from the soil in a frenzy that fed tremendous growth. Soon, where the dense and varied forest once stood was a single species of uniform color, uniform size, and uniform silence. The birds were gone, the animals had fled, and only a few lizards and insects survived as the newly planted trees quietly rustled in the wind.

Today, the alien trees tower over the land. Where the straight edge of the new monoculture meets the original forest, the lush old growth thins from the lack of nutrients. You can see it with your own eyes. The place is the state of Mato Grosso do Sul in Brazil. The alien species is eucalyptus, the oily and fragrant tree from Australia, the leafy home of those cute koala bears. In the 1970s nearly one million acres in three counties of Mato Grosso do Sul were stripped of their forests (*mato grosso* means "thick wood") and replaced with eucalyptus trees. The native forests here were not the vast rain forests of the Amazon basin but the shorter, tangled *cerrado* or scrub forests of the South American central plateau. The destruction of these forests was the first major human assault on this part of Brazil. It was, and still is, the edge, the frontier of "civilization." And it was all for nothing. The clearance and planting of eucalyptus was part of a government scheme giving tax breaks and grants to big landowners in support of a giant paper mill—a mill that was never built.

When the *cerrado* was cleared to make way for the eucalyptus in the 1970s, the wood was just dragged into great piles and burned. Today as another wave of destruction sweeps across the Mato Grosso, the *cerrado* and the eucalyptus are still being burned, but this time the fire turns them into money. The wood is made into charcoal, just like the kind you use in your barbecue. This is a special kind of charcoal, because it is handmade by slaves. The use of wood charcoal to make iron and steel goes back to the eighteenth century and contributed to the deforestation of Europe. In most countries coke, a coal by-product, is used in place of charcoal, but where forests are open to criminal exploitation, or are thought of as having little value, charcoal making is common.

Unemployed workers from eastern Brazil are tricked with promises of paid work and then trapped in charcoal camps far from their homes and the rule of law. The work is grueling—cutting and packing wood into seven-foot-high clay kilns shaped like beehives, then working through the night to adjust the slow controlled burn of wood into charcoal.[18] The slaves suffer burns and cuts, the heat is ferocious, and their flesh wastes away. Without running water, they survive on whatever groundwater they can find; they sleep in open-sided shelters; malaria is common. After burning, the charcoal is heaped up in piles to wait for trucks to carry it to the smelters. Mixed with other fuels, it refines iron ore to pig iron, some of which is exported to the United States. Once here, the pig iron is made into steel and then into a very large range of products, including engine blocks and brackets, exhaust components, and brake drums and rotors for major American car companies. Cars, trucks, and tractors sold in America can be tainted with Brazilian charcoal slavery, as well as sinks, bathtubs, and plumbing fixtures in American homes.[19] Unknowingly, the U.S. consumer provides the incentive for this destruction of both human life and the environment.

MORE IS LESS

When we add together the flow of slave-tainted commodities and products, we see that all of us are touched by slavery in some way, every day. It seems as if we are being swamped by the products of bondage; but strangely, we're not. The fact is that although slave-made products surround us, these products represent only a small proportion of all imported and American-made goods. This points up one of the greatest challenges we face. Unlike the past, when slave-made goods such as cotton held a majority market share, today only a small and insidious fraction of slavery taints commodities and products, making them more difficult to identify and remove. The globalization of the economy has meant a rapid increase in the kinds and variety of slave-made goods that flow into our shops and malls, but that doesn't mean that every shrimp or bathroom tap or shirt or chocolate bar comes from slavery. Only a very small fraction of each commodity or product comes from slave hands. While over $660 million worth of cocoa beans were imported into the United States in 2007, only part of that came from countries where slavery and the worst forms of child labor are known to exist on cocoa farms, and in those countries only a small fraction of farms have slaves. The total fraction of imported cocoa tainted with slavery is probably 2 percent or less.[20] The same applies to cotton, sugar, iron, steel, shrimp, fish, tantalum, timber, and so forth. It is thought that a high percentage of hand-knotted rugs from South Asia are made by enslaved children, but the estimates are not clear. Any amount of slavery in the things we eat, wear, and drive is too much, but in such small proportions, trying to remove slave-made goods from our lives is like looking for a needle in a haystack.

If we look at all the work done by slaves, not just the slave-touched goods that flow into the United States, the actual monetary value of slavery in the world economy is still extremely small. One estimate states that all the work done by slaves worldwide is worth about $13 billion per year, the same amount that spam e-mails cost businesses each year.[21] A recent study by the United Nations estimated that global profits from human trafficking are about $31 billion a year.[22] This sounds like a lot of money, and it is, but to put it into perspective, that's the same amount Warren Buffett donated to the Bill and Melinda Gates Foundation in 2007.[23] In the global economy this is a small drop in a large ocean.

The problem we face as consumers is that it is almost impossible to know which shirt or chocolate bar or chair carries slavery into your home. The criminals using slaves sell their products like everyone else, and they flow into the global market and mix with products of free workers. While the criminals may justify their use of slaves by pointing to economic pressures to reduce labor costs, they never pass the savings from slavery to the consumer, with the possible exception of the Chinese prison factories and the cheap goods they sell to the United States. Normally, the slaveholder just pockets the market price for his slave-made goods—a price set in a market that reflects the presence of free workers. So if slaveholders are feeding on our purchases, it would seem that we should just stop buying those goods. In fact, that may be exactly the wrong thing to do.

We feel a strong revulsion when we think we are eating something or wearing something that comes from slave labor. Our reaction is to push that crime away from us, to distance ourselves, to boycott slave-made goods. The last thing we want to do is support slaveholders. Yet for every criminal using slaves to grow cocoa or cotton or sugar, hundreds or thousands of farmers are producing the same crops without using slaves. Great agribusinesses are involved, as well as individual farmers with just a few acres and every size of farm in between. Small farmers in the developing world have enough problems competing against the vast subsidies given to U.S. and European agribusiness; if the consumers turn against them as well, the result could be the destruction of poor family farms. So while our disgust says, "Boycott," the truth is that boycotts can hurt the innocent more than the guilty. We think of ourselves as consumers. We want to vote in the marketplace for the things we believe in. But this problem usually can't be fixed at the point of purchase.

Of course, there is a place for a carefully targeted boycott. As we saw in chapter 3, the Coalition of Immokolee Workers organized boycotts of Taco Bell and Burger King when these fast-food chains refused to negotiate the punishing wages paid to the workers that picked their tomatoes and other vegetables. Here the boycott had a clear target and a precise aim—to increase the amount paid to workers for every bucket of tomatoes by a single penny, to establish responsibly monitored working conditions, and to ensure that buyers refused to purchase any produce harvested by slave labor. The success of the Taco Bell boycott occurred exactly because its aims were clear and directed at a company that could actually take the needed action. Shareholder pressure, divestment campaigns, demonstrations, and boycotts are all ways to make companies understand our concerns as consumers. But at the same time we have to guard against knee-jerk reactions that can hurt the very people we hope to help. The trick is to be smart about direct action, like the Coalition of Immokolee Workers.

Given the nature of the global economy, however, if we don't want slavery in the things we buy, the best place to stop slavery is not at the cash register but where it happens—on the farm, in the quarry, or in the sweatshop. The $30 you *don't* spend boycotting the purchase of a shirt is worth little or nothing in the fight against slavery in most parts of the world. The slaveholder has already made his profit, and if a boycott leads to a collapse in cotton prices, the slaveholder just moves his slaves to another job or dumps them, or worse. Meanwhile, the boycott drives the poorest farmers, mill hands, and other people out of work, into destitution and vulnerability, and even into a risk of enslavement. A boycott is a blunt instrument that can sometimes be exactly the right tool but can also run the risk of creating more suffering than it cures. What seems to be the immediate and obvious answer isn't always the best one.

Part of the solution is a mental adjustment that Americans can make. It is very easy for consumers to blame corporations, especially big corporations, for many of the world's problems. When we learn that the things we eat, wear, and drive are made with the products of slavery we feel angry, and the companies that sold us those goods are usually the ones we'll blame first. Movies and TV programs often feature the heartless corporate executive as a villain, and certainly companies like Enron don't do anything to dispel that image. In most cases, but not all, slavery is many steps removed from the American companies that sell us things. Should they know their product chain well enough to keep slavery out? It may take some time for companies to dig deeply into their supply chains, but the answer to that question is yes. And consumers should do their best to be aware as well. The moral responsibility for the things we buy does not end at the cash register; every consumer is the last link in the chain that leads back to an enslaved worker. Consumers have to share responsibility with retailers, wholesalers, producers, and the importers of goods and raw materials, all the way back to the ultimate, damning culpability that falls on the criminal who uses slaves. For the average citizen this responsibility is uncomfortable, but the truth is that there would be no slave-made goods in the shops unless people were ready to buy them. Given that most American consumers like a bargain but hate slavery, how do we clean up our product chains? As it turns out, old tools in the form of national laws are ready to break those chains, and new ways of working together offer the hope of an economy unpolluted by slave products. America has a long tradition of banning slave-made goods and an equally long tradition of not enforcing those rules.

A LONG TRADITION OF DOING NEXT TO NOTHING

The United States has laws and regulations that forbid the importation of any slave-made goods, including those made in prison factories. These laws date back more than one hundred years, and they have been tested and ruled on by the Supreme Court. But somehow, as slavery slipped into the darkness and Americans came to believe it was finished forever, these laws fell into disuse and were virtually forgotten.

At the very beginning of the American republic the founding fathers were desperately split over slavery. In the 1787 Constitutional Convention that established the U.S. government, a great deal of effort went into forging two key compromises between the free and slave states. These compromises maintained the fragile unity of the emerging republic but planted the seeds for much greater suffering later. The first compromise was a provision in the Constitution that the government would not be allowed to ban the slave trade until twenty years had past. The second compromise addressed congressional representation by population. The North wanted slaves to be considered chattel, along with horses, mules, and pigs, and not counted as people, whereas the South wanted their slaves to be categorized as humans—not out of a sense of humanity but in order to gain more votes in the House of Representatives. A compromise was hammered out; it ordered that a slave would be counted as three-fifths of a person. Both of these provisions crashed headlong into the ideals of democracy, and both were seen as a price to be paid to keep the new nation together.

While the institution and legality of slavery were not threatened, and the slave trade had a twenty-year reprieve, the new Congress soon began to chip away at slavery in ways that were allowed by the Constitution. In 1790, a law banned U.S. citizens from engaging in the slave trade in foreign ports (almost impossible to enforce), and in 1794 it became illegal to build or equip slave ships within the United States (also difficult to enforce). As the twenty-year deadline approached, Congress passed a series of laws to come into effect on January 1, 1808. One made it illegal to bring slaves into America, another banned supplying ships to the slave trade and allowed slave ships to be confiscated, and another allowed the U.S. Navy to seize slave ships. While on paper these laws virtually wiped out the trans-Atlantic slave trade to America, in reality they were rarely enforced.

Only at the time of the Civil War did the government really address the slave trade. By 1860, the shifting political winds, the swelling abolitionist ranks, and the coming to power of the Republican Party meant that the 1808 law was taken seriously for the first time. For the entire fifty years leading up to the Civil War, the anti–slave trade laws were almost entirely ignored. If a slave ship's captain was arrested and came to trial, he would generally be let off on a technicality or with a derisory fine of just a few dollars. Then in the summer of 1860 a ship's captain from Maine named Nathaniel Gordon was caught red-handed, leaving Africa with 897 slaves packed on board his ship. When he was sent to New York for trial, a new federal prosecutor pressed for the full punishment of the law. Legally, slave trading carried the same penalty as piracy—death; but since the trade had been tolerated for decades, the call for Gordon's execution was extremely controversial. The trial and its aftermath dragged on through the first year of the Civil War, and it came to President Lincoln to decide whether Gordon would be executed or not. Lincoln decided an example had to be made, and Gordon was hanged in 1862.[24]

In 1864, the seizure of more slave ships led to a Supreme Court ruling clarifying the law on bringing slaves into the United States. The Court ruled, citing the 1794 act, that it was not required that U.S. companies actually transport slaves to be liable—just building a ship that was likely to be used in the slave trade was a crime. Essentially, the Supreme Court ruled that it was illegal for an American company or person to profit from the slave trade, no matter where that slavery occurred. What's more, the Court allowed the seizure and sale of a ship even if there was no direct evidence that it had been used to carry slaves, only circumstantial evidence that the ship was *likely* to have been used in the slave trade. That ruling has enormous implications for slavery in the United States today, since it suggests that any car, truck, aircraft, ship, or boat or, for that matter, any house or building that is *likely* to have been used in human trafficking can be seized and sold.

The Emancipation Proclamation of 1863 freed only those slaves behind enemy lines in the Confederate States, so these Supreme Court rulings came before legal slavery was finally and completely banned in 1865. When the Thirteenth Amendment to the Constitution came into force, it stated simply that "neither slavery nor involuntary servitude, except as a punishment for crime whereof the party shall have been duly convicted, shall exist within the United States, or any place subject to their jurisdiction." *Legal* slavery ended with the Thirteenth Amendment; actual slavery did not. Since slavery has never disappeared from America, the Supreme Court has had to rule a number of times on whether other forms of slavery came under the Thirteenth Amendment. The Court has always decided that if a person has lost his or her free will, is under violent control, and is being economically exploited, then the Thirteenth Amendment ban on slavery applies. "Peonage" of African American, white, and Mexican workers, and other forms of debt bondage, have all been ruled to be slavery.

What's important here is that America's most fundamental law, the Constitution, and its interpretation in statutes and by the Supreme Court make it clear that it is forbidden for an American individual or company to take part in slavery in any form or to profit from slavery. This applies wherever in the world the slavery occurs. The implication of this for the situation today, with the products of slavery from all over the planet entering our country, is staggering. What's more, another law, the Smoot-Hawley Tariff of 1930, bans "all goods, wares, articles and merchandise mined, produced, or manufactured wholly or in part in any foreign country by convict labor or/and forced labor or/and indentured labor under penal sanctions," which perfectly describes the Chinese prison-factories. If the Constitution, the Supreme Court, and

Congress all say that profiting from, or bringing into the country, slaves or slave-made goods is a serious crime, why are we confronted daily with slave-made cotton, steel, coffee, sugar, wood products, cocoa, clothing, gold, diamonds, jewelry, and other goods and commodities? It is not as if the law were vague or confusing. Strip away the legalese and American law boils down to this: no slavery in any form, no profiting from slavery in any form, no bringing in or selling the products of slavery in any form; end of story.

BITTERSWEET

Finding a way out of this mess for American companies and consumers will not be easy—but the recent actions of the chocolate industry give us a good example. In 2001 a film made for HBO and British television exposed slave labor on cocoa farms in the Ivory Coast. The footage of young African workers, their backs scarred from whippings, in terrible physical condition after being freed, hit the chocolate industry like a bomb. As they began to get over their shock, chocolate company executives started to assess what they could do about the problem. The challenges were great: almost half the world's cocoa comes from the Ivory Coast. This meant that an immediate boycott of cocoa from that country would have cut world chocolate production in half, as well as destroyed both the economy of that country and the livelihoods of the majority of farmers who didn't exploit slave and child labor. In addition, there was no immediate way to tell which of the country's six hundred thousand farms had slave labor and which didn't, or which cocoa beans were tainted with slavery and which weren't. In the Ivory Coast, chocolate companies are not allowed to buy directly from farmers. The government controls the supply chain, sets the price, and requires companies to buy from registered exporters. By the time the cocoa reaches the export warehouses, all the slave and free cocoa beans are mixed together and indistinguishable.

While consumers pressed for answers, the chocolate companies scrambled to discover what they could do that might be effective. Slavery, after all, is illegal in the Ivory Coast; and the chocolate company executives asked why was it *their* responsibility to enforce the laws of a foreign country. Meanwhile, the government of the Ivory Coast was angry about having their main export threatened by reports of slavery and abusive child labor on a few farms. They also resented calls for the U.S. government to somehow intervene to stop the slavery—not because they condoned slavery but because they didn't like foreigners trying to tell them how to run their country.

Let's think about the shoe being on the other foot. Having read chapter 3 of this book, you know there is slavery in agriculture in South Florida. Now imagine that the government of Ivory Coast announced that it was sending inspectors to Florida to check up on slavery in the tomato fields and orange groves. These inspectors would check farms, interview workers, look for violations, and then decide if America would be allowed to export their tomatoes and oranges. The U.S. government would never allow such a thing; in fact it would be taken as an insult and a provocation. Although Ivory Coast is not a rich country and its government makes mistakes, that doesn't mean that its citizens shouldn't run their own affairs. When you consider that Ivory Coast only gained its independence from France in 1960, it's understandable that they might feel touchy about a rich and mainly white country telling them what to do.

The breakthrough on cocoa slavery came when staffers working for Senator Tom Harkin and Congressman Eliot Engel decided more could be achieved by cooperation than confrontation. Using an amendment to the Farm Bill as a lever, they got the main chocolate companies together with antislavery organizations, consumer groups, trade unions, and anti–child labor agencies. After tough negotiating, all these groups agreed to a kind of treaty. Alternately called the Harkin-Engel Protocol and the Cocoa Protocol, it committed the chocolate industry to work with all the other groups to uncover the amount of slavery and abusive child labor, to fund a foundation aimed at getting slavery out of cocoa, and to develop a way to ensure that no chocolate came from slave or child labor. The protocol was a historic document, the first "treaty" to be struck between an entire industry and the antislavery and anti–child labor movements in the more than two hundred years of their existence.

The result is the International Cocoa Initiative (ICI), a foundation based in Geneva and including the European chocolate companies. The ICI mounts projects in West Africa aimed at taking slavery and child labor out of cocoa. The chocolate companies have put more than $10 million into this work since 2002, money that would never have gone into antislavery work without the protocol. Working the governments of Ivory Coast and Ghana, the ICI constructed a system for inspecting and certifying cocoa, completing the first tests of the system in the summer of 2008. This inspection and certification is tricky since there are more than a million cocoa farms in the region, and who, exactly, should be the group or government that "certifies" that cocoa is slave-free? The certifier needs to be independent, whereas the farmers, exporters, chocolate companies, and even the governments have a big stake in their cocoa crop. Exactly how to inspect and police the farms will take time to work out; sooner is better than later, but at least for cocoa, unlike the other commodities flowing into the United States, there is a vision and a plan.

It is the basic idea of the protocol that is so important—that companies take responsibility for their product chain and work with other groups, including consumers, to clean it up. Since the protocol was hammered out, both Ivory Coast and Ghana have developed programs and asked for foreign help to address their child and slave labor problem. The protocol has also shown how two U.S. politicians could use the bully pulpit of their office to fight slavery around the world. The protocol process is aimed at taking slavery out of a single commodity, cocoa; if this method is successful, it will be a tool that can be used on the other products that bring slavery into our homes. Other industries are looking at the protocol model as a way to clean up their product chains, and when the cost of this work is spread across a whole industry, it doesn't dramatically affect the bottom line or the prices paid by consumers.

MEANWHILE . . .

While procedures like the Cocoa Protocol are worked out and adapted to other commodities like steel, cotton, sugar, and coffee, how can American consumers ensure that they are not buying into slavery? At present, it is hard to know if slavery is in the product you want to buy. "Big box" retailers may know which goods they have imported from Chinese prison factories, or they may not; either way they are unlikely to say. Car companies, grocery store chains, coffee shops, and clothing manufacturers all face the same problem the chocolate companies faced; their raw materials contain some slave-made ingredients all mixed in with legitimate ingredients. Until each of these industries steps up and takes responsibility for the labor link in its product chain, Americans will remain in the dark, knowing the origins of only a handful of products and sources. It is impossible to make an ethical choice about every single purchase. The question is: How do we focus our consumer power in a way that is realistic? Every industry, every company, has to listen to its customers or face disaster. As the last link in the product chain, consumers have considerable power. By speaking in one voice, consumers can bring enough pressure to bear to remove the slavery ingredient from the things we buy. Calling on the companies to work together with consumers and human rights groups to find solutions to the problem can achieve this. Smart companies know that unless they take responsibility for monitoring their product chain and eliminating the element of slavery from their stock, sooner or later they can expect a serious downturn in sales. Antislavery organizations are needed to keep a firm grasp on what is happening on the ground.

There are ways to get businesses to do the right thing. Consumers in England wanted the big grocery store chains to work harder to get slavery out of the food they sold, so they mounted a simple but effective campaign. Thousands of families saved the long receipts they were handed at the grocery store checkout stand. Every month they would attach those receipts to a letter to company bosses. The letter read something like this: "You can see by the attached receipts that we buy our family's groceries at your store. We like shopping at your store, but we would like it a lot more if you would remove slave and child labor from the food and other products we buy." The response from the grocery companies was swift and positive.

You can also be sure you are not buying into slavery with some products if you buy "Fair Trade" goods. Fair Trade goods, like coffee, chocolate, sugar, tea, nuts, bananas, honey, and rice, are inspected and certified by an independent foundation. The basic aim of Fair Trade is to get farmers and artisans in the developing world a fair price for their crops or goods, one that allows them to send their kids to school and have a decent life. The inspection system means that slavery doesn't come into the product. Fair Trade goods can be a little more expensive, since the farmer is getting an agreed-upon and sustainable price as opposed to a market rate that can sometimes be below the cost of production. While Fair Trade doesn't get the publicity of most retail products, you don't have to look too far to find it. Fair Trade coffee, for example, is available at Caribou Coffee, Starbucks, Seattle's Best, Safeway, Giant Foods, Target, Dunkin' Donuts, and many other shops. As more people buy Fair Trade goods, the system expands to cover more producers and more products coming into the market.

The clothing company American Apparel takes a slightly different approach. Based in Los Angeles, the company has a vertically integrated supply chain—meaning that almost all the steps in producing their clothes are taken in the same place by the same company. By assuming a hands-on approach to their product chain and trying to control as much of it as possible, they stop slavery from creeping in. Much of their clothing is available in certified organic cotton as well. Levi-Strauss and other clothing companies have taken still another approach. Working together, they have set required standards for their own factories and all the companies that supply them. In 2008, these companies were working their way down their supply chain, step by step, setting up systems that would eliminate the sort of problem that occurred with the Gap's subcontractor in India.

Yet another approach deals with one of the best known of the slavery-tainted products, handwoven rugs produced by child slaves in India, Pakistan, and Nepal. More than one hundred thousand children are thought to be enslaved in this way, locked in tiny sheds, fed little, forced to work long days, beaten and abused. These rugs are a major export of the region; Pakistan alone exported to the United States more than two hundred million dollars' worth of handwoven carpets in 2007. There is, however, an organization whose efforts ensure that some carpets are made without slave and child labor. Rugmark is an international charity that inspects and licenses carpet looms.[25] When carpet makers apply for a Rugmark license, they promise not to employ children less than fourteen years of age in the production of carpets and to pay adult weavers a minimum wage. In family carpet businesses, regular school attendance is required for children employed as helpers, and only the loom owner's children are permitted to work. Carpet makers promise to allow Rugmark's inspectors to examine their looms and workers at any time. The inspectors carry out random checks to see that the rules are being followed. If they meet these requirements, a license permits the carpet makers to put a Rugmark label, with a unique serial number, on their carpets so that every carpet can be traced all the way back to the loom where it was woven. Companies that import carpets to Europe and America pay about 1 percent of the cost of the carpet to Rugmark. This money supports schools and rehabilitation programs for children who have been freed from slavery in the carpet industry. In this way the former child slaves are safeguarded against being caught and enslaved again. To date, hundreds of child slaves have been freed and rehabilitated by Rugmark.

THE END OF EATING AND WEARING SLAVERY?

America is caught in a strange dilemma. The bitter fruits of slavery are found in our shops and homes, and our marketplace is shot through with slavery. Yet although slavery is ubiquitous, it is also present in very small amounts. If slavery in the U.S. economy were measured like air pollution, it would be registering in "parts per million"—tainting our lives in concentrations that are small but disturbing. When American consumers discover slavery in the products they buy, many are disgusted and want to take action. Recent consumer research showed that more than 80 percent of Americans asked were deeply concerned about slave-made goods. It doesn't matter that the total amount of slave-made goods is small; any amount is too much. Americans understand that their consumption drives much of the global economy, that the flow of goods and raw materials to the United States is vast. That great river of goods, pulled by the purchasing power of Americans, carries slavery into our lives. Somehow that slavery must be filtered out; our laws require it.

So what is going on here? With a strong foundation in our laws and courts, our trade regulations, and rules that govern imports, why are we still eating, wearing, driving, and walking on slavery? A key reason is lack of leadership. No political party, no political leader has made slavery a priority. While the government has clearly, in its laws and regulations, taken responsibility for ending this crime, it has never supported these laws in such a way as to make a difference. Expenditure on all forms of slavery and human trafficking by the U.S. government equals around $200 million a year, only a small fraction of which goes into stemming the flow of slave-made goods.[26] Compare that to the $12 billion spent in 2005 attempting to stop the movement of drugs into the country.[27] If we judge by results, then taking slavery out of the things we buy is a low priority. We have to combat that as consumers by looking hard at the supply chains that bring us our goods.

While it rarely happens now, there are ways to cooperate in managing the supply chain without hurting poor people or honest businesses around the world. This cooperative approach is important because if the existing laws were suddenly and rigidly enforced, the resulting economic havoc would probably increase slavery, at least in the short run, and would certainly harm many farmers, workers, and businesses in other countries who have nothing to do with slavery and hate it as much as we do. No one would want that to happen. Our purchasing power can make or break innocent lives in the developing world; we have to use it carefully.

The lesson of the chocolate industry is that one way forward is to work and organize by economic sector, bringing together the companies that use a particular raw material or product that is known to be touched by slavery. In a globalized economy, many companies will be buying from the same sources and will be able to trace their product chains to the same regions, mines, and even prison factories. That cost of investigating a product chain can be high for a single company but affordable if spread across a number of companies. The government can support industry partnerships by offering incentives for cleaning up product chains. A significant decrease in slave-made imports would occur if the U.S. government required, and helped, businesses to police their supply chains. Tax credits, grants, or tax breaks could help companies to meet the cost of investigating their product chains. Incentives could also apply to funds spent to free and rehabilitate the slaves who will be discovered when the product chain is cleaned up, as well as for setting up ways to monitor and certify commodities and products.

Senator Harkin and Congressman Engel, in bringing the chocolate companies together in forging the Cocoa Protocol, were able to cut through the companies' normally competitive positions and get them working together. The result was positive, but having the occasional politician unilaterally decide to bring companies together is not an organized or efficient way to accomplish this end. Given the antislavery laws of the United States, and the absolute mandate that businesses avoid even the imputation of profiting from slavery, why not set up a small unit, possibly within the corporate social responsibility section of the State Department, charged with helping businesses come together? Government officials could make clear the legal responsibilities of each company and then explain how the businesses could join in a protocol-type agreement to jointly monitor and clean up their product chains. The carrot of cooperation is so clearly preferable to the stick of sanctions that few businesses would choose to go it alone.

Every day brings more information to consumers about slavery in the products they buy. It took some time for shoppers to become aware of environmental concerns and ask for dolphin-friendly tuna and other green products. It will also be some time before consumers fully comprehend the slavery in the goods they buy. But when American consumers figure this out, many will be asking, as many are asking today, why there are not agreements like the Cocoa Protocol in other industries, such as those using cotton, sugar, coffee, or pig iron. Americans will be asking their elected representatives why the Customs Service and other law enforcement agencies don't have the money needed to stop the flow of slave-made goods into the country. As this awareness grows, hopefully people are going to want their retirement funds invested in businesses that police their product chains for slavery.

Consumer movements may be slow to start, but once begun they almost never quit. Businesses that are smart enough to think about what their customers want, and where they are going, are already finding ways to police their product chains.

If, as Calvin Coolidge said, "the business of America is business," how do we build a positive business case for ending slavery and not a risk-based case? In other words, how do we find a way for the end of slavery to be positive for American businesses and consumers, instead of threatening companies for failing to clean up their supply chains? That is a challenge, but it is possible if consumers *and* producers work together and make the collective decision that there is no place for slavery in our shops and homes. Every time we walk into a shop, we vote with our dollars in the marketplace. Often we are voting for or against slavery whether we realize it or not. America is already committed to a strict legal code that absolutely forbids slave-made goods from entering the country. Somehow we have allowed our laws against importing the products of slavery to go unheeded while the flow of tainted goods and raw materials has increased. It is time to put those laws to work and spend the money to get them enforced. When that happens, then Americans will stop eating, wearing, driving, walking, and talking on slave-made goods.

PART II

THE FINAL EMANCIPATION

7

SLAVES IN THE NEIGHBORHOOD

Slavery has been identified in over one hundred of our cities; the real number is undoubtedly much higher. When we hear about slavery in our midst, the tendency is to think, "Not in my town." In a way, we consider ourselves above it, especially if we live in comfortable, relatively trouble-free communities. The harsh truth is, modern-day slavery *is* in your town. You are not protected from it by nationality, race, gender, or income. It can afflict anyone—the gardener down the street, the construction crew on a local office building, your neighbor's housekeeper, your daughter on her way to the mall. Americans are going to have to adjust to the fact that people are enslaved all around us and that the solution to this problem lies, in large measure, within ourselves.

KNOWING IT WHEN WE SEE IT

The message is clear: if you spot a trafficking victim, you should say or do something. It sounds simple; it's anything but. The hard part isn't taking action; it's knowing slavery when you see it. Slavery in America tends to be hidden. Chances are, you could be staring full on at a human trafficking situation and not recognize it. Guidelines are clearly needed. The Washington, D.C.–based NGO Free the Slaves has printed and distributed a handbook entitled *"Slavery Still Exists and It Could Be in Your Backyard: A Community Member's Guide to Fighting Human Trafficking and Slavery* (available at www.freetheslaves.net). In it, they offer a list of things to look for, pointing out that the trafficked person "might be a domestic worker, work in a restaurant, on a farm, in a shop, in a factory, or as a prostitute." The worker "is likely to be enslaved if he or she:

- Is working or being held against his or her will
- Is not free to change employers

- Does not control his or her earnings
- Is unable to move freely or is being watched or followed
- Is afraid to discuss himself or herself in the presence of others
- Has been assaulted, or threatened with assault for refusing to work
- Has been cheated into payment of debt upon arrival
- Has had his or her passport or other documents taken away

"If any of these apply, the person might be a victim of modern-day slavery."[1] And you should consider calling the National Human Trafficking Resource Center's information hotline at 888–373–7888.

The U.S. Department of Education has also provided a list of warning signs of trafficking especially designed for students and young people.[2] Sadly, this is needed; sex traffickers target children because of their vulnerability and gullibility, as well as the market demand for young victims. Recruitment can take many forms, including kidnapping; solicitation by other women or girls recruiting on behalf of the sex trafficker; and the "loverboy" approach of appearing genuinely interested in a romantic relationship while gradually coercing the victim into prostitution. A student or young person caught in human trafficking:

- May have unexplained absences from school for a period of time and may therefore be a truant
- May be unable to attend school on a regular basis
- May chronically run away from home
- May make references to frequent travel to other cities
- May exhibit bruises or other physical trauma, withdrawn behavior, depression, or fear
- May lack control over her or his schedule or identification documents
- May be hungry or malnourished, and inappropriately dressed (based on weather conditions or surroundings)
- May show signs of drug addiction

Clearly, there are a number of warning signs, but we have to take the time to look. In a society in which many of us go through our day avoiding eye contact and keeping human interaction to a minimum, this requires a deliberate commitment and a change in our normal behavior. One antislavery worker explained, "Sometimes as Americans we don't want to be nosy, but really, we could be the person that saves [a] life."[3]

GOOD SAMARITANS

Every day, Americans meet or observe people in slavery situations—usually without knowing what they're seeing. Yet with a little awareness, some sensitivity to the situation, and some genuine perseverance, slaves can be rescued. This is not wishful thinking; it happens with enough frequency to account for about one-third of all slaves rescued in the last few years. The concerned citizens involved in these rescues are often called Good Samaritans, and the only thing that differentiates them from you and me is that they've recognized that someone needs help and have taken action.

What makes a Good Samaritan? At the most basic level, it's openness to the possibility that something isn't quite right. A teenager soliciting on a street corner or in a bar should raise a question in our minds. A domestic servant sitting on a doorstep, or overseeing kids clearly not her own, might simply be a housekeeper or a nanny at her job. Or there could be something in her manner—an overriding sadness or sullenness, a deliberate avoidance of contact with others, a habit of always looking down—that indicates a deeper problem. Establishing contact can be a difficult step, especially if you are unfamiliar with a trafficking situation.

One Man's Tradition, Another's Slavery

In some instances, little action is required—an encouraging word, a suggested direction. Elaine Fletcher (not her real name) lived in an affluent town in Massachusetts, long before the passage of the Trafficking Victims Protection Act (TVPA) in 2000, when very few people were aware of slavery in today's America. She'd had an upper-middle-class New England childhood and had attended a prestigious college. When Elaine was in her late twenties, she became friendly with an attractive, well-off Indian couple in their thirties. The husband was somehow connected to royalty, and his wife was a child of privilege. At the time Elaine knew this couple, they had a young "houseboy" to perform every task they required—from answering the door to cleaning the large, rambling house, maintaining the grounds, and cooking their meals. In fact, after Elaine became friendly with the young man, they exchanged recipes. "He taught me to cook tandoori chicken and palak paneer, in exchange for my pasta primavera recipe." Although the couple had no children, the wife's entire family, including several siblings, lived in the house. Observed Elaine, "He worked his tail off."

Elaine thinks the "boy" was in his early twenties, but "he was slight, bony—he had the look of a much older man." It became clear that the couple had "acquired" their servant while living in India. At one point, Elaine and a few friends asked the couple where the young man slept. "On a mat, on the kitchen floor," was the reply. The guests were shocked, and the husband's explanation was "Oh, but back in India, he'd be living on the street!" "They saw themselves," says Elaine, "as his saviors." She is fairly certain that he received no pay for his work—"and if he did, it surely wasn't much"—and that he was expected to do everything he was told, without talking back. He was illiterate, and when the wife sent him to the supermarket he would match the shapes of the letters on her shopping list with the labels of the items on the shelf. He was also without papers; the couple had taken his documents shortly after he entered the United States.

According to Elaine, the husband—who was well educated, "very cultured, and somewhat passive"—had little to do with the servant, so long as he did what was expected of him. The wife, on the other hand, strenuously controlled all aspects of the young man's life. At one point, she decided it was time he married, so she arranged for friends back in India to send one of their servants to Massachusetts as a wife for her "boy." The couple themselves had an arranged marriage, and an unsuccessful one, as it turned out. The wife was especially unhappy and would take her anger out on her servant. She was, in Elaine's words, "nasty, a dragon woman," whose goal was not the happiness or fulfillment of her servant but rather the total control over a fellow being and the acquisition of a free pair of hands in the house.

When the female servant arrived from India and was wed to the young man, the mistress cleared a small space in the basement for the couple to live. What she didn't anticipate, and what infuriated her, was that the newlyweds actually fell in love. As Elaine describes it, "She was absolutely miserable over their happiness," so much so that when the young wife got pregnant, the mistress told them the baby had to be aborted.

The young couple was devastated. But it points up the psychological state of slaves that it never occurred to them to question or to protest this brutal command. As Elaine observed, "She had so much power over them. . . . I don't know what she was capable of. She's a bad, bad woman."

One evening, while attending a dinner at the house, Elaine saw the change that had taken place in the young man. Questioning him, she learned of the mistress's plans and of the young couple's misery. She arranged to meet with him secretly, and over the course of a long and stressful conversation she convinced him to take his wife and flee. Says Elaine, "Nothing they would encounter in the outside world could have been as horrible as what was happening to them in that house."

With some financial help from Elaine and her friends, the young man and his pregnant wife ran away to New York City, where, despite his lack of documents, he found a job in a food market. At this time, there were practically no organizations devoted to liberating and helping victims of slavery, and there is little likelihood the young man would have known where to look even if there had been. On finding that they had escaped, Elaine recalls, the mistress "went into a rage. She ranted and raved, and if she'd known where they'd gone, she would have pursued them." Elaine never let the woman know the brief, crucial role she'd played in providing the spark for this couple to find their freedom. "I still like to picture him," she says, "running a little restaurant or food market; he was so good with food."[4]

Out of Africa, into Colleyville

Sometimes Good Samaritans aren't even directly involved in rescuing victims of slavery but work to ensure that the liberated victim stays free and receives the love and guidance he or she so desperately needs. In chapter 5, you read about Given Kachepa, the remarkable young man who emerged from enslavement in a boys' choir to become a successful college student and a respected antitrafficking advocate and speaker. Now meet Sandy Shepherd, Given's legal guardian, de facto mother, and a true Good Samaritan.

Recall that Keith Grimes, a Baptist minister in Sherman, Texas, had gone to Zambia and brought home a number of boys' choirs—ostensibly to earn money with which to build schools and improve the lives of the boys' families in their home village of Kalingalinga. (In actuality, nearly all the money ended up in Grimes's pocket, with practically nothing finding its way back to Zambia.) In the early 1990s, after appointing himself pastor of the "Ministry of the Zambian Acapella Boys' Choir," Grimes converted a barn for offices, housed the boys in trailers, and went looking for venues where they could perform. He first focused on the churches. In 1996, he contacted the First Baptist Church of Colleyville, a town outside Dallas. No one in the congregation was more enthused about hosting the choir than Sandy Shepherd.

Sandy was, and is, a devoted churchgoer. She had been deeply involved in church activities since she was very young; in 1969, she had helped write a ministry program called Early Christian Awareness, for children between the ages of six months and three years. She married IBM executive Walter Deetz Shepherd and spent several years moving her family to various cities, both within and outside Texas. Finally, she and Deetz moved to the affluent, predominantly white town of Colleyville, and in 1990 they built a house and settled in with their three daughters. Nothing in her or Deetz's life prepared them for what was to follow.

When the choir was booked to sing in Colleyville, Sandy took on the task of finding "host families"—members of the congregation who would be willing to put up the boys while they were in the area. Sandy herself took in two of the boys only two days after her oldest daughter's wedding. They didn't speak much English, and, as Sandy recalls, "They didn't understand the electric lights, or the bathroom fixtures. They expected to sleep on the floor."[5]

Sandy's church hosted five concerts within a short time, and "by this time, I was hooked. I volunteered, and made lots and lots of calls to find them concerts and host families. I wrote a curriculum for their teacher, since it was obvious that they were getting no education." As it turned out, that wasn't all they weren't getting.

When the boys returned later in the year, their language skills had improved enough for them to make Sandy understand that something was wrong. There was little or no money being sent home, no schools were being built; and the education the boys had been promised had simply never materialized. Further, she discovered that other host families were writing letters to the boys and enclosing telephone calling cards so that they could call their relatives in Zambia, or the host families with whom they had built relationships, but that Grimes was commandeering the calling cards and throwing all the letters away before the boys saw them.

Grimes hired a series of two-person teams—a voice teacher and a choir director—to tour with the boys. The first teams were Zambian. Initially, the teams enforced Grimes's rules, until—one by one—they grew disillusioned over the treatment of the boys and the hypocrisy of Grimes's operation and quit. To an observer, on the surface everything looked all right; Grimes bought the boys uniforms and a school bus to get them to their venues. And, as Sandy recalls, "to hear him speak, you could never believe he'd do anything wrong." But those boys who dared to question him were labeled troublemakers and sent home in disgrace, and new recruits were brought over. It was a juggling act in which Grimes let the parents—and the village community at large—know that the returned boys had been "bad, disobedient, and disrespectful" and that the boys selected to replace them, the "good" choirboys, should avoid all contact with those who had been expelled. As for the parents, "They believed the white pastor, in the white suit, on his proverbial white horse." Some parents were so ashamed of their sons' "misconduct" that they refused to allow their children back home. As a result, some of the boys, whose only offense had been questioning their treatment by Keith Grimes, became homeless.

As Grimes continued to rotate boys for the choir, his rules became increasingly stringent. The boys were regularly awakened at 4:30 a.m., and if there was no time to eat before the bus left they went hungry. They did all the physical work to set up for their concerts, gave their performances, then struck the set afterwards. As Grimes made more and more money from the choir's performances, their treatment worsened. Gifts—items such as clothing and sneakers—that had been given or sent to the boys by their host families were confiscated. The boys were systematically searched for "contraband."

Sandy, thus far unaware of the extent of the maltreatment, decided that new host families would benefit from a guidebook that detailed the boys' history—places they'd visited, foods they liked—so she wrote a host booklet, which was distributed by the boys to the families in the communities where they sang. The host families, who had been hearing from the boys themselves about Grimes's treatment of them, began to annotate the booklets, passing them on to the next families with notes about what they'd learned. When Grimes found out, he confiscated the booklets and forbade their further distribution.

Congregations hosting the choir were becoming increasingly concerned but didn't think these were criminal offenses. After all, says Sandy, "it was a Christian ministry!" After a while Sandy realized that Grimes was a charlatan, and she was resolved to make things better for the boys. Then one boy in the choir was rushed to the hospital by a host family; he was seriously ill with tuberculosis. It became apparent that Grimes had not tested the boys for either TB or HIV/AIDS, two illnesses common to their part of Africa; he claimed to have been "too busy." Sandy responded by closing the First Baptist Church to concerts and home stays until all the boys had been given a clean bill of health. When the Board of Health tested them, twenty-one of the twenty-six boys skin-tested positive for tuberculosis. The state of Texas provided the boys with a free six-month course of medicine, requiring constant supervision, which Keith Grimes was clearly not willing to provide. Within a short time of the diagnosis, he had sent the entire twenty-six-boy choir back to Africa, a few at a time, and brought over another group—this choir containing the eleven-year-old orphan Given Kachepa and ten other boys. He also made plans to bring over one hundred more boys, whom he would house in RVs when on the road (to avoid all contact with host families), and tour the entire country. He put out an impressive marketing effort and raised significant contributions and commitments from across the country. An extraordinary self-promoter, Grimes still found a welcome in many churches, schools, and shopping malls. At one point, Grimes assembled a choir of blind boys from Liberia, with whom he briefly toured, and whom he also abused, until his sponsor got a sense of Grimes's practices, took the boys away, and cut off his funding.

Sandy's First Baptist Church was no longer among the organizations that welcomed Grimes or the choir. Feeling that "it was wrong to let the ministry continue to exploit the boys," she was instrumental in closing the church's doors to Grimes. Comparing notes with others who had contact with Grimes, Sandy called the FBI to request an investigation, while others wrote to the governor and lieutenant governor of Texas, their state and national senators and representatives, the then–attorney general Janet Reno, and Oprah Winfrey. The FBI responded that they saw no reason to pursue an investigation; there were no other replies.

When he got wind of the attempts to investigate his ministry, Keith Grimes was furious. He began to harass Sandy and her pastor and, with the help of his daughter and son-in-law, kept the church families from visiting or speaking with the boys. Calls to Grimes's "ministry" were neither answered nor returned, and the attempts made by Sandy and her friends to help or liberate the boys apparently came to nothing.

By late 1998, Sandy was completely frustrated; believing she could do nothing further for the boys in the choir, she turned her attention to creating the school in Kalingalinga that Grimes had promised years before. She resolved to provide an education for the twenty-six boys who had been sent home in disgrace. With contributions from hundreds of people, Sandy and a few others formed a committee that rented a small building in the village. They hired a teacher and put a sign over the door, reading "Chifundo Junior and High School." In Nyanja—the boys' native language—*chifundo* means "grace." The committee intended to keep the school open for at least three years. The initial contributions paid for books, supplies, rent, and the teacher's salary, in addition to a $15 "soap money" fee for each of the boys who attended the school. Of the original twenty-six boys, twenty-four went to the Chifundo School.

At the end of the three-year period, some of the boys had graduated, and Sandy's committee opened the enrollment to community children. But the contributions were running out, and the school stood in danger of closing. Then a member of Sandy's congregation died and left a generous bequest to build a bigger, better-equipped, and permanent Chifundo School. By 2008 the committee was holding architectural plans and awaiting the approval of the Zambian Minister of Education so they could start construction. The Zambian boys will be working to help build the school, which will offer two classrooms and a computer lab for grades eight through twelve.

Keith Grimes's death from brain cancer and the operation of his ministry by his daughter and son-in-law have been described in chapter 5, as well as his daughter's attempt—foiled by the Immigration and Naturalization Service (INS)—to have four of the boys from the last group deported as "troublemakers." While an INS agent was busy investigating the ministry, the other seven boys contacted him, saying, in effect, "Come get us, we quit."

The agent had placed the original four boys with local families while he conducted his investigation; now suddenly, he had seven more on his hands. He called Sandy's pastor and asked if anyone in the congregation could house the seven boys. The pastor immediately phoned Sandy, whose first reaction was "Why am I being called again? I've closed that door!" But she agreed to help, and because of the urgency she took in all seven boys, keeping them for five days while finding other host families.

The boys were beyond terrified. To keep them in line, Grimes and his family had filled their heads with stories about the cruelty of the American police and had told them that the Colleyville congregation was "wicked" and would abuse them. Grimes had saved the worst vilification for Sandy, categorizing her as a "cruel witch." Sandy knew nothing of this, and as she recalls, "When the boys met me, they thought they were doomed!" They had come out of slavery, and now they feared worse.

While Sandy had the boys as houseguests, the INS agent dropped off seven fourteen-page depositions—one for each of them to fill out. However, since they couldn't read or write, the task fell to Sandy.

Meanwhile, it became necessary for Sandy to install caller ID on her phone in order to warn her when the Grimes family tried to reach the boys—which they often did. Going around to her neighbors she found the boys odd jobs—doing yard work, painting fences—to keep them busy and earn a little money. There were many meetings with the INS agent and health officials, and many of the boys needed inoculations and medical exams. In time, the boys were given "deferred action" status, which granted them social security cards and picture IDs, so that they could work. With their status resolved, Sandy began contacting families who had known the boys when they were touring, trying to arrange more permanent living situations. It took three months, but she managed to find good homes for all seven. Finally, Sandy thought, she could catch her breath.

At this point Given was thirteen, and he and an older cousin went to live with a woman in Childress, Texas. He had been orphaned at nine and had lived in Kalingalinga with his cousin's family until Keith Grimes brought him to Texas two years later. Now he had made new friends, owned his own bike, and was looking forward to attending school. Then suddenly the woman sent Given to visit Sandy "for a few days" and followed up with a letter telling Sandy that the responsibility of raising two boys was too great and that she couldn't handle it. Given was homeless again. His cousin was immediately taken in by a former host family in St. Louis, leaving Given uprooted, without friends or family, in the home of a woman he'd been indoctrinated to fear and hate. Sandy was in the throes of preparing her two younger daughters to go away to college— one for the first time—and she and Deetz had been looking forward to the quiet of an "empty nest." All at once, after having raised three girls, she was responsible for an emotionally ravaged adolescent boy who refused to communicate or even come out of his room. After much deliberation, Sandy told Given he could stay through Christmas. She enrolled him in eighth grade, but the boy found it hard going. Sandy proceeded to spend four to six hours a night, every night, helping him with his homework. And as she says, "My heart changed through the fall." By the time Christmas came, there was no way she would give him up. In the spring, the Shepherds became Given's legal guardians. (They offered adoption, but he preferred to keep his Zambian citizenship.)

Their life together was far from easy. The Shepherds had no idea what was coming next. They feared deportation for Given, as well as other legal problems. The TVPA was brand new, and its provisions were not well known or tested. Sandy set about researching what legal services were available to trafficking victims and applied for a T visa—not just for Given but for several of the other boys as well. Given was awarded his T visa in August 2003; had he not received it, it is likely he would have been deported.

Perhaps hardest of all—on Given and on the Shepherds—was Given's period of adjustment. It combined the painful growth processes of a teenage boy, which the Shepherds had never experienced firsthand, with separation from his cousin, who was his lifeline and his only real family in America. He was also suffering from post-traumatic stress disorder. Given had been a slave, and like many freed slaves he was having a hard time dealing with what had happened to him. "There were times," says Sandy, "where I thought we were going to lose Given, and times when I thought he was going to lose us. We feared he would run away."

Then came the turning point. When Given was sixteen, Sandy took him to a human trafficking conference in Austin, and—after listening to several speakers postulate on how to find and approach victims of trafficking—Given spoke up for the first time as a survivor of modern-day slavery. He so impressed his listeners that he was invited to address the Texas Committee on Jurisprudence. Shortly after that he appeared on the TV news program *Nightline*. Other speaking engagements and appearances followed, and suddenly this troubled high school student had become a respected, sought-after spokesperson on human trafficking. And along the way, he found his inner peace. As Sandy states, "He moved from being a victim to being a survivor." Talking about his experiences helped Given to understand and deal with the trauma he had suffered. He now divides his time between school—he's received a number of scholarships and is studying to become a dentist—and touring the country, addressing colleges, NGOs, and government organizations. Wherever he goes, Sandy accompanies him with support and encouragement. He calls her his mother, and the Shepherds see Given as part of their family. In the most literal sense of the word, Sandy didn't actually *free* Given; but on a much deeper level, she did.

From Massage Parlor to Human Trafficking Activism

Sarah Schell (not her real name) is a remarkable young woman. In 1995, when she was a young teenager, her upper-middle-class parents moved to a major East Coast city to work for a prominent congressman while she remained at home in Brattleboro, Vermont. Living on her own, Sarah earned excellent grades in high school, along with an advanced placement degree. She began to make plans for college but found that she lacked the tuition. Then, on a visit to her parents, she happened to see an ad in the city's newspaper, offering foreign or American college girls work in a massage parlor. "I was naive," she recalls, "that a reputable newspaper would run such an ad."[6] Sarah interviewed with the woman who ran the place, and she took the job. She kept it for nearly ten years. "I made lots of money, and put it towards college. That's how I justified what I did. Nowadays, I'd have been classified as a trafficking victim when I started, because I was underage." But in the mid-1990s, there was no trafficking law in place, so she was merely a young coed, moonlighting in the sex trade.

While working at the massage parlor, Sarah became aware of another operation just upstairs, offering older Asian women for a much lower price. "I was averaging around $600 take-home a day, and these women were only charging $60 per one-hour session. They were given half, and from that, the 'mama-san' who controlled them deducted all sorts of fees—for towels, food, everything. They were making next to nothing." Because of the Asian women's lesser status, Sarah's colleagues looked down on and ridiculed them.

Sarah recalls, "I felt bad for them. We shared a security camera—so that we'd always know when the clients, or the cops, were coming in— and I'd always smile and wave. Then one day, a client of one of the Asian women threw up in our common lounge, and I helped the woman clean it up. She smiled and thanked me, but when she went back upstairs, I heard the sounds of her being beaten. The mama-san used a big wooden spoon to beat her girls, and the sound was very sharp, very distinct. She was being punished for having contact with me."

Sarah's earnings went toward college, where she took courses in negotiation, mediation, crisis management, and human trafficking. "Until then, I was mostly curious, I befriended them." But the more she learned, the clearer it became to her that the Asian women were enslaved. "They never left; the mama-san did all the grocery shopping. They slept in the same space where they worked, they were being paid practically nothing, and the mama-san beat them regularly. And when the police raided the place and arrested the women, a cab would pull up and deliver four or five more, each carrying a single suitcase."

Sarah realized that she wanted to do more for trafficked women, so—while still working at the massage parlor—she volunteered with a local antitrafficking group. "I never told them exactly what I did for a living, that I was still very much 'in the life'; I just said I was a nude dancer; that seemed okay to me. I let them know that I was friends with people in the sex trade and could serve as something of an expert." As a volunteer, Sarah performed direct outreach services, speaking to women from their teens up to their mid-twenties, giving them printed material, and asking trafficking-related questions. "Because I'm white, the organization only wanted me to work with the Caucasian women, but they all seemed to relate to me well."

Sarah makes it clear that her goal at this time was not to free enslaved women: "When I volunteering, I wasn't after freeing prostitutes. I just wanted them to be able to *keep* the money they earned. I mean if they had to do this kind of work, then at least they should be paid for it, as women empowered." One prostitute with whom Sarah worked, aged fifteen or sixteen, was not a good fit at the NGO shelter: "She already had a baby, whom her pimp had taken, her personal hygiene was poor, she was a habitual liar, and she communicated with her pimp, which put the shelter in jeopardy." So the girl had to leave, but when she needed a place to stay, Sarah shared her apartment with her. "I wanted to get her away from her pimp. Aside from taking her kid, he put her in the hospital on a number of occasions and kept most of what she made. I just wanted her to make her money and live her life."

When asked how she came to leave "the life," Sarah responds, "I didn't leave it; it left me!" The massage parlor was raided so often that the owner, sensing that the feds were closing in, closed her doors. "I was really lucky. I was never arrested, never used my real name. As I look back, I realize the woman I worked for was trafficking minors into prostitution. She's now under federal indictment." When the woman was indicted, Sarah's former co-workers, whom she still considers good friends, became alarmed and came to her for counsel—because she had gone to college. Sarah advised them that the government was pursuing cases of human trafficking and had no interest in them.

Sarah, now in her mid-twenties, made a remarkable career decision. Rather than continue in her present life, she chose to make a career working against human trafficking. "When I was 'working,' I was trying to help people; now, I just wanted to carry it on." Believing that the police are "the ones with the power to do something," she went straight to a large organization concerned with the legal affairs and applied for a job. The TVPA had already been passed and reauthorized, and the organization was including trafficking among its public awareness programs. Sarah was hired, and for the past few years she has been in charge of programs concerned with human trafficking. When you call the organization and ask what they're doing in the area of human trafficking, Sarah is the person you'll talk with. Along the way, she earned a master's degree from a major university.

Sarah Schell has covered a lot of ground from underage sex worker in a massage parlor to heading up antitrafficking programs. But she didn't come out of it unscathed. "Anyone who's been in the sex industry comes away with scars," she states. "I still suffer from depression, and I've been diagnosed with PTSS [post-traumatic stress syndrome]. I used to hate being thought of as a survivor—not of trafficking, but of exploitation—but now I realize that it's better to be a survivor than a victim."

TAKE IT UP A NOTCH

Good Samaritans like Elaine Fletcher, Sandy Shepherd, and Sarah Schell would not admit to being anyone special. Yes, they have saved lives and brought freedom to slaves, but ask them about what they have done and they tend to say something like, "Oh come on, *anyone* would do that in the same situation!" They are average citizens confronting something new and dangerous; they're not blind to the danger, but their focus is on the human being in front of them. For most Good Samaritans that focus is combined with a big heart, determination, sensitivity, and common sense. These are self-deprecating, even reluctant heroes in the battle against slavery, but heroes nonetheless. We owe them thanks and support, but grassroots volunteers and well-intentioned individuals can't stop slavery in America by themselves. Ending slavery means that communities have to make collective conscious decisions. Fortunately, many American communities, in the absence of national leadership, have done just that. Some of these are physical communities, others are the virtual communities we share on the Internet, but what they have in common is the conviction that they don't wait for someone else to end the suffering of slaves in America.

In many towns and cities, faith communities have taken the lead. Mark Massey was a lay minister at a small Pentecostal Church in Tulsa, Oklahoma. This was not a rich church; anyone could see that just by its location, facing an oil pipeline welding factory that took up a whole city block. One weekend the church had visitors. Massey explains: "It's a little country-type church and they came into the church one Sunday morning, and you could tell they were kind of uneasy." Two men from India sat in the back for the service, and afterwards Massey approached them. As a lay minister he had done outreach to homeless people and taught English to migrants. He welcomed them to the church and asked how they came to be in Tulsa. The men shied away, suspicious of his interest, but Mark gently stuck with them and they came back to the church again. Over time they came to trust Mark, and from them a remarkable story unfolded.

The owner of the oil pipeline company was a man named John Pickle. Pressured by competition from overseas companies, he had devised a scheme to bring highly skilled welders from India to America under a visa program listing them as "trainees." Dazzled with promises of high wages, comfortable working conditions, and great opportunities, thirty men chose to come to America. Members of the middle class in India, they paid a recruitment fee amounting to a year's salary at home and arrived at the factory in Tulsa. At the factory they were ushered into a warehouse that had been converted into barracks. Here, bunk beds were crammed together, two toilets served for everyone, and there were no tables or chairs. But what most concerned many of the men was the heavy steel door that was the only entrance.

As time passed control over the men increased; guards kept them on the factory grounds, and they were often locked in. Food was in short supply and of poor quality. But in a strange way, and not uncommon among traffickers, Pickle had convinced himself that he was doing these poor men from a poor country a favor. One way he showed his benevolence was to allow a few of the men to go to Massey's church.

In conversations after services, Massey learned more about the men's lives. He says that at first "I thought I must have misunderstood them."[7] Their strong accents, plus some of the workers' poor grasp of English, sometimes made communication hit or miss. In time, Massey asked a friend who had originally come from India to come and translate. Then the whole story came out, and Massey told them that if things got unbearable he would help as best he could. Shortly afterward Pickle said he was going to deport some of the men who had complained about the conditions; they called Massey. That night he parked next to the factory as men began to sneak away, crawling under the fence and rushing to his van. One of the men Massey had not met before; the man told him that he was not a Christian, like the men who had attended church, but a Hindu. "Will you help me?" he asked. "Of course," replied Massey.

In time, fifty-four men were freed from the factory, and a local lawyer began to build a case for back wages. No government office or law enforcement agency got involved, and Massey began to devote all his time to the care of these trafficked workers. He moved his own family out of their big house and into a smaller rental house that they owned in order to give fifty-two of the men a place to live. In his own church, Massey says, "We didn't become popular for doing this or praised really, there's been a lot of hurt. . . . Our churches have been good to help foreign missions, but when the foreign comes into our own comfort area, we're not ready to accept. There were some ministers . . . that felt that it wasn't God's will that I did what I did." Fortunately, other churches, individuals, and charities felt otherwise and began to work together to support the Indian workers. When Robert Canino, a lawyer from the Equal Employment Opportunities Commission, joined the case, the power of government finally arrived on the scene. At first, Canino had to work hard to convince his bosses that employment law was an appropriate way to fight human trafficking. In the process of winning the Pickle case, he set new standards and was later named "Lawyer of the Year" for his breakthrough. In 2003 Pickle was found liable and still owes millions to the Indian men, many of whom have remained in the United States on a special visa.

Many other faith communities have stepped up to help. On Long Island, New York, a couple trafficked sixty-nine people from Peru into forced labor. They were crammed into a suburban home and then placed with a number of businesses, working in a plant nursery, even a cannoli factory. For these workers, freedom came in part from their contact with Catholic charities. They worked tirelessly with the service provider Safe Horizon to find housing and services for the victims. And in San Francisco, Jewish organizations came together to create the Jewish Coalition to End Human Trafficking. They work with the San Francisco District Attorney's Office and promote the passage of strong antitrafficking legislation.[8]

THE COP ON THE (TRAFFICKING) BEAT

In chapter 2, you read how a policeman made his own antitrafficking video to help train other officers. Around the country law enforcement personnel are often the first to encounter cases of modern slavery. When they do, they regularly reach out to the only experts nearby, the faith communities and service providers who are also on the front line. This is most likely to occur where the problem is most prevalent. In Florida's Panhandle, an area rife with human trafficking, the sheriffs of four counties—Escambia, Santa Rosa, Okaloosa, and Walton—formed their own human trafficking task force to investigate "organized criminal enterprises that engage in worker exploitation, . . . labor fraud, . . . identification document fraud and commercial sexual exploitation of minors." Their aim, when they discover human trafficking, is to refer the case to "the appropriate federal agency for prosecution."[9]

Some officers simply come to the decision that finding and liberating trafficking victims is just something they have to do. The Hillsborough County Sheriff's Office in Tampa, Florida, boasts 1,200 officers; since March 2006, two of them have devoted themselves to pursuing human trafficking cases. The point person, Detective Jason Van Brunt of the Criminal Intelligence Unit, had been working computer crime and decided he needed a change. The Crime Prevention Section of the department had been doing "show and tell" presentations on human trafficking. Van Brunt got them to let him take some of their materials out into the community. With a representative of a local faith-based group, he began visiting the Hispanic churches in the area. After services, antitrafficking workers and Van Brunt would speak to the congregation. Van Brunt would ask—through a translator—if people knew of trafficking situations or possible victims. Within a short time, he was getting calls reporting possible trafficking cases.

Since Van Brunt's unit doesn't handle sex-related crimes, he "went down the hall to the Vice guys, to partner up." From then on, when the Vice Unit raided a brothel, Van Brunt and his partner went along to look for human trafficking. Soon he was recruiting informants to probe both labor and sex trafficking. "Most people in that world," he said, "see trafficking and pay no attention to it. It gets confusing."[10]

Van Brunt, who describes himself as "proactive," joined a local human trafficking task force. Funded by a Department of Justice (DOJ) grant, it grew larger. Van Brunt also expanded his work doing antitrafficking presentations at the obligatory annual in-service training for all officers. In his presentation, he explains how to recognize the signs of slavery and focuses on a crucial aspect of the process—the victim interview. "Most law enforcement officers," he observes, "are after admissions or confessions. Interviewing a possible victim of human trafficking is totally different. These are skills that have to be taught. I tell them, 'Know your limitations. If it's not in you, bring in someone else.'"[11] He welcomes the presence of a victim advocate to assist in an interview. After his second presentation, an officer with a possible trafficking case contacted Van Brunt.

By 2008, Van Brunt and his partner had uncovered and pursued five slavery cases—two relating to sex trafficking and three to forced labor.[12]

One involves a Tampa resident, Marcelino Guillen Jaimes, accused of smuggling a Mexican into Florida for a transportation fee of $2,000 and then forcing him into a construction job working seven days a week, ten hours a day, to pay off his debt.[13] But Van Brunt expresses frustration with local prosecutors. "In my judicial circuit," he explains, "not a single prosecutor belongs to the trafficking task force. No one can possibly know all the laws; still it would be nice if at least one attorney was familiar with the state trafficking statutes."[14]

The International Association of Chiefs of Police (IACP) is committed to training and motivating law enforcement on human trafficking. The IACP works to improve the standards and practices of over eighteen thousand police departments nationwide. It offers training seminars, as well as booklets and a handbook on how to recognize and approach human trafficking cases. The challenge of human trafficking, according to an official at IACP who asked not to be named, "is a fairly new one to us. Most policemen believe slavery ended with the Thirteenth Amendment. They feel it can't happen here; it's hard for them to wrap their heads around."

Local cops and their departments have broken big slavery cases, but many in local law enforcement feel that trafficking is a federal affair and that they lack local and state jurisdiction. With the passage of state laws, the same IACP official explained, "it has now become their beat. But still, the awareness and training are missing. Without adequate training, they're not seeing or understanding the crime." And although some city police departments—Houston, San Diego, Atlanta, Seattle, El Paso are good examples—have dedicated significant resources to addressing trafficking, most are "unaware. They frankly don't know what it is. And when they find out, they are easily overwhelmed with the huge need for resources—money, manpower, and time—to wage a successful campaign." With training, however, police "often take it as an opportunity to free people. It can be so satisfying. But the training needs to get out there, and the feds simply aren't putting it there."

Many local police forces are scrambling to find—or invent their own—antislavery training. But for every police department and sheriff's office trying to get a handle on the problem, there are perhaps thousands that remain untrained and unmotivated. Unless local law enforcement takes an active interest in detecting and eliminating human trafficking, protecting the survivors, and punishing the bad guys, and until the federal government beefs up and expands its training programs, the number of prosecutions will remain in the hundreds, while thousands of cases will remain undetected, and the victims will stay hidden and enslaved.

THE THREE "R'S"—RESEARCH, RESCUE, AND RESTORE

It may not be the first place you would expect to find them, but schools and universities have also emerged as leaders in the fight against slavery. In July 2007, Florida Gulf Coast University established the Esperanza Center for Human Trafficking Research, Policy and Community Initiatives, a "national human-trafficking center on campus to block the flow of sex slaves and abused laborers into the country." The center aims to coordinate the several agencies that are "already active in preventing and prosecuting what often is dubbed modern-day slavery." Both federal and grant funding support the center. Florida could use the help. According to Fort Myers–based chief assistant U.S. attorney Doug Molloy, "Southwest Florida has more trafficking cases than many states." He should know; in 2007 Molloy and his staff were working eleven active cases, which ran the gamut from sex and domestic slavery to indentured servitude in the workplace.[15]

It took the arrest of two people for the sex trafficking of two young girls, aged thirteen and seventeen, to awaken Nashville, Tennessee from its complacency—and move Middle Tennessee State University to action. As trafficking cases go it was not unusual: physical force and threats were used against the girls and their families to get them to submit to prostitution. But it made quick work of the attitude that "it can't happen here." A June 2007 newspaper article stated, "People expect to read about it in magazines or watch a prime-time news show special report. But human trafficking in Nashville? It seems unlikely at best." Responding to the case, Middle Tennessee State University hosted a panel discussion on trafficking, featuring two local women who had "long . . . been working to raise public awareness." One was Amber Beckham, coordinator for World Relief's Network of Emergency Trafficking Services, who had provided training to the Nashville police, teaching them to spot cases they would otherwise have missed. Beckham earned high marks with the police. Sergeant Brooks Harris of Nashville's Specialized Investigations Unit explained, "She's bringing us to a keen awareness of the problem and the indicators to be on the lookout for. . . . She's teaching us to take another four or five minutes to dig a little deeper."[16]

One of America's most innovative local antislavery groups is the Rescue and Restore Coalition of Houston, Texas. The coalition has brought together businesses, student groups, religious groups and churches, and community service organizations such as domestic violence shelters. A broad base is important because Houston is not only a well-known point of entry for human traffickers but the site of large-scale slavery cases as well. One of these, the Mondragon case, had more than one hundred victims, most trafficked into sexual exploitation. In collecting information from the victims, the coalition discovered an important fact. "We found that 80 percent of the victims reported being in clubs, bars, or shops where alcohol was sold," explained Stephanie Weber of the coalition, "and we started thinking about how to reach people in that way."[17] In a bold move, the coalition convinced the state legislature to pass a law requiring every business where alcohol is sold to post a bilingual sign listing the national hotline number and an assurance of anonymity, along with a message stating that "obtaining forced labor or services is a crime." After the signs went up and all alcohol beverage control agents received training, the national hotline reported a sharp increase in calls from Houston. By late 2008, Weber reported, "even restaurants and coffee shops that aren't required to put up the sign are posting it."[18]

The coalition also faced the problem of law enforcement investigations that went nowhere. In the large Latino community, there was fear that cooperation with police might lead to deportations, and good tips would be met with stony silence. Six neighborhoods were identified where trafficking cases were likely but underreported. To reach out, the coalition designed a dramatic billboard message: "Stop Modern Day Slavery in Houston," read the headline next to a picture of a young woman, then "Save a Victim of Human Trafficking Today," followed by the national hotline number. Thanks to a printing company in the coalition and a discount from the billboard supplier, ninety large-scale billboards went up in the Houston area, especially near the six neighborhoods with the lowest response rate. In a follow-up effort, similar signs are now being placed on the backs of taxicabs for the next three years. The total cost of these efforts has been low because of the breadth of the coalition; the impact, however, has been significant.

When students and staff at Denver University formed a Task Force on Modern Slavery and Human Trafficking in early 2005, action against human trafficking picked up rapidly. With a base in the university, the task force expanded to cover other organizations, provided training to law enforcement, and moved new laws onto the books. A key player in this work was Claude d'Estrée, a law professor and Buddhist chaplain at the university. D'Estrée was used to hands-on work: with the Red Cross he had coordinated the response at the crash site of Flight 93 on September 11, 2001, and was later recognized for it in a Rose Garden ceremony at the White House. Denver University students under his tutelage became spark plugs, and with others they helped create a Colorado Human Trafficking Task Force and a statewide Network to Eliminate Human Trafficking, as well as to support and advise the Colorado State Patrol's new unit responsible for human trafficking. These and other initiatives, including effective victim identification and support, are carried out in Colorado in cooperation with the Polaris Project.

The role of colleges and universities has been crucial in raising awareness and helping to bring communities together. For example, Free the Slaves, the international antislavery organization based in Washington, D.C., sends speakers to dozens of universities each year, coordinating workshops and advising local and state politicians. Students and teachers are good at getting information before the public, but awareness is just step one. Once achieved, knowledge needs to be put into action, and other groups have been organizing and reinventing themselves to fight slavery in America.

AN EFFECTIVE WEB OF SERVICE PROVIDERS

We've seen how dissension and sometimes downright bitterness exists among many antitrafficking groups. Profound and seemingly insoluble issues relating to policy, philosophy, funding, religion, and the place and performance of government keep organizations from working together, in spite of their shared avowed goal to eradicate human trafficking. Battle lines have been drawn around such questions as the nature of prostitution, the conditions placed on the distribution of money and services, and the very definitions of trafficking and slavery. Such infighting hurts the efforts of these organizations.

This is why it is important to point to a nationwide group of independent service provider organizations that have joined together as the Freedom Network. Formed in early 2001, they are, by their own definition, a coalition of over thirty "non-governmental organizations that provide services to, and advocate for the rights of, trafficking survivors in the United States." Formed not long after the passage of the TVPA in

2000, the Freedom Network works "closely with trafficked persons to ensure that they receive necessary services," and is "engaged in monitoring the implementation of the law."[19]

Florrie Burke, formerly senior director of International Programs at Safe Horizon in New York, credits Lou de Baca with bringing them together.[20] De Baca, who has worn several hats within the DOJ—including involuntary servitude and slavery coordinator, special litigation counsel, chief counsel for the Human Trafficking Prosecutions Unit of the DOJ's Civil Rights Division, and most recently, counsel to the Committee on the Judiciary—was actively involved in virtually every major slavery case that came to light in the 1990s. "I was the vector," he recalls, "the 'Typhoid Mary' of trafficking. I'd worked on everybody's cases—Flores, Ramos, El Monte, the Deaf Mexicans."[21] In early 1998, the DOJ hosted a focus group on trafficking, and de Baca brought together people he had worked with in the different trafficking cases. It made sense, he felt, to introduce them to each other. And when various government agencies began training sessions, it was through de Baca's influence that "we used the folk from the NGOs as instructors."[22]

In 2001, the DOJ's Office for Victims of Crime held their annual conference, and for the first time trafficking was on the agenda. On the panel were such antitrafficking pioneers as senior State Department advisor Amy O'Neil Richard, Maria Jose Fletcher of the Florida Immigrant Advocacy Center (FIAC), and Florrie Burke of Safe Horizon. With so many antitrafficking groups in Washington for the conference, it was the perfect opportunity to come together and look to the future. Ann Jordan, then-director of the Initiative against Trafficking in Persons at Global Rights, convened a meeting in her office that was attended by around twenty professionals. They talked about what each was doing, and discussed how they could be of help to each other.[23]

This handful of organizations decided to form a network of groups that shared the same philosophy and provided direct services to survivors of trafficking. It has grown to include thirty organizations nationwide. In the words of Florrie Burke, "We started small; there weren't that many NGOs back then. The network was loose, and it remains loose to this day. Our strength is in providing services, backed up by solid experience. We're here on the ground—as opposed to those relying only on research and philosophy."[24]

In 2003, with a three-year grant from the Department of Health and Human Services (HHS), the Freedom Network created the spin-off Freedom Network Institute to provide training on human trafficking. It consists of seven of the member agencies, who have created a training curriculum entitled "Human Trafficking and Slavery: Tools for an Effective Response."[25] This program was the first standardized curriculum on trafficking awareness and regional action, and from the beginning the response from law enforcement, government agencies, and service providers was very positive. The curriculum had, according to Florrie Burke, "ongoing technical assistance and capacity building to help people prepare to do and sustain this work structurally." It also featured a substantial resource section and a separate specialized program for law enforcement. Training was conducted by teams, consisting of a service provider, an attorney, a representative of the DOJ, and someone from local law enforcement. "We got really good feedback, especially from the FBI and local police." The courses were taught in a modular fashion, and ended with manuals for the attendees. "Unless you attended the sessions, you didn't get a manual."[26]

By late 2007, thousands of people had attended the courses, and it remains unique. If the institute is criticized for anything, it's for placing its emphasis on foreign-born victims at the expense of domestic victims. However, from the earliest days of the TVPA, the law has applied primarily—and in some instances, solely—to foreign-born victims, and this is where HHS mandated that the institute concentrate its energies. By 2007, the institute was funded entirely by private grants and was updating its curriculum to incorporate domestic trafficking as well. The new, broader approach is also state and region specific: a training program given in New York by Safe Horizon will encompass an understanding of New York State statutes, while an antitrafficking group doing training in Miami will address Florida's laws and how they apply. "It's a great group of people," says Burke about the Freedom Network. "Everyone here is a worker bee. We have no time or money for PR, no glitzy materials, and little time to spend on the 'Hill.'"[27] Nonetheless, federal agencies have come to know and rely on the network.

POLICE UNDER THE MICROSCOPE

Research on American law enforcement sheds light on the widespread need for training like that offered by the Freedom Network. Barbara Stolz, author of a recent study on America's trafficking statutes, points out, "Most law enforcement responsibilities in the United States fall to state and local authorities. Ultimately, trafficking in persons crimes cannot be addressed solely by federal investigative agencies and prosecutors."[28]

Federal government staff cannot ferret out trafficking on our streets and in our communities; they are simply too far removed. That means local police—the "eyes and ears on the ground," as the IACP puts it—must be involved. They are in the perfect position to recognize and address both labor and sex trafficking.

The problem is that most local law enforcement officers don't know any more about modern-day slavery than you do (or did, until you began this book). And those officers who actually do have some awareness of it generally haven't been trained to detect it or to work appropriately with victims. More often than not, they'll miss the signs and mistake a trafficking victim for an illegal alien. Too often, the result is jail and/or deportation. To get a better understanding of this situation, in 2005 the National Institute of Justice funded a study of human trafficking awareness and activity among the nation's police forces. Jack McDevitt and Amy Farrell at Northeastern University's Institute on Race and Justice carried out the study. Both have worked in the area of racial profiling, and they share an interest in gender injustice in the criminal justice system.[29]

The Northeastern survey—"Understanding and Improving Law Enforcement Responses to Human Trafficking"—extended over a two-year period and took as its subjects the chiefs of the nation's police forces or their designees. It also documented the "experiences of multi-agency human trafficking task forces"—the forty-two federally structured groups designed to "help local, state and territorial law enforcement agencies partner with the U.S. Attorney's Office and victim service agencies to ensure a victim-centered response to human trafficking locally."[30]

The report was designed to evaluate the present response of local, state, and county law enforcement to human trafficking and to describe the steps taken by local law enforcement to identify human trafficking. To determine effectiveness, it measured "how often identification of trafficking victims led to their rescue and the prosecution of traffickers." The survey's goal was to provide America's local law enforcement "with the necessary tools to successfully identify, investigate and prosecute cases of human trafficking."[31]

To answer these questions McDevitt and Farrell randomly sampled the country's roughly eighteen thousand police forces, which included municipal departments, county sheriffs' offices, and state police, as well as subsampling all 525 communities with populations over seventy-five thousand. In all, some three thousand agencies, including state police headquarters in all fifty states, 588 county sheriff's offices, and over 2,300 municipal law enforcement agencies, were surveyed.[32]

The task was daunting. Farrell explains, "The whole way in which trafficking is viewed by law enforcement differs from state to state. In the states with trafficking laws, it's a state crime, whereas in the other states, it's federal and requires partnering with federal agencies."[33]

The survey addressed four key questions. The first asked about the perceptions of trafficking held by law enforcement and what preparation agencies had taken to address the problem. The answer to this question was disappointing if not unexpected: "Generally, local law enforcement officials perceive human trafficking as rare or non-existent in their local communities. There is little difference in perceptions of sex trafficking versus labor trafficking among local law enforcement—both types are perceived as non-existent."[34] Larger communities were somewhat more likely to acknowledge human trafficking, though they were also more likely to focus on sex trafficking.[35]

The second question asked about the frequency with which law enforcement identified and investigated human trafficking cases. It turned out that about one in five of the nation's local, county, and state forces had "some type of human trafficking training," fewer than one in ten had a human trafficking protocol or policy, and only slightly more than 6 percent had created specialized units, or assigned personnel, to investigate trafficking cases. In the larger cities the numbers were somewhat higher. Only 7 percent of the agencies in the random survey had actually investigated a human trafficking case, with the numbers ranging considerably higher for the cities larger than 250,000. Farrell and McDevitt estimated from these figures that around nine hundred agencies in the country had investigated at least one trafficking case.[36]

If a law enforcement agency had investigated a trafficking case, they were requested to provide more information, but of those asked, only two-thirds responded. Their answers provided data for the third key research question: What were the number and characteristics of the human trafficking cases investigated? The results showed that the *over-all* number of trafficking cases investigated had grown significantly each year from 2000 to 2006 and that the average number of cases for each agency had risen from three in 2000, to eight in 2006. Nearly three-fourths of these agencies reported that they had only investigated a single *type* of case—sex or labor. Those who found sex cases in their area investigated them and tended to continue to investigate only sex cases; the same was true for the agencies that concentrated on labor trafficking. Of all agencies with trafficking cases, roughly a third had investigated only sex trafficking cases, a third only labor cases, and a third both. All agencies reported that more time *per case* was spent on sex trafficking investigations than on other crimes and that, not surprisingly, most sex trafficking victims were female and most labor trafficking victims were male.[37]

Finally, the fourth research question explored how human trafficking cases were investigated and prosecuted. Over half the respondent agencies reported uncovering human trafficking while investigating other types of crime such as drug offenses or domestic violence. Four out of five agencies indicated that the victim's appearance was "one of the most important indicators . . . particularly whether the victim appeared fearful and non-cooperative." And more than nine out of ten law enforcement agencies connected human trafficking to "other and existing criminal networks such as drug distribution or prostitution."[38]

Since 2000, a little over half the agencies that are investigating trafficking cases have actually brought charges. Of these, a third have filed federal charges, and of *these,* around 60 percent have actually prosecuted cases under the TVPA. Law enforcement agencies stated that "a large number of investigations do not result in arrests, but if an arrest is made" a conviction was likely. As a result, in the reported cases about a quarter of foreign victims received T visas, while roughly the same number were deported. The biggest obstacles to victims' cooperation were reported to be "fear of retaliation to themselves or their family" and "a lack of trust in the criminal justice system"—exactly the same characteristics used most frequently by police to help them identify trafficking victims.[39]

TASK FORCES

The study also set out to assess the federal antitrafficking task forces. Funded by the Bureau of Justice Assistance, the forty-two task forces were designed to incorporate specific government agencies—the DOJ, Immigration and Customs Enforcement (ICE), the FBI, and in some instances, the Department of Labor—along with state, county, and local law enforcement and various service providers and victim advocates. The idea was to bring all the players together in order "to ensure a victim-centered response to human trafficking locally."[40] The research found that the size, composition, and degree of success of each of the forty-two task forces varied depending on the number of service providers, victim advocates, and government agencies available, the amount of trafficking activity in their area, and the level of interest and commitment of the participants.[41] But it was clear that they had a significant effect on prosecutions. Law enforcement agencies affiliated with the antitrafficking task forces "were more than twice as likely to file federal charges (55 percent)" as those who were not (25 percent).[42] And with greater experience under their belts, they were also more likely to recognize human trafficking as a problem in their community, and to identify and pursue more cases, than non–task force agencies.[43]

The importance of these research results is that they show how initially local, state, and federal governments took action against human trafficking in a vacuum. There was little understanding of the crime, much less how best to attack it. It was and is a steep learning curve. This study is the first benchmark of clear results at the local level. Take, for example, the stories of three task forces, each addressing a "different dynamic of human trafficking." The Boston Police Department created its own system of identifying minors at risk of being trafficked for sexual purposes—a process that resulted in the rescue of several girls and the identification of many more. The Human Trafficking Rescue Alliance of Harris County, Texas, which focuses largely on the Houston area, established a set of rules designed to direct activity *after* victim identification has been made, thus getting the victim to the right place in the shortest time. They also agreed on an "emergency protocol"—for both law enforcement and service providers—that comes into effect when "immediate rescue of potential victims" is needed. And the Phoenix Task Force, responding to the severe human smuggling problem in their area, created a training program geared to understanding the differences between human trafficking and human smuggling, and how smuggling can easily become trafficking. This training program is now used nationwide.[44]

While there are success stories, the research also found that "multi-agency task forces struggle to overcome a number of obstacles," especially the sort you get when very different organizations with different goals start to work together. Other problems reflect the vague perceptions of human trafficking. Police, as Farrell says, will tend to look for the types of trafficking cases they expect to find. Law enforcement on the Washington, D.C., task force, for example, is represented by vice squad detectives, who generally look for and uncover sex trafficking. Adds Farrell, "Give someone a hammer, they'll find a nail." Also, there is the issue of "who's in charge." As Farrell puts it, "The degree of success relates directly to the level of leadership."[45] Local law enforcement is funded to convene the task force, but the leadership tends to fall to the DOJ, who are the ones who can direct activity from ICE, the FBI, and the other government agencies and NGOs in the group. If DOJ leadership is weak, little can be expected from the group. The strength of a task force reflects the commitment of each state's U.S. attorney, as demonstrated by those members whom they assign. Farrell points to the Connecticut task force as one with strong direction, through the active participation and guidance of assistant U.S. attorney Krishna Patel. But there are task forces whose members have lost interest and who meet infrequently and perfunctorily. And since it falls to local law enforcement to select the NGOs for task force membership, it is also possible to choose the wrong organization, one with little street experience or perhaps with a distrust of government or other NGOs.

Farrell points out that while "everybody hates slavery and wants to save victims," task force members often can't agree on what human trafficking is or how to define a victim. Not uncommonly, there is friction between groups. Someone from an immigrant rights group might share task force membership with an ICE representative and at the same time be protesting an ICE raid. Perhaps a service provider is seeking victim information from a U.S. attorney or FBI or ICE agent who is reluctant to provide it for fear of jeopardizing or compromising his or her case. And sometimes government agencies themselves are less than cordial toward each other. There is a generic problem of differing expectations of what the people on the task force should know and when they should know it. Service providers lean toward the victim support side, while the goal of a prosecutor or an agent begins with securing a conviction. Certainly there are shades of gray, but old job patterns are hard to break. On the plus side, task forces generally see working with victim service providers as necessary to making their cases, whereas non–task force law enforcement members tend to view NGOs as service providers whose job stops before the courthouse door. Says Farrell: "Task forces change the way the members of the law see NGOs."[46]

Some clear recommendations for local action on human trafficking come out of the research. One is that there should be a "national human trafficking training curriculum targeting local law enforcement agencies." The aim would be to get everyone on the same page, following successful procedures and learning the investigative techniques shown to be the most effective.[47] Even before training arrives, the research suggests that "model protocols"—plans and rules for dealing with trafficking cases—be sent to police around the country. Some of the existing task forces have these plans ready to go.[48]

Looking deeply into America's clumsy response to modern slavery shows that some basic ideas still need serious thought. The complexities of human trafficking cases can be confusing, all the more so when the definition of who is and who isn't a trafficking victim is still unresolved.[49] But if anyone is going to answer this question, according to the research, it will be the multiagency task forces that bring together all the players, know the problem from the ground up, and get the most prosecutions.[50]

ENDING SLAVERY IN THE NEIGHBORHOOD

All over the world, communities are ending slavery. In the developing world, where slavery can be extensive in cities, towns, and villages and the national government is weak or uninterested, the task of ending slavery falls to the local community. Rich and successful countries have a lot to teach the developing world, but we need to remember that often they have a lot to teach us too. Every time a community rids itself of slavery or brings freedom to others, the movement grows. It might be through someone too persistent to ignore, it might be because Good Samaritans have shown the way, it might be because a local cop just had to keep pushing. A conscious and collective decision has to be made to bring slavery to an end, and this is more effectively accomplished at the community than the national level. Remember what Margaret Mead said: "Never doubt that a small group of thoughtful, committed citizens can change the world; indeed, it's the only thing that ever has."

Eradicating slavery in our communities is achievable. We don't face the tough obstacles that exist in other countries: our police are honest, we have viable resources, and while those in power might be slow to act, they oppose slavery. Five steps seem to be needed for communities to rid themselves of slavery. First, whether by neighborhood or community, a conscious and collective decision has to be made that slavery will not be allowed in this place. Second, the community, through a task force or other arrangement, must work together to find the right mix of awareness raising, investigation, and care for survivors that addresses the type—or types—of trafficking and slavery found there. Third, successful community-based solutions need to be *scaled up* as much as possible. To do that, local law enforcement, antitrafficking groups, and their funders need to be always thinking about forming and growing new strategies. Once a successful strategy is tested, it should be proactively offered to other communities as a freely available, "open-source" program.

Fourth, as the research on task forces has shown, antitrafficking groups need to join together and cooperate, forming a wider movement with a shared identity. Collaborating in the world of human rights can be difficult because groups often feel themselves to be in competition for recognition and resources. Like all of us, even the most altruistic antislavery workers have egos that can make cooperation difficult. Fifth, scaling up successful antislavery programs also means shifting more of the responsibility to government at all levels. *Government accountability* for the enforcement of antislavery and antitrafficking laws and for provision of preventive and rehabilitative services needs to be intrinsic to antislavery strategies. If government is truly on board, it can adopt the successful methods and extend the effects of local projects.

The collective decision making of communities is crucial to throwing off the yoke of slavery. Some of the causes of slavery, however, go beyond the reach of any individual community. A community may be able to drive out traffickers, but it needs to join with other groups to change government policies, such as loose visa and guest worker regulations, that may support slavery. Another such policy concerns the treatment of women enslaved in prostitution. Too often women found in circumstances of forced prostitution are arrested and locked up. Clearly, treating a victim of slavery and serial rape as a criminal is not the way to deal with the problem.

No matter what laws are passed, slavery can end only when local communities first decide it will end and then take action. Slavery is woven into the fabric of life at the most intimate levels of our neighborhoods. It has to be cut out of that fabric by those who best understand where its threads are hidden and how they are knotted together with the strands of corruption, indifference, racism, or greed. If you or I live in a community without slavery today, it is possibly because someone in the past turned to his neighbor and said, "This must end." Slavery is too big to be stopped by any individual, no matter how powerful, charismatic, or clever. However, by working together as a community, we can find the slaves in our neighborhoods, and we can set them free. The choice is ours.

HOW TO MAKE YOUR CITY A SLAVE-FREE CITY

Ending slavery in America means making it impossible for slavery to take root anywhere. Once slavery is stopped in a community, region, or country, that place must be "slave-proofed." There is slavery in more than one hundred American cities today. The "Slave-Free Cities" plan shows how we can work together to stop slavery in our communities and make sure it never comes back.

How do you slave-proof a whole city? It takes everyone working together, and it takes leadership. The quickest way to a slave-free city is through community leaders *leading from the front.* But slave-proofing begins with a single citizen.

The following are steps to making your community a Slave-Free City:

1. Community leaders have a lot of demands on them; it will take a dedicated citizen to bring the idea of a slave-free city to her or his community. It can begin when someone raises the idea in a letter to the local newspaper, in a place of worship, in the Chamber of Commerce, or in a high school. When even a small group of people is committed to ending slavery, the process of creating a slave-free city has begun.

2. This group then shares its vision with all the people and groups that will be needed to slave-proof the city—the city council, the mayor, the police chief, heads of education, religious leaders, teachers, service organizations from the Boy Scouts to the Rotary Club, and especially the editors and managers of local newspapers and radio and TV stations. Every one of these community leaders and others will need a visit and an explanation of the plan to rid the community of slavery forever.

3. The Plan for a Slave-Free City has five parts:

   a. *Public Awareness Raising:* The message is, there is slavery in America today, but this community has decided to say "No!" The campaign should include articles in the local newspaper and reports on TV and radio, a proclamation by the city government, and special assemblies in schools. Places of worship and community groups will disseminate information.

   b. *Driving Home the Message:* After the buildup of awareness raising in the schools and the press and on TV and radio, every household should receive a booklet that explains the realities of modern slavery and how to recognize and report suspected cases of human trafficking and slavery.

   c. *On the Streets:* Very early, before the campaign is actually begun, there should be a meeting with local law enforcement and a plan made for officers to receive training on human trafficking and slavery. This training is available from a number of professional sources. The aim should be for the training to take place as the public awareness campaign begins and to be featured in the news of the campaign. Training should also be planned for other workers who are likely to come into contact with victims of human trafficking—nurses and other medical staff, public health and labor inspectors, mail carriers, even gas station employees.

   d. *In the Shops and Retirement Funds:* While the more public part of the campaign is being carried out, a committee—including members of the city council, local business leaders, religious leaders, teachers, bankers, and investment brokers—should be looking into three areas of the city's economy: what local businesses might be using slave-made goods or commodities in their production; what goods are being sold in the community that have a high likelihood of being slave made; and what stocks and shares being invested in for local pension plans and other investments have a high likelihood of deriving profits from slave labor. A city with a plant making car parts, for example, will need to look at the possibility that the raw iron and steel in the plant comes from Brazil and may be tainted with slavery. The aim will not be to suddenly rip these materials, products, and shares out of the community but to make careful decisions about how best to work with suppliers and businesses to remove slavery from shops and investments and to use that process to alert and explain the ideas of a Slave-Free City to businesses and investors.

e. *Ongoing Public Recognition:* The campaign can open with a proclamation that this community is going to become a Slave-Free City. After the major part of the initial campaign is completed, perhaps after three to six months, the mayor or other city leader should report to the community on progress and publicly commit to the ongoing vigilance needed.

8

STATES OF CONFUSION

A SMORGASBORD OF STATES AND SLAVERY CASES

Slavery, in its many forms, exists in every state in the country; the cases don't lack variety. Among the hundreds of cases brought to light over the past eight years have been instances of forced agricultural labor in Florida, New Hampshire, and Colorado; slave-driven sweatshops in American Samoa; enslaved domestics in New York, Michigan, and Washington, D.C.; and women and children forced to engage in commercial sex in Tennessee, California, and New Jersey. Below are a few snapshots of human trafficking cases that have been prosecuted in a handful of states.

In Alaska, in 2001, seven Russian women, two of whom were underage, were given false visas and hired to perform "traditional folk dances." Instead, their "employers" forced them to dance nude at the Crazy Horse strip club and took their passports, plane tickets, and tips. The traffickers housed them in squalid quarters and used the threat of violence to keep them in line. Ultimately, police arrested four people, three of whom admitted to visa fraud and bringing minors into the state. The more severe charges of forced labor and kidnapping were dropped.[1]

In Hawaii in 2004, a jury convicted a man of smuggling seven men to Hawaii from the small Pacific island of Tonga and enslaving them on his pig farm in Waipahu. Here they were forced to work in the man's landscaping business and were frequently beaten with tools. They were fed poorly; sometimes the men were so hungry that they caught and ate dogs. The owner was found guilty on thirty-four counts, among which were forced labor, involuntary servitude, and alien smuggling.[2] He was sentenced to twenty-six years.[3]

In New Jersey in August 2006, two Honduran immigrant sisters entered guilty pleas in a Hudson County federal court. They admitted to bringing dozens of girls, some only fourteen years of age, into the country and forcing them to live together in ramshackle apartments.

To repay their "debts," which ran as high as $20,000, the girls had to dance six days a week at North Jersey bars and drink with the customers. According to one of the traffickers, "prostitution was encouraged," and the girls were beaten if they broke the rules. Their pay was five dollars per hour plus tips, but most of it went to paying what they were told they owed. One of the girls was forced to take an abortion pill after becoming pregnant, and she prematurely delivered a stillborn child.

The two sisters were named as part of a ring that trafficked girls from Honduras over the Mexican border and up into New Jersey. By pleading guilty to charges of forced labor, conspiracy, and harboring illegal aliens, the sisters avoided having to face charges of human trafficking, which bring considerably heavier penalties. Fourteen of the young girls were certified as trafficking victims, and they and their families received visas.[4]

In Georgia in late 2007, thirty-one-year-old Stone Mountain native Jimmie Lee Jones, a.k.a. "Mike Spade," pled guilty to various trafficking charges, including forcing eight young women—two of whom were minors—to "engage in commercial sex acts through force, fraud, and coercion." Representing himself as a casting agent looking for models, Jones was in reality a "gorilla pimp" who recruited his "girls" through misrepresentation and then used physical and mental abuse to keep them in line. He faces a maximum fifteen-year sentence.[5]

A TRIO OF HOUSE SLAVE CASES

In Maryland, a Gaithersburg couple, Rene and Margarida Bonetti, were indicted on violations of various immigration laws relating to the treatment of their sixty-five-year-old "domestic," Hilda Rosa Dos Santos. They had kept the illiterate Brazilian woman enslaved for fifteen years, beating her regularly, scalding her with hot soup, and denying her food, pay, and medical attention. Her rescue came about only after neighbors took her to the hospital with a "stomach tumor that had grown to the size of a soccer ball." Margarida fled the country, but Rene went on trial, claiming as his defense that the old woman "was a costly and horrible housekeeper." Facing a maximum of thirty-five years in prison, Rene was given a six-year sentence and ordered to pay Dos Santos restitution.[6]

In Colorado, a Centennial couple was convicted in August 2006 of enslaving a twenty-four-year-old Indonesian woman for four years. The wife was sentenced to two months in jail and ordered to pay over $100,000 in restitution; her husband was convicted of imprisoning and sexually abusing the woman. Typically, they had commandeered the woman's passport, made her sleep on a mattress in the basement, and forced her to care for their children.[7]

Finally, in Michigan in mid-2007, two Cameroonian naturalized U.S. citizens—Joseph and Evelyn Djoumessi—were sentenced in Detroit to terms of eighteen and six years, respectively. They were also ordered to pay over $100,000 in restitution to a young Cameroonian girl whom they had held in involuntary servitude, forcing her to watch over their children and clean the house, without pay. They had also beaten her—with a spoon, a shoe, a belt, or whatever implement was handy. And Joseph had sexually abused the girl.[8]

These three cases involving enslaved domestics occurred in very different parts of the country, but they show two similarities that apply to almost all slavery cases. The first is the wide disparity in the punishments for what appear to be the same basic offenses. Some of the more serious offenders seem to get off with the lightest sentences. This can happen for various reasons: a plea bargain, a lenient judge or difficult jury, a case that's deceptively difficult to prove despite a long history of abuse, a difference in the nature of the charges from one case to another. If a prosecutor doesn't feel a trafficking charge can be proven, he or she might choose to prosecute on lesser or parallel charges that he or she feels have a greater chance of a guilty verdict. The results are in no way predictable. Trafficking cases are among the hardest to prosecute, relying as they often do on the proof of psychological coercion. The result is that when a slaveholder gets caught in America, there is little certainty that the punishment will fit the crime.

The second common thread running through all these cases, and hundreds more like them, is that they were taken to court by federal, not state, prosecutors. The trials took place in the states where the offenses occurred, but they were all adjudicated on the federal level. While the Department of Justice (DOJ), Immigration and Customs Enforcement (ICE), the FBI, and whatever other federal agencies would have received assistance from state and local cops to make the case, the charges, the prosecutors, and the courtrooms themselves were all federal.

Don't the states have their own antislavery and anti–human trafficking laws? In fact, the majority of them do. Since the passage of the Trafficking Victims Protection Act (TVPA), there has been a growing state-level awareness of trafficking. This growth is reflected in the press:

"Human Trafficking Becomes a Problem in Virginia,"[9] "[Georgia] to Crack Down on Human Trafficking,"[10] "Human Trafficking in North Texas,"[11] "Human Trafficking in Idaho,"[12] "Human Trafficking—in D.C.,"[13] "Human Trafficking, in Minnesota,"[14] "[Florida] Takes on Modern Slavery,"[15] "[Utah] Legislators Target Human Trafficking,"[16] New Law Makes Human Trafficking Illegal in Iowa,"[17] "[California] a Hot Spot for Human Trafficking."[18] Many states have asked themselves tough questions and faced the hard truth that slavery exists within their borders. For most of them, the next step has involved passing their own antislavery and anti–human trafficking statutes; and the federal government has offered help, in the form of a model law.

MODEL ANTITRAFFICKING LAWS FOR THE STATES

In 2004, the DOJ created a model statute for the fifty states, based on the TVPA, in anticipation of an enthusiastic nationwide response. The Model State Anti-Trafficking Criminal Statute was the first such model trafficking law, and it was distributed widely. The model law's purpose, according to the DOJ, was to ensure "seamless partnerships in combating human trafficking."[19] The DOJ cited three objectives in their template: "prevent gaps between federal and state laws; promote a national legal strategy to combat trafficking that would facilitate greater coordination and reduce confusion on the part of both victims and law enforcement; and provide examples of the most effective legislative approaches to address trafficking."[20]

From a criminological standpoint, the model was fairly comprehensive in that it addressed both "labor," with its qualifying force and coercion, and "services," which included—among other unlawful activities—forced prostitution. It went a step further by suggesting that the induction of minors into prostitution should constitute trafficking, without the need to prove force, fraud, or coercion. However, because the DOJ's main area of focus is prosecution, only minimal provisions were made in their model statute for victim services. Shortly after the DOJ came out with its template, two victim-centered organizations— Polaris Project and the Freedom Network—constructed and released their own models, which, despite some differences, both added victim provisions not found in the DOJ model: "access to state crime victims compensation fund, shelter, medical and mental health treatment, translation services, and protection for the safety and privacy of victims."[21] By combining the DOJ's model—with its focus on the *crime* of trafficking—with the NGOs' recommendations to support victims, the states had everything they needed to write a complete slavery and trafficking law.

Since most state laws begin with a section that defines human trafficking, the DOJ model included in its template specific legal definitions for such terms as *blackmail, commercial sexual activity, financial harm, forced labor or services, sexually explicit performance,* and *trafficking victim*. The Freedom Network added some definitions for *debt bondage, minor,* and *venture,* while Polaris weighed in with *debt coercion, person, minor,* and *sex act*.[22] Despite this semantic road map, the states that have written their own laws show "great variation in their definitions."[23] Few state laws would be considered comprehensive.

THE THREE COMPONENTS THAT EVERY STATE LAW NEEDS . . . AND FEW HAVE

According to Amy Farrell of Northeastern University's Institute on Race and Justice, a state trafficking law should have three main components. The first is problem identification and planning: pinpointing the issue and deciding how to tackle it. Predictably, the DOJ model recommends assigning these tasks to federal agencies—specifically, the Attorney General's Office in the state and the Department of Health and Human Services (HHS). The NGOs' models recommend a broader membership base, utilizing all available agencies and organizations. A logical extension of this idea is the statewide, interagency task force, which is discussed below.

The second component of a state law focuses on criminal provisions and penalties. The DOJ's model defines three main offenses: involuntary servitude, sexual servitude of a minor, and trafficking of persons for forced labor or services. The two NGO models added their own; both Polaris and the Freedom Network suggested that accomplice liability—aimed at those who deliberately aid or abet trafficking and slavery—be considered a crime, and the Freedom Network added provisions for "unlawful conduct with documents" where it furthered trafficking.[24] Overall, the states with trafficking laws have had no problem establishing criminal provisions. The overwhelming majority have implemented provisions and penalties for human trafficking. This is not surprising, since it is "consistent with the public framing of human trafficking as a criminal justice problem."[25]

Every state has its own set of rules about determining criminal sentences. Some use required sentencing ranges, guidelines, or grids for determining the sentence, and/or mandatory minimum sentences. Because of that, Farrell points out, "it is difficult to describe the average type of sentence proscribed by statute."[26] The result is that penalties for human trafficking vary radically from state to state, often depending on each state legislature's definition and interpretation of the crime itself. A felony offense that could bring a sentence of several years in, say, Illinois might receive a one-year judgment or a slap on the wrist in Texas.

Nearly all the state trafficking laws assign liability only to individuals. Only two states—Georgia and Virginia—have made provisions that allow businesses or corporations to be found criminally liable for slavery or trafficking. If a state doesn't have this provision, it short-circuits any attempt to hold the large agricultural buyer corporations accountable for slavery in the fields or to hold sweatshops or factories accountable for enslaving their workforce. All three models recommend that "asset forfeiture" be included in the state laws, a strategy clearly supported by Supreme Court rulings, as seen in chapter 6. Despite this, only two states—Illinois and Pennsylvania—have elected to allow the seizure of assets held by human traffickers. The Illinois law provides for the seizure of "any profits or proceeds and interest or property" that derive from specific acts of human trafficking. These include involuntary servitude, involuntary servitude of a minor, and trafficking for the purpose of forced labor.[27] The absence of asset forfeiture from most state laws is odd, since law enforcement agencies are strongly in favor of such provisions and normally push hard for their inclusion. Across the country, assets seized from criminals, especially drug dealers, help fund law enforcement efforts. And while trafficking and slavery are defined as crimes against the person, they also have a central economic dimension and generate profits and assets. It is appropriate that the convicted trafficker or slaveholder be made to surrender the fruits of slave labor, and even more appropriate that the proceeds of that forfeiture be given to the ex-slave. The profits and assets represent labor stolen from the victim; compensation from seized assets should be returned to the "rightful owner."

The third recommended component—victim protection—is by far the most complex, and the least evident, of the three. Even the crime-focused DOJ model advised that "prosecution without victim protection is unworkable." Nonetheless, fewer than one-fifth of the states "provide resources or make explicit provisions for victim services such as shelter, mental and physical health services, translation, and legal assistance."[28] An even smaller number of states included provisions for immunity for victims who commit a crime as a result of their enslavement. And only one state—California—has included in its trafficking law a provision for caseworker privilege to ensure the confidentiality of information shared by a victim with a service provider or advocate.[29]

Some states, including Florida, Texas, and Arizona, jumped the gun and passed their own versions of trafficking legislation before the model statutes came out. According to Lou de Baca, counsel to the House Committee on the Judiciary and former prosecutor for the DOJ, they failed to get it right. The Arizona law, for example, confuses trafficking with smuggling, and prosecutors still pursue cases as slavery that have nothing to do with the issue.[30]

By early 2008, thirty-nine states had passed anti–human trafficking laws. The speed with which these laws were passed is impressive, given the slow pace at which state governments usually work.[31] Many of these laws, however, are noteworthy for their incompatibility with federal law and with each other. Some states used the DOJ model as a template, but most modified it to suit their own views of human trafficking or ignored it completely. As Amy Farrell points out, a major characteristic shared by many of the laws is their concentration on the criminal aspects— definitions of the crime, levels of misdemeanor or felony for specific types of trafficking—and their lack of attention to victims' needs and services.[32] Operating from the premise that just having a law to punish the traffickers is sufficient, state legislators have managed to create laws that not only leave the victims out in the cold but generally fail to acknowledge their existence at all.

In some cases, states have passed antitrafficking laws without appropriating funds for their implementation. In their discussion of state trafficking laws, Jim Finckenauer and Min Liu of Rutgers University describe this as "symbolic politics." "In a nutshell," they write, "symbolic politics refers to a policymaking situation wherein perceptions trump substance; where the appearance of action, sometimes without actually doing or intending to do anything, becomes paramount in reassuring political constituents. According to this particular view, such political acts as the passage of legislation with respect to certain issues are largely symbolic."[33] They suggest that the primary reason for some states' reluctance to pass legislation, and for others to put muscle behind it, is the states' "belief that human trafficking is a 'federal problem' and thus not something to be made the subject of state jurisdiction." And although states acknowledge that trafficking does occur within their borders, the "absence of data fuels opposition to the need for anti-trafficking legislation, permitting the argument that the prevalence of trafficking is not large enough to warrant new laws and financial appropriations."[34]

While the laws vary dramatically from state to state, interest groups have their own take. The New York law, for example, is seen by Mark Lagon, director of the Office to Monitor and Combat Trafficking in Persons (TIP Office), as "far and away" the best state law to date.[35] Abolitionist groups, however, would prefer to see the "force, fraud, and coercion" provision removed from that law, while the human trafficking sphere is concerned that the state has defined sex and labor trafficking as two separate issues, with sex offenses seen as the more serious of the two. In New York, "sex trafficking" is now punishable as a "B" felony (maximum sentence twenty-five years), whereas "labor trafficking" warrants only "D" felony status (maximum sentence seven years). So disparate are the views and positions among government agencies, service providers, and advocates that no state law could possibly please everyone.

Looking across the country, some questions arise: To what extent do the state laws address all forms of trafficking and address them equally? What state laws have made provisions for the care and safety of the victim rather than just criminalizing the offense? And exactly how effective are the various state laws?

Clearly, the state legislatures didn't communicate with each other when they framed their respective trafficking laws. A number have created bifurcated statutes, separating sex and labor servitude. Among these are Minnesota, Arizona, Florida, New York, and Missouri. Others, such as Texas, Illinois, Arkansas, and Washington, have taken a more generalist approach and have "criminalized the broader offense of human trafficking." Some states, including Florida and Missouri, have followed the federal lead in specifically criminalizing the trafficking of minors. The unlawful use of government documents is included in the laws of Missouri and Minnesota. And a handful of states have made "bride trafficking" and sex tourism a part of their antitrafficking statutes.[36]

Why the wide disparity? It is certainly not for a lack of models from which to work. Aside from the DOJ's 2004 template and the models put forth by Polaris Project and the Freedom Network, there are several options to choose from. The federal government also put out the U.S. Department of State Model Anti-Trafficking Law, the TVPA itself and its three reauthorizations, and the Prosecutorial Remedies and Other Tools to End the Exploitation of Children Today (PROTECT) Act of 2003. From the private sector, there is the Center for Women Policy Studies' *Resource Guide for State Legislators—Model Provisions for State Anti-Trafficking Laws,* which—while not a model statute—offers in-depth suggestions as to what such a law should contain. There is no lack of reference material. Admittedly, the emphasis differs from one source to another. The Center for Women Policy Studies stresses the law's impact on women and girls, while the DOJ takes a broader approach, geared more to dealing with the actual crime of trafficking. Still, it appears that the state legislatures have tended to go it alone in drawing up their slavery laws.[37]

FLUNKING HUMAN TRAFFICKING 101

All of this points up the absence of—and need for—accurate documentation. In a recent study, Anthony Shorris, of Princeton's Policy Research Institute for the Region, said, "There is very little [research] work done on trafficking, and much of the research that does exist is focused on one element of the problem: the need for more and better data."[38] The Center for Women Policy Studies has answered this need by creating a comprehensive evaluation of each state and its trafficking laws. They call it a "Report Card on State Action to Combat International Trafficking," and it is just that—an old-fashioned report card, complete with letter grades for a variety of categories and explanations to go with them.[39]

The center has worked on human trafficking on the state level since 1998 and frequently consults with the various state legislatures. It is primarily concerned with how the states' antitrafficking efforts affect women and girls, and this is reflected in some of the survey's categories. They do not, however, subscribe to the antiprostitution school of thought. According to the center's president, Leslie Wolfe, "Our work is about human rights, not antiprostitution. It's about what public policy can do to end the oppression of women."[40] Despite its gender emphasis, the center's report card is comprehensive enough to evaluate each state's legislative overall response to trafficking. It covers five areas: criminalization of trafficking; victim protection and assistance; creation of statewide interagency task forces; regulation of international marriage brokers; and regulation of travel service providers who facilitate sex tourism. All fifty states were surveyed. Their report from early 2007, when only half the states had passed felony trafficking legislation, provides an overall—and sobering—picture of the trend in state-level trafficking legislation. As for the grades, on the whole, there are very few As—you can count them on two hands—and an alarming number of Fs, indicating that the state in question has made no effort to date in a particular category. An F in the "Criminalization of Trafficking" column, for instance, would mean that that particular state had not yet passed a trafficking law. A student receiving such a report card would have to repeat the school year.[41]

Under the "Criminalization of Trafficking" section of the report card, the areas surveyed included an impressive list of criteria on which the states were evaluated.[42] In this category, no state received an A, and those with a B grade—including such states as Iowa, California, Illinois, and New Jersey—are all seen, in one way or another, as lacking. In the case of California, the center recommends that it revise the provisions to "include a definition of 'forced sexual exploitation' that criminalizes all forms of sex trafficking, not just 'prostitution.'"[43] Illinois is advised to add "corporate liability for traffickers, and mandatory training for local and state law enforcement."[44]

The "Victim Protection and Assistance" section of the report card survey defines appropriate care and services for survivors: access to safe and secure housing; protection of victims from intimidation, threats, and reprisals; competent physical and mental health care; legal and immigration assistance; translation services; educational and job readiness programs; policies and procedures to provide access to services; and the right of private action. Under this category, fourteen of the states that have trafficking laws in place received an F, while six more earned a D, indicating that the majority of states have done little or nothing to provide help or services for the victim. Again, no state got an A, and only three—California, Indiana, and Illinois—got Bs. The center commends California for "its exceptional efforts to provide social services to victims of trafficking" but goes on to recommend that it provide "other forms of assistance," such as safe housing, health services and trauma counseling, immigration and legal assistance, and translation services. One victim service provision in the California law has rankled law enforcement agencies from the local level all the way up to the DOJ. The statute stipulates that "within 15 days of first encountering a trafficking victim, law enforcement agencies must complete and submit the Law Enforcement Agency Endorsement (LEA) documents. If the LEA Endorsement is found to be 'inappropriate,' the law enforcement agency, within 15 days, must provide the victim with a letter explaining why it was denied."[45] Says one high-ranking official at the DOJ (who asked to remain anonymous), "Law enforcement thinks this a bad provision; it's inflexible and makes fixed schedules of reporting for continued presence and the like. Victim services are important, but it's not law enforcement's primary objective; the main thing detectives should be doing is, they should be out there being detectives."

Two of the report card's categories, "Regulation of International Marriage Brokers (IMBs)" and "Regulation of Travel Service Providers" for sex tourism, are almost exclusively women's issues, and they show a nearly unbroken field of Fs, with only the occasional passing grade. Only four states had enacted laws against marriage brokering, with Texas getting the only A, while Missouri, Hawaii, and Washington got As for their work in legislating against sex tourism–based travel services.[46]

Under the final category in the survey—"Creation of Statewide Interagency Task Forces"—seven states received top marks: California, Colorado, Hawaii, Connecticut, Idaho, Washington, and Maine. This can be misleading at first, since at the time of the study neither Maine nor Hawaii had a trafficking law in place. But in the center's estimation, the existence of a thoughtfully constructed, forward-moving task force in both states speaks well for a considered approach being taken toward passing one.[47]

THE IMPORTANCE OF STATEWIDE INTERAGENCY TASK FORCES

Both the Freedom Network's and Polaris Project's model statutes advocate for the creation of interagency statewide task forces—with a broad membership base drawn from both government and NGOs. Center president Leslie Wolfe has strong opinions in favor of the task forces. "Some states aren't ready to pass a trafficking law yet, some aren't familiar with the issues, and some are studying the issues, or have passed statewide task force laws."[48] For all the states—those with and without a trafficking statute—she believes that a state legislature–approved interagency task force is the key to a successful war on human trafficking. The establishment and membership of the statewide task force are mandated by the state legislature, and the task force is most effective when composed of a broad spectrum of involved professionals: victim service providers and advocates; researchers; human rights, immigration rights, and domestic violence services; and members of state and local law enforcement and government. The most vital functions they can provide are to research and ascertain the types and extent of trafficking within their respective states, develop state human trafficking response plans, review existing services, and establish policies.

Wolfe sees Connecticut's statewide task force as the model for other states. It is the creation of Democratic state senator Andrea Stillman, who brought the various members together and remains actively involved. However, since each state faces its own specific set of problems regarding human trafficking, it is unrealistic to expect that the task forces should adopt a "one-size-fits-all" approach. Idaho has a "small-ish" task force, says Wolfe, when compared to that of Connecticut, "but both have the same mission." Washington, one of the first states to pass a trafficking law, "keeps evolving, amending their task force, working to improve victim protections. They're the kind of state where the legislators are committed to doing the work." Wolfe was not concerned that Maine was one of the fourteen states that had no anti–human trafficking statute by early 2008 because their statewide task force was, in her opinion, providing a comprehensive study of the problem and recommending the best possible way of addressing it.[49]

Just assembling a task force does not ensure success. In the wake of the passage of their 2007 human trafficking statute, the New York State Legislature passed a law mandating the creation of an interagency task force. The specified members are the New York State Department of Labor, the Division of State Police Office of Children and Family Services, the Crime Victims Board, the Department of Health, the Office of Alcoholism and Substance Abuse Services, the Office of Mental Health, and the Office for the Prevention of Domestic Violence. The task force is co-chaired by the New York State Office of Temporary Disability Assistance, to address victim services, and the New York State Division of Criminal Justice Services, to deal with the legal end. There are two subcommittees, to which have been added still more agencies. Yet despite this impressive list of participants, their collective experience in the area of human trafficking is minimal to none. The logical thing would have been to include victim service providers in the task force, yet not a single NGO is on the list. Although the task force has set up hearings to get testimony from the NGOs ("asking NGOs to do their work for them," in the words of one service provider), they have essentially denied a seat at the table to the people with real experience in the field. The legislature wheeled out the heavy agency guns without providing them with the ammunition they will need to understand the problem and get the job done.

Letter grades aside, Leslie Wolfe is emboldened by the states' response. "It is judgmental to say the laws are good or bad. Given that the state legislators' awareness of the issue began as recently as 1998,

I'm rather pleased with the progress made in so short a time." In her opinion, the report card is only a "snapshot in time," helping to both chronicle and provide incentive to the states' efforts. The low grades, Wolfe says, "encourage the various state governments who have done something to do more, and those who have done nothing to do something." She is currently working with the Arizona legislature to give their law a much-needed facelift. "They have an awful law," she admitted, "and now they're working on a better one."[50]

Wolfe is more positive about state trafficking laws than Finckenauer and Liu. She sees the various state legislatures much as a strict teacher views her class. She applauds their efforts, knows they can do better, and provides the tough love to motivate them to excel. "Some of these legislators are real heroes," she says. "I've watched them learn to see the reality of trafficking in a human rights context rather than as a mission to 'end sin and promote law enforcement.' And I've watched them take on this issue as courageous and powerful spokespeople and policy leaders. They've taken on something that their colleagues aren't familiar with, and don't really care about, and they've gotten laws passed. None of these state statutes is perfect—but then, what is?"[51] Some, however, would suggest that the relevance and comprehensiveness of the various state laws are more at issue than the courage and inspiration it might have taken to get them passed.

LOOKING FOR HELP AMONG THE STATES

One former member of the DOJ Programs Office (who requested anonymity) commented that state victim services laws are "redundant and inefficient. With the federal government funding victim services through HHS and other agencies, the states should have no need to enact their own victim-centered legislation as well." Leslie Wolfe sees this as a "typical federal bureaucratic response. I wouldn't want to rely on only federal money for victim services. It seems foolish to suggest the federal government should stand alone in their responsibility to victims."[52]

To what extent does the federal government look to the states for legislative assistance in fighting human trafficking? According to Amy Farrell, the TVPA was created in 2000 to "provide a legal structure for prosecuting individuals engaged in human trafficking activities." The federal government, says Farrell, was never meant to go it alone. Despite the efforts of the various federal agencies to uncover trafficking cases, prosecute traffickers, and assist survivors, "it was understood at the time of drafting the legislation that the TVPA was insufficient to prosecute all human trafficking operations throughout the United States." The federal government acknowledged that state and local authorities were the likeliest to locate and identify instances of trafficking at the community level. Therefore, it was imperative that state and local law enforcement agencies be armed with the appropriate statutes to prosecute these cases within their own borders. This, states Farrell, was the federal government's understanding and intention when they framed the 2000 law.[53] A parallel can be drawn with another serious felony—kidnapping. Kidnapping and human trafficking share certain characteristics, primarily the violent control exercised over the victim. Every state has a law against kidnapping, as does the federal government; there is no debate about whether states should have their own kidnapping statutes.

RAISING THE MORAL BANNER . . . AGAIN

The antiprostitution movement has influenced states' efforts to activate trafficking legislation in much the same way that it has been lobbying Congress for changes in the federal laws. Says Amy Farrell, "The limited research to date on human trafficking policymaking and legislation suggests advocacy organizations specifically concerned with commercial sex trafficking and child prostitution called upon political elites to address the perceived growing threat of exploitation."[54] State legislators have likely been responding as well to newspaper stories on human trafficking. A review of 1,350 news articles for the period 1990–2006 that use the phrase *human trafficking* or *trafficking in persons* points to an increased emphasis on sex trafficking. The review focused on articles relating to "sex trafficking," "labor trafficking," and "sex and labor trafficking." While there was an increased overall recognition of the trafficking problem, media coverage was "dominated by articles focused explicitly on sex trafficking." The stories' common theme featured young women and girls "forced into prostitution by conspiracies of foreign organized criminal networks."[55]

Over several years the number of articles on all forms of trafficking grew moderately, but in the mid- to late 1990s sex trafficking articles increased dramatically. Whereas the number of articles on sex trafficking, labor trafficking, and a combination of the two ran fairly even until around 1995, after that year media coverage of sex trafficking took off. By 2000 sex trafficking articles were increasing rapidly, and in 2006 they were practically off the chart—while the number of labor trafficking articles remained relatively flat and even showed a downturn. This trend, along with abolitionist lobbying, is likely to have had an effect on legislators when they framed trafficking laws.[56]

Some statutes include a "findings" section, naming the type of trafficking the legislators see as specific to their state; Nebraska named prostitution. The 2006 Nebraska antitrafficking law states, "Increasing prostitution in Nebraska has become harmful to communities and neighborhoods, often contributing to both incidents of crime and fear of crime." The Nebraska law ostensibly addresses both labor and sex trafficking; nonetheless, the "findings section is specific to prostitution and commercial sex."[57]

As in the TVPA and the DOJ model, forced prostitution of minors is a major component of most state trafficking laws. In seeking a broad definition of the crime of trafficking, says Lou de Baca, the federal government turned their gaze to prostituted children, and the states followed suit. "Typically, state cases are just repackaging of what once were categorized as child prostitution. By conflating child prostitution with trafficking in the 2000 TVPA, we've created low-hanging fruit—easy crimes to detect and to prosecute. It's really old wine in new bottles."[58]

OF BLIND MEN AND ELEPHANTS

There are several angles from which the states should examine, or reexamine, slavery and human trafficking: as an issue of immigration, crime, human rights, national security, economic justice—or all of the above. Framing a single statute to encompass them all is a daunting challenge. Of the roughly two-thirds of the states that have made the leap and passed antitrafficking laws, a few address a wide range of issues well, some are more issue specific and "morally" inclined, and some shoot considerably wide of the mark.

It is gratifying that most of the states have rallied and, in a very short time, have initiated, supported, and passed laws outlawing slavery within their borders. And if there is always room for improvement, there is also the sense that as living, breathing things the laws can grow and improve with increased knowledge and experience. But just passing a law doesn't necessarily entitle the state legislators to feel that they've done all they could to fight human trafficking. For one thing, it is evident that few states have thought beyond the criminalizing of human trafficking to address the vital issue of victim care and services. Yes, it is essential to catch and punish traffickers, but that is only one part of the equation. The list of things needed by—and owed to—the victims must not be ignored or dismissed. If a state law excludes the victims of human trafficking, the law should be changed to encompass them. Now that the state legislators have assumed the DOJ's aggressive position on the actual crime of trafficking, they should take a page from the Freedom Network, or Polaris Project, or any of hundreds of organizations that provide care and services to America's slaves, and should make their laws more victim centered.

Some practical issues are inherent in widening the scope of the state laws. As Farrell points out, "External factors beyond problem definition . . . may facilitate or hamper the passage of more comprehensive legislation." The more extensive the list of provisions, the greater the likelihood of delays and disappointments in committee. And the wider the range of proposed services—training, outreach, victim services—the greater the likelihood of fiscal competition with other state priorities. States have limited budgets and political agendas, and the issue of modern slavery is comparatively new. It is unrealistic to presume that the lion's share of the money would go to human trafficking legislation.[59]

In framing their laws, the state legislatures should also include monitoring programs. The absence of viable research data must be addressed. While the passage of state laws is a laudable first step, the only way to ascertain their success is to "monitor and understand how legislative mandates are translated into action."[60] A system of tracking the actual implementation of the state laws is needed. The Center for Women Policy Studies' "Report Card" and Farrell's paper "State Human Trafficking Legislation" are tremendously helpful, but ultimately they will suffer from the same pitfall that afflicts all research material in dealing with topical issues: they will soon be outdated. Research, to be relevant, must stay current.

There is no doubt that ultimately every state will pass anti–human trafficking legislation. But it's better to do it right than to do it right now. There is considerable merit to Leslie Wolfe's suggestion that the states take the time—and use the right resources—to explore and understand the issue in its entirety before passing a law. As Finckenauer and Liu suggest, "State policy makers should proceed cautiously and judiciously in considering anti-trafficking legislation. Symbolic actions should be avoided. And it should be recognized that half-way measures may well be worse than no measures at all."[61]

9

THE FEDS

It is important to look at the federal government's actions—both positive and negative—in its relatively new war against human trafficking in America. Many federal officials have taken on the task of rooting out and prosecuting traffickers, as well as coordinating with service providers and victim advocates providing care for survivors. We'll speak with representatives of some of the federal agencies whose job description has been expanded to include modern-day slavery and get a sense of how they feel the campaign is going. We'll also examine some cases that seem to stand in direct contradiction to the antitrafficking position taken by the government—cases in which administration politics and inaction have actually increased human trafficking on American soil—both here and abroad. One of the worst of these cases involves taxpayer money supporting slavery as part of Operation Iraqi Freedom.

BRINGING DEMOCRACY TO IRAQ—ON THE BACKS OF SLAVES

First Kuwaiti General Trade and Contracting Co., a billion-dollar construction company, was hired to build the new U.S. Embassy in Baghdad—after no American company would agree to the government's terms.[1] The project is worth $592 million to First Kuwaiti and encompasses a 104-acre, twenty-one-building complex, making it the largest U.S. embassy in the world. When completed, it will be six times larger than the United Nations and the same size as Vatican City.[2] From the beginning First Kuwaiti had difficulty in fulfilling the terms of its contract. Serious problems piled up: faulty wiring, fuel leaks, and poor construction. Some of the problems were determined to be "life safety issues." And while the day-to-day firefight was going on in Baghdad, a war of words was being waged between the State

Department in Washington, who defended their contractors, and those on the ground in Iraq, who were suffering from substandard work and delays.[3]

Boondoggles, pork barrels, and shoddy work are scandalous, but it was another, uglier issue that brought First Kuwaiti to the world's attention. Some of their contract workers had been trafficked to Iraq against their will, held by force, and paid little or nothing. First Kuwaiti—and by association, the U.S. Department of State—were using slave labor to build the embassy. Taxpayers were footing the bill. The idea of a U.S. subcontractor trafficking enslaved workers into the country where we are waging a war to introduce freedom and democracy is disturbing. Yet in case after case the construction company hired workers, normally through subcontractors, from India, Pakistan, Nepal, Sri Lanka, Sierra Leone, Egypt, Turkey, and the Philippines under false pretenses. Promised work in Dubai—indeed, their boarding passes for the flight to Iraq actually *read* Dubai—they landed in a combat zone. Once the workers were in Iraq, contractors confiscated their passports and forced them to live in squalid conditions and work long hours for little or no pay. And, says journalist David Phinney, "It was all happening smack in the middle of the US-controlled Green Zone—right under the nose of the State Department."[4]

The issue came to light after the murder of twelve Nepali workers who had been "recruited under false pretenses from rural villages . . . before being trafficked illegally into Iraq." En route to a U.S. base in Iraq, all twelve were kidnapped and executed by insurgents. The subcontractor had "sent them into the war zone, and along one of the most dangerous roads in the world, in what basically amounted to taxi cabs." Ali Kamel al-Nadi, the man who allegedly assembled the unprotected caravan, commented when asked about the incident, "If they were my workers, maybe I should be compensated for losing them."[5]

Though foreign workers had been complaining of abuses since early 2003, the problem was first flagged in a news report in late 2005. The report provoked a flurry of base inspections by the government. In April 2006, the Pentagon, without naming any of the subcontractors to Halliburton/KBR, concluded that "doing business in this way" was common in Iraq and Afghanistan.[6] The confiscation of workers' passports kept the laborers from leaving Iraq, the report stated, or from seeking jobs with other contractors. No penalties were assigned to the contractors. Nonetheless, the Pentagon ordered that all passports be returned and that such practices "cease and desist" immediately.[7]

They didn't. In July 2007, two American civilian contractors who had worked on the embassy testified before the House Committee on Oversight and Government Reform, chaired by California congressman Henry A. Waxman. One of the two, native Floridian John Owens, had worked for twenty-seven years building U.S. embassies around the world, sometimes in areas troubled by violence and corruption. But after working for seven months as a foreman in Iraq, he quit. "I've never seen a project more fucked up. Every U.S. labor law was broken," he said.[8] Owens testified that the workers' living and working conditions were "deplorable" and described how workers were "verbally and physically abused," forced to live in cramped trailers, denied basic needs like shoes and gloves, and made to work twelve-hour days, seven days a week, with time off only for prayer, and how they "had their salaries docked for petty infractions."[9]

The second contractor to testify was Rory J. Mayberry. He told the committee that First Kuwaiti managers had asked him to escort fifty-one Filipino workers onto a flight to Baghdad. The plane, Mayberry recalled, was an unmarked fifty-two-seater—"an antique piece of shit."[10] Mayberry noted with surprise that "all of our tickets said we were going to Dubai," whereupon a First Kuwaiti manager told him not to let any of the laborers know they were going to Iraq. John Owens recalled the same experience when he saw the workers' boarding passes: "I thought there was some sort of mix up and I was getting on the wrong plane."[11] In Mayberry's words, the workers were "kidnapped by First Kuwaiti to work on the U.S. Embassy." After their passports were taken in Baghdad, they were "smuggled into the Green Zone."[12]

Mayberry, an emergency medical technician, was horrified at the number of injuries and ailments among the 2,500 or so foreign laborers. Infected, unattended sores and unbandaged wounds were common. There was a lack of disinfectant, hot water, any form of hygiene. Prescription pain killers, he testified, "were being handed out like a candy store . . . and then people were sent back to work. . . . I told First Kuwaiti that you don't give painkillers to people who are running machinery and working on heavy construction, and they said, 'That's how we do it.'" After he requested an investigation into the deaths of two laborers as a result of what he believes could have been "medical homicide," Mayberry was fired.[13]

Owens confirmed the inhumane treatment. He testified that health and safety measures were nonexistent and that serious injuries took place as a result. When he advised workers to seek medical help for their injuries and illnesses, he was accused by the firm's managers of "spoiling the workers and allowing them to simply skip work." At one point, seventeen laborers tried to escape by climbing over the wall; they were recaptured—with the help of a State Department official—and put in "virtual lockdown."[14]

First Kuwaiti responded in writing that the charges were "ludicrous."[15] State Department Inspector General Howard J. Krongard disputed the charges in a follow-up hearing, stating that his "limited review" and two visits to Baghdad had failed to verify the claims: "Nothing came to our attention that caused us to believe that trafficking-in-persons violations"—or any other serious abuses—"occurred at the construction workers' camp at the new embassy compound."[16] In a written submission the antislavery organization Free the Slaves pointed to serious flaws in Krongard's report. They noted that the State Department's own Trafficking in Persons (TIP) Report for 2007 revealed "a structure conducive to trafficking in persons" throughout much of the Middle East. This includes sponsorship laws that give employers control over workers' ability to leave the work site, their job, or the country. The TIP report observed "Employers commonly do not provide workers with documents legitimizing their employment in the country . . . and refuse to sign exit permits allowing victims to leave the country, effectively holding the worker hostage." Most damning, the Free the Slaves submission showed that while Krongard had gone to investigate a charge of human trafficking, he failed

> to recognize the significance of, and appropriately characterize as warning signs: . . . the contractor's practice of holding employee passports; terms of employment that raise concerns about exploitation, including the amount of payment relative to national standards, payment by the month rather than the day or hour, and a 14 day workweek, with no days off; the requirement to prepay recruitment, travel or other fees before obtaining control of earnings; and the fact that most workers interviewed either originated in countries whose laws prohibit work in Iraq, because of the strong possibility of abuse, and/or whose countries are identified by State's TIP report as having a significant number of victims of severe trafficking to the Middle East.[17]

For his part, Chairman Waxman was also dissatisfied with Krongard's methodology and conclusions. The inspector general, said

Waxman, "had followed highly irregular procedures in exonerating the prime contractor, First Kuwaiti Trading Company, of charges of labor trafficking."[18] On September 18, 2007, Waxman began an inquiry into accusations that Krongard had repeatedly hindered fraud and abuse investigations in both Iraq and Afghanistan. The allegations were supported by information from several of Krongard's current and former employees, some of whom sought whistle-blower status to protect them from punishment for malfeasance. Congressman Waxman stated to Krongard, "One consistent element in these allegations is that you believe your foremost mission is to support the Bush administration, especially with respect to Iraq and Afghanistan, rather than act as an independent and objective check on waste, fraud and abuse on behalf of U.S. taxpayers."[19] Playing politics may be business as usual, but when politics and business combine to abet slavery and then hide it, something is terribly wrong in our government.

IN THE WAKE OF KATRINA

Any American who is not aware of the dismal federal response to Hurricane Katrina has not been paying attention. A significant part of our country lay in ruins, and much of it still does. In the aftermath of the hurricane a door opened to abuse and human trafficking. The need for immediate, cheap labor to help repair the storm's damage—and to rebuild order in the devastated region—was met with an influx of thousands of laborers. Some were U.S. citizens, others foreigners— documented and not. Some came on their own, seeking work, while others were brought in by smugglers, with the usual promises of steady work at a decent wage. Meanwhile, the combination of physical devastation and government negligence fostered a breakdown of order, and as human rights attorney Cathy Albisa puts it, Mississippi and Louisiana were "like the Wild West all over again."[20] The opportunities for forced labor were rife, and opportunist criminals wasted no time. When the rule of law breaks down, exploitation and slavery flourish, imposing the control of the weak by the strong, the hopeful by the greedy.

It is sometimes difficult to distinguish between a case of trafficking and one involving harsh labor conditions. This is especially the case with undocumented, "illegal" workers. "The very act of criminalizing a person's existence," says Albisa, "creates these blurry lines."[21] In a number of instances, the government determined that, while unconscionable, the conditions under which workers suffered were really nothing more than instances of unfortunate working arrangements—some of which included labor law violations—and did not impede the workers from leaving to find other employment. Some cases, such as the Imperial Nurseries case in Connecticut, leave room for doubt.[22] Still, while the seeds of trafficking might exist within worker exploitation, they don't always blossom into full-blown slavery—at least to the extent that they can be proven in court.

In November 2005—shortly after Katrina hit—the online magazine *Salon.com* published a report by journalist Roberto Lovato entitled "Gulf Coast Slaves." It documented the Halliburton company's deceptive hiring, mistreatment, and discarding of hundreds of undocumented Latino workers brought in for post-Katrina cleanup on U.S. naval bases in Louisiana and Mississippi. KBR was the main subcontractor.[23]

According to Lovato, President Bush paved the way for labor abuses by relaxing labor standards immediately after the hurricane through his suspension of the Davis-Bacon Act, a law that requires contractors to pay workers the "prevailing wages" for government contract work. Bush also removed the requirement that laborers had to fill out employment eligibility forms. Without them, Halliburton and its subcontractors were free to hire undocumented laborers and to pay them as little as they chose—or, as happened in some cases, nothing at all. Finally, under pressure, Bush reinstated both policies, but not before a tremendous amount of money had been made on the backs of abused workers.

Remarkably, given that these are paid for by tax dollars, the Halliburton contracts are secret. Despite the number and size of the jobs awarded the megacontractor, "there is an utter lack of transparency."[24] Laborers' International Union of North America vice president James Hale said, "To my knowledge, not one member of Congress has been able to get their hands on a copy of a contract that was handed out to Halliburton or others. There is no central registry of Katrina contracts available. No data on the jobs or scope of the work." Although his legislative staff have attempted to obtain copies of contracts, they were refused for reasons of "national security." He adds, "If the contracts handed out to these primary contractors are opaque, then the contracts being let to the subcontractors are just plain invisible. . . . This is an open invitation for exploitation, fraud and abuse."[25]

What we do know is that Halliburton hired KBR—which hired subcontractors, who hired subcontractors, until the list of companies with initials for names formed a "shadowy labyrinth . . . a no man's land where nobody seems to be accountable for the hiring—and abuse—of these workers."[26] This line of deniability ran all the way to the job brokers who hired the workers. These job brokers customarily find workers by frequenting job fairs and advertising in Spanish-language newspapers in various cities with large Hispanic populations. According to Lovato, the ads "typically promise room, board and pay in the range of $1200 a week."[27] One worker later said, "They gave us two meals a day and sometimes only one."[28] Said another, "Mr. Donaldson [CEO of KBR subcontractor DRS Cosmotech] promised us we'd live in a hotel or a house. We lived in tents and only had hot water that smelled of petroleum."[29] A third man, who had been working on the naval base at Belle Chasse, Louisiana, reported, "The food was going to be free, and rent, but they gave us nothing. They weren't feeding us. We ate cookies for five days. Cookies, nothing else."[30] Ultimately, when the workers received no pay whatsoever for their weeks of work, the job brokers claimed they themselves had not been paid by the subcontractors who had hired *them,* and so on up the ladder, with avowals of nonpayment at every rung, all the way to Halliburton—which denied the "existence of undocumented workers providing labor for their operations on the Gulf Coast bases."[31] This was a lie. Logging phone calls from workers, the Mississippi Immigrant Rights Alliance estimated a presence of over five hundred undocumented laborers on Belle Chasse alone. And an October 2005 raid on Belle Chasse by Immigration and Customs Enforcement (ICE) established the presence of undocumented workers, as did "visits to the naval bases and dozens of interviews by *Salon.*"[32]

The physical conditions under which the laborers worked are numbingly familiar. For those who didn't sleep in tents, there were run-down trailer parks, reminiscent of those in which migrant farmworkers are forced to live, where "up to 19 unpaid, unfed and undocumented KBR site workers inhabited a single trailer for $70 per person, per week." The workers suffered from a number of maladies—sprains, cuts, bruises, stomach problems—for which they got no medical help, "despite being close to medical facilities on the same bases they were cleaning and helping to rebuild."[33] And, after several weeks on the job, the workers were turned out into the street without ever having received their pay.

On learning of the abuses on our Gulf Coast bases, Louisiana Senator Mary Landrieu commented, "It is a downright shame that any contractor would use this tragedy as an opportunity to line its pockets by breaking the law and hiring a low-skilled, low-wage and undocumented work force."[34] But exactly what law were they breaking? Here's where the line blurs. Isn't this, awful though it might be, simply a case of worker exploitation and not human trafficking? As we know, the Trafficking Victims Protection Act (TVPA), in defining trafficking, calls for the presence of force, fraud, or coercion. And without clear evidence of force, fraud, and coercion, prosecutors rarely bring a case into court. So where is the evidence of forced labor, the pressure that denied the workers the right to leave to seek other employment? In Lovato's article, a single sentence states that the Mississippi Immigrant Rights Alliance "received phone calls from several Latino workers who complained they were denied, under threat of deportation, the right to leave the base at Belle Chasse."[35] Could this take us from a case of worker abuse into the realm of modern-day slavery? Possibly, but it would require more evidence. We know that the workers were undocumented, so deportation could indeed have been a viable threat. But in what context was it made? Were they truly unable to simply walk away, despite being threatened with return to their own country? The short term of their confinement, if they were in fact held against their will, could lead a jury—and a prosecutor—to dismiss the idea that this was true slavery, especially in the light of several recent cases in which people were kept in bondage for years. Given the federal government's reluctance to take on possible trafficking cases that aren't surefire wins, this probably wouldn't make it to court.

As Laura Germino of the Coalition of Immokalee Workers says, "Slavery doesn't happen in isolation."[36] It is generally part of a sequence of many abuses. In retrospect, perhaps "Gulf Coast Slaves" is a reasonably accurate title for Lovato's article; then again, perhaps it is too presumptive for an article that chronicles a situation of egregious worker exploitation, made possible in part by the federal government but falling just outside the legal definition of human trafficking. In time, as more cases are uncovered and prosecuted, it is to be hoped that the definition of slavery will become less blurred. What is clear is that when the government suspends basic worker protections and gives a free hand to contractors behind a smokescreen of "national security," people will be abused, cheated, demeaned, and, potentially, enslaved. The lesson of Iraq and Katrina seems to be that while America professes to abhor slavery, in an emergency anything goes, including the denial of fundamental human dignities. That this would be the case is disturbing given the large number of federal workers now deployed in the fight against trafficking and slavery.

SOME OF THE KING'S MEN

Who specifically forms the national battle line in the war against slavery in America? The federal government has no shortage of agencies addressing human trafficking. Our intention here is not to examine each agency and department but rather to focus on those that are most directly involved in fighting trafficking.[37]

The Department of Health and Human Services

When victims of human trafficking and slavery are found, the Department of Health and Human Services (HHS) is supposed to help them out. As the State Department explains:

> HHS is responsible for certifying foreign victims of human trafficking once they are identified. HHS issues certification letters for adult non-U.S. citizens to confer eligibility for certain benefits and services under any Federal or state program or activity to the same extent as a refugee. Benefits and services include: housing or shelter assistance, food assistance, income assistance, employment assistance, English language training, health care assistance, mental health services and assistance for victims of torture. HHS issues similar letters of eligibility for non-U.S. child victims of human trafficking (under age 18), who are immediately eligible for services and benefits to the same extent as refugees, once HHS has received proof that the child is a victim of trafficking. HHS funding focuses on TIP [Trafficking in Persons] victim assistance and increasing awareness and identification of foreign and internally trafficked victims in the United States. HHS funds the Rescue & Restore public awareness campaign and the National Human Trafficking Resource Center with an information hotline at 888–373–7888.[38]

THE HAND THAT GIVETH—OR NOT

In the antitrafficking world, HHS is the agency most involved in building coalitions among, and affiliations with, NGOs. HHS is a vast agency; with its approximately fifty thousand employees, it ranks as the second largest, just behind the Department of Defense.[39] As the State Department description indicates, HHS is largely responsible for the allocation of funding to the various NGOs working in the field of human trafficking. As such, the agency has come in for a lot of criticism, both because of the organizations chosen—and not chosen—to receive the money and because of the policies and procedures for the allocation and distribution of funds. The controversy takes us back to the thorny question of prostitution.

A section added to the 2003 law reauthorizing the TVPA requires that NGOs wishing to receive—or *continue* to receive—federal funding sign a statement that they do not "promote, support or advocate the legalization or practice of prostitution." Some NGOs never deal with sex trafficking cases; nonetheless, they are obliged to sign or go unfunded. Of the organizations who do offer services to victims of trafficking and forced prostitution, many also provide services to "sex workers" of all kinds, some who would describe themselves as voluntary. In such cases, the requirement seems contradictory. Some NGOs have likened the provision to a witch-hunt, others to a violation of the right of free speech. Since there is no federal antiprostitution law with the exception of the Mann Act, it is difficult to understand how "promoting" or "supporting" any nonviolent policy can lead to a denial of participation in a government program under the First Amendment. Though the controversy concerns prostitution, the principle concerns free speech. If this pattern were reflected in other areas of debate, then environmental groups could be denied governmental participation or funding for "promoting" the idea of global warming and schools could have their funding cut for "supporting" the theory of evolution.

However, Vanessa Garza, associate director for trafficking policy in HHS's Office of Refugee Resettlement (ORR), responds that the provision is neither outrageous nor inappropriate: "The money is a gift from the American people, and we have to make sure it goes to the right people." She adds, "The government places conditions on funding all the time; this is just one among many. Our goal is to rescue victims of human trafficking, and the administration feels prostitution is an enabler. The policy is in place to protect the organizations. They don't have to sign it; they just won't get the money. If you take government funding, you have to play by the government rules. We have this little pot of money, and it's our job to make sure the best organizations get it."[40] Steve Wagner, who was director of HHS's Human Trafficking Program from 2003 to 2006, feels very strongly that the requirement is essential to recognizing prostitution as a form of trafficking. He sees the provision as "totally appropriate. If you don't get the exploitation here, you don't belong in the antitrafficking business."[41]

Another bone of contention for a large number of NGOs is the change in the funding procedures. In the past grants were awarded to a range of service providers, but in 2005 HHS went to a per capita system—so much money allocated per victim helped. According to Vanessa Garza, the government's initial approach was to throw money at the problem:

"In the beginning, we were funding organizations that never found a victim; now we're putting our money into servicing victims and tailoring case management to the victims' needs."[42] Says Steve Wagner, who was director at the time the decision to go to a per capita system was made, "The system I inherited involved a series of grants both to provide services to victims and to do some vague community outreach. I found this to be extremely insufficient." The grants, says Wagner, had nothing to do with the caseloads. "We had agencies with more victims than they could handle, and more than they were provided for," while others "were receiving money and didn't have a single case. There was no incentive for grantees or [other] organizations . . . to go out and find victims." Wagner states that at the time he took office he was "distressed at the lack of accountability" and assumed the per capita system would "incentivize" NGOs and create its own automatic accountability: if you brought in a victim, you got the money. When an official at the agency who chose to remain anonymous was asked why HHS didn't go to a hybrid system, which would have automatically continued the grant money to organizations with real caseloads while cutting or putting on the per capita system those without trafficking victims, the official replied, "Ask Steve Wagner." Says Wagner, "The per capita system was the only way we could achieve our objective. With a hybrid system, certain incumbents would be given noncompetitive grants because of caseloads. We would be put in the position of picking a priori who the grantees would be. The per capita system makes it an empirical issue. Besides," he adds, "I'm not convinced there *were* grantees who had a caseload that justified the extent of their grant."[43] A number of NGOs who had viable caseloads and who lost funding take exception.

But how is the per capita system working out? Although Wagner states, "I'm out of it; I don't know how it's working," he acknowledges that the "number of victims found and certified during my time was small, and it's inadequate now. The per capita system, as I envisioned it, is not a 'silver bullet.' It's very disappointing. I thought there'd be a tremendous proliferation of agencies receiving help, and correspondingly, there would be a large number of victims. . . . I was hoping we were moving towards some sort of breakthrough; that may still be the case. There's a certain inevitability to a breakthrough."[44]

While it is true that some NGOs served more victims than others and that there was considerable fiscal waste, the per capita policy had a negative impact on many victim service organizations. This system puts the onus on the NGO to go out and find trafficking victims, which, they say, is not really their job. They argue that this should be done by state, county, and local law enforcement, who are in a much better position—and have an obligation—to investigate and uncover trafficking cases. Many service providers and victim advocates feel that the fiscal pressure to leave their service role in order to "bring in" victims is a wrongheaded approach that hurts everyone in the long run—including victims. With the per capita approach, several organizations that previously had viable caseloads have had to reduce both staff and services. In some cases, they have simply closed their doors.[45] Garza echoes the department line that both law enforcement agencies and NGOs should work toward finding victims of trafficking. The police can benefit from NGO tips and help in "bringing them forward." She also concedes, however, that through the per capita system "Some good NGOs were penalized." Garza, who inherited the system from Wagner, admits, "We've been accused of killing programs."[46]

Wagner takes a much harder line: "NGOs who voice that opinion [that NGOs are not equipped to go out and find victims] should talk to the NGOs who are in the business of *finding* victims. The issue is, what is the NGO's mission? I don't accept the argument that NGOs have a different role. I see them as the most effective detectors of victims, because they're in the community." He does agree with Garza, however, that the effort should be a joint one, uniting NGOs with local law enforcement.[47]

Looked at objectively, investigating trafficking situations can be dangerous. This is fieldwork, and hazardous fieldwork at that. Should a service provider—a counselor, say, or a psychologist, or even a college-level volunteer—be required to take such risks in order to qualify to receive government funding? Further, asks Ann Jordan of Global Rights, "Why is HHS's Office of Refugee Resettlement funding investigations in the first place? Aren't investigations the job of law enforcement, and not of unaccountable, untrained members of the public? I thought HHS's mandate was to provide support for services to victims. It seems that someone at HHS has a clear misunderstanding here of the different and distinct functions of NGOs, law enforcement, and the Department of Health and Human Services."[48] An HHS representative responded that the NGOs aren't actually *required* to find victims; they just won't receive funding without them.

At one point, HHS took the unconventional step of hiring Ketchum Public Relations, a worldwide PR firm better known for clients such as Kleenex, to implement its Rescue and Restore campaign, with its "Look beneath the Surface" slogan. "We gave them a goal—who they should contact and partner with: faith-based and community, law enforcement and legal, social services, ethnic organizations," says Vanessa Garza.[49] In 2005, the PR campaign was given the Silver Anvil award by the Public Relations Society of America. The success of the agency's efforts, however, has been called into question by various NGOs and officials at other government agencies, and it has been suggested that their contract was renewed only so that they could correct mistakes made in the first go-round. According to one anonymous Washington area victim service provider, "We're giving money to Ketchum so they can train people who can train people who can train people to serve victims. Trafficking victims are hidden. They're not really going to be affected by a big, splashy PR campaign. They're not watching Lifetime television."[50] A high-ranking government official spoke more succinctly of Ketchum on condition of anonymity: "They should be gone."

Steve Wagner, however, who was in some measure responsible for bringing Ketchum aboard, has nothing but praise for the agency. "They're fantastic," he states. "I have the highest regard for Ketchum. They did a fantastic job, which was recognized by a Silver Anvil award, their [Look beneath the Surface] video won awards. They're great. And no," he adds, in response to a persistent rumor that followed him out of office, "I didn't go to work for Ketchum after I left government."[51]

HHS is responsible for "certifying" foreign-born victims of trafficking. "Certification" means that the government recognizes a person as a human trafficking victim under the criteria set out in the TVPA. It is no secret that finding such victims has been difficult and that the results have been disappointing. Meanwhile, a shift in focus has occurred, toward U.S. citizen victims. Some victim advocates and service providers who have been working with foreign-born victims maintain that it is a policy shift brought about by an administration desperately seeking trafficking victims and finding that trafficked American children are easier to find than foreign victims. One Washington NGO member takes a harsh view: "Because of the government's failure to ID victims, they're dumping tons of money into IDing U.S. children and reconceptualizing it as trafficking. U.S. 'victims' are much easier to identify." HHS insists that this is not the case. "I don't see that at all," responds Vanessa Garza. "I've heard U.S. victims are the 'low-hanging fruit,' but I don't see it that way. Even though we might find tens or hundreds of thousands of U.S. child prostitutes, that doesn't mean we should stop funding for foreign-born victims. It's not a case of either/or. We're trying to get back to the middle."[52] Steve Wagner believes that there are ten times more U.S. than foreign-born victims; he places their number between two hundred thousand and four hundred thousand a year, "exclusively juvenile victims of sex trafficking," and adds, "A report will be coming out shortly to support those numbers." As to the plight of U.S. victims, Wagner states, "The TVPA is a fantastic piece of legislation; most of its faults are in the implementation. The TVPA [which was written to apply exclusively to foreign-born trafficking victims] says that U.S. victims already *have* access to systems. But the most important service we could give them is to establish a relationship between victim and service provider. U.S. victims don't get this service."[53] Garza agrees. "U.S. citizens, by virtue of their birth, are entitled to services already—but a good case manager can help walk them through it." But, she adds, "there are disconnects. We *do* fund case management for foreign victims; we don't do that for domestic victims. HHS has asked Congress for five million dollars for the past two years for this, and we haven't gotten it. Meanwhile, we're doing the best we can to see that our programs are responsive to the field."[54]

HHS, through ORR, also created a number of "grassroots coalitions," twenty-one of them, since 2005. Their purpose, according to the HHS Web site, is to "enlist local community organizations in the task of abolishing trafficking within the community," in order to "disseminate information on the phenomenon of trafficking, to train organizations of intermediaries, and to otherwise galvanize the community to identify and rescue victims." As distinct from the forty-two Department of Justice (DOJ) task forces that, according to Steve Wagner, focus totally on law enforcement, the HHS coalitions ostensibly seek to connect with "local coalition members and available resources for victims."[55] "Coalitions," he states, "were implemented to get the movement out of Washington and into the community. We were after a community response."[56] The degree to which they are succeeding varies, depending on whose opinion is heard. Some, including a former DOJ official, claim that there is considerable redundancy in having both the coalitions and the task forces. One HHS official, speaking on condition of anonymity, acknowledges, "Both [coalitions and task forces] provide services; there's replication across the board, and now the Department of Labor is coming in to do some of the work. There is some confusion." Steve Wagner disputes this, and Vanessa Garza—who inherited this program as well—states, "We put a lot of money into building them, but they have been self-sustaining ever since. Whereas DOJ can't control who applies to their task forces, the HHS coalitions pick their member organizations." It is, she says, a "network of care." Membership is voluntary, there is no compensation, and some of the coalitions, Garza points out, have actually morphed into subcommittees of the federal task forces.[57] Some members of the DOJ, who asked to remain anonymous, expressed the view that the HHS coalitions were unnecessary, redundant, and politically motivated.

One sticking point at HHS is the frequent delays in the treatment of child trafficking victims. The child is sent to ORR. Once here, he or she often floats in limbo, as the case is shuttled from ORR to the DOJ, along with the FBI and ICE. Meanwhile, months can pass before resident status is awarded, during which time the child is held in detention or simply cut loose to run away. The 2007 reauthorization bill proposes that ORR be allowed to issue temporary custody of the child to the Unaccompanied Refugee Minor Program, to provide services and housing *before* certification and the award of a visa. This could do a great deal to shrink the size of the hole in the system through which many child victims fall.

USCCB: THE CATHOLIC CHURCH AND THE SERVING OF VICTIMS

In 2006, HHS decided to contract with an outside organization to distribute funds according to the newly formed per capita system. After soliciting proposals, they selected the U.S. Conference of Catholic Bishops (USCCB) and awarded them a multi-million-dollar contract, totaling one-third of HHS's annual trafficking budget, to oversee and provide funding to subcontractors. According to Vanessa Garza, HHS meets weekly with representatives of USCCB, which is using federal funds to support a list of organizations. When asked about the appropriateness of having one particular religious denomination wield so much financial control over a national campaign, she replied, "Faith-based organizations do great work on the ground. USCCB is the most effective contractor I've ever worked with. They know their stuff, they're very victim centered, and they have strong relationships with their partners. They solely advocate for the rights of the victim."[58]

Indeed, USCCB has been involved in the antitrafficking campaign since actively advocating for the passage of the TVPA in 2000. They immediately began to build coalitions, one of which—the Catholic Organization Against Trafficking—still functions and is doing very well, according to Sister Mary Ellen Dougherty, coordinator of education and outreach for USCCB's Anti–Human Trafficking Program. In 2002, they received a three-year grant from HHS to provide educational and technical assistance to migrant farmworkers, urban groups, local law enforcement, medical centers, and the general and religious populations. In one of the earlier trafficking cases—the Kil Soo Lee case on American Samoa—they served several victims through Catholic Charities.[59] That same year, they focused on trafficked children, advising agencies on how to recognize the victims and place them in the Unaccompanied Refugee Minor Program. They created a service-to-adults program in 2003, entitled "Anytime, Anywhere," through another three-year HHS grant. In 2004, they were awarded grants from the DOJ to develop an antitrafficking response in two areas—the Mid-Atlantic states and Oregon. This entailed establishing task forces and providing communication, training, and community outreach. The following year, they oversaw an HHS outreach grant, managed by Catholic Charities in Camden, New Jersey, and funded to identify victims of both sexual exploitation and agricultural servitude in the southern part of the state. Prior to the award of the 2006 per capita contract, they had received an HHS grant to provide services to victims anywhere in the country where they were found and identified. When the Request for Proposals for the per capita contract was announced, says Sister Mary Ellen, "we felt experienced, and we applied."[60]

Says Anastasia Brown, director of Refugee Programs for USCCB, "We'll work with anyone who subscribes to the regulations of the contract," adding that this presupposes an organization of sufficient experience, size, and commitment to warrant funding. "We don't really deny funding to an agency if capacity and the financial viability to front the services are issues; we just say, 'Not now,' and suggest they affiliate with a larger, more experienced local agency that's already a provider—a shelter, for example—in order to receive funding." Unless an NGO can demonstrate the immediate need to serve victims, there is no funding. As Brown states, "Not all our subcontractors have seen a victim, but they are all ready to receive victims. There is a preexisting contract mechanism pending finding victims. This allows for accountability."[61]

As to the actual role of the NGO in finding victims themselves, Nyssa Mestes, USCCB assistant director for trafficking, believes that there are "many types of agencies qualified as NGOs. Some are better suited to find and identify victims than others." Mestes doesn't place the responsibility solely with the NGOs: "Victims don't come into the [NGO] offices looking for help. So the involvement of local law enforcement is very important." She sees the need for the NGOs to "build networks of relationships in order to find and service victims," and she considers the police vital to these networks.[62]

USCCB has been allocated up to $6 million for regranting over a five-year period. This does not mean they automatically have the full amount to distribute; as they are quick to point out, it is conditional on numbers of victims found and appropriated funding. In 2007, they were asked by the government to provide research to help determine how long victims should receive services and how much they should be allotted.

The unreality of this "one size fits all" approach is immediately obvious. No two victims are alike. Aside from the fact that there are different kinds of exploitation within human trafficking, each victim carries his or her own history, problems, and needs. There is no "average" trafficking victim; no one can predict the amount of psychological support needed by a victim of months or years of beatings, rape, and slavery, or what amount of bilingual help a non-English speaking victim might need. USCCB based their research on the average length of time victims have been in care in the past. Basing their determinations on data from USCCB and other sources, HHS came up with a period of up to nine months of service for precertified victims, with a monthly allotment of $1,300, and four months for certified victims, at $900 per month. Not surprisingly, there are serious problems, beyond language and adjustment issues. "Trials," says Brown, "are times of incredible trauma and mental anguish" for trafficking victims, when they could most benefit from counseling. However, if their allotted time for service has expired by the opening of a trial, they are basically out of luck. Another time of stress is during family readjustment. This is a time when a victim needs service—even if the allotted period has expired. In emergency situations, USCCB can go to HHS's ORR and ask for dispensation to spend more time, and more money, on a given victim, but a positive response is by no means guaranteed. Without question, the time limits placed on the distribution of services impose an artificial and frustrating qualifier, especially, says Brown, when service is contingent on the involvement of law enforcement.[63]

To further complicate matters, there is inconsistent service at different levels of government—something USCCB is currently documenting and attempting to correct. Says Brown, "Victims who have already been serviced and are eligible for refugee benefits might not receive them because in many places it's difficult to get city, state and county offices to understand the system. For example, the federal government doesn't require that victims have photo IDs, but a lot of local welfare offices ask for them anyway. This can delay the process tremendously." Delays are also a result of slow processing of T visas. Logistically, Brown says, "there must be some limitation to funds and services; still there's a lot of dependency on law enforcement to get these people a T visa, and although the turnaround can be as fast as one month, it can take upwards of ten to twelve months." And there is often ignorance, she points out, on the part of law enforcement. For instance, "Most Border Patrol agents have no knowledge of trafficking, and none of them feels it's their responsibility to ID victims. And this is Homeland Security territory!"[64] Sister Mary Ellen sees an enormous degree of "pragmatism" on the part of law enforcement. She spoke of a recent case reported by an NGO in which dozens of victims were brought to the attention of the FBI, of whom the bureau selected only eight, on the premise that this was the number they needed to make their case. And although local and state police are required to apply to the federal government for a victim's "continued presence"—their right to stay in the United States—very few are actually doing it.[65]

To their credit, USCCB doesn't feel that the per capita system is the end-all and be-all for the provision of services. Although she sees benefits in the system—built-in accountability, tighter control of funds—Sister Mary Ellen acknowledges the absence of valuable service providers and concedes, "The field feels the loss of these agencies. We've lost some very fine, valuable colleagues who are no longer able to do the work. It's a shame."[66] Nor is USCCB averse to a viable hybrid system; Nyssa Mestes sees it as potentially "a good thing, to budget some and put others on per capita." Still she feels, "The sites that have the large caseloads are the same as would succeed in the per capita system. It's the agencies with medium-size caseloads who don't do well; there's too much fluctuation."[67]

Apparently, USCCB is satisfied with its list of subcontractors. "The agencies providing services are doing very good work," says Mestes. "It's tough work; some of these victims have had their whole world turned upside down. They come with only the clothes on their backs."[68] Still, USCCB staffers have no illusions regarding the small number of victims found. As do so many victim advocates, Sister Mary Ellen points to the hidden nature of the crime itself as a reason why more victims don't come forward. She adds, however, "They're driven even further underground when the national conversation on immigration is as hostile as it's become." She stresses community education as a means of finding victims, pointing to the mailman and the "guy delivering alcoholic beverages to a bar" as typical people who can be trained to know what—and whom—to look for.[69]

Overall, the number of victims found in the United States, when compared to the multiagency press and expenditures, is alarmingly small. And as defined by the parameters of their contract, USCCB is empowered to fund services only to foreign-born victims of human trafficking. Still, they are proud of their record and of the results of their recent efforts within the framework of the current contract. In the eighteen months between April 2006—when the contract was awarded—and the end of October 2007, 569 victims of trafficking were identified. Of these, 322 were victims of labor trafficking, 184 of sex-related trafficking, and 63 of both. They came from sixty-nine different countries, the most predominant of which were Thailand, Mexico, South Korea, Russia, and the Philippines.

USCCB makes no secret of the fact that it is a faith-based organization. This has raised concern among some service providers, who feel that the organization (and, by implication, HHS) tend to lean toward supporting organizations whose thinking is more in line with their own. There are, according to Sister Mary Ellen's records, currently ninety-two subcontractors, thirty-three—or 35.8 percent—of which are Catholic agencies. However, she points out that they have never solicited strictly religious organizations but have "advertised the contract to just about everybody in the world. Many of the smaller organizations wouldn't take the contracts because there was no money in it for them." Besides, she stresses, a lot of social service agencies, by definition, are faith based.[70]

Still, one provision of the contract is particularly unsettling to a number of service providers. Found in both the proposal and the contract, it reads, "As we are a Catholic organization, we need to ensure that our victims services funds are not used to refer or fund activities that would be contrary to our moral convictions and religious beliefs. . . . Specifically, subcontractors could not provide or refer for abortion services or contraceptive materials for our clients pursuant to this contract."[71] In a situation where a trafficking victim—either adult or minor—is raped and made pregnant by her trafficker, USCCB will deny related services to that victim should she choose to have an abortion. She is forced to either bear her trafficker's unwanted child or seek alternatives on her own, without benefit of government financial assistance. Abortion is legally available in the United States in exactly these circumstances, but if you have been trafficked, enslaved, and raped, our government's system of "victim support" denies it.

At a time when the line separating church and state has been crossed and recrossed throughout the tenure of the Bush administration, many see it as unacceptably blurred here. What business, ask several NGOs, does a church-based group have in determining civil policy? It's a valid question, and one that the USCCB addresses head on. "It is a church-based consideration," acknowledges Sister Mary Ellen. "We were up front with the federal government when we submitted the proposal, and the government was okay with it. Your question shouldn't be 'Why did we include it?' It should be, 'Why did the government approve it? Why did they give us a contract with that clause in it?'"[72]

Steve Wagner, who was director of HHS's Human Trafficking Program at the time the USCCB contract was awarded, is an antiabortion advocate and served in George W. Bush's Faith Based Office. When asked what he thought of a church-driven provision that would leave a pregnant trafficking victim figuratively if not literally out in the cold, he responded, "You don't want to ask me what I think of abortion."[73]

Federal Bureau of Investigation

The FBI is the DOJ's main investigative agency. One hundred years old in 2008, it acts as the government's primary federal investigative branch as well as a domestic intelligence agency. These are the guys we stereotypically picture in dark suits and short hair. Known as the agency of J. Edgar Hoover, the bureau has long been viewed in polarized terms: by some as a heroic force standing to preserve the American way of life and by others as a group of gruff, humorless functionaries who often can't get out of their own way and stand aloof from other agencies.

OFFICE OF VICTIM ASSISTANCE

The FBI is one of the government's vanguard agencies in its human trafficking campaign. It divides its efforts mainly between two departments—the Office for Victim Assistance (OVA) and the Civil Rights Unit. OVA, as a prominent NGO member described it, is the "warm and fuzzy" branch. By definition, it "manages and supports victim assistance operations across the FBI."[74] According to OVA program director Kathryn Turman, it works with NGOs and state and local service providers. "Our function is to see that victims of crimes receive the rights and services due them and the assistance to help them cope with the crime." The department's job, says Turman, is "strictly humanitarian." Their victim specialists go to the crime scenes with the field agents. "It helps the agents, and it's satisfying to see victims get help, to cope and do better."[75]

Of the nearly two hundred thousand crime victims identified by the FBI in fiscal 2006, Turman acknowledges that only a small handful were victims of human trafficking. She attributes this to the legal definition of trafficking, the difficulty in getting victims to come forward, and the fact that many apparent trafficking cases end up being alien smuggling cases. Turman sees stumbling blocks in bringing trafficking cases and helping victims. "There's no time to get to know the victims and build their trust. Also, most human trafficking cases—forced labor, households, small businesses—are harder to find." Turman adds that about half the bureau's "take-down cases" are labor based and half sex related.[76]

One facet of trafficking that frustrates Turman involves juvenile victims of forced prostitution. "A lot of well-meaning NGOs and police want to help, but the services these kids need just aren't there. You can't send them home, you can't put them in foster care, and they don't belong in jail. They need medical and mental health care, help with substance abuse, counseling to get over relationships with pimps. Most agencies don't want them and aren't set up for it. A lot of these kids are going to run. They're going to end up back on the street, or they'll get killed. There's no cocoon for them."[77]

According to Turman, the trafficking cases brought by the bureau are fairly evenly divided between foreign-born and domestic victims. She holds the not uncommon view that a lot of attention has been paid to international victims—as per the provisions of the TVPA—with minimal focus on U.S.-born victims. "Training and funding," she states, "are framed to look at foreign citizens. It all gets stove-piped."[78]

Turman speaks freely on her department's involvement in the federal antitrafficking task forces. "We encourage our OVA victim specialists to be members," she says, although she sees the same weaknesses in the task force system described by others: "Although they are useful out in the field, some of them are more useful than others. Members often don't speak the same language—law enforcement and NGOs, agencies who don't trust each other. Somehow they have to break down barriers." A frequent NGO complaint, she says, is the need for better FBI and ICE training on how to "address and interview victims, especially when they're from countries where the police are to be feared. Investigations require time to get to know the victims and earn their trust. We want to treat these people well; they're not tissues to be discarded." Turman's department handles all continued presence victims, ensuring they get help finding jobs, housing, ESL classes, and counseling. Working with ICE, it also addresses visa issues.[79]

Turman believes in her department's work; however, there are things she would see changed: "We need better training, and lots more of it. 'What are victims? How did they become victims?' Many don't even believe they're victims of slavery—it's a survival skill. Both NGOs and government need greater awareness as to the nature of victims. It's a multifaceted problem." Turman recalls a time when coordinating councils, mandated by Congress, met regularly and coordinated policy and training. "It forced the various agencies to work together. With DOJ guidance, each task force could become more of a model and give people a process to problem solving."[80]

Not surprisingly, Turman echoes the generic call for additional manpower and funding. "These cases take a lot of time and require many more services than are needed for a straightforward gun or drug case." It would be beneficial to have an "emergency fund to help in cases of trafficking victims when we need to fly in services, do TB testing, find housing, and so on."[81]

CIVIL RIGHTS UNIT

The Civil Rights Unit of the FBI is responsible for the "guidance and direction" of the bureau's Civil Rights Program. The unit oversees four programs, of which Human Trafficking ranks third in order of importance, behind Hate Crimes and Excessive Force by Law Enforcement but ahead of Freedom of Access to Clinic Entrances (FACE). But, we are assured, Human Trafficking is growing in importance, having climbed to 20 percent of the unit's cases in 2007, up from only 1 to 2 percent in 2002.[82]

While Kathryn Turman speaks for OVA, Unit Chief Carlton Peeples was assigned to speak for the bureau's Civil Rights Unit. It is impossible—gender aside—to confuse the two. Both are clearly professionals; however, where Turman does come across as slightly "warm and fuzzy," Peeples has a straight-on, no-nonsense federal agent's delivery. "Our role," he states, "is to investigate credible cases of human trafficking." He echoes Turman's statement concerning the small number of cases and victims found but points to a slow but steady increase: "In 2002, we opened only 58 cases, we made 65 arrests, and obtained 15 convictions; In fiscal 2006, the number of cases opened grew to 216, the number of arrests to 125, and convictions to 63." Peeples has an interesting take on why there are still so few cases uncovered. Aside from the standard response that trafficking is a hidden crime, he believes that victims have no incentive to come forward, largely because "their state of captivity is still better than their lives in the country they're coming from. Part of it," he adds, "is psychological trauma as well—and fear of harm to their families in the country of origin."[83]

In describing the bureau's involvement with other agencies involved in the antitrafficking campaign, Peeples makes no bones about the tension between ICE and the FBI. "Our relationship with ICE needs some work." While he describes ICE's function as "protecting the borders," he points to a "territorial war at the upper levels" that, he perceives, "comes down to funding. Foreign-born victims come through ICE's domain. There's an intelligence gap between ICE and FBI to work for the greater good and to provide victim assistance through both agencies." He states, however, that this is mainly an administrative conflict and that "on the ground we tend to get along."[84]

In discussing the issue of foreign-born as opposed to U.S. citizen victims, Peeples "can't concur" with former HHS director Steve Wagner's estimate of two hundred thousand to four hundred thousand American child victims per year. "Of the 216 cases opened in 2007, only 11 percent involved U.S. citizens. The numbers speak for themselves." Of the cases the bureau has opened in the past six years, about half involved "recruitment for the commercial sex industry"; of the remaining half, the most prevalent number involved domestic servitude. "Domestics," says Peeples, "are given more freedom than other types of victims. They have the opportunity to build relationships, and sometimes that other person helps get them out of their situation. In other forms of trafficking, the 'Big Eye' is always watching you." Peeples sees the Good Samaritan as the victims' best—and sometimes only—hope for rescue. "I don't know how these government programs are reaching [the victims]. It's the Good Samaritans who play the big role. Maybe they've seen an NGO's public service announcement or awareness campaign."[85]

Peeples sees the need for interservice communication in addressing trafficking cases. "We encourage the agents at our fifty-six field offices to build relationships. When we have a takedown, or need to relate to victims, we need to outreach to NGOs. They are in a unique position to provide intelligence and victim services." Most leads, he states, come directly from the victims, through the NGOs. Peeples agrees with Turman that agency training is vital but states that FBI training is strictly internal, with no training given either by the federal government or by the various NGOs. "Since 2002, we've trained 650 agents and 1,200 local officials on what constitutes a human trafficking violation and how to investigate a case."[86] (In fact, the FBI's agents and field offices have attended various training programs since the passage of the TVPA, some of which were given by the Freedom Network and the Coalition of Immokalee Workers.) He also believes that local police are in the best possible position to find victims.

On questions of victim services, Peeples defers to OVA but says, "We need the victim to cooperate, so we need the victim to be comfortable. We have to overcome the victim's perception that police are bad; for this, we rely on OVA and the NGOs." The NGOs, he adds, "are bringing awareness to the public," and he concedes that "there needs to be a better relationship between FBI and the NGOs."[87]

NGOs give the FBI a mixed report card. Some service providers point to situations in which agents were constantly on site, offering help to both the NGO and the victim and working in close conjunction with other federal and local agencies. Others express frustration and anger over instances when FBI agents have been unavailable and uninterested. When asked about agent accountability, Peeples insists that a review process makes all agents accountable. "It's extremely important for Americans to know that the FBI takes human trafficking and civil rights very seriously. We will vigorously investigate any possible human trafficking situation. If an allegation is made by an NGO, it would go to the management of that agency in the field." Sometimes, however, the field office itself has received the criticism. Peeples places some of the responsibility for agent nonresponse on the fact that "not every case brought forth by an NGO is human trafficking. Each agent makes that determination. That might be taken as uncooperative; but if we make a decision not to proceed, it's because we don't see a case. And we don't make that determination lightly; we talk to DOJ Civil Rights before making that decision. And if an NGO brings us too many of these, they will lose the trust of the agent, who will be a lot more skeptical next time."[88] While there is, no doubt, validity to this scenario, many NGOs feel that some agents are simply better at the job than others, that some "get it" while others lack a grasp of—and a commitment to—the issue of human trafficking.

Another factor is at work here. In *The War on Human Trafficking: U.S. Policy Assessed*, Anthony M. DeStefano compares the number of potential trafficking cases reported to the DOJ by such agencies as the FBI and ICE with the number prosecuted. The disparity is staggering.

In case after case, the DOJ declined to bring criminal charges. The impact this can have on even the most dedicated of agents is obvious: Why pursue human trafficking cases when they are almost certain to be denied prosecution? As to why the government rejects the large majority of cases brought it, DeStefano states that "prosecutors in all federal court districts declined to proceed to criminal charges for reasons that seemed constant from year to year: lack of evidence of criminal intent, weak or insufficient admissible evidence, 'office policy' (which was not defined), problems with jurisdiction or court venue, no evidence of a federal offense, 'minimal' interest of prosecutors because a prosecution wouldn't have deterrent value, and problems with witnesses," such as fear, inability to identify their traffickers, and failure to remember all the details of their experience.[89] Although the federal government is proud of its record of convictions based on the TVPA, by selecting the slam-dunks and weeding out the doubtful cases, the DOJ mathematically increases its chances of success. As DeStefano points out, "Clearly . . . if prosecutors do not decline a referral, there is a strong likelihood that the resulting prosecution will lead to a conviction."[90]

Bureau of Immigration and Customs Enforcement

The events of September 11, 2001, changed many things and led to the formation of ICE. For decades there had been two distinct agencies, the Immigration and Naturalization Service (INS) and the U.S. Customs Service. Before 9/11 both agencies had taken steps to develop antitrafficking and antislavery strategies. They came at this work from very different perspectives. For the Customs Service, antislavery work centered on the enforcement of the laws forbidding the importation of slave-made goods that are described in chapter 6. The INS was primarily concerned with the control of people entering the country, and that naturally included concerns about smuggling and human trafficking. The new visa for trafficking victims was just being brought into force in September 2001 when the world changed.

In the aftermath, the Department of Homeland Security was formed and a reorganization of agencies began. In these changes the INS and the U.S. Customs Service were combined to form ICE. The "shotgun marriage" of the two agencies required major adjustments. And for both agencies work on slavery and trafficking slowed to a crawl as staff were reassigned to border security and antiterrorism jobs.

In some ways the difficult transition to a combined agency has been good for ICE's antislavery and antitrafficking work. By late 2007 it was possible to point to three types of antislavery work done by ICE. The first was the interdiction of goods or commodities made by slaves or prison labor. Stopping the flow of slave-made goods into the country is difficult. Many of the products discussed in chapter 6 are the subjects of ongoing ICE investigations. The second is Operation Predator, ICE's comprehensive initiative to safeguard children from pedophiles, international sex tourists, Internet child pornographers, and human traffickers. The December 2007 conviction of a Maryland man to fifty years' imprisonment for the production of child pornography was typical of the joint operations ICE does with local law enforcement and the Postal Service to bring down child sex abusers. Finally, ICE has its own program against human trafficking, and more than other agencies has been issuing Civil Asset Forfeiture Reform Act (CAFRA) notices to property owners whose properties have been identified as being used to facilitate smuggling or harboring aliens. This is an important tool because many employers and landlords turn a blind eye to the facilitation of criminal activity on their properties, though U.S. law clearly allows the confiscation of property used in slavery or trafficking.

Department of State

The State Department explains its role in the fight against human trafficking and slavery in this way:

> DOS chairs the information-sharing, interagency working group and Cabinet-level task force responsible for coordinating anti-trafficking policies and programs. The Bureau of Population, Refugees, and Migration (PRM) and the Office to Monitor and Combat Trafficking in Persons (G/TIP) fund international anti-trafficking programs. G/TIP also produces the Annual Trafficking in Persons Report which spotlights modern-day slavery around the world, encourages the work of the civil sector, and is the U.S. government's principal diplomatic tool used to engage foreign governments. PRM also funds the Return, Reintegration, and Family Reunification Program for Victims of Trafficking. The Human Trafficking and Smuggling Center (HTSC) is an interagency fusion center and clearinghouse that disseminates information and prepares strategic assessments. It brings together law enforcement, intelligence, and diplomatic communities to work together to take action against criminals moving people around the world for profit, exploitation, or in support of terrorism.[91]

THE TIP OFFICE

The State Department's Office to Monitor and Combat Trafficking in Persons (usually called the TIP Office) was established by the TVPA. Its duties are to support the Interagency Task Force on Trafficking and to prepare an annual report on all countries, evaluating how well they're doing in fighting human trafficking. Soon after it was established, the TIP Office also became a conduit for the funding of antitrafficking and antislavery projects overseas. The annual Trafficking in Persons Report, using data gathered by embassies, consulates, and other sources, including NGOs, assesses 170 countries on their efforts to fight human trafficking and slavery. It is the most comprehensive global measure of trafficking and slavery and is used by the U.S. government to guide its diplomatic efforts to encourage and support antislavery work. The researchers who compile the report in the TIP Office face enormous challenges in collecting reliable information but have developed systems of careful validation, making this a report that is relied on around the world. Sadly, the report regularly faces two criticisms that have nothing to do with the professional researchers who bring it together; both criticisms concern requirements set by Congress in the TVPA law.

The first criticism concerns the provision that all countries be ranked into one of three categories, or "tiers." According to the law, countries that languish in the lowest category and show no sign of improvement over time can be sanctioned. Many people feel that for the United States to set up a scoring system, which only they control, to rank all other countries is not a helpful way to move forward. Several governments have reacted strongly to what they felt were unfair rankings. Moreover, an examination of those placed in the lowest tier and slapped with sanctions since 2001 shows political concerns creeping into the process. Cuba, North Korea, Sudan, and Burma are regularly sanctioned; "friendly" countries with significant amounts of slavery and trafficking (India, Pakistan, or Nigeria, for example) are not sanctioned. The second criticism hits closer to home: America has set itself up as judge over all other countries but has made no provision to have its own work assessed. The United States is not included in the report, and no effort has been made to commission an independent evaluation. It would make the excellent work of the annual TIP Report much more palatable to the rest of the world—and much more viable—if the United States were evaluated by the same standards as everyone else.

In many ways the most important work of the TIP Office is the least known: the funding of antitrafficking and antislavery projects in other countries. Some of these projects are designed to educate potential victims so that they are never tricked and trafficked. Others train the police and border patrols to better identify and prosecute traffickers. Still other projects support the rehabilitation and reintegration of victims of trafficking. In 2007, the TIP Office awarded $16.5 million for sixty-three projects in forty-six countries, making it one of the largest funders of antislavery work in the world. These funds are carefully monitored and tend to be effectively used. In northern India, for example, funds support the rescue and rehabilitation of enslaved children kidnapped and trafficked from their home villages into the "carpet belt" of Uttar Pradesh. Locked into small dark rooms, the children work long days, weaving carpets for export. They suffer beatings, malnutrition, sexual abuse, and lung disease from the dust and fibers. TIP Office funds support workers who find and liberate the children, as well as a residential center where they get the medical, psychological, and educational help they need to rejoin their families. Ginny Bauman, who manages this project for the NGO Free the Slaves, explains, "This is a large-scale problem of internal trafficking, but with solid support the children return and help organize and 'slave-proof' their villages, and that means no more children can be enslaved."[92]

President Bush appointed Mark Lagon to be ambassador at large and director of the TIP Office in 2007. Much of Lagon's attention is focused on the international scene, and he spends a lot of his time traveling abroad. In addition to his office evaluating the performance of the world's nations with regard to human trafficking, Lagon's responsibilities include monitoring trafficking within the United States. As chair of the Senior Policy Operating Group on Human Trafficking—a role he describes as "more cat-herder than director of the different agencies"— he meets with representatives of nine major government agencies, including the Departments of Labor, State, Justice, Homeland Security, Education, Defense, and Health and Human Services. According to the State Department, "This interagency working group coordinates the implementation of the Trafficking Victims Protection Act and addresses emerging interagency policy, grants, and planning issues."[93]

Lagon's predecessor was former congressman John Miller. During the course of his tenure, Miller engendered controversy among the members of the various human rights organizations. He was under extraordinary pressure from those responsible for his appointment, both in Congress and in the conservative and controlling Bush White House, to represent the position that all prostitution is slavery and that all human trafficking equates with prostitution. In the words of author Anthony DeStefano, he "used his job as a pulpit for abolitionism." But another writer on the subject, E. Benjamin Skinner, paints a more nuanced view. He notes that Miller's "staff, who parsed the issue very closely, understood that American law, and human morality, dictated that no one form of slavery was any more tolerable than any other. Miller, for his part, tried to strike a balance by speaking out against prostitution, but also by pressuring countries like India and Saudi Arabia to combat debt bondage and domestic slavery. Overall, he broadened the scope of American concern for the enslaved."[94] He also was among the first to make Americans aware of the link between human trafficking and slavery.

There have been other concerns about the TIP Office, and one is a lack of strategy and coordination. In 2006 the Government Accountability Office (GAO) reported that the "U.S. government has not developed a coordinated strategy to combat trafficking in persons abroad, as called for in a presidential directive, or evaluated its programs to determine whether projects are achieving the desired outcomes. . . . The lack of a coordinated strategy and evaluation plan prevents the U.S. government from determining the effectiveness of its efforts to combat human trafficking abroad or to adjust its assistance to better meet needs."[95] One victim advocate states that under Miller "there was no accountability, transparency, assessments, or evaluations of what was happening in the field, and no reorganization or restructuring of programs. In order to have a positive impact—and do no harm—it's necessary to have all your programs founded on objective, evidence-based analysis. This was not happening."[96] It is difficult to hang all the blame for this on Miller. Ugly battles between career staffers and political appointees wracked the TIP Office before he arrived and in the early part of his tenure, derailing attempts to build a coherent and rational strategy. The GAO investigation itself was sparked by concerns over political and ideological influence in the award of grants. Under his directorship, by the time Miller had left office the battles had ended and heads had rolled, but the government's lead international agency was behind where it might have been.[97]

Some hoped that when Miller left office his replacement would assume a more balanced approach to trafficking into labor versus prostitution. Ambassador Lagon certainly had the diplomatic experience needed to broker such a compromise. For over a decade, he climbed from one position of governmental responsibility to another, including deputy staff director of the House Republican Policy Committee, senior staff member of the Republican staff at the Senate Foreign Relations Committee, and deputy assistant secretary of state for international affairs. As director of the TIP Office, he also serves as senior advisor to the secretary of state.

Arranging an interview with the ambassador initially proved to be difficult. A request came for a list of questions to be submitted for approval. This is not unusual; with the various government and NGO representatives interviewed thus far, the process has been a formality. However, our proposed questions for Dr. Lagon, on issues such as the federal balance between sex and labor trafficking and the nature of funding to NGOs, were found unacceptable and were rejected. Following the submission of a revised list of questions, the interview was confirmed.

As it turned out, this screening process wasn't necessary; Dr. Lagon addressed all our questions (including those that had been rejected) fully and without hesitation. Intelligent and well spoken, he gave clear and concise answers. The subject of federal prioritizing of sex trafficking over other forms of slavery was one to which he'd clearly given thought, as he had the question of foreign-born versus U.S. citizen victims. Acknowledging that there had been an imbalance, he responded, "Sex trafficking is in some ways the most stark and salacious story that animates the movement. But we're trying—from [the NGO] Free the Slaves, to the U.N. Office on Drugs and Crime, to my office—to make sure that people understand that forced labor—indeed, what I would call slave labor—is a very important part of this as well. I'm concerned with making it a matter of policy that the TVPA was meant to cover all victims of trafficking equally—those victims of sex trafficking and slave labor, those victims—men and women—who are both foreign and nationals and U.S. citizens. There may be more of one than another in any of these pairings, but it's important that we not forsake any of them. In particular, I hope to work with my colleagues to more vigorously get access to the benefits and protections for victims that they already have rights to."[98]

Lagon defines himself as victim centered; in fact, he credits the TVPA for his involvement in the antitrafficking campaign. "The bill had one thing that captured it for me: it opened my eyes to what the victim-centered approach should be, and that was the idea of having a visa for people we found as victims, even if technically speaking they were illegal aliens. If they're so grossly exploited and controlled, that trumps all other issues." Lagon expressed concern for the welfare of the victim, which is often less of a consideration than the successful prosecution of the case itself: "It's natural for law enforcement to pursue hot leads, to want to get going, but we need to make sure we have a victim-centered approach first. . . . We need to give special care to child sex victims, and while we should encourage them through interviews by law enforcement to be witnesses, if you take care of them first, then their value as an asset will follow. The best way to get a witness for the prosecution is to give comfort and succor—rehabilitation and protection—to a victim. That part of [police] training—of the realization process on how to attack the problem—needs some work."[99]

He has no illusions about the need to train local law enforcement. While acknowledging that they're not the only ones who can spot a victim or a trafficking situation (he names social workers, emergency room staff, and church volunteers as potential Good Samaritans), he sees the police as "probably number one. We need to train more and more police. [Training] clearly has to be targeted in certain areas, so that those police who are exposed to areas where there is sex trafficking, where there are migrant workers in agriculture, or in restaurants, or factories, will have the tools to identify the victim."[100]

When asked what would head his wish list for additional federal funding, Lagon replied, "The first place I would devote more funding is to intense case management, to help someone who is a victim of human trafficking get access to what they have legal rights to already. You can't expect someone who is hamstrung by lack of language, or who has been traumatized by human trafficking—whether they're a foreign national or a U.S. citizen—to walk through all those bureaucratic steps to get access to what they need. Notably," he added, "foreign nationals are afforded the certification process, a T visa, intensive case management. Social workers can help them negotiate the intense bureaucracy that is the U.S. government. I just want to make sure that we do a bit more for U.S. citizens who happen to be the victims of human trafficking. There is a clear provision of benefits for U.S. citizens, but that helping hand in navigating the benefit structure of the U.S. government would be enhanced by efforts to give intensive case management." A request for funds to accomplish this, he says, was placed before Congress by the executive branch for the past two years and was rejected. "Congress feels that what we've had is enough, and they haven't taken that extra step; we're working to get the extra dollars we've been asking for."[101]

Referring to his own family history, Lagon stated, "I believe deeply in America being the land of migrants. I don't believe we should be helping U.S. citizens *instead* of foreign nationals; we should be helping both.

It's only natural that some NGOs look at things from their own parochial perspective; we all do. If an NGO's self-defined mission is to help foreign nationals, they may be concerned that something might happen to cut into their ability to service victims. There is no need, however, to have a sense that there must be a trade-off." Lagon is correct, but it is also true that the "mission" of most NGO antitrafficking projects is shaped by the TVPA, which—as we know—was created specifically to serve foreign-born victims. By expanding beyond the terms of the law, an NGO can risk loss of funding.

Lagon says he is working closely with Homeland Security's Citizenship and Immigration Services (CIS) to create a "technical way that someone could cross the threshold and become a U.S. citizen, by regulations that allow the T visa to be adjusted to permanent legal resident status." His comments regarding the embarrassingly low number of certified victims to date offer no surprises. The TVPA provides for T visas to be issued to up to five thousand trafficking victims per year. Since its passage in 2000, however, only slightly more than one thousand T visas have been issued. "Our head hasn't even brushed that ceiling," he states. "The existence of the T visa is a wonderful symbol of the nature of the regime. We need to go out and find all the more victims. The biggest obstacle is the victims' fear to come forward. They're afraid they'll be treated as illegal aliens or as criminals. In the sex industry, they may feel the blame will go to them rather than their exploiter. There is," he stresses, "a need for more awareness: public awareness, police awareness, immigration awareness, so that fear is reduced."[102]

The ambassador sees public awareness as the area where he can make the most progress. "We need to look at whether more can be done to raise awareness in communities, whether the training that is being given to local communities, while very well crafted, could do even more. And here, the multiplier effect of a dynamic NGO coalition is important. I hope to go out into the communities and help encourage the building of operational partnerships. . . . One has to assume it's going to be a difficult business finding victims; this is a learning process. . . . I'm not going to be afraid to go out and raise issues about sex trafficking . . . and additionally for people to understand that there is forced labor." Lagon envisions himself in a "bipartisan bubble in a time of poisonous partisanship," and sees the "robust bipartisan nature" of the fight against human trafficking as "one of the great strengths of the movement."[103]

Some critics view Lagon as old wine in a new bottle—saying all the right things but still believing that the most important aspects of human trafficking are related to prostitution and pimping. In his glowing appraisal of the New York State law, quoted in a previous chapter, Lagon praised the law for the way in which it addresses "all aspects of human trafficking, in particular on the sex trafficking front." No one would doubt his sincerity, and when he says, "I'd like to see thousands and thousands of victims found, and I'd like to see the market changed," you believe him.[104] Still, in an early-2008 interview on National Public Radio's *Tell Me More* program, Lagon stated, "Human trafficking is about people losing control over their lives and being bought and sold. And women and girls in prostitution fit that description."[105] In fact, that is only true insofar as it pertains to minors; there is no law—at least, thus far—that defines a prostitute as a slave, unless forced prostitution can be proven.

Ultimately, the TIP Office is the face of America's global war against human trafficking; as such, its imperative should lie not in an adherence to a glitzy political agenda, dictated by the moral crusade du jour, but rather in an unbiased recognition of slavery as it applies to all real and potential victims. Some of these men, women, and children are hard to find and harder to identify, but this very difficulty calls for an even greater commitment on the part of the federal government's antitrafficking efforts. The parts of the TIP Office that don't make the news, the research into trafficking and the support for foreign law enforcement and antislavery projects around the world, are excellent. It is a shame when that work is interrupted or distracted by politics.

As to the tier program, it is always easier to assign blame than to accept it; but the old adage concerning people in glass houses comes to mind. Our own house is far from clean, yet we have set ourselves up as the world's moral arbiters. Perhaps if the government spent the time and money addressing human trafficking in the United States that it spends in studying and judging other nations, we would see a more significant impact on slavery at home. The TIP Office is effective as far as it goes; it could go a lot further.

Department of Justice

The State Department Web site describes the role of the DOJ in this way:

> The DOJ Civil Rights Division's Criminal Section has the primary responsibility for the forced labor, sex trafficking, involuntary servitude and peonage statutes. It works closely with the FBI, DHS/ICE, other federal

and local law enforcement agencies, U.S. Attorneys Offices, and the Criminal Division's Child Exploitation and Obscenity Section (CEOS) to investigate and prosecute cases of trafficking in persons and worker exploitation. The Civil Rights Division also funds and staffs its national complaint line for reporting trafficking crimes at 1–888–428–7581. CEOS, in conjunction with federal and local law enforcement agencies, focuses on cases involving child sex trafficking, such as children exploited in prostitution in the U.S. and child sex tourism. The Bureau of Justice Assistance funds domestic programs such as the anti-trafficking Task Forces. The Office of Victims of Crime provides assistance to TIP [trafficking in persons] victims prior to certification. The National Institute of Justice and the Bureau of Justice Statistics conducts TIP research. The Office of Legal Policy produces the Attorney General's Report Annual Report to Congress on U.S. Government Activities to Combat Trafficking in Persons and the Assessment of U.S. Government Activities to Combat Trafficking in Persons.[106]

In fact, DOJ has been chasing down slavery cases for well over a century. As Lou de Baca tells it:

> While the term *trafficking* didn't come on the scene until the late 1990s, the Justice Department began to prosecute "trafficking" cases when it was founded in 1870, dismantling rings that enslaved Italian children as street beggars, Native American miners, Hispanics and Asians in prostitution, and African Americans kept in servitude in agriculture and domestic service through debt bondage, despite the Thirteenth Amendment.
>
> The Civil Rights Division has been prosecuting trafficking cases since it was started as a section in the Criminal Division during the Roosevelt administration, under the Peonage Program and later the Involuntary Servitude and Slavery Program. Those efforts took up the bulk of the office's work in the 1940s. Federal agents' and prosecutors' activities in conjunction with the NAACP were instrumental in dismantling the sharecropping system in the American South. But once the seminal Thirteenth Amendment cases were resolved, the civil rights movement's focus turned to education, housing, and voting efforts under the Fourteenth and Fifteenth Amendments. The 1970s and 1980s saw a shift from exploitation of African American U.S. citizens in the field, to exploitation of immigrants, especially in agriculture.
>
> A renewed antislavery effort by DOJ, FBI, INS, and DOL in the early 1980s received a crippling blow from the Supreme Court in the Kozminski case (involving a white American farmhand held in servitude through psychological coercion and exploitation of his mental illness), when it ruled that psychological coercion was not enough to prove a violation of the servitude statutes. Going into the Clinton administration, the Involuntary Servitude and Slavery Program was an important but diminished part of

the Civil Rights Division's work. That began to change in the wake of high-profile garment factory cases in the late 1990s and the increased international women's rights movement to stop trafficking for sexual exploitation, often from the former Soviet Union. When the Clintons needed to fight trafficking, they turned to their antislavery experts in the Civil Rights Division, who worked with DOL to put together an interagency task force and formulate legislation and policy responses.[107]

Early on, the Criminal Section of the DOJ's Civil Rights Division was chosen to lead the federal government's war on human trafficking. At the time, Al Moskowitz was section chief, and he recalls that toward the end of the Clinton administration, after the passage of the TVPA, the approach to trafficking was "balanced. Clinton spearheaded the new statute, with an emphasis on trafficking that wasn't there before. There wasn't a sense that we should move resources from other types of cases into trafficking." After the election of George W. Bush, however, Moskowitz witnessed an administration-mandated shift in the agency's priorities. The time, staff, and resources that the Civil Rights Division had been directing toward hate crimes and police abuse cases were now being reallocated to fighting trafficking. The reasons were twofold, says Moskowitz. First, there was a genuine interest in investigating and prosecuting a crime that was supposed to have ended 150 years earlier. There was a sense of moral outrage, combined with a real desire to find and help victims. Another reason, however, was less altruistic and reflected a purely political agenda. The federal government found a campaign against slavery to be more "politically attractive" than cases involving race issues or the prosecution of police officers. According to Moskowitz, "More and more resources were being pushed into trafficking" as the government urged the DOJ to investigate and prosecute more trafficking cases. "They were clearly making a choice on priorities, and there was a lot of pressure to produce. We were accountable for results."[108]

Inevitably, in the frenzy to produce results, cases of human smuggling and visa fraud were erroneously lumped in with trafficking cases. "The administration," says Moskowitz, "was after numbers. Cases were being counted very carefully. Awards and speeches were being given for successes in trafficking prosecutions, but not in those relating to hate crimes or police cases."[109] Results were evident in the steadily increasing number of prosecutions, although when compared to the huge number of potential cases estimated by the federal government to exist, the successful prosecutions represented "a drop in the bucket," according to Moskowitz. That points up four problems.

First, it is not the Civil Rights Division's responsibility to actually uncover cases; they can only act on what is brought to them by outside organizations: government agencies, local law enforcement, and NGOs. "Most of our cases came from escapees, and a few hot line calls—rarely from pro-active police work. A lot of time, money, and effort were spent pursuing cases that were initially thought to involve trafficking, but in the end, couldn't be established as such."[110]

Second, the nature of trafficking cases requires much more time and resources than most other types of crimes. Without cooperative victims, says Moskowitz, it's virtually impossible to make a trafficking case. "Victim services are a necessary corollary to success in court. You often don't know you have a trafficking case until you spend a lot of time speaking with victims who aren't forthcoming. These are very complex cases; they take special skills. A lot of prosecutors don't have these skills, and they don't want them. They're busy doing other things. The crime of trafficking, as defined, requires proof of enforced labor; it's hard to prove, and finding and IDing victims is also turning out to be very difficult. If we could have known in advance which were the real cases—which of course is an impossibility—it would have reflected a better result."[111]

Third, the very numbers the government has been feeding the public over the past eight years—aside from being all but indefensible in terms of research or degree of accuracy—have been working against any true perspective regarding the DOJ's actual rate of success. "The numbers were killing us," recalls Moskowitz. "The public was accepting them without question. We made good efforts, but ultimately we could never do enough cases, in the face of the numbers, to make an impact in the eyes of the public. Trafficking is a worthy problem; but without knowing how big the problem is, it's hard to know what resources to focus on it or how to make a good policy decision."[112] He anticipates that the government's vacillating numbers game will eventually invite a backlash. Resources will be withdrawn. And without consistent information or solid data—a virtual impossibility given the hidden nature of the crime—the public will eventually see trafficking as an empty cause and lose patience with and interest in it.

Finally, there is a built-in mechanism for failure in the system: limited resources. "The government is simply not capable of doing thousands or tens of thousands of trafficking investigations. The FBI doesn't have the manpower, and DOJ doesn't have the prosecutors." The government, Moskowitz argues, initially didn't think that far ahead; there was a trafficking problem, and the Criminal Section of the DOJ's Civil Rights Division was assigned the vanguard position. "Little thought was given to resources in the event that thousands of cases came in." When this eventually became clear, the federal government encouraged each state to pass its own trafficking law, drawing up a model statute toward this end, in order to take up some of the slack. Further, though the Criminal Section was leading the charge, the administration made an effort to involve the U.S. attorneys around the country in trafficking cases—an effort that met with mixed success.[113]

Moskowitz has a difficult time understanding how HHS—an agency by definition outside the realm of law enforcement—came to be involved in what he refers to as "criminal investigative response." Their methodology escapes him. "I've never seen anything like it. You had a crime, but couldn't find victims, so you paid people to find them! It boggles the mind. HHS came up with this scheme to find victims, and it's the only program I know of where the work of finding victims is allocated to a non–law enforcement agency. It's strange, and dangerous. [Investigating trafficking] is the job of the FBI or DOJ. The horror and validity of the crime should not be undermined by harebrained schemes and bad numbers."[114]

Moskowitz also sees as wrongheaded the pressure placed on the NGOs by HHS's per capita system to locate their victims. "We've had a number of cases from NGOs. But it's not their job [to go looking for them]. We're forcing them to ID victims without actually becoming victims; it's inappropriate, and fraught with danger. This ought to be led by FBI or some other law enforcement agency." By and large, he has very positive recollections of working with NGOs. "Our view of NGOs was that they were often very important partners to a successful investigation and prosecution. We fostered good relations with many of them. There were also fringe NGOs with close ties to the administration who were hard to deal with; but the majority worked with us well, tried to help and to not get in the way."[115]

The issue that gave Moskowitz the greatest concern was the shift in emphasis toward prostitution as a form of human trafficking. From the beginning, he notes, "I got a strong sense that the sex cases were much more interesting to the Bush administration." He sees it as fallout from the foreign-versus-domestic victim issue. "This was just starting during my tenure. There was some media criticism of the overemphasis on foreign victims and all the benefits they're entitled to, and the administration is sensitive to criticism. It's possible that their sensitivity is responsible for the switch to local victims and to instances of pimps beating prostitutes, violations of the Mann Act, and so on, being charged as trafficking cases. It's kind of a creative way of looking at them. I looked at these cases and said, 'We're not here in the Civil Rights Division to drive pimp and prostitution cases.' That's what disturbed me the most. They didn't belong in the Civil Rights Division." And if prostitution is made a federal offense, he asks, "Where are the resources? There aren't enough federal prosecutors in the country to prosecute these cases."[116]

What in the system would he like to see changed?

> Ideally, the DOJ should have a separate antitrafficking section consisting of lawyers from the Criminal Division to deal with immigration fraud, Mann Act violations, and trafficking-related prostitution; the Criminal Section to address the crime of servitude; the Asset Forfeiture Section, to seize criminally obtained assets and instrumentalities (cars, etc.) used to commit the crime of trafficking; and the Child Exploitation and Obscenity Section—CEOS—to address child-related trafficking issues. Part of the mandate would be to bring training to U.S. attorneys in the various states throughout the country. And a vital component would be an investigative arm attached to the unit within the FBI or somewhere. Maybe the volume wouldn't be there, but I think it is. And the government could then say, "We're making our best efforts." I always thought this was inevitable, but it never happened, they never did that. Instead, they shifted the main agenda of the Civil Rights Division from hate crimes and official misconduct cases; some members of the administration saw trafficking as a convenient way out—leading the civil rights charge without actually doing any civil rights cases. My question is: Should this effort have been focused on the Criminal Section of the Department of Justice in the first place? The priority of the Civil Rights Division needs to be civil rights. Although I was an integral part of the effort, in retrospect I have doubts as to whether this shift in priorities from the section's traditional civil rights mission was the wisest course. While the extent of the trafficking problem is unclear, there is no doubt that there are many thousands of victims in the country—and the world—who are experiencing the most horrendous forms of physical and psychological abuse, day after day, month after month. These are serious crimes that need to be addressed by law enforcement, but it must be done in the most effective way possible.[117]

GAUGING PERFORMANCE

It is difficult to evaluate the federal government's success in the trafficking war. Apparently, accountability is something that the government itself finds elusive. A report put out by the Government Accountability Office in July 2006 states, "U.S. government-funded anti-trafficking projects often lack some important elements that allow projects to be monitored, and little is known about project impact due to difficulties in conducting evaluations." While disagreeing that "monitoring of programs was limited," the State Department did concede that "better information is needed."[118]

From interviews with members of both NGOs and government agencies, many of whom asked to speak anonymously, there is a sense that the quality of commitment and performance from federal agencies—including the FBI and ICE—does not always measure up to the trafficking-related policies and practices that they are responsible for implementing. As with so many things, it all comes down to the man or woman in the field. Some are truly exceptional. In the words of human trafficking consultant Florrie Burke, "Both DOJ and ICE have amazing victim witness coordinators—Sue Shriner at ICE, and Lorna Grenadier at Justice. Both have gone on site following raids and rescues and have had direct contact with victims to assess their needs and provide support. They're not your armchair bureaucrats. They have also been an incredible resource to NGOs. They know how criminal justice and immigration systems work, and most NGOs rely on them for technical assistance. They walk it like they talk it."[119]

However, one state's NGOs might be thrilled with the level of competence and enthusiasm from an DOJ or ICE agent, while those in a bordering state are frustrated, angered, and appalled. Same agency, same job definition, different approach to the job. This is also true of U.S. attorneys. Some are real ground shakers when it comes to pursuing cases of human trafficking, while others merely go through the motions—or not. How frustrating to rescue victims and work to provide for their care, and to devote your energies to seeing their traffickers put away, only to run into apathy or reticence at the state's highest judicial level. It has happened.

Granted, the fight against human trafficking in the United States is only recently begun. Nonetheless, it is essential that some viable standards of accountability be applied when it comes to monitoring our response to this crime. There are victims of modern-day slavery throughout America; no one denies this. Attention should be focused on finding them and helping them, not on grandstanding, moral crusades, or waving unsupportable numbers like battle flags. By quoting unsubstantiated estimates of foreign-born victims, or American-born children at risk annually, or women forced into prostitution, the government is not only acting irresponsibly but doing harm in the long run to the public perception of trafficking. Its very nature as a hidden crime belies the accuracy of any of the "official" numbers; but this should not deter the federal government from structuring a reliable system of evaluating its own efforts. The aim we all should share, government and citizens, should include but transcend the immediate need for arrests of traffickers and the support of those enslaved; it should be nothing less than the end of slavery in America.

10

A FUTURE WITHOUT SLAVERY

We hold these truths to be self-evident, that all men are
created equal, that they are endowed by their Creator
with certain unalienable Rights, that among these are
Life, Liberty and the pursuit of Happiness.
Declaration of Independence, July 4, 1776

All persons held as slaves . . . shall be then,
thenceforward, and forever free.
Emancipation Proclamation, January 1, 1863

The last time America brought slavery to an end, the price was high.
Over six hundred thousand Americans died in our Civil War—more
than the total loss of American life in all our other wars combined. Not
every Union or Confederate soldier was fighting to end or preserve the
institution of slavery, but make no mistake: slavery was the spark that
ignited the war. After the war the emancipation of four million
Americans, promised by the Thirteenth Amendment to the Constitution,
was badly handled and incomplete. The government's failure to offer
freed slaves the full rights of citizenship was a mistake that America is
still paying for today. Legal slavery in America ended in 1865, but slavery continued, pernicious, hidden, and cruel. There has been slavery in
America from the moment of the country's birth; and just as it has been
America's greatest burden, the true eradication of slavery could be
America's greatest triumph. Ending slavery in America would also be a
victory for all humanity, for slavery has dogged our steps from the beginning of history. Nothing shows this better than the interweaving of slavery into the tapestry of civilization.

A WORLD OF SLAVES

Walk through the cool marble halls of the world's great museums: the
Smithsonian, the British Museum, the Louvre. The lofty ceilings and
enormous galleries make them more than a little awe-inspiring, and an
automatic hush often falls on those who grasp what they are seeing. The
honey-colored columns and the tall marbled-walled rooms contain the

treasure chests of empire and the accumulated store of human knowledge. They hold the finest and most durable glimpses into our distant past. From the Acropolis come the stirring marble sculptures of horses and men in battle. Huge stone lions that graced the palace gates of ancient Assyria now look down on gaggles of wide-eyed schoolchildren. A stone pharaoh, impassive as the day he was raised as a god-king over his river empire, glows with the last remnants of the desert sun. And in all of this, there is slavery.

From Uruk in Mesopotamia comes a six-thousand-year-old clay cylinder. On it are etched images of war captives roped at the elbows and knees, over whom stands a man raising a whip. Here are the wall paintings of the ancient Maya; under the eye and club of a warrior in a feather headdress are neck-bound slaves marching to their deaths on the sacrificial altar. A victory celebration is carved into the golden stone of Babylon, and chiseled slaves crawl along its base. From a tomb overlooking the Nile come the lush colors of a mural, still bright after thousands of years. It depicts an oversize pharaoh stepping forward to meet the jackal-god Anubis, gatekeeper to the afterlife, who will present him to Osiris for a welcome into paradise. Beneath the pharaoh's feet are long lines of tiny slaves—hundreds of them—chosen to serve him after death. Behind these ranks are men carrying baskets of grain, and beneath the baskets slave girls fight for the gleanings. Hebrew slave musicians march along a Babylonian wall painting, guarded by a soldier with a drawn sword. Here are the exquisite terracotta vases and cast bronze statues of ancient Greece, showing slaves spinning, weaving, and stacking finished cloth. Here is Homer's Ulysses with the seven women he enslaved on the island of Lesbos. In a Roman triumph the victor's chariot is followed by hundreds of shackled slaves. In a medieval illuminated manuscript stands a feudal lord, one foot resting on the neck of his slave. Here is the carved and painted statue of an African king; his footstool is the back of a kneeling slave. In a Renaissance painting, a slave boy holds the musical score while sumptuously dressed men and women play and sing.

In other galleries are the printed records and illustrations of the eighteenth and nineteenth centuries, documenting ships packed with slaves, slaves in coffles, standing on auction blocks, bent in labor in the fields, whipped, burned, and hanged from trees. Like a cancer in the blood, slavery has infected every society, every culture that we admire for artistry and genius. The cool, dim halls of these magnificent museums stand as a monument to human achievement and, if you look more closely, a reminder of the endless suffering of slaves.

The inspiring history of humanity's climb out of the Stone Age and into a wondrous world of our own construction runs parallel to the story of enslavement. For thousands of years, we have loved, dreamed, sung, and built lives of security and beauty. We have also murdered, starved, tortured, and denied the common humanity of millions. Our vaunted civilization has been, and is today, nourished by the lives of slaves. But for the first time, we are seeing that the same genius for creativity and innovation that led to our greatest achievements, combined with compassion, can finally bring slavery to an end.

WE HOLD THESE TRUTHS . . .

America was founded on the principle that personal liberty is a natural right. Without question, our attempts to embody this concept have been flawed. We established ourselves as a slaveholding republic, and this inherent contradiction has plagued us ever since. Yet for all our faults, and even in times when partisan bitterness and confusion are at their worst, the thread that binds us all together is the concept of freedom. It is the rock upon which our nation was built and the light that has guided our good laws and our progress. Now, if we choose to accept the challenge, we can end slavery in America once and for all; and if we are true to our ideals, anything less would be unacceptable.

Ending slavery requires making commitments and taking action. In this last chapter we outline a number of actions that can be taken by each of us as individuals and community members, as well as by the government, to help bring slavery to an end.

BY OUR OWN HANDS

If we want to eliminate slavery from this country, we must do it ourselves, one citizen at a time, and working together. Almost every major positive change in our country was accomplished through grassroots effort. From the antebellum abolitionist movement, to the legal recognition of the rights of women, to the civil rights movement, the demand came first from the people, not the politicians. It is within our grasp to end slavery in America once and for all, but each of us has to reach for it; if we wait for it to be handed to us, people will live and die in slavery for many years to come.

As citizens, one of the first things we need to do is learn to recognize slavery in our communities. We can all learn to recognize human trafficking, what to do with our suspicions, how to help victims once they've been rescued, and how to take an active role in ending slavery in America. Slavery has been around for a long time and requires a serious, long-range commitment to make it go away. When we read about a child being victimized or a woman being kept, beaten, and sexually abused, we become angry. It's a natural impulse to want to batter down a door and dramatically rescue a victim. But that's not a job for the average citizen. Joining the fight against human trafficking means accepting that we each have a job to do and that our job might not include being the action hero. Attempts at dramatic action by the average citizen can hurt the victim's chance at freedom and the government's ability to prosecute traffickers and can be dangerous to the citizen and the victim. The organizations that make up the Freedom Network, after years of victim service, base their efforts on the simple directive "Do no harm." If we follow this all-important mandate, we can't go far wrong. The needs of the victim should always come first. If we can't all be action heroes, there are still many things we can do to help. The question is which options work best for you. What follows is a list of the key skills we must cultivate to rid our country of slavery.[1]

Spotting a Trafficking Victim

Many clues can spark suspicion that a person is a trafficking victim. Some, such as confiscation of passports, debt bondage, and lack of control of earnings, tend to be revealed only during the course of careful investigation by victim advocates, service providers, and trained and sensitive police officers. Any of us, however, can pick up on other indications of human trafficking. One is the presence of trauma—injuries, bruising—that might indicate a pattern of physical abuse. Not all instances of physical abuse point to slavery, but it bears watching. Untreated infections can also be a sign that a person might be enslaved.

Another possible indicator is a person's demeanor. Does he or she appear fearful, reluctant to communicate, or generally withdrawn? A trafficking victim has been programmed to fear outside contact. The victim is likely to believe that the police are cruel and corrupt and that any connection with the outside world could result in jail or deportation. In many instances, the trafficker has warned the victim that an attempt to escape or communicate with the authorities will mean injury or death to the victim's family. In addition, trafficking victims may be unable to answer very simple questions because of their isolation. They may not know what city or state they are in, their street address, or their phone number. If more communication is possible, trafficking victims often show the deep psychological signs of enslavement. One of these is self-blame, the assumption that their suffering is their own fault. Another is a seemingly contradictory emotional attachment to the trafficker at the same time that the victim is physically afraid. Isolation, dependence, and trauma breed this confusion and leave the enslaved person mixed up and erratic in his or her answers to questions. Confusion can also occur because some victims will be coached to assume another identity if they are questioned. Traffickers will often pass off an enslaved person as their own wife or child, or explain that the person is a tourist or student, and expect the victim to back up the story.

Yet another warning sign is the victim's inability to move about freely; often he or she is watched or followed. Trafficked people are often forced to live and work in the same place. Many domestic slaves are kept in the house at all times, while those who are allowed out to shop, or to take their "employer's" kids to the playground, are so thoroughly conditioned as to make escape unlikely. The trafficked construction workers on the U.S. Embassy site in Iraq were compelled to sleep within the walled compound where they worked. And the immigrant farm workers enslaved in Florida by the Ramoses and Abel Cuello were kept locked in trailers or shabby huts and were overseen by gun thugs. In one case an important clue was concertina wire facing *in* toward a factory—to keep workers in rather than to keep intruders out.

Looking for Victims

The best defense against modern-day slavery is a vigilant public. Be a nosy neighbor. Slavery often comes to light because a member of the public sees something odd and speaks up. There are a surprising number of places on the job and in the community where you might come across a human trafficking victim. Doctors and nurses, for example, are in a prime position to encounter a victim of modern slavery. In fact, health care professionals have rescued several victims, especially when they have shown up in emergency rooms. The fact that a trafficker or slaveholder brings in a victim for medical attention doesn't imply concern for the person's welfare; it could simply be motivated by the possibility of lost revenues or fear that the person might die or be permanently disabled, leaving the "employer" facing serious legal charges in addition to trafficking. For anyone working in public service, such as in a hospital, be aware that a third party insisting on interpreting or being present for conversations with a patient or client is a sign of control that can indicate enslavement. The same is true if a person who comes into a hospital or clinic seems to be "guarded" by someone else. If the victim comes in without the trafficker, and the warning signs are recognized, then with the right questions the story of his or her enslavement might emerge.

Brothels can be anywhere; women enslaved in prostitution can be locked away in nice suburban neighborhoods as well as in rough areas that feature strip clubs and massage parlors. As we saw in chapter 7, a "legitimate" massage parlor can also front for a brothel with enslaved women. In the case of a brothel set up in a residential area, a tip-off is the constant activity of cars and individual men coming and going at all hours.

Bus and train stations, gas stations, and truck stops are also logical places to look for trafficked people. Traffickers often move their victims from place to place and from state to state. As the Miguel Flores case showed us, agricultural crew chiefs move their laborers with the harvest. A picker might start in South Florida and in the same season move to Georgia, the Carolinas, and eventually as far north as Pennsylvania and Delaware. Traffickers that exploit women in forced prostitution frequently transport their "girls" from state to state to avoid discovery. Some of them sell their victims' services at way stations for truckers as well as at train and bus stations. Some are just passing through. Since the vans transporting victims have to stop for gas, service stations are natural stop-offs for traffickers. Station attendants can be especially helpful if they learn to look for large numbers of fearful people being guarded as they use the restrooms. These same restrooms are good places to display information, in several languages, offering immediate help to victims, in the form of the phone numbers of local NGOs, police, and the trafficking hotline. Along with these numbers, it should be made absolutely clear that the victims will in no way be held legally liable or accountable; what is being offered is help, not apprehension by the law.

You can sometimes find victims on landscaping crews. A major Connecticut nursery allegedly turned twelve Guatemalan guest workers, here on H-2B visas, "into a captive labor force," confiscating their passports, working them eighty hours a week at minimum pay, denying them medical attention, and threatening them with arrest and deportation if they complained.[2] If you were a customer of this nursery, perhaps with a little diligence you might have seen that something wasn't right.

These victims were being hidden in plain sight, and a little added awareness on the part of the public could have made all the difference.

Construction is another field that is ripe for trafficking. One Immigration and Customs Enforcement (ICE) agent commented, "I've seen kids as young as ten from India who'd been sold . . . for $2,000 . . . working on construction sites holding jackhammers."[3] One would think that seeing any preteen operating a jackhammer would send up a warning flag. In 2006, a California case involved dozens of skilled Thai welders, brought here to be guestworkers for Trans Bay Steel Corp., only to find that they'd been enslaved. The usual violations occurred: exorbitant "debt," confiscated papers, shabby living quarters with several men to a room with no heat, electricity, or furniture, total restriction of movement, and threat of arrest and deportation. But there was a twist. There was only enough work for nine of the welders, so the rest were channeled into menial work for thirteen hours a day, at no pay, throughout Los Angeles and Long Beach. Apparently, no citizens noticed, and if they did, nothing was said. Eventually, these workers rescued themselves and, through the U.S. Equal Employment Opportunity Commission (EEOC), brought suit against the corporation. When the case was settled, $1.4 million in compensation was awarded to forty-eight Thai workers, along with several benefits, including college tuition and books for further education, relocation costs, minimum wage, and guaranteed work on the project they had come for in the first place.

One of the most insidious forms of trafficking—the enslavement of domestics and nannies—occurs under our very noses. Here you must be vigilant. It is being practiced by your neighbors and community members, and with awareness you can spot it. Enslaved domestics will have many of the same warning signs: someone else holds their documents, and their movement and communication are restricted and controlled. With domestics, one of the warning signs is actually the fact that they are rarely seen. Sometimes a neighbor will become aware that one person who lives in a nearby house is only glimpsed occasionally, never seems to leave with other residents, or is never seen wearing a coat outdoors. Sadly, most survivors of domestic servitude who find freedom do so through their own courage and desperation; they escape. Many more would be rescued if the public learned to look for and recognize the warning signs.

These are just a few of the situations in which you might encounter a victim of trafficking; there are many more—restaurants, sweatshops, laundries—limited only by the innovativeness of the trafficker. And please remember: if you hear about or uncover what you think could be a trafficking situation, great care and sensitivity must be shown in speaking with possible victims, and the best course is to call a trained professional. The appendix gives a list of organizations recognized as the best in the victim services field; if none is near you, either call one and ask for a local referral, or dial the national Human Trafficking Resource Center hotline, 888–373–7888, any time day or night, or the U.S. government hotline, 888–428–7581, Monday through Friday, nine to five.

Helping the Survivors

Once free of their enslavement, survivors need a lot of assistance, and there are specific, hands-on ways you can help them. One of the keys to helping former victims is through giving, both of yourself and of your money. If your personal or professional skills are applicable, or if you have items that are needed, be generous with them. Talk with local organizations that work with trafficking victims, and let them know you'd like to play a role. Survivors of human trafficking often walk away from their slavery with nothing, and there is no doubt you can help.

DONATE CLOTHES AND EQUIPMENT

One of the easiest things you can give is clothes. The ability to dress appropriately and attractively not only helps the survivor move on toward finding a job and making a life in the real world but has a positive impact on his or her self-image. Clean clothes in good condition are generally accepted by such service organizations as Dress for Success. Also, computers, cell phones, and other personal electronic devices are welcome.

OFFER YOUR LANGUAGE SKILLS

Since many victims come from abroad and enter the country with little or no capacity to speak English, language is a major issue. The ability to speak, read, and write English is important for those survivors seeking to make a life in America. People from dozens of countries have been enslaved in our country, and your ability to speak one of their languages can be invaluable. If you have a language skill, talk to your local service provider about acting as an interpreter for intake interviews with the staff attorney or legal director. Or you can help antislavery and anti-trafficking organizations translate materials so that they can reach a greater number of people in slavery. If you can teach, consider teaching English as a second language. Perhaps the service provider can set up classes or tutorials for you.

OFFER YOUR PROFESSIONAL SKILLS

Many professions can be of significant value to those freed from slavery. A health care background enables you to provide the physical and mental attention that virtually all victims need. Nurses, doctors, and other medical professionals are much sought after, and low- or no-cost mental health care providers are desperately needed. If you are a lawyer, or work with a law firm that does pro bono work, consider volunteering your services. If you have a banking and finance background, please share it. And in today's world, what could be of greater use than computer skills? A local service provider organization can help you schedule classes and focus your abilities.

DONATE MONEY

You knew we'd come to this point eventually. All through this book are listed local, state, and national groups fighting human trafficking. All of them need your help and support. Many are helping people freed from slavery, and they are most likely operating on a shoestring, lacking resources to do as good a job as the survivors of trafficking and slavery need and deserve. When you look at the list of these groups in the Appendix, decide which one matches your interests and talents; they will be glad to hear from you, and they can give you a clear picture of where your money will be going. Once people escape from slavery, they usually have no money at all. Many need support while they await the trial of their abusers. This includes food, shelter—the basics. Others need help to buy an airplane ticket home. Donations sometimes go to programs in emerging nations to help curb some of the root causes that drive individuals to take the risks that result in slavery here.

BUY SURVIVOR-MADE GOODS

Purchasing products made by survivors of human trafficking will work toward creating economic empowerment and moving survivors toward self-sufficiency. Check out survivor-made products sold by the Emancipation Network (TEN) online at www.madebysurvivors.com or at http://freetheslaves.madebysurvivors.com. TEN sells products made by clients of many of the leading antitrafficking organizations around the world.

GET CREATIVE!

Think outside the box. There are people around the country who don't wait for permission or approval to create their own programs and initiatives. A group of women in Collier County, Florida, has taken a unique approach to fighting the growing problem of human trafficking by concentrating their efforts on feminine products. The Florida Council of Catholic Women is writing letters to the makers of Tampax and other feminine products, encouraging them to put an emergency hotline message on their packaging. This will let women know—in different languages—that if they're being held to work against their will there is a twenty-four-hour number they can call. "In human trafficking, these people are owned and sold from person to person and they're never free," said Janet Mitchell of the Council of Catholic Women. "If they see that phone number, they know somewhere out there people are trying to help them. It will give them hope if nothing else." The women say they chose feminine products because women of all backgrounds and languages use them, and they use them in private—away from the eyes of their captors.[4]

Led by an inspired teacher, a group of fifty eighth graders in Crescent Springs, Kentucky, made it possible to rescue and rehabilitate dozens of trafficked children abroad. Their teacher was inspired by an Oprah Winfrey program about children forced to do dangerous work on fishing boats in Ghana. She shared the story with her class, who adopted the issue for their service project. They set a high goal—to rescue and rehabilitate forty kids, half a world away. The students learned how to design and put up a Web site. They created brochures and slide shows on slavery to educate other students, business leaders, and faith congregations. They donated baby-sitting money and allowances; they baked cookies and sold lemonade. And in six weeks, they raised over $28,400. This same energy can be directed toward helping trafficking victims in America, and—with the right incentive and direction—it can be done on a massive scale.[5]

Spreading the Word

Now that you're familiar with the issue of human trafficking in today's America, don't keep it to yourself. You can help educate people in your community about how to identify slavery and trafficking, particularly those who are most likely to come into contact with victims: law enforcement officials, medical workers, restaurant inspectors, transit workers, service station employees, and others who regularly interact with the public. If you go to MeetUp.com, you will find antislavery and antitrafficking MeetUp groups in several cities around the country. This is a great way to meet other people who are working to end slavery in America. Below are some other ways to get the word out and to join with others who want to end slavery in America.

WRITE YOUR CONGRESSMAN

It's no secret that our politicians tend not to move on an issue without pressure from their constituency; that's us. Write or e-mail your local, state, and federal government representatives. Don't assume they are familiar with the issue; tell them what you think they should know, and encourage them to act. We will shortly list a number of actions you can suggest they take.

JOIN OR CREATE A MEDIA CAMPAIGN

Many antitrafficking groups carry on Internet awareness campaigns. MoveOn.org did an impressive job of it, and they started with just a person and a message. They need people like you to take part, share information, and bring other people into the discussion. The investment can be minimal, and the number of potential recipients is vast and growing. Look at YouTube! And while you're at it, write an OpEd column or a letter to the editor of your favorite newspaper or magazine.

JOIN OR CREATE A NEIGHBORHOOD WATCH
OR INTEREST GROUP

For this, you will want to involve local service providers, law enforcement, teachers, librarians, parents, faith leaders, and government officials. You should meet regularly, stay up to date on all trafficking-related issues and developments, and create strategies for monitoring possible trafficking activity within the community. If there are already Neighborhood Watch groups in your community, make sure that human trafficking is included in what members are watching for.

SPONSOR PROGRAMS

You can arrange with local men's and women's clubs, PTA groups, high schools, colleges, faith leaders, and community centers to sponsor speakers who are professionals in the antitrafficking field and to screen relevant DVDs. The thirty-minute film *Dreams Die Hard* is a powerful introduction to slavery in America and is available from Free the Slaves. It can be shown free and can be previewed on the Internet (YouTube style) and purchased at www.freetheslaves.net.

SHARE WHAT YOU'VE LEARNED

Make certain that resource materials, including this book and the *Slavery Still Exists* pamphlet, are available at municipal, school, and college libraries, bookstores, senior citizen and community centers, police departments, and places of worship. Include your name as a community member willing to discuss and support efforts to stop human trafficking.

Improving Government Performance

Nearly a decade ago, the government declared war against human trafficking. Dedicated professionals in a number of agencies have applied their skills to uncovering cases, prosecuting traffickers, and providing services to victims. And as with any new cause—and any political agenda—there is tremendous need for growth. Experience has shown, in the words of a high-ranking official at the Department of Justice, that there is simply "not enough—of everything: time, money, resources."[6] And while progress has been made, at times money has been wasted and focus lost. Here, then, are some suggestions, made in the interest of keeping the government on track, as well as pointing out specific areas that could benefit from serious attention.

ELIMINATE SLAVE LABOR FROM GOVERNMENT CONTRACTS

Contracts awarded by the U.S. government have fueled human trafficking in the building of the new U.S. Embassy in Iraq and on military bases here at home. Despite warnings from Congress, there are concerns that the practice may be continuing. The federal government must back up its zero-tolerance policy on the use of forced labor in its works and monitor and debar any contractors who directly or through subcontractors use tax dollars to enable human trafficking. It should make those contracts transparent. We have to keep our own house clean if the fight against slavery is to succeed.

PUT FAIRNESS IN THE VISA PROGRAM

There are blatant inequalities in the award of visas for workers entering the United States. For example, a nineteen-year-old French or British girl coming here as an au pair receives a J-1 visa and with it monitoring, orientation programs, a guaranteed salary, and money for education—all the care and attention that we would hope for if our own children were traveling as workers abroad. Meanwhile, a nineteen-year-old Cameroonian girl coming to the United States for the same job receives a B-1 visa and a quick visual inspection at the airport. There is no record made of her address in the United States, no monitoring, no guaranteed salary, nothing to prevent her from becoming enslaved. This imbalance must be corrected.

PROTECT AND RESPECT OUR GUEST WORKERS

At various times, America requires outside labor, and the Guest Worker Program helps to meet that need. But it fails miserably in caring for these guests in our country. While the program provides for the support and protection of our guest workers, in case after case these provisions are not enforced. As a result, a system designed to import free labor at a fair wage is delivering men and women into slavery, with little or no government supervision to prevent it. This program must be monitored and its rules enforced. The program requires more labor inspectors, tighter employer screening, and a provision that allows workers the freedom to seek new employers should they be dissatisfied or mistreated.

GIVE LABOR RIGHTS TO OUR FARMWORKERS
AND DOMESTICS

When it was passed in the 1930s, the National Labor Relations Act brought fair working conditions to millions of workers in America. Largely because of pressure from southern congressmen, two categories were excluded—farmworkers and domestics. Sadly, these two groups of workers are still denied the rights enjoyed by all other workers. The provisions and protections of the NLRA should be immediately extended to cover these workers; otherwise, as recent history has shown, they will continue to be more susceptible to enslavement than other workers in America.

ADDRESS THE ISSUE OF SLAVE-MADE GOODS

America has an excellent law that provides for the seizure of suspicious, or "hot," goods, but only if they were made within the United States. This means that if the Customs Service doesn't catch slave-made goods at the border there is no second chance. The "hot goods" seizure law should be immediately extended to encompass all slave-made goods, regardless of the place of origin, so that they can be stopped and confiscated before they reach our homes.

The Cocoa Protocol, described in chapter 6, has shown that an industry working together with human rights groups, consumer groups, and labor unions can remove slavery from the products we buy. This model needs to be fostered and extended to other American industries whose products are tainted with slavery: sugar, cotton and clothing, fish and shrimp, iron and steel (in such goods as cars and car parts, plumbing fixtures, furniture), wood (everything from houses to fine cellos), electronics, handwoven rugs, and many others. Government can encourage businesses and the antislavery movement in this process so that stakeholders come together to clean up supply chains.

TO THE VICTIMS SHOULD GO THE PROFITS

Slavery is the theft of labor; it's usually a crime about profit. Yet the assets seized from convicted traffickers go into law enforcement's budget, not into helping the slaves rebuild their lives. Imagine for a moment that a burglar takes your television and is later arrested, and the *police* get to keep or sell your TV. Absurd and unfair though that might sound, the current slavery law, the Trafficking Victims Protection Act (TVPA), does just that. It is right that police have the authority to seize the assets of slaveholders, but these assets represent what was stolen from the slaves and should be returned to them, in the form of either services or straightforward restitution.

PROVIDE BETTER VICTIM SERVICES

Beyond locating victims of slavery, the government has a responsibility to provide better care and services for them once they're free. A number of areas need immediate attention. As the system is now structured, each survivor is allowed the same amount of time and services, regardless of the nature and period of enslavement. This policy is both unrealistic and severely limited in its effectiveness. It is the government's responsibility to ensure that no one is trafficked into slavery within our borders; therefore, when a victim of slavery is found, the government must be prepared to give that person whatever services are needed—and all the time required—for recovery and readjustment. Each survivor of human trafficking is entitled to physical and mental health services, housing, language training, and legal and employment counseling. It will mean additional funding across the board, but considering how low the existing budget is, it would be money well spent. Anything less is dereliction.

Another practice that needs immediate replacement is the per capita system. As you read in chapter 9, it provides piecemeal funding only as each victim is found, thereby placing undue responsibility and danger on the NGOs. This system was wrongheaded from the start and has proven to be a lopsided failure. Bona fide victim service providers with long-standing records have had funding cut so severely that many are struggling to remain open, as pressure is put on them to find their own victims—a job that is better left to local and state law enforcement. And allocating funding on the basis of religious or political agendas is a sure way to deny victims access to some of the best nonprofit organizations in the country.

QUANTIFY THE RESULTS

Since the passage of the TVPA, the government has been handing out money—under one program or another—with little accountability. Among NGOs and government agencies alike, the consensus is, there is too much we simply don't know. One sure way to determine the success or failure of the current war on human trafficking is through an independent, structured program of monitoring and regular evaluation. This means that we need to require that contracts be awarded transparently and competitively, consistent with current law. It is also important that antitrafficking efforts encompass reintegration efforts, place further emphasis on individual care plans for each survivor, and provide realistic and properly resourced programs for local follow up and monitoring of survivors. Performance goals must provide sufficient flexibility to ensure this. In addition, as recommended by the U.S. Government Accountability Office report, performance indicators should measure the extent of local community engagement in preventing trafficking, since the lack of community involvement where antitrafficking programs are targeted will likely undermine the success of such programs.

TRAIN POLICE TO FIND VICTIMS

If the government's numbers can be believed, only a small fraction of human trafficking cases are being uncovered. And although the number of prosecutions has increased over the past few years, these prosecutions are only a tiny fraction of the total estimated number of trafficking cases. When compared to the prosecutorial success rate of such crimes as homicide, this is alarming, and the responsibility falls largely on state and local law enforcement. Yet only a small fraction of America's law enforcement officers have been trained to recognize and stop this serious crime. As one survey makes clear, most state and local police either have no idea that human trafficking actually occurs or don't believe it happens within their jurisdiction. Yet these are the people who are most directly responsible for uncovering slavery in America. If the police are to be more effective, an intense and comprehensive nationwide training program must be given, and soon. Good training programs exist; the Freedom Network Institute gives one of the best.

They have experience instructing both NGOs and government agencies. There are over eighteen thousand police departments in this country, in addition to state agencies; training them all is a tall order, but it's the only way to get the job done. If each department established an anti-trafficking unit, as they do for homicide and other crimes, the number of cases uncovered, and of victims rescued, would increase dramatically. And the training should include those *federal* agencies involved in fighting trafficking as well. Agents from the FBI, ICE, and the Departments of State, Labor, and Justice would all benefit from a comprehensive, job-specific training experience.

PROVIDE ADEQUATE FUNDING

The government has stated repeatedly that human trafficking is the world's second- or third-largest crime, along with drugs and guns. Yet the resources that law enforcement devotes to the war on trafficking pale when compared to those dedicated to the other two.[7] We have a Drug Enforcement Agency; perhaps it's time for the government to consider an Antislavery Enforcement Agency. Other countries, such as Brazil, have shown that a dedicated antislavery force can be powerful and effective. Those parts of the government that do actively work against slavery have to do so on a shoestring. Take ICE, for example. They are charged with stopping slave-made goods flowing into the United States, but to do that they must determine which goods come from the hands of slaves. That makes sense, but then they are given so few agents to make that determination that they cannot begin to investigate any more than a tiny fraction of possible cases. They work hard and do a good job with the scant resources they get, but it is no wonder our country is still importing slave-made goods.

DO THE NEEDED HOMEWORK

We need to know the size and scope of problem. That means a commitment to data collection and analysis and also outreach to other information gatherers. By early 2008 the CIA, State Department, Justice Department, and a number of other government agencies had been collecting and organizing information on human trafficking for almost ten years—and not sharing it. International agencies like Interpol and the UN also have large-scale trafficking databases that they don't share. If this problem were a health issue, epidemiologists would be combining every data set available to crack it; but for reasons that are not clear, the information about human trafficking in America has been sealed off behind bureaucratic walls. It is time for those walls to come tumbling down.

BUILD AN ANTISLAVERY PERSPECTIVE
INTO GOVERNMENT POLICY

Some large-scale and joined-up thinking needs to be done to align U.S. policies and assistance with antitrafficking goals. This should encompass aid, trade, investment, debt relief, law enforcement, and military cooperation with other countries, and a well-plotted course for America within the UN. It should also include procurement of goods and services by the government. Put simply, someone—perhaps the Office to Monitor and Combat Trafficking in Persons—needs to look at the work of the U.S. government from a "slavery perspective." If this is going to be a free country in every sense of the word, then we need to examine how everything we do can be part of the effort to end slavery.

CONCLUSION

We could probably fill another book with suggestions for improving the campaign against slavery in today's America. It's especially easy to find fault when the awareness of the problem is so recent and the mechanism responsible for addressing it is so cumbersome. Our goal here is not to point fingers but rather to find more and better ways to locate cases of human trafficking in this country, to rescue and help victims, and to punish perpetrators. Sometimes the issues of the moment, such as the conflict between the antiprostitution faction and the human rights faction, and the question of foreign-born versus U.S. citizen victims, grab government and public attention. But then such issues take the emphasis away from where it is most needed—the total elimination of slavery in America. No one form of slavery is more unacceptable than another; they all represent the complete elimination of choice, the violent removal of personal liberty. As such, they are against not only the law but the very precepts upon which this nation was founded. All victims must be given adequate services, regardless of their country of origin. If the laws for helping victims are out of balance, they can be amended. That's the beauty of our system; what doesn't work can be fixed.

There must be a symbiotic approach to wiping out slavery in America. Government cannot possibly succeed without the full awareness and support of the public, any more than we can make an impact without the government's commitment. Go back a few pages, and read over your options once again; choose one that you feel you can commit to, and follow through. And please write to your representatives, tell them what you know, and ask them to provide more community awareness programs, more training for law enforcement, more victim services, and more money, and to do it in a more balanced way. You are now an active participant in the war against human trafficking and slavery in America. Welcome to the fight. With your help, it's one we can win.

APPENDIX

FOR FURTHER INFORMATION

ANTISLAVERY ORGANIZATIONS AND AGENCIES

Free the Slaves
P.O. Box 34727
Washington, DC 20005
Phone: (202) 638–1865
Fax: (202) 638–0599
info@freetheslaves.net
www.freetheslaves.net

Free the Slaves is a nonprofit organization dedicated to ending slavery around the world. It is the main antislavery organization in the United States with a global focus. Free the Slaves works with partner organizations around the world to address slavery at a local level, raises awareness of the issue, promotes businesses and goods that do not have ties to slave labor, educates government officials about slavery, and conducts research on contemporary slavery.

Coalition of Immokalee Workers
P.O. Box 603
Immokalee, FL 34143
(941) 657–8311
(941) 657–5055
workers@ciw-online.org

CIW is a community-based worker organization. Its members are largely Latino, Haitian, and Mayan Indian immigrants working in low-wage jobs throughout the state of Florida. CIW has been extensively involved in bringing enslaved agricultural workers to freedom. It organizes actions and boycotts of companies that will not take responsibility for the human cost of the fruit and vegetables they buy. The CIW Web site holds a large number of published reports and press releases and a large collection of materials for student action, including sample press releases and reports from boycotts and demonstrations at universities around the country. It is an invaluable resource for understanding the reality of slavery in modern America.

ECPAT USA
157 Montague Street
Brooklyn, NY 11201
Phone: (212) 870-2427
Fax: (212) 870-2055
info@ecpatusa.org
www.ecpatusa.org or www.ecpat.net

ECPAT is an international institution dedicated to eliminating child pornography, child prostitution, and "the trafficking of children for sexual purposes." ECPAT is nonpolitical and nonreligious; it works with other organizations and governments to support its goals. It has a number of books that are basic and fundamental explanations of child prostitution and trafficking, particularly *The ECPAT Story*, by Ron O'Grady (1996); *The Rape of the Innocent*, also by Ron O'Grady (1994); *Enforcing the Law against the Commercial Sexual Exploitation of Children*, by ECPAT (1996); and *Child Prostitution and Sex Tourism: A Series of Research Reports*, by Dr. Julia O'Connell Davidson and Jacqueline Sanchez-Taylor (1996).

Polaris Project
Headquarters
P.O. Box 77892
Washington, DC 20013
Tel: (202) 745-1001
Fax: (202) 745-1119
info@polarisproject.org
www.polarisproject.org

Polaris Project's comprehensive approach to combating human trafficking includes operating local and national crisis hotlines, conducting direct outreach and victim identification, providing social services and housing to victims, advocating for stronger state and national antitrafficking legislation, and engaging community members in local and national grassroots efforts. Through these efforts Polaris Project seeks to aid victims and increase awareness at both the grassroots and policy level.

GOOD ORGANIZATIONS FOR RESOURCES

National Underground Railroad Museum and Freedom Center
www.freedomcenter.org

The National Underground Railroad Museum and Freedom Center opened in Cincinnati, Ohio, in September 2004. It chronicles the history of the Underground Railroad and the fight for freedom of slaves in America before 1865. The Freedom Stations on the Web site are an interactive learning area where you can do in-depth research on a very large database of photos and documents.

Office to Monitor and Combat Trafficking in Persons, U.S. State Department
www.state.gov/g/tip

The U.S. government's main antislavery agency is the Office to Monitor and Combat Trafficking in Persons. Its Web site provides an introduction to anti-trafficking work around the world. The office publishes an annual report on global human trafficking, listing the situation in almost every country.

Rugmark
www.rugmark.org

Rugmark is a global organization dedicated to taking child and slave labor out of carpet making and to offering educational opportunities to children in India, Nepal, and Pakistan. The Web site has a wealth of information on child labor and the rehabilitation of child workers. It explains the Rugmark certification process and lists shops that sell Rugmark rugs.

Child Labor Coalition (CLC)
www.natlconsumersleague.org/clc.htm

Since 1989 the CLC has worked to end exploitation of child labor and to encourage education, health, safety, and general well-being for working children. The CLC researches child labor abuses and publishes its findings to influence policy concerning child workers.

The CLC Web site offers advice on what consumers can do to combat child labor, other background information, and links to other child labor organizations.

SERVICE PROVIDERS

In addition to these national organizations, there are groups that work directly with human trafficking victims in many cities and states. So that you can find the professional nearest you who can help with cases of human trafficking and slavery in America, the list below is organized by location.

Arizona

Arizona League to End Regional Trafficking (ALERT)
P.O. Box 57839
Phoenix, AZ 85079
Tel: (602) 433–2441
Fax: (602) 433–2441
www.traffickingaz.org

California

Asian Pacific Islander Legal Outreach
1188 Franklin Street, Suite 202
San Francisco, CA 94109
Tel: (415) 567–6255
Fax: (415) 567–6248
www.apilegaloutreach.org

Catholic Legal Immigration Network, Inc.
564 Market Street, Suite 416
San Francisco, CA 94104
Tel: (408) 554–5368
www.cliniclegal.org

Coalition to Abolish Slavery and Trafficking (CAST)
5042 Wilshire Boulevard, #586
Los Angeles, CA 90036
Tel: (213) 365–1906
Fax: (213) 365–5257
www.castla.org

Legal Aid Foundation of Los Angeles
(LAFLA)
5228 Whittier Boulevard
Los Angeles, CA 90022
Tel: (213) 640–3900
Fax: (213) 640–3911
www.lafla.org

National Immigration Law Center
405 14th Street, Suite 1400
Oakland, CA 94612
Tel: (510) 663–8282
Fax: (510) 663–2028
www.nilc.org

Florida

Coalition of Immokalee Workers
CIW Anti-Slavery Campaign
P.O. Box 603
Immokalee, FL 34143
Tel: (239) 657–8311
Fax: (239) 657–5055
www.ciw-online.org

LUCHA: A Women's Legal Project Florida
Immigrant Advocacy Center
3000 Biscayne Boulevard, Suite 400
Miami, FL 33137
Tel: (305) 573–1106
Fax: (305) 576–6273
www.fiacfla.org

Georgia

Tapestri Inc.
PMB 362
3939 Lavista Road, Suite E
Tucker, GA 30084
Tel: (404) 299–2185
Fax: (770) 270–4184
www.tapestri.org

Hawaii

Na Loio—Immigrant Rights and Public Interest
Legal Center
810 N. Vineyard Boulevard
Honolulu, HI 96817
Tel: (808) 847–8828
Fax: (808) 842–0055
www.naloio.org

Illinois

Counter-Trafficking Services
National Immigrant Justice Center (a Heartland
Alliance partner)
208 S. LaSalle Street, Suite 1818
Chicago, IL 60604
Tel: (312) 660–1370
Fax: (312) 660–1505
www.immigrantjustice.org

International Organization for Adolescents (IOFA)
4305 N. Lincoln Avenue, Suite K
Chicago, IL 60618
Tel: (773) 404–8831
Fax: (773) 404–8842
www.iofa.org

Maryland

Boat People SOS—Maryland Office
7411 Riggs Road, Suite 328
Adelphi, MD 20783
Tel. (301) 439–0505
Fax (301) 439–6644

Casa de Maryland
734 University Boulevard East
Silver Springs, MD 20903
Tel. (301) 431–4185
www.casademaryland.org

New York

The Door
121 Avenue of the Americas, 30th Floor
New York, NY 10013
Tel: (212) 941–9090
Fax: (212) 941–0714
www.door.org

Immigrant Women and Children Project
City Bar Justice Center
New York City Bar Association
42 West 44th Street
New York, NY 10036
Tel: (212) 382–1370
Fax: (212) 354–7438
www.citybarjusticecenter.org

Safe Horizon
2 Lafayette Street, 3rd Floor
New York, NY 10007
Tel: (212) 577–7700
Fax: (212) 577–3897
www.safehorizon.org

Texas

MOSAIC Family Services
4144 N. Central Expressway, Suite 530
Dallas, TX 75204
Tel: (214) 821–5393
Fax: (214) 821–0810
www.mosaicservices.org

Political Asylum Project of Austin (PAPA)
One Highland Center
314 E. Highland Mall Boulevard, Suite 501
Austin, TX 78752
Tel: (512) 478–0546
Fax: (512) 476–9788
www.papaustin.org

Boat People SOS—Houston Office
11205 Bellaire Boulevard, Suite B22
Houston, TX 77072
Tel: (281) 530–6888
Fax: (281) 530–6838

Virginia

Boat People SOS
6066 Leesburg Pike, Suite 100
Falls Church, VA 22041
Tel: (703) 538–2190
Fax: (703) 538–2191
www.bpsos.org

**Center for Multicultural Human Services Program
for Survivors of Torture and Severe Trauma**
701 W. Broad Street, Suite 305
Falls Church, VA 22046
Tel: (703) 533–3302
Fax: (703) 237–2083
www.cmhs.org

Tahirih Justice Center
6066 Leesburg Pike, Suite 220
Falls Church, VA 22041
Tel: (703) 575–0070
Fax: (703) 575–0069
www.tahirih.org

Washington, D.C.

Break the Chain Campaign
Institute for Policy Studies
P.O. Box 34123
Washington, DC 20043
Tel: (202) 234–9382
Fax: (202) 387–7915
www.breakthechaincampaign.org

FAIR Fund Inc.
P.O. Box 21656
Washington, DC 20009
Tel: (202) 986–5316
www.fairfund.org

**Initiative Against Trafficking in Persons,
Global Rights**
1200 18th Street NW, Suite 602
Washington, DC 20036
Tel: (202) 741–5033
Fax: (202) 822–4606
www.globalrights.org/trafficking
www.globalrights.org/tratadepersonas

**Legal Momentum: Advancing Women's Rights
Immigrant Women Program**
1522 K Street NW, Suite 550
Washington, DC 20005
Tel: (202) 326–0040
Fax: (202) 589–0511
www.legalmomentum.org

Ayuda, Inc.
1707 Kalorama Road NW
Washington, DC 20009
Tel: (202) 387–4848
Fax: (202) 387–0324
www.ayudainc.org

NOTES

1. THE OLD SLAVERY AND THE NEW

1. "Girl Reunited with Parents," *Laredo Morning Times*, May 17, 2001.

2. "Woman Sentenced to Life in Prison for Torturing 12-Year-Old Maid," *Amarillo Globe News,* October 20, 2001.

3. U.S. Department of State, *Trafficking in Persons Report,* June 2006, www.state.gov/g/tip/rls/tiprpt/2006/.

4. U.S. Department of Justice, *Attorney General's Annual Report to Congress on U.S. Government Activities to Combat Trafficking in Persons for Fiscal Year 2006,* May 2007, www.usdoj.gov/olp/human_trafficking.htm, 17. Other cases were brought by Immigration and Customs Enforcement.

5. Only one man in U.S. history, a Portland, Maine, sea captain named Nathaniel Gordon, was ever hanged as a slaver, despite the fact that slave trading— sailing to Africa, loading your hold with captives, and selling them in America, Cuba, or Brazil—had been made a capital offense by the Piracy Act of 1820. Thousands of slave ships sailed to Africa with impunity, as the government and the navy looked the other way, and the courts did practically nothing to enforce the slave trade laws. Not until the election of Abraham Lincoln and the advent of the Civil War was an attempt made to exact the death penalty for this crime that had led directly to the deaths of millions. For the complete story, see Ron Soodalter, *Hanging Captain Gordon: The Life and Trial of an American Slave Trader* (New York: Atria, 2006).

6. Jacqueline Jones, *The Dispossessed: America's Underclasses from the Civil War to the Present* (New York: Basic Books, 1992), 107.

7. Lutheran Immigration and Refugee Service, "Case Study," available from LIRS, 700 Light St., Baltimore, MD 21230.

8. Slavery is a patterned relationship that achieves exploitative ends including appropriation of labor for productive activities resulting in economic gain, use of the enslaved person as an item of conspicuous consumption, sexual use of an enslaved person for pleasure and procreation, and the savings gained when paid servants or workers are replaced with unpaid and unfree workers. Any particular slave may fulfill one, several, or all of these outcomes for the slaveholder. Slavery is a relationship between two people. It is both a social and economic relationship, and like all relationships it has certain characteristics and rules. The key characteristics of slavery are not about ownership but about how people are controlled. The core characteristic of slavery throughout history, whether it was

legal or not, is *violence.* The slave master or slaveholder controls a slave by using or threatening violence. Slavery is about having no choices at all, having no control over your life, and living in constant fear of violence. This is the key to slavery. Violence brings a person into slavery. Many people who become slaves are tricked into it. Many people, following a trail of lies, walk into enslavement, but what keeps them there is violence. Once enslaved, there are all sorts of ways that slaves are held in slavery—sometimes it is the way the slave gives up and gives into slavery, sometimes it is about the personal relationships that develop between slaves and slaveholders—but the essential ingredient is violence.

The second key characteristic of slavery is *loss of free will;* slaves are under the complete control of someone else. There is no other person, authority, or government the slave can turn to for protection. Slaves must do as they are told or they will suffer. The third characteristic is that slavery is normally used to *exploit* someone in some kind of economic activity. No one enslaves another person just to be mean; people are enslaved to make a profit. Most slaveholders see themselves as normal businesspeople. They have little interest in hurting anyone, in being cruel or torturing people; it is just part of the job. Slavery is about money. If we put these characteristics together we can define slavery in this way: *Slavery is a social and economic relationship in which a person is controlled through violence or its threat, paid nothing, and economically exploited.*

Slavery has been defined in many ways—within the social sciences and history, as well as in legal and international instruments. Many of these definitions vary significantly from each other. Kevin Bales and Peter Robbins explore the development of many of these definitions in "No One Shall Be Held in Slavery or Servitude: A Critical Analysis of International Slavery Agreements," *Human Rights Review* 2 (January 2001): 18–45.

9. Free the Slaves and Human Rights Center, University of California, Berkeley, *Hidden Slaves: Forced Labor in the United States* (Washington, DC: Free the Slaves, 2005).

10. Ben Schmitt and Suzette Hackney, "Sex Ring Busted by Kidnapped Girl's Tip," *Detroit Free Press,* January 15, 2003; Suzette Hackney, "Abducted Teen's Mother Describes House of Horrors," *Detroit Free Press,* January 16, 2003; Suzette Hackney, "More Sex Ring Arrests Likely Today," *Detroit Free Press,* February 4, 2003; Ben Schmitt, "More Charges in Sex Ring," *Detroit Free Press,* February 15, 2003; Suzette Hackney, "Man Sentenced in Sex-Ring Case," *Detroit Free Press,* September 16, 2003.

11. Deborah J. Daniels, "Remarks of the Honorable Deborah J. Daniels, Assistant Attorney General, Office of Justice Programs, at the National Conference on Human Trafficking, July 15, 2004, Tampa, Florida," www.ojp.usdoj.gov/aag/speeches/ncht.htm. It is not clear whether Ms. Daniels was referring to the proportion of cases known to and prosecuted by the U.S. government or to all cases in the United States.

2. HOUSE SLAVES

1. The great majority of household slaves in America are young women, so we will usually refer to enslaved domestics as "her" and "she."

2. Free the Slaves and Human Rights Center, University of California at Berkeley, *Hidden Slaves: Forced Labor in the United States* (Washington, DC: Free the Slaves, 2004) (can be downloaded at www.freetheslaves.net).

3. The story of Ruth Gnizako was related by Joy M. Zarembka in "America's Dirty Work: Migrant Maids and Modern-Day Slavery," in *Global Woman: Nannies, Maids, and Sex Workers in the New Economy,* ed. Barbara Ehrenreich and Arlie Russell Hochschild (New York: Metropolitan Books, 2002), 143–53. Joy Zarembka is the director of the Break the Chain Campaign in Washington, DC. For more information about that organization's work for migrant domestic worker rights, visit www.ips-dc.org/campaign/index.htm.

4. "A Slavery Case Nears Hearing in Manhattan: Servant Accuses Kuwaiti Diplomat," *New York Sun,* August 10, 2004.

5. Quoted in Melissa Dittmann, "What Makes Good People Do Bad Things?" *Monitor on Psychology* 35 (October 2004): 68.

6. "Indonesian Received Less Than $2 a Day, Authorities Say," Associated Press, July 28, 2006, www.msnbc.msn.com/id/4080380/.

7. "Wisconsin Couple Convicted on Human Trafficking Charges," U.S. Newswire, May 27, 2006.

8. U.S. Department of Justice, "Two Milwaukee Doctors Each Sentenced to Four Years in Prison for Forcing Woman to Work as Domestic Servant for 19 Years," press release, November 16, 2006, www.usdoj.gov/opa/pr/2006/November/06_crt_772.html.

9. "Man Sentenced to 16 Months in Prison in Human Trafficking Case," Associated Press, May 12, 2006.

10. "Woman Sentenced to Probation in Human Trafficking Case," KGBT 4, May 12, 2006.

11. Florrie Burke, human trafficking consultant, interview, December 21, 2007.

12. Frank Eltman, "NY Couple Convicted in Slavery Case," Associated Press, December 17, 2007.

13. Robert E. Kessler, "Muttontown Woman in Slave Case Sentenced to 11 Years," Newsday.com, June 27, 2008.

14. Frank Eltman, "Second NY Millionaire Convicted of Enslaving Indonesian Workers Sentenced to Prison Time," Associated Press, June 27, 2008.

15. U.S. State Department, "Report of the Visa Office 2007," Table XVIb, "Nonimmigrant Visas Issued by Classification," http://travel.state.gov/visa/frvi/statistics/statistics_1476.html.

16. Quoted in Helena Smith, "Slaves in the Land of the Free," *New Statesman,* September 9, 2002.

17. Briefly, four arguments can be made for denying diplomatic immunity in slavery cases: (1) slavery violates the Thirteenth Amendment to the U.S. Constitution, and no treaty can overcome the provisions of the Constitution; (2) slavery and trafficking are fundamentally commercial activities and thus not covered by the Vienna Convention; (3) slavery and trafficking laws and international agreements are accepted as *jus cogens* laws, norms that transcend and trump any other laws, including the treaty concerning diplomatic immunity; and (4) the U.S. Trafficking Victims Protection Act guarantees to all victims the

right to pursue civil remedies. For further information, see Mani Kumari Sabbithi, Joaquina Quadros, and Gila Sixtina Fernandes, plaintiffs, v. Major Waleed KH N. S. Al Saleh, Maysaa KH A. O. A. Al Omar, and State of Kuwait, Case No. 07-CV-00115-EGS, U.S. District Court for the District of Columbia, www.aclu.org/pdfs/womensrights/20070530sabbithioppositiontomotiontodismiss.pdf.

18. Quoted in Frank Langfitt, "Servants: Diplomat Held Us as Suburban 'Slaves,'" National Public Radio, March 1, 2007, www.npr.org/templates/story/story.php?storyId=7626754.

19. Quoted in ibid.

20. "Congressional Briefing on Migrant Domestic Workers (Bill H.R. 3244: Trafficking Victims Protection Act of 1999)," testimony of Xiomara Salgado at the Campaign for Migrant Domestic Workers' Rights Public Briefing, Washington, DC, February 15, 2000, www.montgomerycountymd.gov/content/hhs/vasap/domesticworkerscongressionaltestimony.pdf.

21. Ibid.

22. Workers in social service agencies helping victims of trafficking and slavery told the authors of these tough choices. Most did not want to be identified with this complaint against government policy lest it threaten the resources they did receive.

23. Free the Slaves, *Hidden Slaves*.

24. "Christina: Narrative as Told to Peggy Callahan for Free the Slaves, February 24, 2005, Washington, DC," excerpted from "In Their Own Words: Christina Elangwe," interview, www.freetheslaves.net/NETCOMMUNITY/Page.aspx?pid=349&srcid=208, in *To Plead Our Own Cause: Narratives of Modern Slavery*, ed. Kevin Bales and Zoe Trodd (Ithaca: Cornell University Press, 2008).

3. SLAVES IN THE PASTURES OF PLENTY

1. Laura Germino, Coalition of Immokalee Workers (CIW), interview, January 6, 2007.

2. Greg Asbed, "Coalition of Immokalee Workers: '¡Golpear a Uno Es Golpear a Todos!' To Beat One of Us Is to Beat Us All," in vol. 3 of *Bringing Human Rights Home*, ed. Cynthia Soohoo, Martha F. Davis, and Catherine Albisa (New York: Praeger, 2007), 1–24.

3. Lucas Benitez, CIW, interview, January 7, 2007.

4. Ibid.

5. Greg Asbed, CIW, interview, January 8, 2007.

6. Lucas Benitez, interview, January 7, 2007.

7. John Norris, U.S. DOL wage and hours inspector, Ft. Myers, FL, interview, March 28, 2007.

8. Greg Asbed, CIW, interview, January 8, 2007.

9. Oxfam America, "Like Machines in the Fields: Workers without Rights in American Agriculture," Report, March 2004, www.oxfamamerica.org/newsandpublications/publications/research_reports/art7011.html/OA-Like_Machines_in_the_Fields.pdf, 36.

10. Cindy Hahamovitch, *The Fruits of Their Labor: Atlantic Coast Farmworkers and the Making of Migrant Poverty, 1870–1945* (Chapel Hill: University of North Carolina Press, 1997), 123.

11. *Dying to Leave,* dir. Chris Hilton, "Wide Angle" special, PBS, 2003.

12. Antonio Martinez, CIW, interview, December 2, 2007.

13. Asbed "Golpear a Uno."

14. Laura Germino, interview, January 20, 2007.

15. Ron Soodalter, *Hanging Captain Gordon: The Life and Trial of an American Slave Trader* (New York: Atria Books, 2006), 254.

16. Lucas Benitez, interview, January 7, 2007.

17. Laura Germino, interview, February 2, 2007.

18. Greg Asbed, interview, January 8, 2007.

19. Lucas Benitez, interview, January 7, 2007.

20. Laura Germino, interview, January 6, 2007.

21. Asbed, "Golpear a Uno."

22. Ibid.

23. Laura Germino, interview, January 20, 2007.

24. Asbed, "Golpear a Uno."

25. Laura Germino, interview, January 6, 2007.

26. Greg Asbed, interview, January 8, 2007.

27. Allen Davies, formerly sergeant of the Hendry County, FL, Sheriff's Office, interview, February 14, 2007.

28. Mike Baron, formerly Border Patrol agent-in-charge, Pembroke Pines, FL, interview, March 27, 2007.

29. Laura Germino, interview, February 2, 2007.

30. Armando Brana, former U.S. DOL senior investigator, interview, April 3, 2007.

31. United States v. Miguel A. Flores, Sebastian Gomez, Andres Ixcoy, Nolasco Castaneda, indictment, Criminal No. 2:96–806, U.S. District Court of South Carolina, Charleston Division, October 10, 1996.

32. Transcript of sentencing hearing, Criminal No. 2:96–806, 59–60.

33. Armando Brana, interview, April 3, 2007.

34. Ibid.

35. Ibid.

36. Mike Baron, interview, March 27, 2007.

37. Ibid.

38. Laura Germino, interview, February 2, 2007.

39. Greg Asbed, interview, January 8, 2007.

40. Soodalter, *Hanging Captain Gordon,* 254.

41. "Labor Camps Kept Workers in Servitude with Crack Cocaine," *Naples News,* September 23, 2006.

42. "Labor Camp Owner Given 30 Years in Prison," *Florida Times-Union,* January 27, 2007.

43. CIW, "CIW Anti-Slavery Campaign," 2008, www.ciw-online.org/slavery.html.

44. Greg Asbed, interview, January 8, 2007.

45. Mike Baron, interview, March 27, 2007.

46. Laura Germino, interview, February 2, 2007.

47. Ibid.

48. Soodalter, *Hanging Captain Gordon,* 262.

49. "CIW, McDonald's, and Their Suppliers Reach Agreement to Improve Farmworkers Wages and Working Conditions," April 9, 2007, www.escr-net .org/news/news_show.htm?doc_id=483476.

50. Interview with Lucas Benitez, April 12, 2007.

51. "Statement from Burger King," February 7, 2007, www.namcnewswire .com/releases/content/view/845/2/.

52. Lucas Benitez, "CIW Response to Burger King Statement of 2/5/07," press release, February 6, 2007 (no longer available on the CIW Web site).

53. "Statement from Burger King."

54. "Burger King Pledges Cage-Free Food," *New York Times,* March 28, 2007.

55. Quoted in Soodalter, *Hanging Captain Gordon,* 262.

56. Amy Bennett Williams, "Burger King Puts Self on Grill," *Ft. Myers News-Press,* April 28, 2008.

57. Eric Schlosser, "Burger with a Side of Spies," *New York Times,* May 8, 2008.

58. "Brutal Farm Labor Bosses Punished, but Not the Growers Who Hire Them," *Miami Herald,* April 3, 2007.

59. Lisa Butler, attorney with Legal Services, Florida Rural Legal Services, interview, March 1, 2007.

60. Dan Werner, legal director, Workers' Rights Law Center, interview, March 12, 2007.

61. Ibid.

62. Kevin O'Connor, U.S. attorney for the State of Connecticut and DOJ chief of staff, interview, April 2, 2007.

63. Michael Wishnie, clinical professor of law, Yale Law School, interview, March 13, 2007.

64. O'Connor, interview, April 2, 2007.

65. "Suit Charges That Nursery Mistreated Laborers," *New York Times,* February 8, 2007.

66. Kevin O'Connor, interview, April 2, 2007.

67. "Settlement Ends Workers' Suit," *Hartford Courant,* June 26, 2007.

68. Michael Wishnie, interview, July 24, 2008.

69. Kathleen Kim and Dan Werner, *Civil Litigation on Behalf of Victims of Human Trafficking* (Los Angeles: Legal Aid Foundation, 2005), www.lafla.org/ clientservices/specialprojects/VictimsTrffcking0405.pdf.

70. U.S. DOJ, "Jury Convicts New Hampshire Couple of Forced Labor," press release, September 2, 2003.

71. Mary Bauer, "Close to Slavery: Guestworker Programs in the United States," report, Southern Poverty Law Center, 2007, www.splcenter.org/pdf/ static/SPLCguestworker.pdf, 7.

72. Mary Bauer, director of Southern Poverty Law Center's Immigrant Justice Project, interview, July 23, 2008.

73. Bauer, "Close to Slavery," 42.

74. Ibid., 39.
75. Ibid., 15–17.
76. Quoted in ibid., 27.
77. Ibid., 17.
78. Complaint, Muangmol Asanok et al., Plaintiffs, v. Million Express Manpower, Inc. et al., Defendants, U.S. District Court for the Eastern District of North Carolina, Western Division, Case 5:07-cv-00048-BO, filed February 12, 2007, 8.
79. Kate Woomer-Deters, staff attorney, Legal Aid of North Carolina, Farmworker Unit, interview, March 14, 2007.
80. Complaint, Asanok et al. v. Million Express Manpower et al., 1.
81. Ibid., 2.
82. Ibid.
83. Ibid., 8–9.
84. Ibid., 1.
85. Kate Woomer-Deters, interview, March 14, 2007.
86. Ibid.
87. Ibid.
88. Mary Bauer, interview, March 16, 2007.
89. U.S. House of Representatives, Committee on Education and Labor, "GAO Investigation Finds Labor Department Not Effectively Fighting Wage Theft, Department Not Using All Its Tools to Collect Back Wages," press release, July 15, 2008.
90. "Wage Theft, Bush Style," *People's Weekly World,* July 23, 2008, www.pww.org/article/articleview/13416.
91. Bauer, "Close to Slavery," 28.
92. Ibid., 29.
93. Mary Bauer, interview, March 16, 2007.
94. Patricia Medige, attorney, Colorado Legal Services, Migrant Farm Worker Division, interview, March 20, 2007.
95. See Moffat County Sheriff's Office, "Mission Statement" and "Vision Statement," 2007, www.moffatcountysheriff.com.
96. Kevin Bales and Steven Lize, "Trafficking in Persons in the United States: A Report to the National Institute of Justice," August 2005, www.ncjrs.gov/pdffiles1/nij/grants/211980.pdf, 140.
97. Patricia Medige, interview, March 20, 2007.
98. Mary Bauer, interview, March 16, 2007.
99. Bauer, "Close to Slavery," 41.
100. Laura Germino, interview, February 2, 2007.
101. Bauer, "Close to Slavery," 41.
102. Robert J. Allison, "The Origins of African-American Culture," *Journal of Interdisciplinary History* 30 (Winter 1999): 475–81.

4. SUPPLY AND DEMAND

1. Lutheran Immigration and Refugee Service, "Case Study #3," available from LIRS, 700 Light St., Baltimore, MD 21230. According to Annie Sovcik,

staff attorney at LIRS, the "Maria" story is a composite of cases involving a few girls, whose histories were combined both to protect the individual victims and to educate various groups as to "how many potential opportunities there often are for identifying and rescuing victims that go unrealized."

2. Kevin O'Connor, U.S. attorney for Connecticut, interview, June 13, 2007.

3. Interestingly, prior to the Civil War, when slave trade cases were being heard in northern federal courts, a number of lawyers who made their living by defending accused slavers had been U.S. attorneys and assistant U.S. attorneys before going into private practice.

4. 18 U.S.C. § 1591.

5. The court ruled that for their personal safety only the first letter of the victims' last names would be used.

6. Alex Wood, "Ex-prostitute Describes Pimp's Domination, Violence," *Journal Inquirer* (Hartford, CT), June 6, 2007.

7. Lee Sawyer, "Defendant Denies His 'Escort Service' Was a Prostitution Ring," *Journal Inquirer* (Hartford, CT), June 13, 2007.

8. U.S. DOJ, "Tenth Defendant Found Guilty for Role in Human Trafficking Ring," press release, June 14, 2007, www.usdoj.gov/usao/ct/Press2007/20070614–3.html.

9. Assistant U.S. attorney Krishna R. Patel, interview, April 13, 2007.

10. Lois Lee, "The Pimp and His Game," unpublished paper written "in partial fulfillment of the requirements for the degree of Doctor of Philosophy in sociology/anthropology," 1979, 9; also Lois Lee, founder, Children of the Night, interview, July 23, 2007.

11. Ibid., 10.

12. Ibid., 11.

13. Krishna R. Patel, interview, April 13, 2007.

14. U.S. Attorney's Office, Department of Justice, State of Connecticut, to Diane Polan, Esq., representing Shamere McKenzie, August 22, 2007.

15. Dorchen Leidholdt, co-founder, Coalition Against Trafficking in Women, interview, October 8, 2007.

16. Rachel Lloyd, Girls Educational and Mentoring Services, interview, July 25, 2007.

17. Lois Lee, interview, July 23, 2007.

18. Ronald Weitzer, "The Social Construction of Sex Trafficking: Ideology and Institutionalization of a Moral Crusade," *Politics and Society* 35 (September 2007): 452.

19. Ibid.

20. Michael Shively et al., "Final Report on the Evaluation of the First Offender Prostitution Program," Abt Associates, March 7, 2008, www.ncjrs .gov/pdffiles1/nij/grants/222451.pdf.

21. Bradley Myles, "'The World Famous Players Ball' at-a-Glance," unpublished briefing document to Polaris, July 2005, 1.

22. Ibid., 6.

23. Ibid., 2.

24. U.S. Department of Health and Human Services, "Sex Trafficking Fact Sheet," November 2004, www.acf.hhs.gov/trafficking/about/fact_sex.html.

25. "U.S. Must Link AIDS, Anti-Trafficking Efforts," Standard Newswire, August 1, 2007.

26. Government Notice of Filing, U.S. District Court, Southern District of Florida, Case No. 05–20444-CR-Seitz(s), United States v. Justin Evans, 13–19.

27. United States v. Justin Evans, 476 F.3d 1176 (11th Cir. 2007), 1177–78.

28. Myles, "Players Ball," 9.

29. Ibid., 3.

30. Richard J. Estes and Neil Alan Weiner, "The Commercial Sexual Exploitation of Children in the U.S., Canada and Mexico," University of Pennsylvania, September 18, 2001 (amended April 2002), Abstract, www.sp2.upenn.edu/~restes/CSEC_Files/Abstract_010918.pdf, 2.

31. Richard J. Estes and Neil Alan Weiner, "The Commercial Sexual Exploitation of Children in the U.S., Canada and Mexico," University of Pennsylvania, September 18, 2001 (amended April 2002), Executive Summary, www.sp2.upenn.edu/~restes/CSEC_Files/Exec_Sum_020220.pdf, 10.

32. Lisa M. Jones and David Finkelhor, "The Decline in Child Sexual Abuse Cases," *OJJDP Bulletin* (Office of Juvenile Justice and Delinquency Prevention), January 2001; Lisa M. Jones, David M. Finkelhor, and Kathy Kopiec, "Why Is Sexual Abuse Declining? A Survey of State Child Protection Administrators," *Child Abuse and Neglect* 25 (2001): 1139–58.

33. Rachel Lloyd, interview, July 25, 2007.

34. "Connecticut Man Pleads Guilty for Role in Human Trafficking Ring," Standard Newswire, August 21, 2007.

35. Statement of Chris Swecker, assistant director, Criminal Investigative Division, Federal Bureau of Investigation, before the Commission on Security and Cooperation in Europe, United States Helsinki Commission, June 7, 2005, www.fbi.gov/congress/congress05/swecker060705.htm, 2.

36. Rachel Lloyd, interview, July 25, 2007.

37. Lois Lee, interview, July 23, 2007.

38. U.S. Department of Justice, "Man Sentenced to Life in Prison for Producing Video of Toddler Being Sexually Assaulted," press release, April 16, 2007, www.usdoj.gov/criminal/ceos/Press%20Releases/DID%20Banks%20sentence%20PR_041607.pdf.

39. Statement of Chris Swecker.

40. "Life Term for Trafficking Juveniles," *Washington Post,* March 18, 2006.

41. Nancy Ramos, CATW, interview, October 10, 2007.

42. Andrew Oosterbaan, CEOS, interview, June 30, 2007.

43. Wendy Waldron, trial attorney, CEOS, interview, July 16, 2007.

44. Ibid.

45. Ibid.

46. Ibid.

47. The NGO was Agir pour les Femmes en Situation Precaire (Acting for Women in Distressing Situations).

48. U.S. Department of Justice, "Man Convicted of Sex Tourism, Child Pornography Charges," press release, April 5, 2007, www.usdoj.gov/usao/fls/PressReleases/070405-02.pdf.

49. Anna Rodriguez, director, Florida Coalition Against Human Trafficking, interview, September 18, 2007.

50. Andrew Oosterbaan, interview, August 7, 2007.

51. Wendy Waldron, interview, July 16, 2007.

52. Rachel Lloyd, interview, July 25, 2007.

53. Dorchen Leidholdt, interview, October 8, 2007.

54. ECPAT stands for "End Child Prostitution and Child Pornography and Trafficking of Children for Sexual Purposes," perhaps the most unwieldy name in the antitrafficking world.

55. Carole Smolenski, ECPAT, interview, August 13, 2007.

56. Ibid.

57. Rachel Lloyd, interview, July 25, 2007.

58. Carole Smolenski, interview, August 13, 2007.

59. Christa Stewart, the Door, interview, July 20, 2007.

60. Ibid.

61. Ibid.

62. Ibid.

63. Lois Lee, interview, July 23, 2007.

64. Alison Boak, president of IOFA, interview, August 13, 2007.

65. Florrie Burke, human trafficking consultant, interview, June 26, 2007.

66. Lois Lee, interview, July 23, 2007. In fact, several NGOs offer beds to victims of trafficking, but they keep this information confidential for the victims' and the NGOs' security. Nonetheless, the shortage of accommodations is a huge problem.

67. Christa Stewart, interview, July 20, 2007.

68. Testimony of Ann Jordan, former director, Initiative Against Trafficking in Persons, Global Rights, before the House Subcommittee on Border, Maritime and Global Counterterrorism, March 20, 2007, http://homeland.house.gov/SiteDocuments/20070320165954-38416.pdf, 5–6.

69. Dorchen Leidholdt, interview, October 8, 2007.

70. CarlLa Horton, executive director, Northern Westchester Shelter, interview, October 10, 2007.

71. Testimony of Ann Jordan, 6–7.

72. Lois Lee, interview, July 23, 2007.

73. Florrie Burke, interview, August 3, 2007.

74. Lois Lee, interview, July 23, 2007.

75. Dorchen Leidholdt, interview, October 8, 2007.

76. Bradley Myles, Polaris Project, interview, July 31, 2007.

77. Ibid.

78. Ibid.

79. Mark Lagon, director, TIP Office, interview, October 3, 2007.

80. Carole Smolenski, interview, August 13, 2007.

81. Alison Boak, interview, July 30, 2007.

82. Ibid.

83. Lou de Baca, U.S. House Judiciary Committee, interview, August 14, 2007.

84. Andrea Powell, FAIR Fund, interview, August 8, 2007.

85. Ibid.

86. Lou de Baca, interview, August 14, 2007.

87. Bradley Myles, interview, July 31, 2007.

88. Detective Lieut. Edward P. Reilly, interview, October 17, 2007.

89. Edward J. Schauer and Elizabeth M. Wheaton, "Sex Trafficking into the United States: A Literature Review," *Criminal Justice Review* 31, no. 1 (2006): 1.

90. Norma Ramos, interview, October 10, 2007.

91. Schauer and Wheaton, "Sex Trafficking," 2.

92. Coalition Against Trafficking in Women, *Primer on the Male Demand for Prostitution* (N. Amherst, MA: Coalition Against Trafficking in Women, 2006), http://action.web.ca/home/catw/attach/PRIMER.pdf.

93. Norma Ramos, interview, October 10, 2007.

94. Anthony M. DeStefano, *The War on Human Trafficking: U.S. Policy Assessed* (New Brunswick: Rutgers University Press, 2007), 109.

95. William F. McDonald, quoted in Barbara Ann Stolz, "Interpreting the U.S. Human Trafficking Debate through the Lens of Symbolic Politics," *Law and Policy* 29 (July 2007): 322.

96. Ethan A. Nadelman, quoted in ibid.

97. Ibid.

98. Ibid., 319.

99. According to Swedish law, the economic and social relationship between a woman selling sex and a man buying sex is not a relationship that even approaches equality. The rationale behind the law is that as long as society remains male dominated, women selling sex will be in a more vulnerable position than men buying sex. Men's right to buy women's bodies is seen as a form of male dominance to be resisted and controlled. This law leaves the sale of sex as legal; it is only the purchase that is made illegal, thus attempting to redress the imbalance of power between men and women. An official report by the government concerning the law explained: "The proposal by the Prostitution Report to criminalize both buyer and seller has been subjected to extensive criticism by almost all referral bodies. The government also deems that, even if prostitution in itself is not a desirable social activity, it is not reasonable to prosecute the party that, at least in most cases, is the weaker party, exploited by others to satisfy their sexual drive. This is also important if prostitutes are to be encouraged to get help to leave prostitution and can feel they will not have to worry about the consequences of having been prostitutes." Quoted in Maria-Pia Boethius, "The End of Prostitution in Sweden?" Swedish Institute, October 1999.

100. Dorchen Leidholdt, interview, October 8, 2007.

101. Norma Ramos, interview, October 10, 2007. The validity of these figures has been questioned by other organizations. DeStefano cites New York City's Urban Justice Center's report that "fewer than 25% of the immigrant women served by the center's sex workers project fit the criteria for being labeled a trafficked person." DeStefano, *War on Human Trafficking*, 115.

102. Stolz, "Interpreting," 323.

103. Ibid.

104. Ibid., 324.

105. Testimony of Ann Jordan, 1–2.

106. DeStefano, *War on Human Trafficking*, 116.

107. Stolz, "Interpreting," 326.

108. DeStefano, *War on Human Trafficking*, 108.

109. Ibid., 109.

110. Ibid., 128.

111. It is in fact difficult to identify any other policy area where such a requirement has been made. Any number of advocacy groups, in many areas of social and environmental policy, call for changing existing laws. The right to call for a change in law, through peaceful and democratic means, seems to be clearly guaranteed under the First Amendment to the Constitution. The authors are adamant in our support for the right to peacefully question and call for reform of any law or policy within a context of free speech and democratic process.

112. Testimony of Ann Jordan, 2.

113. Ibid., 3.

114. Florrie Burke, interview, September 13, 2007.

115. DeStefano, *War on Human Trafficking,* 129.

116. Jacqueline Berman, "The Left, the Right, and the Prostitute: The Making of U.S. Antitrafficking in Persons Policy," *Tulane Journal of International and Comparative Law* 14 (Spring 2006): 274.

117. Quoted in ibid.

118. Dorchen Leidholdt, interview, October 8, 2007.

119. Norma Ramos, interview, October 10, 2007.

120. Mark Lagon, interview, October 3, 2007.

121. Dorchen Leidholdt, interview, October 8, 2007.

122. Ann Jordan, interview, October 24, 2007. The ILO quotes within this quote are from Lin Lean Lim, "Trafficking, Demand and the Sex Market," International Institute for Labour Studies, International Labour Organization, presented at the International Symposium on Gender at the Heart of Globalization, March 12, 2007, www.sexworkeurope.org/site/index.php?option=com_docman&task=cat_view&gid=41&Itemid=198, 7.

123. Untitled, unpublished position paper, Coalition to Abolish Slavery and Trafficking (CAST), Los Angeles, October 19, 2007.

124. Heather Moore, CAST, interview, September 14, 2007.

5. NEW BUSINESS MODELS

1. Quoted in Brian Donahue, "Three Charged in Hair Salon Human Trafficking Ring," *Newark Star-Ledger,* September 6, 2007.

2. Quoted in "Authorities: West Africans Used as N.J. Hair-Braiding Slaves," AP report, September 9, 2007, NBC10.com, www.nbc10.com/news/14064841/detail.html?rss=phi&psp=news.

3. See Thomas R. Dew, *Review of the Debate in the Virginia Legislature of 1831 and 1832* (Richmond, 1832). Another slavery apologist who regularly repeated that slaves were better off in America than free in Africa was George Fitzhugh; see ch. 5, "Negro Slavery," in his *Sociology for the South, or the Failure of Free Society* (Richmond, VA: A. Morris, 1854).

4. Quoted in Adrienne Packer, Lynnette Curtis, and Francis McCabe, "China Star Acrobats: Trio Face Slavery Charges," *Las Vegas Review-Journal,* July 4, 2007.

5. Quoted in ibid.

6. "US Court Opens Trial on Slavery Charges," *Zou Di,* August 6, 2007, www.china.org.cn/english/China/219946.htm.

7. Florrie Burke, Human Trafficking Consultant, interview, September 17, 2007.

8. Lou de Baca, counsel, U.S. House of Representatives Counsel on the Judiciary, interview, September 13, 2007.

9. "Suffering in Silence," *Time,* August 4, 1997.

10. Ibid.

11. "Deaf Mexicans Recount Enslavement in the City," *New York Sun,* September 28, 2006.

12. Lou de Baca, interview, September 13, 2007.

13. Florrie Burke, interview, March 2, 2007.

14. "Suffering in Silence."

15. Florrie Burke, interview, March 2, 2007.

16. "Suffering in Silence."

17. Lou de Baca, interview, September 13, 2007.

18. Ibid.

19. "Suffering in Silence."

20. Lou de Baca, interview, September 13, 2007.

21. "Deaf Mexicans Recount Enslavement."

22. Florrie Burke, interview, September 17, 2007.

23. "Deaf Mexicans Recount Enslavement."

24. Lou de Baca, interview, September 13, 2007.

25. Ibid.

26. Florrie Burke, interview, September 17, 2007.

27. Sandy Shepherd, interview, August 21, 2007.

28. Given Kachepa, interview, May 15, 2007.

29. Ibid.

30. Quoted in Ron Soodalter, *Hanging Captain Gordon: The Life and Trial of an American Slave Trader* (New York: Atria, 2007), 255.

31. Quoted in ibid.

32. Sandy Shepherd, interview, August 21, 2007.

33. U.S. District Court for the District of Kansas, Case No. 04–40141 SAC, Second Superseding Indictment: United States v. Arlan Dean Kaufman and Linda Joyce Kaufman, 14.

34. "Breaking Down Doors to a Human Nightmare," *Topeka Capital-Journal,* June 27, 2005.

35. Ibid.

36. Indictment, Arlan Dean Kaufman and Linda Joyce Kaufman, 18.

37. Ibid., 2.

38. Ibid., 4.

39. "Kaufman House Stun Gun Incidents Focus of Testimony," *Topeka Capital-Journal,* October 18, 2005; also, U.S. Department of Justice, "Kansas Couple Convicted of Involuntary Servitude Charges for Abusing Mentally Ill Patients," press release, November 7, 2005.

40. Indictment, Arlan Dean Kaufman and Linda Joyce Kaufman, 5.

41. Ibid., 17.

42. Ibid., 16–17.

43. Ibid., 19.

44. Ibid., 6.

45. Ibid., 15.

46. "Breaking Down Doors."

47. Ibid.

48. "Kaufmans Receive Restitution Orders," *Kansan,* June 15, 2006.

49. Jim Cross, public information officer, U.S. Attorney's Office, Topeka, KS, interview, May 26, 2007.

50. Currently the United States holds nine territories: the Midway Islands, Puerto Rico, the Northern Mariana Islands, the Virgin Islands, Micronesia, the Marshall Islands, Palau, Guam, and American Samoa, where this story takes place.

51. Soodalter, *Hanging Captain Gordon,* 257.

52. Federal Bureau of Investigation, "Anatomy of an International Human Trafficking Case, Part 1," FBI Headline Archives, July 16, 2004, www.fbi.gov/page2/july04/kisoolee071604.htm.

53. Krishna Patel, assistant U.S. attorney, Bridgeport, CT, interview, April 13, 2007; also U.S. District Court, District of Connecticut, Indictment, Criminal No. 3:03CR350 (PCD), United States v. Hussein Mutungirehe, Abiba Kanzayire.

54. Indictment, Arlan Dean Kaufman and Linda Joyce Kaufman.

55. U.S. Attorney's Office, District of Connecticut, "Rwandan Child Smuggler Sentenced," press release, February 24, 2005.

56. Krishna Patel, interview, April 13, 2007.

6. EATING, WEARING, WALKING SLAVERY

1. See Michael Smith and David Voreacos, "The Secret World of Modern Slavery," *Bloomberg Markets,* December 2006.

2. See National Marine Fisheries Service, "Fish Watch: U.S. Seafood Facts," n.d., www.nmfs.noaa.gov/fishwatch/trade_and_aquaculture.htm (accessed August 2007).

3. Shrimp imports also reported at ibid.

4. See, for example, Environmental Justice Foundation, "Dying for Your Dinner," June 26, 2003, www.csrwire.com/PressRelease.php?id=1932; International Labour Organization, "Forced Labor in Burma," Report No. 32, September 8, 1998, http://burmalibrary.org/reg.burma/archives/199809/msg00281.html.

5. Anti-Slavery International, "Indonesian Fishing Platforms," report, London, 1998.

6. See "Indonesia Hopes to Increase Fish Export Earning to US$ 5 Billion," *Indonesian Commercial Newsletter,* March 2004.

7. Smith and Voreacos, "Secret World," 60.

8. Quoted in ibid.

9. Australian Anti-Slavery Society, "Was Your Sparkling Diamond Produced by Child Slaves or Polished by Bonded Children?" 2003, www.anti-slaverysociety.addr.com/diamonds.htm.

10. Quoted in Smith and Voreacos, "Secret World," 64.

11. Quoted in ibid.

12. Ibid., 65.

13. Ginny Baumann, director of partnerships, Free the Slaves, Washington, DC, interview, July 12, 2007.

14. Dan McDougall, "Indian 'Slave' Children Found Making Low-Cost Clothes Destined for Gap," *Observer*, October 28, 2007.

15. Ramin Pejan, "*Laogai:* 'Reform through Labor' in China," *Human Rights Brief: A Legal Resource for the International Human Rights Community* 7, no. 2 (2000): 22.

16. Ibid., 23.

17. See, for example, Greenpeace, "Cyanide, Gold Mining's Devastating Killer," August 30, 2006, www.greenpeace.org/seasia/en/press/reports/cyanide-gold-mining-s-devasta.

18. You can see a Brazilian charcoal camp in Mato Grosso do Sul, using Google Earth and its satellite and aerial photographs. The beehive-shaped domes of the low ovens used to burn the forests into charcoal for use in the steel industry are lined up on each side of a dirt road. Smoke is rising from the ovens, and the ground is blackened near the road where charcoal has been spilt. To the east of the camp you can see where the forest has been clearcut to feed the ovens. Looking at satellite images, you cannot tell if the workers in this camp are free or enslaved, but you do know exactly where it is. If you would like to see this camp, the GPS coordinates are 19°52′14.22″ South, 53°03′30.84″ West.

19. Smith and Voreacos, "Secret World," 58.

20. See U.S. Department of Agriculture import figures at "Tropical Products: World Markets and Trade," March 2001, www.fas.usda.gov/htp/tropical/2001/03–01/troptoc.htm.

21. See Kevin Bales, *Disposable People: New Slavery in the Global Economy,* rev. ed. (Berkeley: University of California Press, 2004).

22. International Labour Organization, *A Global Alliance against Forced Labor* (Geneva: ILO, 2005).

23. Yuki Noguchi, "Gates Foundation to Get Bulk of Buffett's Fortune," *Washington Post,* June 26, 2006, A01.

24. Ron Soodalter, *Hanging Captain Gordon: The Life and Trial of an American Slave Trader* (New York: Atria, 2006).

25. You can learn more about Rugmark at www.rugmark.org.

26. Expenditure on antitrafficking work within the United States is around $150 million; the international work of the Office to Monitor and Combat Trafficking in Persons in the State Department costs up to $100 million per year. See, for example, Jerry Markon, "Human Trafficking Evokes Outrage," *Washington Post,* September 23, 2007, and the annual *Trafficking in Persons Report* of the Office to Monitor and Combat Trafficking in Persons, the latest of which, *Trafficking in Persons Report 2006,* is available on their Web site at www.state.gov/g/tip/rls/tiprpt/2006/.

27. See, for example, Petri Raivio, "The War on Drugs: The U.S. Approach to the Drug Problem," U.S. Institutions Survey Paper, FAST Area Studies Program, Department of Translation Studies, University of Tampere, April 2001, www.uta.fi/FAST/US2/PAPS/pr-drugs.html.

7. SLAVES IN THE NEIGHBORHOOD

1. Free the Slaves, *Slavery Still Exists and It Could Be in Your Backyard: A Community Member's Guide to Fighting Human Trafficking and Slavery* (Washington, DC: Free the Slaves, 2004), http://66.216.83.171/files/Community_Guide.pdf, 2.

2. U.S. Department of Education, "Human Trafficking of Children in the United States: A Fact Sheet for Schools," June 2007, www.ed.gov/about/offices/list/osdfs/factsheet.pdf.

3. "Middle Tennessee Sees Rise in Human Trafficking," WBIR.com, June 22, 2007.

4. Elaine Fletcher, interview, August 20, 2007.

5. Sandy Shepherd, interview, August 21, 2007. All of the subsequent details and quotations from Sandy Shepherd regarding this story come from this interview.

6. Sarah Schell, interview, September 11, 2007. All the subsequent details and quotations from Sarah Schell regarding this story come from this interview.

7. Quotations from Mike Massey come from "The Competition," *This American Life,* Public Radio International, December 3, 2007. For a detailed discussion of the Pickle case, see John Bowe, *Nobodies* (New York: Random House, 2007).

8. "Don't Sweep Human Trafficking under the Rug," *Jewish News Weekly of Northern California,* September 18, 2006.

9. "Sheriffs Focusing on Human Trafficking," Pensacola News Journal.com, August 20, 2007, www.pensacolanewsjournal.com/apps.

10. Jason Van Brunt, Hillsborough, FL, Sheriff's Office, interview, September 6, 2007.

11. Ibid.

12. Ibid.

13. Hillsborough County Sheriff's Office, "Marcelino Guillen Jaimes Arrested for Human Trafficking," news release, March 15, 2007, www.hcso.tampa.fl.us/Press_Releases/2007/3/07–142.htm.

14. Jason Van Brunt, interview, September 6, 2007.

15. "FGCU Could Aid Trafficking Fight," *News Press,* July 5, 2007, 3.

16. "Middle Tennessee Sees Rise," 3.

17. Stephanie Weber, Houston Rescue and Restore Coalition, interview, August 28, 2008.

18. Ibid.

19. Freedom Network USA, home page, 2008, www.freedomnetworkusa.org.

20. Florrie Burke, human trafficking consultant, interview, August 28, 2007.

21. Lou de Baca, counsel, House Committee on the Judiciary, interview, September 13, 2007.

22. Ibid.

23. Florrie Burke, interview, August 28, 2007.

24. Ibid.

25. The founding organizations are Safe Horizon, Break the Chain, Coalition to Abolish Slavery and Trafficking (CAST), Coalition of Immokalee

Workers, Florida Immigration Advocacy Center (FIAC), International Organization for Adolescents (IOFA), and Midwest Immigrant and Human Rights Center.

26. Florrie Burke, interview, August 28, 2007.

27. Ibid.

28. Barbara Ann Stolz, "Interpreting the U.S. Human Trafficking Debate through the Lens of Symbolic Politics," *Law and Policy* 29 (July 2007): 331.

29. Amy Farrell, interview, October 5, 2007.

30. Jack McDevitt and Amy Farrell, "Understanding and Improving Law Enforcement Responses to Human Trafficking," Final Report, June 30, 2007, Institute on Race and Justice, Northeastern University, prepared for National Institute of Justice.

31. Ibid., 3.

32. Amy Farrell, interview, October 5, 2007.

33. Ibid.

34. McDevitt and Farrell, "Understanding and Improving," 4.

35. Ibid.

36. Ibid., 5.

37. Ibid., 6.

38. Ibid.

39. Ibid., 7.

40. Ibid.

41. Kathryn Turman, program director, Office of Victim Assistance, FBI, interview, October 11, 2007.

42. McDevitt and Farrell, "Understanding and Improving," 7.

43. Ibid.

44. Ibid., 8.

45. Amy Farrell, interview, October 5, 2007.

46. Ibid.

47. McDevitt and Farrell, "Understanding and Improving," 9.

48. Ibid.

49. Ibid.

50. Ibid.

8. STATES OF CONFUSION

1. Sheila Toomey, "Russians Brought by a Chugiak Man Were Supposed to Be Tourists, Officials Say," *Anchorage Daily News,* January 6, 2001.

2. Vicki Viotti, "Waipahu Man Accused of Human Trafficking," *Honolulu Advertiser,* June 14, 2003.

3. U.S. Court of Appeals for the Ninth Circuit, United States v. Lueleni Fetongi Maka, June 14, 2007.

4. "Immigrant Sisters Admit Charges in Human Trafficking," *Star-Ledger,* August 4, 2006.

5. U.S. Department of Justice, Civil Rights Division, "United States v. Jones (Georgia)," *Anti-Trafficking News Bulletin,* Summer/Fall 2007, www.usdoj.gov/crt/crim/trafficking_newsletter/aug_07.htm#12, 9.

6. iAbolish American Antislavery Group, "Slavery in the United States," 2008, www.ibolish.org/slavery_today/usa/states.html, 5.

7. Ibid., 2.

8. U.S. Department of Justice, Civil Rights Division, "United States v. Djoumessi (Michigan)," *Anti-Trafficking News Bulletin,* Summer/Fall 2007, 8.

9. "Human Trafficking Becomes a Problem in Virginia," WSLS-TV, April 30, 2006.

10. "State to Focus on Human Trafficking," *Atlanta Journal-Constitution,* April 15, 2006.

11. "Human Trafficking in North Texas," CBS 11, Dallas, June 12, 2006.

12. "Human Trafficking in Idaho," KBCI, July 25, 2006.

13. "Human Trafficking—in D.C.," *Washington Times,* August 23, 2006.

14. "Human Trafficking, in Minnesota," *Star Tribune,* October 8, 2006.

15. "State Takes on Modern Slavery," *Press Journal,* April 7, 2006.

16. "Legislators Target Human Trafficking," *Deseret News,* September 19, 2006.

17. "New Law Makes Human Trafficking Illegal in Iowa," WHO-TV, April 21, 2006.

18. "State a Hot Spot for Human Trafficking, Panel Says," *Mercury News,* December 5, 2007.

19. Amy Farrell, "State Human Trafficking Legislation," in *Marshaling Every Resource: State and Local Responses to Human Trafficking,* ed. Dessi Dimitrova (Princeton, NJ: Policy Research Institute for the Region, 2007), 21.

20. Ibid.

21. Ibid.

22. Ibid., 22.

23. Ibid.

24. Ibid., 24.

25. Ibid.

26. Ibid., 25.

27. Ibid.

28. Ibid., 26.

29. Ibid.

30. Lou de Baca, counsel, U.S. House of Representatives Judiciary Committee, interview, December 19, 2007.

31. Leslie Wolfe, president, Center for Women Policy Studies, interview, December 21, 2007.

32. Farrell, "State Human Trafficking Legislation."

33. Jim Finckenauer and Min Liu, "State Law and Human Trafficking," in Dimitrova, *Marshaling Every Resource,* 5.

34. Ibid., 8.

35. Mark Lagon, interview, October 3, 2007.

36. Finckenauer and Liu, "State Law," 9.

37. Ibid.

38. Quoted in Dimitrova, *Marshaling Every Resource,* 1.

39. Center for Women Policy Studies, "Report Card on State Action to Combat International Trafficking," May 2007, www.centerwomenpolicy.org/documents/ReportCardonStateActiontoCombatInternationalTrafficking.pdf, 7.

40. Leslie Wolfe, president, Center for Women Policy Studies, interview, December 21, 2007.

41. Center for Women Policy Studies, "Report Card."

42. The criteria are the definition of trafficking as a felony; the use of comprehensive language to define the trafficker, e.g., "recruits, harbors, transports or obtains" persons; the use of "force, fraud, or coercion" as hallmarks; the criminalization of all forms of trafficking for forced labor and involuntary servitude—sweatshops, agricultural fields, brothels, households, etc.; enhanced penalties for trafficking of minors; mandatory restitution to victims/survivors and asset forfeiture of the trafficker's goods; affirmative defense for victims (so they are not prosecuted for crimes committed under duress); corporate liability for traffickers; and mandatory training for state and local law enforcement. Ibid., 6, 3.

43. Ibid., 16–17.

44. Ibid., 32–33.

45. Ibid., 16–17.

46. Center for Women Policy Studies, "Report Card," 7 ff.

47. Ibid.

48. Leslie Wolfe, interview, December 21, 2007.

49. Ibid.

50. Ibid.

51. Ibid.

52. Ibid.

53. Farrell, "State Human Trafficking Legislation," 18.

54. Ibid., 19.

55. Ibid., 20.

56. Ibid., 19.

57. Ibid., 22.

58. Lou de Baca, interview, December 19, 2007.

59. Farrell, "State Human Trafficking Legislation," 30.

60. Ibid.

61. Finckenauer and Liu, "State Law," 12.

9. THE FEDS

1. "Blame Somebody Else," *Exposé: America's Investigative Reports,* September 21, 2007.

2. David Phinney, "A U.S. Fortress Rises in Baghdad: Asian Workers Trafficked to Build World's Largest Embassy," *CorpWatch,* October 17, 2006, 1.

3. "Construction Woes Add to Fears in Iraq," *Washington Post,* July 5, 2007.

4. Phinney, "U.S. Fortress," 1.

5. "Dodging on Human Trafficking?" *The Swamp, Chicago Tribune,* June 22, 2006, 2.

6. KBR (formerly known as Kellogg Brown and Root), the largest contractor in Iraq, is a subsidiary of Halliburton, the Texas-based firm that Vice President Dick Cheney formerly helmed. KBR has a multi-billion-dollar deal

with the U.S. military to provide a wide range of support services for the soldiers, including meals, housing, and laundry.

7. Phinney, "U.S. Fortress," 2.

8. Ibid.

9. "Foreign Workers Abused at Embassy, Panel Told," *Washington Post*, July 27, 2007, 1–2.

10. Phinney, "U.S. Fortress," 2.

11. Ibid.

12. "Foreign Workers Abused," 2.

13. Ibid., 4.

14. Ibid., 5.

15. "Foreign Workers Abused," 2.

16. Ibid., 3.

17. Copies of the Submission to the Committee on Oversight and Government Reform by Free the Slaves, July 26, 2007, are available from info@freetheslaves.net.

18. "Blame Somebody Else," 2–3.

19. "State Dept. Official Accused of Blocking Inquiry," *New York Times*, September 18, 2007, 1.

20. Cathy Albisa, interview, September 26, 2007.

21. Cathy Albisa, interview, October 25, 2007.

22. See chapter 3 above.

23. Roberto Lovato, "Gulf Coast Slaves," *Salon.com*, October 25, 2007.

24. Ibid., 5.

25. Ibid., 6.

26. Ibid., 3.

27. Ibid., 10.

28. Ibid., 2.

29. Ibid., 10.

30. Ibid., 7.

31. Ibid., 9.

32. Ibid., 3.

33. Ibid., 4.

34. Ibid., 6.

35. Ibid., 4.

36. Laura Germino, interview, October 26, 2007.

37. For a comprehensive description of the functions of the various federal agencies and their history in the twenty-first-century antislavery campaign, see Anthony M. DeStefano, *The War on Human Trafficking: U.S. Policy Assessed* (New Brunswick: Rutgers University Press, 2007).

38. U.S. Department of State, Office to Monitor and Combat Trafficking in Persons, "Overview of U.S. Government Federal Agencies' Principal Roles to Combat Trafficking in Persons (TIP)," fact sheet, June 29, 2007, www.state.gov/g/tip/rls/fs/07/87547.htm.

39. Vanessa Garza, former director of the HHS Trafficking in Persons Program (A/TIP), currently associate director for Trafficking Policy in the Office of Refugee Resettlement (ORR), interview, October 26, 2007.

40. Ibid.

41. Steve Wagner, interview, November 19, 2007.

42. Vanessa Garza, interview, October 26, 2007.

43. Steve Wagner, interview, November 26, 2007.

44. Steve Wagner, interview, November 19, 2007.

45. Florrie Burke, interview, November 15, 2007.

46. Vanessa Garza, interview, October 26, 2007.

47. Steve Wagner, interview, November 19, 2007.

48. Ann Jordan, interview, November 21, 2007.

49. Vanessa Garza, interview, October 26, 2007.

50. Jerry Markon, "Human Trafficking Evokes Outrage, Little Evidence," *Washington Post,* September 23, 2007.

51. Steve Wagner, interview, November 19, 2007.

52. Vanessa Garza, interview, October 26, 2007.

53. Steve Wagner, interview, November 19, 2007.

54. Vanessa Garza, interview, October 26, 2007.

55. U.S. Department of Health and Human Services, "Annual ORR Reports to Congress—2005," www.acf.hhs.gov/programs/orr/data/05arc6.htm.

56. Steve Wagner, interview, November 19, 2007.

57. Vanessa Garza, interview, October 26, 2007.

58. Ibid.

59. See chapter 5 above for a description of the case.

60. Sister Mary Ellen Dougherty, USCCB, interview, December 4, 2007.

61. Anastasia Brown, director of refugee programs, USCCB, interview, December 4, 2007.

62. Nyssa Mestes, assistant director for trafficking, USCCB, interview, December 4, 2007.

63. Anastasia Brown, interview, December 4, 2007.

64. Ibid.

65. Sister Mary Ellen Dougherty, interview, December 4, 2007.

66. Ibid.

67. Nyssa Mestes, interview, December 4, 2007.

68. Ibid.

69. Sister Mary Ellen Dougherty, interview, December 4, 2007.

70. Ibid.

71. USCCB, "Proposal for Services to Victims of Human Trafficking," submitted to HHS, RFP #06Y007781, February 23, 2006, 23.

72. Sister Mary Ellen Dougherty, interview, December 5, 2007.

73. Steve Wagner, interview, November 19, 2007.

74. FBI, "Victim Assistance," n.d., www.fbi.gov/hq/cid/victimassist/home.htm.

75. Kathryn Turman, program director, OVA, FBI, interview, October 11, 2007.

76. Ibid.

77. Ibid.

78. Ibid. According to the "Double-Tongued Dictionary" (www.double-tongued.org), the verb *to stove pipe* means to "develop or be developed in an

isolated environment; to solve narrow goals or meet specific needs in a way not readily compatible with other systems."

79. Ibid.

80. Ibid.

81. Ibid.

82. Carlton Peeples, unit chief, Civil Rights Unit, FBI, interview, November 11, 2007.

83. Ibid.

84. Ibid.

85. Ibid.

86. Ibid.

87. Ibid.

88. Ibid.

89. DeStefano, *War on Human Trafficking,* 134.

90. Ibid., 133.

91. U.S. Department of State, "Overview."

92. Ginny Bauman, Free the Slaves, interview, August 30, 2008.

93. U.S. Department of State, "Overview."

94. Ben Skinner, interview, January 3, 2008.

95. U.S. Government Accountability Office, "Human Trafficking: Better Data, Strategy, and Reporting Needed to Enhance U.S. Antitrafficking Efforts Abroad," Report to the Chairman, Committee on the Judiciary, and the Chairman, Committee on International Relations, House of Representatives, July 2006, www.gao.gov/new.items/d06825.pdf.

96. Ann Jordan, interview, October 11, 2007.

97. For a full discussion of John Miller's tenure in the TIP Office, see E. Benjamin Skinner, *A Crime So Monstrous: Face-to-Face with Modern-Day Slavery* (New York: Free Press, 2008).

98. Mark Lagon, interview, October 3, 2007.

99. Ibid.

100. Ibid.

101. Ibid.

102. Ibid.

103. Ibid.

104. Ibid.

105. Mark Lagon, interview with Michelle Martin, *Tell Me More,* National Public Radio, January 7, 2008.

106. U.S. Department of State, "Overview."

107. Lou de Baca, interview, April 2, 2008.

108. Albert Moskowitz, former section chief, Criminal Section of the Civil Rights Division, U.S. Department of Justice, interview, December 12, 2007.

109. Ibid.

110. Ibid.

111. Ibid.

112. Ibid.

113. Ibid.

114. Ibid.

115. Ibid.

116. Ibid.

117. Ibid.

118. Anthony M. DeStefano, "Study: Trafficking Project Unchecked," *Newsday.com,* July 26, 2007.

119. Florrie Burke, interview, March 25, 2008.

10. A FUTURE WITHOUT SLAVERY

1. The list and discussion of indicators that follow represent a compilation of information from Free the Slaves, human trafficking consultant Florrie Burke, and members of the Freedom Network Institute, including Break the Chain, the Florida Immigrant Advocacy Center, Safe Horizon, and the Coalition of Immokalee Workers.

2. "Suit Charges That Nursery Mistreated Laborers," *New York Times,* February 8, 2007.

3. "In the Field with a Real ICE Agent" [Supervisory Special Agent Anthony Scandiffio], n.d., Turmoil Leads to Hope, www.TLTH.org/ht.htm.

4. Kara Kenney, "Group Wants Tampons to Display Anti-trafficking Hotline," NBC-2.com. (Collier County, FL), January 17, 2007.

5. "I Am the Change—Leslie Hughes," 2007, www.freetheslaves.net/NETCOMMUNITY/SSLPage.aspx?pid=354&srcid=381.

6. Andrew Oosterbaan, U.S. Department of Justice, Child Obscenity and Exploitation Section (CEOS), interview, August 7, 2007.

7. According to White House budget figures, the federal expenditure on drug enforcement, not counting any incarceration costs, was just under $12.5 billion in 2006. Expenditure on all antitrafficking and antislavery projects by the federal government in 2006 was about $200 million, or less than 2 percent of the expenditure on drugs.

INDEX

Text: Sabon
Display: Franklin Gothic
Compositor: International Typesetting and Composition
Indexer: Indexing Specialists (UK) Ltd.
Printer and Binder: Maple-Vail Book Manufacturing Group